SAGE was founded in 1965 by Sara Miller McCune to support the dissemination of usable knowledge by publishing innovative and high-quality research and teaching content. Today, we publish more than 750 journals, including those of more than 300 learned societies, more than 800 new books per year, and a growing range of library products including archives, data, case studies, reports, conference highlights, and video. SAGE remains majority-owned by our founder, and after Sara's lifetime will become owned by a charitable trust that secures our continued independence.

Los Angeles | London | Washington DC | New Delhi | Singapore | Boston

Embattled Media

Embattled Media

*Democracy, Governance and
Reform in Sri Lanka*

Edited by
William Crawley
David Page
Kishali Pinto-Jayawardena

⑤SAGE   www.sagepublications.com
Los Angeles • London • New Delhi • Singapore • Washington DC • Boston

First published in 2015 by

 SAGE Publications India Pvt Ltd
B1/I-1 Mohan Cooperative Industrial Area
Mathura Road, New Delhi 110 044, India
www.sagepub.in

SAGE Publications Inc
2455 Teller Road
Thousand Oaks, California 91320, USA

SAGE Publications Ltd
1 Oliver's Yard, 55 City Road
London EC1Y 1SP, United Kingdom

SAGE Publications Asia-Pacific Pte Ltd
3 Church Street
#10-04 Samsung Hub
Singapore 049483

Published by Vivek Mehra for SAGE Publications India Pvt Ltd, typeset in 10/12 Minion Pro by Diligent Typesetter, Delhi and printed at Saurabh Printers Pvt Ltd, New Delhi.

Library of Congress Cataloging-in-Publication Data Available

ISBN: 978-93-515-0062-9 (HB)

The SAGE Team: Shambhu Sahu, Sandhya Gola, Vaibhav Bansal and Rajinder Kaur

In memory of
Tilak Jayaratne
who ably represented a generation of
honourable and committed broadcasters

Thank you for choosing a SAGE product! If you have any comment,
observation or feedback, I would like to personally hear from you.
Please write to me at contactceo@sagepub.in

—Vivek Mehra, Managing Director and CEO,
SAGE Publications India Pvt Ltd, New Delhi

Bulk Sales

SAGE India offers special discounts for purchase of books in bulk.
We also make available special imprints and excerpts from our
books on demand.

For orders and enquiries, write to us at

Marketing Department
SAGE Publications India Pvt Ltd
B1/I-1, Mohan Cooperative Industrial Area
Mathura Road, Post Bag 7
New Delhi 110044, India
E-mail us at marketing@sagepub.in

Get to know more about SAGE, be invited to SAGE events, get on
our mailing list. Write today to marketing@sagepub.in

This book is also available as an e-book.

Contents

CHAPTER 14
Conclusion: Media Reform in a National and Global Context 341

List of Abbreviations

ABC	Asia Broadcasting Corporation
ACJ	Asian College of Journalism
AFP	Agence France Presse
AHRC	Asian Human Rights Commission
AMIC	Asian Media Information and Communication Centre
ANCL	Associated Newspapers of Ceylon Ltd
BASL	Bar Association of Sri Lanka
BBC	British Broadcasting Corporation
CDN	Ceylon Daily News
CFA	Ceasefire Accord
CPA	Centre for Policy Alternatives
CPC	Civil Procedure Code
CPJ	Committee to Protect Journalists
COPE	Committee on Public Enterprise
CSN	Carlton Sports Network
DPT	Department of Posts and Telecommunications
DRC	Dispute Resolution Council
ECHR	European Convention on Human Rights
EPDP	Eelam People's Democratic Party
ER	Emergency regulations
FMETU	Federation of Media Employees Trade Union
FMM	Free Media Movement
FTTP	Fiber-to-the-premise
GCE	General Certificate in Education
GMMP	Global Media Monitoring Project
GOBU	Government-owned business undertaking
GSP	General System of Preferences
IBA	International Bar Association
IBAHRI	International Bar Association's Human Rights Institute
ICCPR	International Covenant on Civil and Political Rights
ICJ	International Commission of Jurists

ICTs	Information and communications technologies
IFEX	International Freedom of Expression Exchange
IFJ	International Federation of Journalists
IMF	International Monetary Fund
IMPACS	Institute for Media, Policy and Civil Society
IMS	International Media Support
IPDC	International Programme for the Development of Communication
IPKF	Indian Peace Keeping Force
ISP	Internet Service Provider
ITN	Independent Television Network
ITU	International Telecommunications Union
JDS	Journalists for Democracy in Sri Lanka
JVP	Janata Vimukhthi Peramuna
LBO	Lanka Business Online
LLRC	Lessons Learnt and Reconciliation Commission
LISL	Lanka Internet Services Limited
LST	Law and Society Trust
LTTE	Liberation Tigers of Tamil Eelam
MCNS	Media Centre for National Security
MCR	Mahaweli Community Radio
MDA	Media Development Authority
MRTC	Media Resources and Training Centre
NES	New Education Service
NFEP	Non-formal education programme
NGO	Non-government Organisations
OPA	Organisation of Professional Associations
OUSL	Open University of Sri Lanka
PA	Peoples' Alliance
PCCSL	Press Complaints Commission of Sri Lanka
PEMRA	Pakistan Electronic Media Regulatory Authority
PSO	Public Security Ordinance
PTA	Prevention of Terrorism Act
RCT	Rehabilitation and Research Centre for Torture Victims
RSF	Reporters Sans Frontieres
RTI	Right to information
SI	Social indicator
SLBAB	Sri Lanka Broadcasting Authority Bill
SLBC	Sri Lanka Broadcasting Corporation
SLCJ	Sri Lanka College of Journalism

SLFP	Sri Lanka Freedom Party
SLMMF	Sri Lanka Muslim Media Forum
SLPI	Sri Lanka Press Institute
SLRC	Sri Lanka Rupavahini Corporation
SLTTI	Sri Lanka Television Training Institute
SLWJA	Sri Lanka Working Journalists Association
SVIAS	Swami Vipulananda Institute of Aesthetic Studies
TID	Terrorism Investigation Division
TNA	Tamil National Alliance
TRAI	Telecoms Regulatory Authority of India
TRC	Telecommunications Regulatory Commission
TRCSL	Telecommunications Regulatory Commission of Sri Lanka
TULF	Tamil United Liberation Front
UCR	Uva Community Radio
UNESCO	United Nations Educational, Scientific and Cultural Organisation
UNF	United National Front
UNFPA	United National People's Freedom Alliance
UNHRC	United Nations Human Rights Council
UNP	United National Party
VoIP	Voice over IP

Preface

The idea for this book has had a long gestation. It emerged originally from discussions with colleagues in the Media South Asia network at a conference in Delhi in May 2004. We were reviewing a two-year programme of workshops which had explored issues of common interest and concern to media practitioners in different South Asian countries in the wake of the satellite revolution. The issues included the development of community radio, the use of media for development, the relationship between broadcaster and audience and the dynamics of terrestrial and satellite broadcasting. We all agreed that the workshops had demonstrated the value of a South Asian approach and the potential for cross-fertilisation in these specific areas. But when asked to prioritise issues for future collaboration and research, our colleagues were almost unanimous in answering 'Media Policy and Law', the framework of law and regulation within which media operate, the interface between government, media and the public.

The years that straddled the millennium had been a watershed for broadcasting in South Asia. Decades of state broadcasting monopolies had been brought to an end by the satellite revolution, which ushered in new investment, new TV and radio channels, new choices, and new aspirations, and kicked off a consumer revolution across the region. With the help of an experienced team of researchers from across the region, we had tried to document those changes in *Satellites over South Asia: Broadcasting, Culture and the Public Interest*, which was published by SAGE in 2001. At several levels, the revolution had been immensely liberating, but it had also thrown up a huge range of cultural, social and political issues. Some of these related to cross-border cultural influences (particularly of India on its neighbours), some to changing cultural norms within societies, some to the changing balance between the state and the citizen as viewer and listener.

For a period, that balance seemed to have swung wildly in the citizen's favour. For a variety of reasons, South Asian governments stood back as cable networks mushroomed and entrepreneurs seized the new technical opportunities to launch satellite channels from beyond South Asian shores. But it soon became clear that the nation state should not be underestimated. South Asian governments had not attempted to prevent the emergence of a multi-channel television universe, as had happened in China and Iran, but the majority of them continued to exercise tight control over the state broadcasting sector and to restrict the expansion of commercial radio and other private media as well. The Indian Supreme Court had ruled in 1995 that the airwaves were 'public property' but the Indian government had shown no sign of acting on that seminal judgement. In Sri Lanka not long afterwards a progressive judgement by the country's highest court was also brushed aside by policy makers. Considerations of security, long-established bureaucratic reflexes and informal systems of patronage all militated against the formal creation of a more liberal media regime, in which freedom of expression is not an opportunity seized from a state caught off guard by technological change but a right underpinned by the state's own legal and administrative structures. These same factors also held back the creation of systems of media regulation in the public interest, in which state and commercial media are required to acknowledge wider responsibilities than to the party in power or the profitability of private companies. It was for these reasons that colleagues in the Media South Asia network, many of them representatives of civil society or pressure groups for media change, put media policy and law so high up their agenda.

In response to this clear expression of interest, we began a scoping study in 2006 with the support of the British Academy's Society for South Asian Studies and the help of colleagues in four South Asian countries: India, Pakistan, Bangladesh and Sri Lanka. The aim was to examine the constitutional and legal basis for media freedoms in each country and potential common ground for the development of new frameworks for the media, to take full advantage of new technologies at different levels of public communication, to allow scope for diversity and to promote the use of the media to advance the public interest and promote economic development across South Asia.

The study examined a variety of key issues and the opinions of different stakeholders in each country—government officials, international bodies, politicians, lawyers, media organisations, community and linguistic interests and civil society pressure groups. Issues examined included constitutional guarantees of media freedom, restrictive laws, the interpretive role of the judiciary, different approaches to licensing and regulation, the balance between the state and the commercial sectors, scope for community media, cross-media ownership, convergence, self-regulation and media ethics. The study also looked at sources of expertise and the extent to which universities and colleges were advancing public knowledge of these issues.

The exercise demonstrated the value of a South Asian regional approach and the importance of shared administrative and judicial systems. India, Pakistan and Bangladesh had all been part of the same country in colonial times, and Sri Lanka had many similar features, though the island had been administered from London rather than New Delhi. After Independence, governments and judiciaries in each country pursued their own paths, in constitution making, in the introduction of new legislation, the amendment of old laws and in judicial interpretation. But there were some striking common elements reflecting their shared history and experience, common geo-political and cultural factors, the impact of global technological developments, as well as the influence of international legal conventions and agreements which uphold human and civil rights. In terms of the development and diversification of the media, the effect of the satellite and other technological revolutions and the regulatory challenges which they pose, the study established the value of a comparative perspective. It also showed that in specific areas, such as efforts to reform Contempt of Court legislation, to introduce Right to Information legislation, or to establish regulatory systems for media and for telecommunications, South Asian countries faced very similar challenges and had much to learn from each other.

At the same time, the study highlighted a paucity of expertise on these issues in most South Asian countries. While there were individuals, mostly lawyers, with knowledge of media law in each country, few of them combined knowledge of media law with an awareness of media developments and the actual and potential role of the media in society. Moreover, though the media was taught as a subject in many colleges and universities, media policy and law in this wider sense rarely featured as a module. Expertise in the comparative state of media policy and law across South Asia was an even rarer commodity. This remains the case today.

The scoping report pointed us in important new directions. It underlined the urgency of developing Media Policy and Law as a curriculum subject at university level and the need for appropriate source material for teaching purposes. It also pointed to the need to work more closely with the universities in the work of curriculum development and with a range of different experts—academics, lawyers, media practitioners and others—to put together a body of relevant information. The aim would be to provide students of the subject in each country with the necessary historical and legal background, detailed information on the constitutional and legal framework for media governance, expert treatment of key themes and issues, an annotated bibliography and compendium of relevant legal judgements. The information would be aimed not just at teachers and students but at other interested groups, including lawyers, journalists, broadcasters and members of civil society. The emphasis would be on the specifics of the national situation but there would also be a comparative dimension, drawing on issues of common interest across the region.

In 2009, the Ford Foundation provided us with a grant to explore some of these themes in greater depth, working mainly on Sri Lanka but with some scope to work on India as well. It was not the wider South Asian comparative study we had initially proposed, but it was too tempting an offer to resist. It gave us the opportunity to examine the role of the media in a state committed to democracy and the rule of law which had suffered extraordinary stresses as a result of ethnic strife, insurrection and civil war. Media liberalisation from the 1990s onwards had extended the range of choice for viewers and listeners and created a more diverse media landscape. But the war in the north and insurrections in the south had taken their toll of media freedoms. The island had lived under a permanent state of emergency for nearly three decades. The balance of power between government, judiciary, the media and the public had been put under immense strain.

In 2009, with the end of the war in the north, all this seemed about to change, increasing the relevance of our enquiries and raising hopes of media reform and greater freedom of expression. But progress towards a different sort of normality has been slow. The war and its aftermath have continued to cast a long shadow, which has limited the scope of our research. Over the past few years, universities have been closed for long periods. University teachers have been engaged in disputes with the government, which has affected their teaching and their research. The NGO sector has been heavily criticised by the government for pursuing foreign-funded agendas and finds itself under fire and on the defensive. Many media proprietors and journalists have maintained their long-established habit of self-censorship, for fear of inviting reprisals of one sort or another. Though not on the same scale as previously, there have been killings and disappearances of journalists since 2009 and the memory of past abuses still affects people's thinking. All this has made the study more challenging.

Kishali Pinto-Jayawardena, who had contributed to the earlier scoping report, has been our principal research associate in Sri Lanka for what we have called the 'Media Reform Lanka Initiative'. As co-editor of this book, she has brought extensive knowledge of the working of the law in Sri Lanka, with regard to its impact on the operation of the media, and long experience of writing on these issues for international and national audiences. She coordinated the research in Sri Lanka and has been our principal interlocutor with the Sri Lankan universities. She has helped to identify contribrutors for this volume and, with Gehan Gunatilleke, has contributed three authoritative chapters herself.

We would also like to acknowledge the significant contribution of the late Tilak Jayaratne, the former Director of Educational Broadcasting at the Sri Lanka Broadcasting Corporation, to whose memory this book is dedicated. Although already unwell when the project began, he and his friend and former colleague, Sarath Kellapotha, willingly accepted our commission and dedicated themselves to producing a comprehensive analysis of the working of the electronic media, much of it based on their own experience, which is also a moving personal testament.

Dr Jayantha de Almeida Gunaratne PC provided critical input at different stages of the development of the work. He has also contributed an article examining the need for Freedom of Information legislation.

There are a number of academics whom the editorial team would like to thank for their advice in shaping the research. We had helpful conversations at an early stage with Sasanka Perera, Professor of Sociology at Colombo University, who has since become the Dean of the Faculty of Social Sciences at the new South Asian University in New Delhi, and with Professor Selvakkumarran, Dean of the Colombo University Law Faculty. We visited the Colombo University Journalism Unit and met the department's three senior lecturers—Mr Kamal Waleboda, Mr Samantha Herath and Dr Ajantha Hapuarachchi—to discuss the scope of their syllabus. We also visited Kelaniya University and discussed curriculum development with members of the Mass Communications Department, including Wijayananda Rupasinghe and Professor Sunanda Mahendra de Mel. A number of staff at Peradeniya University in Kandy expressed interest in the project, including Athula Samarakoon and his colleague, Sudesh Mantillake, in the Fine Arts Department, Dr Sumathi Siva Mohan, who teaches English literature, and Dr W.A.D.P. Wanigasundara, who heads the Agricultural extension department. We are also grateful to all those who provided interviews for our research, whose names are listed in the bibliography.

In the research phase, Wijayananda Rupasinghe played a valuable coordinating role, assisting us in collecting curricula from different university departments and providing a link with the university lecturers' mass media group, which proved a useful sounding board for some of our initial findings. He and Sunil Senevi of Sabaragamuwa University helped us to convene a meeting of university lecturers in September 2012 to share some of the project's findings and launch the project website: www. mediareformlanka.com. Kishali Pinto-Jayawardena visited a number of universities in Sri Lanka and in India for discussions with their academic staff and is particularly appreciative of the support extended by the Asian College of Journalism in Chennai and the Centre for Media, Culture and Governance, Jamia Millia Islamia University, New Delhi. Dr Raguram welcomed the research team to the Eastern University, Trincomalee Campus, where we had a valuable discussion with Rev. Dr C.P. Rajendram, the first Director of the Faculty of Communications. Dr Raguram also contributed an article on educational curricula in the north and the east of the island. Towards the end of the project, as the website was being launched, we visited the Uva Community Radio station and had discussions with the staff.

We made two useful visits to the Sri Lanka Press Institute (SLPI), which was set up by representatives of the proprietors, editors and journalists, to speak for the industry, to improve training facilities and to provide a means of redress for the public. The SLPI also manages the College of Journalism and the Press Complaints Commission. Our thanks go to Kumar Nadesan, then Chair of the SLPI, who is also the Managing Director of Express Newspapers; Sinha Ratnatunga, the Editor-in-Chief of the *Sunday Times*, who has been a key figure in the emergence of the Institute and is a contributor to this volume; to Imran Furkhan, a past Executive Director and to Namal Perera, former Director of the College of Journalism.

We benefitted from conversations with a number of journalists, broadcasters, development and communication professionals and media analysts. We would particularly like to thank Nalaka Gunawardene, Ameen Izzadeen, Amal Jayasinghe and Namini Wijedasa, who have all contributed to this volume. We are also grateful to Vinya Ariyaratne, Dr P.H.J. Arunasiri, Iqbal Athas, Michael David, Asoka Dias, Elmo Fernando, Dilrukshi Handunetti, Sanjana Hattotuwa, Hana Ibrahim, Frederica Jansz and Rohan Samarajiva.

Segments of the preliminary core research on print and electronic media were published in the *Law and Society Trust Review* edited by Kishali Pinto-Jayawardena to obtain perspectives from the Sri Lanka–based legal and media community with the aim of fine-tuning the work. We are grateful to those who responded to that request.

In Bangalore, Lawrence Liang at the Alternative Law Forum contributed to the earlier scoping study and has been a valued source of advice throughout the project. We also benefitted from discussions with his colleague, Siddharth Narain, and Sunil Abraham at the Centre for Internet and Society.

In Colombo, Kishali Pinto-Jayawardena was ably assisted in her research and in the coordination of the project by attorney and television producer, Radika Gunaratne, who also designed the cover of the book, and by attorney, Prameetha Abeywickreme. Duminda Wijerathna built the website.

In London, the project was based at the Institute of Commonwealth Studies, where we received encouragement and support from the Director, Philip Murphy and from Professor James Manor. We are also indebted to Paul Sullivan, who was exemplary in managing our reporting requirements to the Ford Foundation.

We are grateful to Dr Ravina Aggarwal of the Ford Foundation in New Delhi for her interest in the project and her willingness in the best traditions of the foundation to let us get on with the job once the funding decision had been made. We hope the results meet at least some of her expectations.

We would like to thank SAGE India for encouraging us to publish the book, for their unfailingly professional support and for the useful review of an earlier manuscript which they commissioned. Our thanks in particular to our Commissioning Editor Shambhu Sahu, Production Editor Sandhya Gola, Associate Vice President R. Chandra Sekhar and Senior Vice President Sunanda Ghosh.

There is a good deal more to be done to put Media Policy and Law on the university map in Sri Lanka. But we hope that this book will provide some of the tools required to make the subject more accessible to teachers and students and all those Sri Lankans interested in creating a better regulated media and a better informed society.

William Crawley
Institute of Commonwealth Studies, University of London

David Page
Institute of Commonwealth Studies, University of London

Kishali Pinto-Jayawardena
Colombo

August 2014

1

Democracy, Governance and Media Reform: Sri Lanka and the Wider Region

For a long time, Sri Lanka had an enviable international reputation as a country with strong democratic traditions, a high level of literacy and its own welfare state, providing free education and food security for all its citizens. Compared with India and Pakistan, which emerged from British colonial rule through the trauma of partition, mass migration and killings, Sri Lanka seemed to glide effortlessly to independence in 1948 with little or no confrontation with the departing imperial power. Unlike in India, where the Indian National Congress became the dominant political party for nearly 20 years, or Pakistan, where the Muslim League began to fracture even before the death of the state's founder, Sri Lanka soon developed its own version of the British two-party system, with power alternating with a degree of stability between the United National Party (UNP) and the Sri Lanka Freedom Party (SLFP) through the 1950s and 1960s. The decision to deprive the tea workers of their citizenship in 1948 was vociferously opposed by Tamil politicians, but in the early years, the Sri Lankan Tamil community played a full part in politics and in the professions, including the law and the civil service. The legal profession attracted many of the island's brightest pupils and the judiciary developed a reputation for independence and for checking government excesses and upholding individual rights. The Sri Lankan press—English, Sinhala and Tamil—played its own part in this democratic process, though radio remained a government monopoly until the 1990s.

The 'divide-and-rule' policies of the colonial rulers had always been resented by some Sinhalese, who felt that their language and culture had been neglected, and this became a more significant factor after independence. With the stirrings of Sinhala populism in the 1950s, the elite politics of the English-speaking class were gradually superseded by a more ethnically driven political agenda. The Sri Lankan Freedom Party of S.W.R.D. Bandaranaike championed a policy of 'Sinhala only' and represented Sri Lanka increasingly as a Sinhala Buddhist nation, which left other communities feeling marginalised. The 1957 Bandaranaike–Chelvanayakam pact was perhaps the last best hope of a genuine political accommodation with the Tamils, though it provoked so much opposition that eventually it was abrogated by Bandaranaike himself, who not long afterwards was assassinated by a Buddhist monk.

The UNP continued to attract support from both the main communities but as the party of business interests, it was considerably weakened in the 1970s, when Mrs Sirimavo Bandaranaike's left-wing coalition government nationalised many of the country's leading industries, including the powerful Lake House newspaper group owned by the Wijewardene family. An insurrection by Sinhala youth in the south of Sri Lanka in 1971 had signalled a major challenge to the country's established political parties and heralded a period of political and economic turbulence. The Public Security Ordinance, which was enacted in 1947 to deter leftist trade unions, was used against the insurrectionists and ad hoc legislation was enacted to try them. In 1972, the coalition government recast the country's constitution, severing the links with the British crown and replacing the Governor General with a President as nominal head of state. The constitution removed the notion of an independent civil service and paved the way for the politicisation of the bureaucracy. The independence of the judiciary was weakened by several provisions that tilted the balance of power firmly towards the legislature. Judges were deprived of their traditional trappings of office, such as their robes and wigs. The right of appeal to the Privy Council was abolished. The previous system of judicial review by the courts was replaced by a new mechanism—a constitutional court with more limited powers to scrutinise bills. Even so, tensions between parliament and the newly established court were apparent from the start. At its first sitting over the Press Council Bill, there was a clash with parliament. The entire court resigned and the government was compelled to appoint a fresh set of judges. The enactment of the Press Council Bill containing draconian provisions for the regulation of the country's print media was a clear sign of emerging authoritarian trends.

Minority rights were affected by the abolition under the 1972 constitution of safeguards provided under the previous one. Violence escalated in the north with the assassination in July 1975 of the Mayor of Jaffna, Alfred Duraiyappah, by Tamil youths, who were later to form the Liberation Tigers of Tamil Eelam (LTTE). Senior Tamil politicians, who regarded Duraiyappah as a government collaborator, did not condemn the assassination, though it highlighted an extremist trend among both Tamil and Sinhala parties which was to have increasingly divisive consequences. Within a year, the newly formed Tamil United Liberation Front (TULF) passed a resolution calling for the formation of a separate state of Tamil Eelam.

With the Sri Lankan economy in a state of siege, youth unemployment rising, minority parties in ferment and freedom of expression restricted, parliamentary democracy seemed suddenly much more fragile. Mrs Bandaranaike extended her period of office without electoral approval and by the time she called the general elections of 1977 had become very unpopular. In those elections, the SLFP and its allies were swept away in J.R. Jayawardene's landslide victory and with them the policies of economic self-reliance and state control which had proved so ineffective. It was a 'winner takes all' scenario and Jayawardene used his enormous mandate to introduce a new Gaullist-style constitution, becoming the country's first directly elected President. With International Monetary Fund (IMF) backing, Sri Lanka embarked on a new experiment in economic liberalisation, with Singapore as its ideal. An impressive new parliament building was commissioned at Kotte but parliamentary democracy had in effect been superseded. The centralisation of power which had begun under Mrs Bandaranaike was now institutionalised in a formidable new way in what Jayawardene bizarrely called a Democratic Socialist republic. Junius Richard Jayawardene was a man of Christian antecedents and upbringing with no real sympathy for Sinhala populism but he had introduced a system of government which accentuated the country's already distinct majoritarian and authoritarian tendencies. He had resigned from parliament in protest at Mrs Bandaranaike's extension of her term of office, but he later deprived her of her civic rights and extended the UNP's parliamentary term by means of a referendum. This manipulation of parliamentary terms has become an unfortunate feature of Sri Lanka's democracy.

The judiciary was also weakened. Some constitutional amendments ensured security of tenure for judges, but the new constitution also included a clause specifying that all judges of the appellate courts, on the commencement of the new constitution, shall cease to hold office. President Jayawardene used this clause to 'reconstitute' the higher courts by not appointing 7 out of the 19 sitting judges. This measure undermined their guaranteed tenure and established an unhealthy precedent. The 1978 constitution also did nothing to address Tamil demands for more autonomy, despite rising militancy in the north. Nor did it declare the Tamil language an official language, despite the fact that this was a key concern of the Tamil-speaking minorities. The Tamil language was only given official status through amendments a decade later.

Jayawardene hoped that his new open-door economic policy would bring prosperity to Sri Lanka and help to solve its unemployment problems but it took time to get going and brought more benefits to the south than to the north, which had suffered low levels of investment for years. Politically, Jayawardene tried to buy off the Tamil political and parliamentary elite with privileges of various kinds, but he made few real concessions to their demand for greater political autonomy. They showed their willingness to work with him but received little in return and were eventually brushed aside with great brutality by younger, more militant groups. By 1983, when 14 soldiers were killed in Jaffna by Tamil insurgents and armed mobs were let loose on Tamil property and businesses in Colombo in retaliation, the scene was set for a deepening ethnic rift and perpetual insurgency in the north and the east.

By 1985, Tamil insurgent groups had taken control of Jaffna and in May that year, the LTTE, which was becoming the dominant group, staged a massacre at Anuradhapura, which horrified Sinhalese opinion. Massacres of Sinhalese civilians by the LTTE were matched by the killings of Tamil villagers by the Army in the north, often in retaliation for the deaths of soldiers through roadside bombs and ambushes. In 1987, as the Sri Lankan army began an operation to retake the Jaffna peninsula, India, which was providing moral and material support to some of the Tamil groups, intervened to try to bring about a settlement. The Indo-Lanka Accord, signed on 29 July, brought an Indian Peace Keeping Force (IPKF) to the north and ushered in the 13th Amendment to Sri Lanka's Constitution, setting up Provincial Councils and offering the prospect of political autonomy for the north and the east. Under the agreement, the Sri Lankan army withdrew to barracks and the Tamil insurgents were supposed to lay down their arms. But the leader of the LTTE, Velupillai Prabhakaran, ultimately refused to comply and launched a military offensive against the Indian troops.

In the south of Sri Lanka, exploiting the presence of Indian troops and the strong nationalist reaction among Sinhalese people, youth militants of the Janatha Vimukthi Peramuna (JVP) launched their second offensive against the government, leading to thousands of extra-judicial executions and disappearances at the hands of both state and non-state actors. This insurrection, which paralysed government in the southern provinces for more than two years, was quelled with considerable brutality and the killing of the JVP leadership by early 1990. In the same year, with a change of government in Delhi, the IPKF withdrew from Sri Lanka and the war in the north resumed.

In 1994, the UNP, which had ruled the country for nearly 16 years under three Presidents, was finally rejected at the polls. Chandrika Kumaratunga became the Prime Minister of Sri Lanka at the head of an SLFP-led coalition, and was later elected President. She had campaigned on the basis of bringing peace to the country after years of war and was handed a convincing electoral mandate, though the promise of peace was not fulfilled during her 10 years in office. Instead, after a honeymoon period of two or three years, the trend towards authoritarianism continued. Executive interference in the judiciary became pronounced. Editors were targeted with criminal defamation charges and journalists were subjected to physical threats and assaults.

In 2001, her government lost the national parliamentary elections to a UNP-led coalition known as the United National Front (UNF) with Ranil Wickremasinghe as the Prime Minister. This ushered in an unusual two-year period of 'co-habitation', which brought some relaxation of restrictions on the media and renewed efforts to find a peaceful solution to the country's civil war. A Norwegian-brokered ceasefire accord was signed between the LTTE and the UNF, but it became notable for infringements of its various provisions by both parties. In November 2003, Kumaratunga dismissed the Prime Minister when he was out of the country and in April 2004, after fresh elections, her party re-captured power in a United People's Freedom Alliance, which included the JVP. On her retirement as President in 2005, her Prime Minister, Mahinda Rajapaksa, was elected as her successor, with strong backing from the Buddhist clergy. The conduct of the war in the north and the east was then intensified, leading ultimately to the military defeat of the LTTE, which was achieved with serious loss of life not only among the combatants, but also among Tamil civilians, putting Sri Lanka at the centre of international scrutiny.

These eventful decades brought a transformation of what had earlier been an elite-dominated, consensus-driven, lightly regulated society into one living almost permanently under Emergency laws. The courts continued to function but were under growing political pressure and limited by legislation suspending constitutional freedoms in the furtherance of the state's efforts to subdue its militant opponents. With the appointment in 1999 of a former Attorney General, Sarath Silva, to the office of Chief Justice by President Kumaratunge, the Supreme Court was taken in politically driven directions, attracting the censure of the United Nations and monitoring bodies such as the International Bar Association. The 17th Amendment to the constitution was passed by the parliament in 2001 in an effort to stem the politicisation of the country's judiciary, civil service and police. It provided for a Constitutional Council, representing not only politicians, but also eminent men and women in public life, which was to be responsible for the key appointments to public and judicial office. But though the council was formed in 2002, it was soon made unworkable by politicians irritated at the restraints on their powers.

Militarisation of the civilian administration became a common pattern, particularly in the war-affected areas. The Sri Lankan army, which only consisted of a few battalions at independence, grew to a regular fighting force of over 200,000 men, made up of 13 divisions and many specialised brigades, recruited to deal with internal insurgencies both in the south and the north. Efforts to persuade the LTTE to civilianise their struggle and to accept political autonomy in the two merged Tamil-majority provinces were twice rejected and a series of military campaigns ensued, culminating in the victory of May 2009, the death of the LTTE leader and of many thousands of civilians caught in the crossfire.

These were years of extraordinary civil unrest, insecurity and anxiety, in which many young people grew up not knowing what their rights were in normal times—because there were no normal times. The business of government continued; elections took place, but many leaders were replaced by the bullet rather than the ballot. The assassination of S.W.R.D. Bandaranaike in 1959 was an early instance of what later became a worryingly regular phenomenon. Leading UNP politicians, such as President Ranasinghe Premadasa, Lalith Athulathmudali and Gamini Dissanayake, and the People's Alliance Foreign Minister, Lakshman Kadirgamar, were all assassinated by the Tamil Tigers, and virtually all the moderate TULF politicians, including Amirthalingam, Yogeshwaran, Dharmalingam, Alalasundaram and Neelan Thiruchelvam, were also assassinated, either by the Tigers or as a result of political rivalries within the Tamil community. It was through such internecine warfare and the brutal elimination of other Tamil resistance groups that the Tigers acquired their dominance by the late 1980s.

The death toll in the war against the Tigers rose to over 60,000 people by 2009, of which at least 20,000 were Sri Lankan soldiers, an equal number if not more were Tamil Tigers, and a similar number were civilian casualties, many caught up in the last months of the conflict. Independently of the Tamil conflict, death tolls in the two major JVP uprisings of 1971 and 1988 in the south of Sri Lanka also ran into tens of thousands. From a model democracy and island paradise, Sri Lanka had been transformed into a country at war, in which democracy and human rights could no longer be taken for granted.

The implications of this transformation for freedom of expression, which is a critical component of democracy, for the exercise of that freedom by the country's media, and for its constitutional underpinning through parliament and the courts have been widespread and severe. In the aftermath of the victory over the Tamil Tigers, President Rajapaksa was returned to power in 2010 with an overwhelming mandate. Yet, democracy was weakened still further when the 18th Amendment to the constitution removed many salutary features of the 17th Amendment as well as abolishing the term limits for the re-election of the President. If a functioning democracy and a thriving civil society require a sense of confidence among all citizens that they are free to air their views and go about their business without let or hindrance, providing they do no harm to others, then Sri Lanka has not been measuring up to that ideal for some time. If it requires an independent judiciary, which is able to review the acts of the executive, interpret the constitution and uphold the rights of citizens without fear or favour, then the hasty and ill thought out impeachment of Sri Lanka's Chief Justice, Dr Shirani Bandaranayake, in 2013, was only the latest of a series of developments which cast doubt on that essential division of powers. As to the fourth estate—the print media, television and radio, the Internet and the proliferating social media—it has been working under serious constraints, legal and illegal, overt and covert, for many years. Sri Lankan journalism has a long and distinguished pedigree, stretching back well over a century, but its practitioners never faced such serious challenges as during the last phase of the long civil war. Between 2004 and 2009, according to the international agency, the Committee to Protect Journalists, 16 journalists, both Tamil and Sinhalese, were assassinated. In 2007, a leading commercial TV company had its newsroom smashed up by an armed gang. In addition to the legal constraints imposed under anti-terrorism legislation, Sri Lankans learnt to be wary of the 'white van syndrome', of armed men acting with impunity to curb the critics of the regime. Over 30 journalists fled the country for fear of their lives, taking refuge in neighbouring India and Nepal, and in 2014, many had still not returned.

The government's response to continued international pressure has not been encouraging. The passing of resolutions by the United Nations Human Rights Council (UNHRC) urging the Sri Lankan government to pursue accountability for acts committed during the war by state agents and to restore the Rule of Law has been met by further restrictions on the media. In 2014, the UNHRC passed a resolution mandating an international inquiry led by the Office of the High Commissioner for Human Rights into abuses alleged to have been committed by both the government and the LTTE during the final stages of the conflict. This was followed by an increasingly severe government crackdown on journalists, particularly Tamil journalists living and working in the former conflict areas in the north and the east.

As part of this crackdown, organisers and participants at media training workshops received death threats. Tamil journalists travelling to the capital city for workshops were stopped and harassed at army checkpoints. In an unprecedented occurrence, mobs demonstrated in front of the press industry-run Sri Lanka Press Institute in central Colombo, demanding the halting of an ongoing workshop. Police investigation and action against such mobs have been ineffective.

The intimidation of the media has gone beyond the specific targeting of journalists of Tamil ethnicity. Journalists reporting on situations of unrest have been increasingly subjected to assaults and abuse. During the 2013 protests by villagers for clean water in Weliwerya (located close to Colombo) where the army was called out, resulting in two bystanders dying from indiscriminate firing, journalists reporting on the scene were chased by army officers, abused and attacked. After the eruption of communal violence between Sinhalese and Muslims in Sri Lanka's south-western towns of Aluthgama and Beruwala in 2014, journalists who reported on the incidents were questioned by the Criminal Investigation Department (CID). Journalists reporting on court proceedings involving acts of human right abuses by state agents have also been subjected to threats and abuse.

The government's inaction in bringing those responsible for the intimidation of journalists before the courts carries with it the implication of governmental involvement. The use of national security laws to suppress freedom of expression on the part of the media has continued, while militant Buddhist priests have engaged in hate speech provoking communal and religious hatred without hindrance. In July 2014, the government issued a directive calling for non-governmental organisations to cease holding training programmes for journalists. There has been an evident hardening of the government stance towards dissent, including the continued blocking of websites perceived as being 'anti-government'.

This troubled history raises a number of important questions about the future of democracy and the role of the media in societies divided by civil war and afflicted by the breakdown of inherited constitutional and legal norms. Is what has been happening in Sri Lanka, a reversion to pre-colonial norms of government and a rejection of the paraphernalia of democracy which Britain introduced—with colonial modifications—in Sri Lanka and other Asian and African countries? Or is it a temporary aberration, an abnormal situation brought about by the extraordinary pressures of ethnic division and civil war, which can be restored to normality by the will of the people and the re-establishment of those norms? Sri Lanka's lawyers and journalists have a preferred answer to these questions and their support for valued freedoms is a powerful element of Sri Lankan civil society. But in a highly polarised society at the time of civil war, the appeal of personality and ethnicity has tended to be stronger than the niceties of constitutions, rights and the ideal of equality before the law. Maintaining an inherited system of rights is one thing; restoring it in adverse circumstances quite another.

Throughout the long years of conflict, the Sri Lankan government remained an active member of the international community. It is a signatory of many international charters, conventions and protocols, such as the UN charter or the International Convention on Civil and Political Rights, which commit it, like other signatories, to respect the civil and political rights of individuals, including the right to life, freedom of religion, freedom of speech, freedom of assembly, electoral rights and rights to due process and a fair trial. It is also a signatory of dozens of other international agreements which underpin its relations with the rest of the world in a whole range of spheres of activity, from trade to the environment, from the law of the sea to the rights of the child and discrimination against women. As a member of the Commonwealth, Sri Lanka subscribes to the Harare declaration of 1991 and the Latimer House principles endorsed at Abuja in 2003, which set out Commonwealth values, including commitment to the rule of law, the division of powers between different branches of government, the independence of the judiciary and the importance of the principle of accountability. It has not abrogated these agreements, though it has been called to account by its critics at the bar of the United Nations Human Rights Committee and in other international fora on account of its human rights record during the war as well as for attacks on the judiciary and the media in the post-war years. Its suitability to chair the

Commonwealth Heads of Government meeting in Sri Lanka in 2013 was questioned on the same grounds.

The Rajapaksa Presidency had always maintained that it was fighting a terrorist war which threatened the existence of the state and that ultimately it had the overwhelming support of the predominantly Sinhala Buddhist electorate in eliminating that threat. Whatever his critics may say, President Rajapaksa was returned to power with a substantial majority in 2010. Since then, however, public concern has increased regarding the wastage of public funds for projects, including a commercially questionable international airport in his hometown as well as a proliferation of ministries expending vast resources while the cost of living for ordinary citizens has risen steeply. The unprecedented concentration of power in the hands of the President and his brothers, the growing disregard for Sri Lanka's parliament and the virtual decimation of the political opposition have brought Sri Lanka dangerously close to authoritarian if not dictatorial rule. In 2013, the holding of provincial council elections in the northern province was a positive development, even if prompted by external pressures, but the sweeping victory of the Tamil National Alliance, which stood in opposition to government, indicated that the policy of post-war development at the expense of the civil rights of the Tamil population had not paid dividends.

Internationally, in suppressing the Tamil insurgency, the Sri Lankan government benefitted from the global 'war on terror' declared by the United States in the wake of the September 2001 attacks on New York. The LTTE, which had been widely supported by the Tamil diaspora, was declared a terrorist organisation. The conduct of the war in its brutal final months opened up allegations and evidence of war crimes against civilians on both sides, with the Sri Lankan army under particular scrutiny. But the Sri Lanka government responded robustly to its 'western' critics, accusing them of subjecting it to a type of scrutiny to which even developed countries are not subject, a view that found some sympathy among other Asian and African countries. The end of the long civil war has been generally welcomed internationally, though criticism of the government's human rights records remains. At the same time, enhanced military and logistical—as well as political—support from China is apparently changing Sri Lanka's perceptions of its international and regional strategic interests. China's increased presence in and around the Indian Ocean region is creating new geopolitical realities.

The curbing of freedom of expression in Sri Lanka, by whatever means, has been part of a complex series of changes in governance, brought about by the persistence of the civil war and the state's response to it. But it has also highlighted the importance of constitutional freedoms to a thriving and inclusive democracy and the role of the judiciary in upholding them, as well as the dangers inherent in their suspension or gradual decline. It has focussed attention on the role of the Sri Lankan state as regulator, newspaper proprietor, broadcaster and enforcer of last resort, as well as the implications of such a concentration of power for the public interest, the reflection of diverse opinions and the role of the fourth estate in holding government to account. The balance between state and private media, the roles of the proprietor and the editor, the working conditions of journalists and their own training and commitment to a free media are other parts of the same jigsaw. Most important of all, however, is the role of Sri Lankan civil society and the Sri Lankan public, their perception of the role of the press and of the electronic media and the extent to which they have prized these freedoms. It is these interrelated issues which this book seeks to explore through the experience and understanding of a number of leading Sri Lankan lawyers, journalists and academics. The aim is to identify what reforms may be required to restore freedoms which have been suspended or curtailed, to improve the quality of media regulation and to provide for more effective media education and media literacy for university students and for other citizens.

Sri Lanka's Media Development from a Regional Perspective

This analysis is provided in the context of regional and international developments and comparisons. Sri Lanka is not alone in facing challenges both to its constitutional and legal systems and media freedoms. It shares a common history with other countries of South Asia, in particular, in terms of the colonial provenance of some of its basic laws and regulations, including those affecting freedom of expression and freedom of information. Among these are the Official Secrets Acts originally drawn up by colonial governments with the aim of protecting and strengthening their own authority. The extent to which the various South Asian Official Secrets Acts have been changed since independence provides one measure of how much new thinking went into building the legal and moral foundations of the independent states. Some of the continuity, however, reflects the persistence of systems and procedures which have been retained by most states, whatever their ideological basis or political and cultural origins.

The monopolistic character of broadcasting legislation was common to all the South Asian states until it was overturned by new communication technologies in the 1990s. Laws derived from colonial legislation also provided the means to influence and control or manipulate the print media but did not envisage state control of the press. Post-colonial governments in South Asia went further than their colonial predecessors: for example, in Pakistan under military rule, in India under the emergency in the 1970s, and in Sri Lanka, where the Lake House group was nationalised. The techniques of press control may have been learned from the former colonial regimes but they were not restricted by colonial precedents in their application. In India, the foundational premises of free speech and the kind of principles that have been established emerged in the context of the print media. And the freedom of the broadcast media depends crucially on the degree to which the print media can exercise those freedoms.

Fundamental to the constitutional foundations of freedom of speech and expression in contemporary South Asia has been the extent of independence of the judiciary and its ability in different states to interpret and actively extend these rights. Here, the experience of India, Pakistan, Bangladesh and Sri Lanka has been different. Sometimes, the ability or otherwise of the judiciary to enforce constitutional rights has been a two-edged weapon for the South Asian media. In some contexts, it has been empowering and a strong protection against the arbitrary encroachment of government on civil and political rights. In others, it has reinforced its own authority and that of governments in ways which have not been friendly to the freedom of the media. The ways in which the doctrine of Contempt of Court—another legacy from colonial times and UK practice—has been applied and developed by the judiciaries of India, Pakistan and Sri Lanka, and the implications for the freedom of the media, are one area of innovation and comparability which is more than a matter of academic interest.

In comparing the impact of constitutional rights on media law in South Asia, the relative strength of the Indian courts is apparent in their ability to challenge government decisions both in normal circumstances and in an emergency or when extraordinary powers are in force. From the judiciary's role in standing up to government during Indira Gandhi's period of Emergency rule in 1975–1976 to its 1995 decision in declaring the airwaves to be public property, India's activist judiciary has set a powerful domestic and regional example. In Pakistan, where for more than 30 years since independence the country has been under military rule, constitutional rights are more vulnerable to emergency provisions. In Bangladesh, the constitution provides an even weaker foundation.

Commenting on the situation in India, Lawrence Liang focuses on the restrictive rather than the enabling influence of the judiciary for media freedoms.[1] He argues that the rulings of the courts on Contempt issues have had the effect of suppressing a critique of judicial pronouncements. In viewing judicial activism as the defining aspect of a new construction of media restrictions rather than freedoms, he also indicates a promising comparative perspective across the countries of South Asia. In Pakistan, it is recognised that members of the public may in good faith criticise judicial acts. The courts have held that this right must not be exercised in pursuance of improper motive or malice or in an attempt to impair or impede the course of administration of justice. However, in the November 2007 emergency provisions, it was the government itself rather than the media which mounted a radical attack on the judiciary. In Bangladesh, the courts have taken conservative positions and Contempt of Court legislation has increasingly come to be used against the media. In Sri Lanka, the sub-judice rule has seriously impeded discussion on matter of public interest.

Among the changes in the international legal environment which have been affecting media laws in South Asia are attitudes to Freedom of Information. In Pakistan, Freedom of Information was regarded as a subsidiary of the right to freedom of expression expressed in Article 19 of the Constitution. Pressure from international organisations led to the promulgation of the Freedom of Information Ordinance of 2002. But the positive features of this law are marred by a broad list of exceptions. Government can classify embarrassing or revealing documents, or set a prohibitively high cost on accessing information. Protection for whistle blowers, who expose confidential information in the public interest, is another issue on which international practice is increasing awareness in South Asia, where the concept enjoys less recognition and protection than in some other countries.

The increasing use of the Internet and of mobile phone technology has in some respects greatly increased the range and participation in journalistic activity by ordinary citizens. It also presents a formidable challenge to systems of censorship. Internationally—as the Chinese government has demonstrated—it has not proved as difficult to censor Internet traffic as was once thought. An international consensus on the evils of child pornography, and international political cooperation against terrorism, appears to have had some impact. In Pakistan, while in some respects government has been able to censor Internet traffic, blocking mainly pornographic and anti-government websites, citizens can still access information which the government would prefer to censor. South Asian experience in this area is part of a global picture.

Public Interest Broadcasting is another concept which is commonly recognised as being important and valid in South Asia, even when the interpretations of its content and meaning may differ. It has been the commonest defence of the value of the state broadcasters, which except in Sri Lanka still dominate or monopolise the terrestrial networks. The historic control and manipulation of the state media by governments for their own propaganda purposes has always been the biggest flaw in that argument. The justification of the claim on the grounds of superior reach became harder to prove as satellite TV expanded into the rural areas and state broadcasters in all countries adopted the same commercial practices as their competitors. However, the commercial TV channels have done little to reinforce their own claim to national legitimacy by moving into the area of public interest broadcasting, arguably a missed opportunity. In the current situation, it is not possible to revert to the development communication model that prevailed in the early history of broadcasting in India. But the virtual disappearance of issues of development in mainstream media in almost all South Asian countries certainly alerts us to the need to think about issues of public interest broadcasting. This is a challenge for all the South Asian countries which requires further analysis and discussion both nationally and regionally.

National responses to the problems posed by converging communications technologies form another useful point of comparison. In some countries, new media regulatory institutions have challenged the authority of the ministries which previously had the power to regulate broadcasting and communications. In India, this has put the Information and Broadcasting (I & B) Ministry and the Communications Ministry to some extent in competition with the quasi-independent Telecoms Regulatory Authority of India (TRAI). The TRAI took over responsibility for broadcasting and cable TV regulation in January 2004. The Communications Convergence Bill of 2000 had been aimed at creating a single regulatory authority, the Communications Commission of India or CCI, to replace the TRAI, with the power to regulate content in any media. The bill was pending in India's Parliament for years until it lapsed with the dissolution of the Lok Sabha in 2005. Subsequently a further attempt was made with the Indian Broadcasting Services Bill of 2007 to create a new regulatory authority with enhanced powers, but this met with vigorous opposition and was not enacted into law.

In Pakistan, a regulatory body for the electronic media was set up shortly before the February 1997 election. In 2002 under General Pervez Musharraf's military government, it was renamed the Pakistan Electronic Media Regulatory Authority (PEMRA) by an ordinance. In addition to being the media licensing authority, it was given a brief to improve access to mass media at the local and community levels and to ensure good governance by optimising the free flow of information. It was ostensibly independent of the Communications ministry, though it continued to be subject to official pressures. In the aftermath of the October 2005 earthquake, PEMRA's action in issuing local radio licences in the disaster-affected areas was a major boost to the liberalisation of information in Pakistan and enhanced its reputation. But when PEMRA imposed drastic restrictions on broadcasters under the emergency of November 2007, its role at that time—despite its denials that it was acting on the government's orders—severely undermined its credibility with the industry and with the public.

In Bangladesh, there is no equivalent law for licensing of the broadcast media or for the regulation of private radio and television. Licensing decisions are made by government and subject to negotiation by the bureaucracy and private entrepreneurs. An initiative to set up an autonomous broadcasting commission made by a high-powered government-appointed committee in 1996 came to nothing. Bangladesh media continue to be subject to direct government control in the case of the state broadcasters and to more covert but no less direct pressure in the case of the private TV channels. Compared to India or Pakistan, Bangladesh has some way to go in promoting freedom of the airwaves or confidence that it is moving in that direction.

In Sri Lanka, there has been a long-standing demand for structural reform of the state electronic media to protect them from political pressures. But the recommendation of a government-appointed commission to make them autonomous was not implemented in the mid-1990s and looks further away today. Sri Lanka was ahead of other South Asian countries in creating diversity in its media regime both in FM radio, the provision of community radio under the state umbrella, and in licensing both terrestrial and satellite TV channels. But the institutional and legal structures for protecting a diverse media system in Sri Lanka leave much to be desired. Government continues to license stations directly itself and in times of insecurity to restrict media freedoms by recourse to emergency legislation. For these and other reasons, the judicial underpinning of media freedoms is also more in doubt than for some years, which is a cause of increasing concern to the journalistic community. Sri Lanka has shown with its telecommunications authority that an autonomous body can prove effective, but in present circumstances, there seems little likelihood that it will embark on the same path for the broadcasting industry.

Aims and Contents of the Book

This book aims to present an authoritative analysis by Sri Lankan writers of the legal and regulatory environment affecting the Sri Lankan print and electronic media and to examine the role of media education and training in the shaping of the professional journalist and wider civil society. The authors have varied and complementary experience and perspectives on the development of the Sri Lankan media. They are aware of the threats and challenges to it playing an effective democratic role and the value of a comparative perspective. The analysis illustrates the importance of the professional issues involved, the range of matters needing reform and the principles at stake. It also touches on the reciprocal implications for Sri Lanka of the media policies of other South Asian countries. In the light of changes in the media environment both regionally and globally, it asks whether the policies that Sri Lanka has been pursuing towards the media represent a simple variant of the frameworks set up in other democratic societies or a significant departure from widely accepted democratic values and principles.

The book incorporates the outcome of a research initiative started in late 2009 by the Institute of Commonwealth Studies in London University with the support of the Ford Foundation. The principal objective was to work with educational institutions in Sri Lanka to contribute to the development of new curricula in Media Policy, Regulation and Law, with the aim of providing an accessible guide to the issues and to promote greater understanding of problems specific to Sri Lanka and in some cases common to other South Asian countries.

The book is divided into five sections. The first deals with the Sri Lankan print media, the second looks at electronic and new media, the third at legal and institutional reforms, the fourth at media education and the fifth at future prospects. The conclusion draws the various strands together and assesses Sri Lanka's experience in the context of regional and international developments.

The Print Media

The first section on the print media consists of four essays by print media practitioners who provide an historical introduction to the development of the media in Sri Lanka and some personal reflections on the challenges of being a journalist in recent decades.

In Chapter 2, Sinha Ratnatunga, the Editor-in-Chief of the *Sunday Times*, reflects on the development of the Sri Lankan media over more than 200 years, the battles of the print media with successive governments to preserve its autonomy and the wider issues of freedom for the electronic media and new online sites. He argues that media freedoms are a sine qua non of a modern liberal democracy, but that patience is required in convincing a sceptical and increasingly powerful government of the need to promote and protect them.

In Chapter 3, Ameen Izzadeen, a senior media practitioner, analyses the behaviour of the minority media in different phases of the country's history and the challenges they face today. The term 'minority media' refers to the print and electronic media catering to the minority communities—the Tamils, who make up 17 per cent of the country's 20 million population, and the Muslims, who are 8.5 per cent of the population. He concentrates mainly on the Tamil media, which is further divided into three categories— independent Tamil media owned by Tamils, independent Tamil media owned by Sinhalese and Tamil media run by the state. The development of the minority media in Sri Lanka is examined in three phases: the early history, the minority media during the civil war and the minority media after the civil war. The paper looks at the challenges the sector has faced and the threats to journalists from state and non-state actors. It also explores the concept of embedded journalism in Sri Lanka and the development of the modern media.

In Chapter 4, Amal Jayasinghe writes of his personal experience reporting for an international news agency on different stages of the conflict in Sri Lanka over the past 30 years. He describes the impact of physical threats to Sri Lankan journalists, and the effect of emergency laws and other legal instruments in controlling and restricting the media. He assesses the sensitivity of the government and sections of the Sri Lankan media to foreign reporting on the conflict in Sri Lanka and the extent to which it assists or handicaps the local assertion of media freedoms and the practice of independent journalism. He writes of the need for professional standards and the cooperation of media institutions in providing training, and the challenges ahead for the Sri Lankan media following the end of the war against the LTTE and Tamil separatism.

In Chapter 5, Namini Wijedasa writes on the contribution that women make to journalism and the media in Sri Lanka and the particular difficulties that they face in the profession. She observes that while there are fewer women in journalism than men, they are gradually taking on more influential roles. Women journalists face many of the same constraints as their male counterparts, as well as particular issues of sexual harassment in the workplace. But she says the breakdown of law and order in Sri Lanka is all-encompassing; and the control or suppression of rights is not restricted to the media industry.

Electronic and New Media

The second section of the book begins with the chapter 'The Political Economy of the Electronic Media' by the late Tilak Jayaratne, a former Director of Educational Services at the Sri Lanka Broadcasting Corporation (SLBC), and Sarath Kellapotha, senior researcher and broadcaster.

This chapter takes a practical perspective based on the authors' own experience as senior broadcasters in the state-controlled electronic media. They review the history of the electronic media in Sri Lanka, its colonial origins and the post-independence political context, which has underpinned and in some cases distorted its development. They provide a theoretical framework to their discussion of media practice but give less weight to legal issues, which are covered extensively elsewhere. Since 1971, insurgency and conflict have had a major impact on the development of the media, drawing attention to the potential power of the media both as an instrument for government and as a threat to the stability of the state if it were to fall under insurgent influence or control. It is argued that political parties took advantage of this dilemma. In opposition, they would agitate for media rights and promise reform. In power, the same parties changed their position.

The authors examine the changes in the media landscape of the 1980s and 1990s, some positive and some negative. The case of the New Education

Service (NES) set up by the SLBC in 1994 is examined in detail as an initiative which set out to extend the best traditions and practice of Sri Lankan broadcasting, but was abruptly cancelled when it appeared to be too critical of aspects of government policy. One of the authors was closely involved in setting up the NES and the account provides a strong personal perspective on what went wrong and why. The staff of the state broadcaster was strongly unionised and the authors argue that there was competition between the unions and management as to who should exercise the role of gatekeeper of the public interest.

A subsequent 'see-saw phase' in relations between the government and the media showed that the pressures for media control and media liberalisation were not all one way, and that even in a time of conflict there was significant support for media freedoms in society at large which governments were in part willing to recognise. Under the unprecedented but short lived 'cohabitation' government of 2002–2004 in which the President and Prime Minister were of rival parties, Prime Minister Ranil Wickremasinghe took some significant steps towards enhancing media freedoms, notably with the repeal of provisions relating to Criminal Defamation in the Penal Code and the Press Council Law, though the authors argue that he was motivated as much by political rivalry as by a commitment to media freedom.

The record of President Mahinda Rajapaksa has been one of consolidating his authority by an appeal to the very different constituency of Sinhala Buddhist nationalist opinion, for which it seems a liberal and open media as an ideal indicated in Sri Lanka's constitutional and legal system has less attraction. The continuance of tough media restrictions even after the defeat of the Tamil Tigers has incurred extensive international criticism. But despite these pressures, the reporting environment remains insecure, with many media outlets only reporting what those closely affiliated with the ruling party wish to make public.

The authors argue that media ownership is crucial to the way in which society is organised and economic decisions are taken. The private electronic media in Sri Lanka are owned by people whose wider business networks are vulnerable and who are not focused principally on serving the public interest. They argue that a fresh look at the entire media ownership framework is required to encourage more diversity of ideas and voices.

At a time when traditional space for independent journalism has been shrinking, the proliferation of new media and the principle of open access to digital platforms on the Internet has been a potent means both of extending journalists' sources of information and the ability of members of the public to disseminate information and opinion without being subject to editorial control. But the space thus made available to a responsible 'citizen journalist' becomes equally accessible to false or untested assertions, extremist views and potentially subversive or socially disruptive propaganda. Kishali Pinto-Jayawardena and Gehan Gunatilleke note (in Chapter 8) that in Sri Lanka 'news websites have flourished whereas freedoms of the [mainstream] media have drastically declined'. They write:

> On the one hand, the 'website culture' has provided badly needed space for the circulation of news and opinion without repercussions for individual journalists or publishing houses. On the other hand, unrestrained by the law or by effective self-regulation, gossip and slander masquerade as 'news' on some of these websites. In the context of the consistent suppressing of conventional news gathering by the intimidation, threatening and killing of journalists, these developments have been unfortunate but hardly surprising.

Students of the digital media have argued that a new generation of users, which has grown up with the Internet, has very different perceptions of the nature of the media and its relationship to state and society. These so-called 'digital natives' are less impressed with the globalised nature of the media so apparent in television and radio broadcasting than with the possibilities and implications of applying digital technology to an immense variety of local circumstances. The Internet has been a key medium of protest and mobilisation as well as a means of transforming interpersonal relations and social communication.[2]

Efforts by governments to counteract these influences, ostensibly to protect individual rights and the integrity of public institutions, threaten to create whole new areas of surveillance, censorship and media control, though the technical challenges remain considerable. The danger to the media may be seen more in setting new benchmarks for online media outlets which are more restrictive than those in place for the print and broadcast media.

For the established print media, self-regulation has been the preferred option, although in practice it has been seriously flawed. With the new media there has been even greater resistance to self-regulation. The success of the Internet has depended on its freedom and flexibility. It has been able to innovate by dispensing with the governing institutions and editorial control which determine the content of the print and broadcast media. Any attempt to regulate content would undermine confidence in the accuracy of the information provided.

In Chapter 7, science writer and new media watcher Nalaka Gunawardene offers a perspective on how Sri Lankan policy and regulatory systems, and society as a whole, are responding to the proliferation of new media, principally mobile telephony and the Internet. He argues that the rapid growth in new communication technologies, expansion in their service coverage and the lowering of access barriers have not been accompanied by adequate policy preparedness or societal acceptance. This mismatch has led to an uneasy coexistence of analogue-era thinking with digital tools, platforms and opportunities, creating distrust and friction.

Gunawardene says that resolving these post-connectivity challenges is crucial to harnessing the full potential of new media for socio-economic development, national integration and democratic pluralism. Policy makers, law reformers, researchers and social activists operate in a difficult environment. But advocates of a right to information and freedom of expression have to communicate better the tangible benefits of their conceptual ideals, so that the currently apathetic public appreciate and demand such freedoms. Gunawardene concludes that there are many opportunities in the networked world to promote the public interest and achieve better social and cultural cohesion—but only if fundamental freedoms are valued and defended.

Legal and Institutional Reforms

The third section of the book begins with a detailed chapter by co-editor Kishali Pinto-Jayawardena, in association with Gehan Gunatilleke, a lawyer and independent researcher. This analyses issues of media policy from a legal and institutional perspective with a view to identify where reform might be needed or possible, both in protecting the rights of individuals and in the operation of the media industry and relevant social and legal institutions.

The authors stress the high literacy rate and strong traditions of professional journalism practised in Sri Lanka in the early years of the country's independence but argue that a number of factors have weakened independent journalism in recent decades. High among these is the impact of two major insurgencies, mainly among Sinhalese youth, and the long civil war against the LTTE to prevent Tamil separatism.

As a result of the war and persistent reliance on emergency regulations, there has been growing hostility between the state and the private media, accompanied by intimidation and in some cases assassination of local journalists and editors. The constitutional and legal framework has been turned against media institutions and has contributed to the erosion of media freedoms. Issues of media regulation and media law reform in Sri Lanka reflect a debate in many other countries and the authors explore comparisons both with India and with countries outside the South Asian region. Formal censorship imposed by tight security laws has been reinforced by self-censorship in the face of extra judicial killings, violence and real personal threats against media personnel, for which no authority would take responsibility or even investigate.

The ending of the war against the LTTE in 2009 brought hope of a fresh start. Pinto-Jayawardena and Gunatilleke write that 'ideally, Sri Lanka's post-war years should have heralded the opening up of a vibrant media culture with all its potential to aid reconciliation between communities'. In reality, the Sri Lankan media has struggled to re-establish its integrity and independence in the face of 'an over-mighty state' and the weakening of traditional checks and balances.

State policy relating to media law reform in Sri Lanka has often been dictated by expediency. There is a process of bargaining between the media industry bodies and the government in power at the time. Outdated laws and regulations are an obstacle to media professionalism. Criminal defamation has been one area where a measure of reform has succeeded. But there are other areas of reform in which there has been little progress. These include Contempt of Court, the creation of an independent broadcasting regulator and the passing of Right to Information legislation.

Initiatives for media reform in Sri Lanka owe a great deal to what is usually known as 'the R.K.W. Goonesekere Committee Report' of 1996. This government-appointed parliamentary committee drew up a 'Legislative and Regulatory Framework for the Media' using a 'bipartisan approach' and identified areas where reform was necessary. After more than 18 years, many of its recommendations are still not implemented. But they constitute a landmark in progressive consideration of media reform, and have remained relevant in a political environment in which despite occasional periods of attempted relaxation, restrictions on the media have been tightened. The committee argued that the constitution on its own was not adequate to protect freedom of speech and expression. The principle of open government would be best protected by a Freedom of Information Act. Pinto-Jayawardena and Gunatilleke examine these recommendations and the initiatives to respond to them in the years since the committee reported.

The emergency laws and restrictions that operated in Sri Lanka during the long years of conflict have not stifled debate about media reform. Over the years, there have been times when support for media reform has been articulated vigorously by media lawyers and a wide spectrum of civil society, for whom liberal institutions have been seen not as an alien ideology, but as one rooted in the independence movement and supported by advocates of political and cultural autonomy.

The symposium held in 1998 which led to the Colombo Declaration on Media Freedom and Social Responsibility marked a high point of public support for media freedoms. This was the first of three so-called Colombo declarations that have continued to provide a framework for long-term policies for ensuring media freedoms. It was primarily a media initiative which showed that even while government was tightening its grip, the media could take a strong stand to assert its independence. For the electronic media, it was a time when the case for an autonomous status for the state broadcasters seemed to be most urgently demonstrated. But it never happened. In more normal times, these declarations might have been accepted and enforced by governments. Currently, however, the prospect of achieving a more liberal policy framework looks bleak.

Although the state has been slow to respond to the main concerns of the media industry, civil society continues to attach considerable importance to what is known as the 'Tholangamuwa Declaration'. This was the outcome of an initiative of key Sri Lankan journalists' associations in adopting a Media Charter in September 2005. The charter asserted that 'a professional media with a responsibility to the public interest, independent of government or partisan influence and interference, is a vital part of the series of checks and balances central to democracy'.

The Tholangamuwa Declaration places great emphasis on the citizen's right to know and freedom of information at all levels of government. It calls on the Sri Lankan government to promote transparency, open government and freedom of information and ensure the participation of all citizens in developing a democratic culture to strengthen the cohesion of all communities. The charter also emphasises the journalist's right to work in conditions of safety and security, without undue pressure, direct and indirect or interference.

The need for freedom of information legislation is also underlined from a more purely legal perspective in Chapter 9, in which senior practitioner in public law, Jayantha de Almeida Guneratne, assesses the concept of judicial activism as an influence on the practical workings of the Sri Lankan legal system, and in particular on the implementation and protection of media freedoms. Although Sri Lankan courts have the power to enforce fundamental rights as defined in the Sri Lankan constitution, he argues that this power is in practice limited. From a detailed review of the relevant case law and judicial observations on issues of media freedom, he concludes that a Right to Information Act is essential to support the country's commitment to basic democratic values.

Media Education

The fourth section of the book looks at media teaching and training—in universities and professional training institutions; how it has shaped the industry and the wider understanding of the media's role in society and what might be done to make it more effective.

Kishali Pinto-Jayawardena and Gehan Gunatilleke examine the teaching of media studies at university level in Sri Lanka and offer a critical analysis of its effectiveness in fulfilling these broad objectives. After a review of the curricula of different Sri Lankan universities, they highlight in particular a serious lack of attention to media policy and law. As a vibrant new generation seeks to enter the profession, they argue there is a real need for more effective professional training and more course content on media freedom and contemporary issues.

The chapter also compares the teaching of media law and policy in Sri Lanka to that in India, based on Pinto-Jayawardena's discussions with colleagues in media teaching institutions during a visit to south India. She argues that the expansion of the Indian media during the last two decades has transformed media education. But she finds that efforts to reform curricula have met with obstacles. While the laws governing the Internet now occupy an important part of the curriculum, constitutional aspects of the courses have become less important. The linking of human rights with the teaching of media law and policy has a lower priority.

The chapter discusses the sequencing of content in university courses and the difficulty of finding the right balance between theory and practice. Case studies are often taken from foreign examples, which are neither contemporary nor relevant to the local media. In the authors' view, the approach to media law in these courses lacks an interdisciplinary dimension and a critical study of the role and impact of the media is often missing.

Chapter 11 deals with media education in the north and the east of Sri Lanka. Dr S. Raguram of the Eastern University, Trincomalee Campus, explains that progress over the past few decades has been seriously affected by persistent insecurity and civil war. He looks at the development of media studies curricula in three universities, the role of language, the balance between theoretical and vocational approaches and links with the job market. He also underlines the need for more critical approaches to the role of media in society and concludes with some recommendations for future changes.

There is broad agreement that the scope of media education includes two important dimensions which are sometimes contradictory. One is to encourage a theoretical understanding of the place of the media in society. This includes a consideration of ownership, audiences and impact, the relationship with government and the policy framework both for freedom of expression and for regulation or control of the media. The second is to provide training in the practical skills required for working in the print or electronic media, the digital media or a combination of all of them. For most training institutions, practical training for a professional qualification is the priority and the more academic aspects of media training take second place. More specifically, the training is oriented towards an existing job market, and when, as in Sri Lanka, many jobs in journalism are dominated by government that objective will almost inevitably determine the nature of the training provided, especially in university and training institutions which are themselves controlled by government. In these circumstances, reconciling the need for technical professional skills with the study of more fundamental or more philosophical issues such as media governance and media ethics becomes a central concern.

In Chapter 12, in their discussion of media literacy and curriculum development in Sri Lanka, Tilak Jayaratne and Sarath Kellapotha put forward the view that media education lacks a national policy and reflects the needs of the industry rather than the country as a whole. In their view, media issues are not much discussed in the media itself, which focuses more on entertainment than on the real issues facing society. Media education needs to be less about professional training and more about encouraging a reflective, critical approach to the media and society.

Drawing on the experience of UNESCO and other organisations, they argue that media literacy should be taught in schools as well as in universities; that it is essential to enable citizens to make sense of the daily flow of information from different media outlets, old and new. They see it as critical to the creation of a vibrant democracy, in which citizens are capable of evaluating the credibility of media content and messages, comprehending and sharing ideas and making informed decisions. They say that media literacy is critically important to media freedom, not just for human rights activists and legal affairs professionals, but for all Sri Lankan citizens. They also contribute their own ideas towards the development of new university curricula which will look beyond the purely theoretical or the purely practical and provide media education which is needs-based and culturally appropriate and draws on the reality of Sri Lankan experience as well as best practice elsewhere.

Future Prospects

In the fifth and final section, Kishali Pinto-Jayawardena and Gehan Gunatilleke take a broader look at the successes of the media industry and the challenges it faces, combining a theoretical analysis with practical observations by media practitioners and by the public at large. They argue that there is a crucial link between efforts towards reform and the overall democratic structure of governance. They point to an unfortunate culture of dependency, as private media organisations in Sri Lanka have become heavily reliant on the government for loans as well as revenues from advertisements.

In reviewing the long-standing reality of government regulation of the media as opposed to the idea of self-regulation, they note that the concept of professional self-regulation of journalistic standards has been described as a 'novel' one for Sri Lanka. But it has been a point of contention as to whether the government was within its rights to regulate television programming on the grounds of national security. The authors have no doubt that the Press Complaints Commission of Sri Lanka (PCCSL), the media industry's self-regulatory body, carries out an indispensable function within the media sector today; and that the allocation of effort and resources to maintain its institutional integrity and efficiency is justified. The main issue with the PCCSL, as they see it, is that some newspaper editors and journalists have been unwilling to accept its decisions—a lack of commitment that could cast doubt on the legitimacy of the concept of self-regulation. The overall media environment is one of excessive governmental control. Additional pressures placed on editors by owners accentuate the already severe constraints on editorial freedom.

Lack of personal and job security and inadequate and often delayed pay have resulted in the failure of the media industry to achieve any real solidarity. For the editors and managers, the Code of Practice of the Editors' Guild is a significant improvement on the previous Press Council Code, but provides limited protection. The practice of self-censorship is universal.

Despite its reputation for being a pioneer in community radio, Sri Lanka does not have an extensive community radio industry, even compared with India which was a late starter in allowing this form of communication. In both countries, there are major ethnic and linguistic divisions between communities, and in a polarised environment there have been few attempts to break these barriers. In Sri Lanka, diversity of ethnic representation in media houses is a key issue which needs to be addressed. So is the wide disparity of representation of women in the profession of journalism, especially at the higher managerial and editorial levels. Here, the authors argue that the reform agenda should be mainly focused on education and training for the future, as they believe that changing the mindsets of the present generation of media professionals is improbable.

Looking at the market, the authors identify a dearth of information on media economics in Sri Lanka. They say the media industry is heavily dependent on advertising and the maximisation of profits leads to irresponsibility. They argue that media stakeholders have a social responsibility in relation to the content of advertisements, which needs to be taken more seriously. On the issue of media censorship, they argue that there has been a big change in the past 10 years. Though censorship is rarely imposed, self-censorship is routinely practised. The government is blamed for creating a climate of fear, but the media are criticised for being too malleable and to a great extent apathetic to the erosion of media freedom. The instances of the disappearance or killing of media personnel, though much fewer than before, coupled with the implementation of prevention of terrorism laws, have contributed to this.

The end of the long civil war brought legitimate expectations of an improvement in media freedoms, which have not yet been fulfilled. In the context of continued media restrictions and curtailment of the freedom of speech and expression, the authors say two issues require special attention. One is the protection of journalists, which should be given the highest priority. The other is to improve the conditions for public debate, extending background reporting and political analysis. Reform is needed and as memories of decades of conflict recede, the hope is that civil society will become stronger, democratic space will broaden and the opportunities for journalists to play an effective role as the fourth estate will increase. As of now, however, this remains an aspiration rather than a reality.

Notes

1. Media Policy and Law in South Asia Scoping Report (2008), http://mediasouthasia.org/research_report.asp (accessed on 25 August 2014).
2. For a discussion of these issues, see Shah and Jansen (2011). See also http://cis-india.org/digital-natives/blog/dnbook (accessed on 25 August 2014).

Part I

The Print Media in Sri Lanka

2

The Erosion of Media Freedoms: Some Historical Reflections

Sinha Ratnatunga

It is no exaggeration to say that in recent times the media in Sri Lanka have themselves been at the centre of the news. Recently, the state-controlled *Daily News* had a front page lead story under the heading 'Under Hand Move to Destabilise Sri Lanka—Hidden Agenda Evident' about a demonstration organised by media unions protesting against the failure of the government to investigate violent attacks on journalists. The Police had gone to the local magistrate to stop the march and got an order that the demonstrators should not obstruct traffic. A counter demonstration was quickly put in place by the government and men carrying intimidating batons were photographed forcing the media demonstrators to switch venues. A week later, the President of the country invited national newspaper editors to breakfast and foreign correspondents to dinner as if asking what the fuss was all about. Such is the facade, if not the farce, of contemporary government–media relations.

Early History

In Sri Lanka, historically, like in all other countries, it was the printing press that formed the media with religious, cultural and local literature. There were numerous pamphleteers and small printing presses made their money rolling out hymn sheets for churches, and their local language equivalent, the '*kavi kola*' or poems praising the dead at funerals.

It was in 1739 that the Dutch occupiers of the island nation introduced the first printing presses to the country. The main purpose of these machines was to print their laws and Christian literature in the vernacular languages, Sinhala and Tamil. With the ouster of the Dutch by the British, these presses fell into the hands of the new settlers. Thus, in 1802, the *Government Gazette* came into existence and is considered as the first newspaper in Sri Lanka (then known as Ceylon). It contained news from the British and Indian press, some local news, public notices, obituaries, a few articles and advertisements. The *Government Gazette* exists even today, though not as a newspaper, but as a communicator of new laws passed by Parliament, of regulations under these laws, notifications treated as 'official' and recognised by courts of law, and even appointments and transfers of government servants and judicial officers.

The Colebrooke Commission established in 1829 was one of the earliest commissions of inquiry into British rule in Sri Lanka. It said that the powers of the British Governor were too wide and there must be independent newspapers in the island. The *Colombo Journal* (1832) could be called the first free newspaper in the country, as it was devoid of official propaganda, but it was frowned upon by officialdom at the time. Ironically, the Editor was George Lee, the Governor William Horton's Private Secretary and son-in-law. In 1834, the first non-government newspaper, the *Observer*, came into being. It was begun by two British merchants in the island, G. Ackland and E.J. Darley, and commercial advertising was seen for the first time in this newspaper. Its first Editor, George Winter, was charged in court for criticising a police officer but was later freed. Soon to become the *Colombo Observer* and then the *Ceylon Observer*, this newspaper exists today, albeit under government control, and is sometimes referred to by its detractors as the 'Government Gazette' for its political leanings.

As newspapers began taking root in Sri Lanka, the colonial administration introduced the Registration of Newspapers Ordinance No. 5 of 1839 to 'regulate the printing and publishing of newspapers', a law still in force after amendments in 1951, 1973 and 1976. The *Times of Ceylon*, under British ownership, was the first large scale newspaper with an almost island-wide circulation. This was launched in 1849 mainly to cater to the British community in the country, especially those in the far flung tea plantations in the central highlands, starved for news from 'back home' and those in the mercantile sector in Colombo interested in markets in London, shipping and other commercial news. In 1862, the first Sinhala language newspaper, *Lakminipahana*, was registered under this ordinance.

A Sinhala language press already existed, printing largely pamphlets containing local poetry and tidbits of news. But by the turn of the 20th century, this vernacular press was churning out tabloids with a nationalistic and religious bent aimed at moulding public opinion against colonial domination. The *Jaffna Freeman* was the first newspaper published outside the capital of Colombo. Other Tamil language newspapers then sprouted in the northern citadel of Jaffna for the local populace. It is recorded that in 1901, there were 30 newspapers—13 in English, 10 in Sinhala and 7 in Tamil—catering to a population of 30,000 Europeans, 2.5 million Sinhalese and 1 million Tamils.

The inter-war period saw the early modern era of newspapers in Sri Lanka. The first major indigenous newspaper group, Associated Newspapers of Ceylon, was launched in 1918. Its founder was an English-educated Sri Lanka barrister, D.R. Wijewardene, and his empire is known even today as Lake House because of its proximity to an inland lake. A Tamil publication, *Virakesari*, was begun in 1930 to cater mainly to the increasing number of people of Indian origin in the country. In many ways, the major English and Tamil newspapers in the country had their beginnings in catering to the community of planters (Englishmen) and workers (Tamils) in the tea plantations of Ceylon.

Independence and After

While the *Virakesari* had limited competition from the Tamil language publications of the Times and Lake House stables, the rivalry and stiff opposition between the latter two groups for the English and Sinhala language readership continued for a considerable period until a third major player entered the fray. In 1960, Independent Newspapers Ltd was begun by Sepala Gunasena, whose father owned a bookshop and a small press. In 1981, another newspaper group, Upali Newspapers Ltd, made a grand entry. Launched by a young and adventurous tycoon, Upali Wijewardene, with business interests around the world, connections to powerful political families by birth and marriage, and a flamboyance that had excited the public but rattled long-standing politicians of the day, this new entrant added a fresh dimension to journalism in the country, breaking the conservative mould that had existed for half a century with racy and populist stories. By then, however, the old Times group was on its last legs, embroiled in boardroom battles, to be eventually acquired by the government under an obnoxious Business Acquisition Act, and liquidated soon thereafter.

From time to time, governments in Sri Lanka, unable to tolerate virulent attacks by rival political party organs, would shut them down or drag their editors to court. The major onslaught on media freedom came in the early 1960s with the appointment of a Press Commission by a left-wing government unable to stomach the 'independence' of the powerful, conservative Lake House group. Clearly, that group had become partisan, supporting one of the country's major political parties, with some of its directors well entrenched in the party's hierarchy and decision-making process. The Commission recommended stern action against the group and thus the Newspaper Corporation of Ceylon Bill was introduced in 1964 for the 'broad basing' of the ownership of Lake House. With it they introduced the Press Council Bill, a law that was to ensure government appointees inquired into public complaints about matters published in newspapers with powers to jail journalists and even publishers.

These moves in 1964 were scuttled by some deft political manoeuvring spearheaded by the directors of Lake House. A well-orchestrated and well-financed campaign saw the downfall of that left-wing government as many legislators switched sides. The Press Council Bill, when put to the vote, was defeated and the government fell with it. The same left of centre coalition was, however, returned to power in 1970 and, fortified with a very large majority in Parliament, passed the laws in 1973. The enemies of the state, the private media, were put in their place.

The takeover of Lake House was soon to follow. In 1974, Independent Newspapers was sealed under emergency regulations that had been originally introduced to quell an armed insurgency by under-privileged youth in 1971. Then, the government wrested control of the already weakened Times group. By the time the 1977 general elections came along, it had the print media under tight control but faced a humiliating defeat at the hustings, proving the point that the people were unwilling to believe in state propaganda and everything that is printed in government controlled newspapers.

The new government of 1977 did not repeal the Press Council Law, even though they felt it was worth walking out of Parliament when it was introduced in 1973. They lost no time in stamping their authority on any notions that an era of press freedom had dawned. An antiquated Parliament (Powers and Privileges) Law was dusted off and used to summon two senior editors of the government-controlled Lake House group to the well of the House for a disgraceful display of 'justice by the mob', a show trial by government MPs for some mix-up of photo captions. Lake House remained in the hands of the ruling party.

It was around this time that I was penning a political column for my newspaper, *Weekend*, under the pseudonym 'Migara'. It is difficult to keep a secret in Sri Lanka and very soon my cover was blown. I was, however, the last person who could afford to complain, as my speciality was in ferreting out cabinet secrets from Ministers willing, and in fact, wanting to leak. The government of the day found some of the sensitive information out in the public domain inconvenient. And so, when I wrote critically of the national carrier and revealed how the Cabinet Secretary, who wore two hats, being a director of the airline, wrote to a public institution asking for fuel concessions on behalf of the airline on his Cabinet Secretary stationery (which I said was an attempt to influence the public institution), the gentleman concerned promptly lodged a case before the Magistrate's Court under the Press Council Law (Section 16) for divulging cabinet secrets in some other unrelated column. Fortunately at the time, friends in high places helped prevent the ignominy of a custodial sentence or some other form of punitive justice for my editor, but not without him having to share a dingy cell before our case was called with another accused, a fellow Sri Lankan who was being tried for the slightly more heinous crime of hijacking an Alitalia flight to Bangkok.

Such were the trials and the tribulations of journalists in that period. And yet, despite the inconveniences of the times, there was no real physical danger in practising one's profession. Such days, and nights, were yet to come.

Though the same UNP government liberalised radio and television, when the1994 elections came around, media freedom or more to the point, the lack of it, still remained an issue, with a populist President, Ranasinghe Premadasa, turning virulently against the free media. This gave rise to the birth of the Free Media Movement (FMM) consisting of media practitioners, academics and rights' activists who had carried the opposition candidate, Mrs Chandrika Kumaratunga, to high office on their shoulders. They were prepared to overlook the fact that she was the daughter of Mrs Sirimavo Bandaranaike, who as Prime Minister presided over all those repressive deeds against the press of the previous decades.

Within a few months, the supporters of the FMM were forced to admit that they had made a big mistake. Their supposed fairy tale had turned into a nightmare. President Chandrika Bandaranaike Kumaratunga's rise to high office was phenomenal. She had only been on the fringes of politics, first as the younger daughter of high profile parents, both former Prime Ministers, and then in the shadow of her actor husband, Vijaya Kumaratunga. It was upon his assassination by extreme Marxist-nationalist elements and because of the physical incapacitation of her mother, that the young socialist, who had frequented the Latin quarter of Paris during her student days at the Sorbonne, came into prominence. After ousting her brother from her parents' party, then sidelining her mother, she became first the Chief Minister of the Western Province in 1993, then Prime Minister and Executive President in 1994. It was a heady rise to power and power went straight to her head.

Hardly had she assumed the office of President when newspapers began to write critically about her allegedly bohemian lifestyle. Stories of late night parties were said to have compromised her standing as President. For her part, she wanted the best of both worlds: the people's respect for her as the President of the Republic and the lifestyle to which she was accustomed. And then, she picked on a gossip item that was factually incorrect. The story appeared in two Sunday newspapers, the *Sunday Times* (English) and the *Lakbima* (Sinhala) on the same day.

The story in the English Sunday said that the President had attended a birthday party hosted by a government MP 'in the heat of the silent night' at a five star hotel. It referred to her 'Epicurean tastes'. Innocuous as it may have sounded, it was the last straw for the President, though she later said that it was her then Justice Minister and one-time university professor of law who advised her to institute criminal defamation proceedings against both newspapers.

Section 479 of the Penal Code was drafted by the British during the subjugation of India and Sri Lanka; the same provision with the exact same wording appearing in both countries' criminal laws. Historically, the law was interpreted so as to ensure that there was no breach of the peace as a result of the publication of any material that was detrimental to the colonial administration. That was an important element in the law; there had to be civil commotion that resulted from such a publication. It gained a life of its own as the years rolled by, and even the rulers of independent India and Sri Lanka found it a convenient law to keep in their armoury. For several years, the law was used sparingly, mainly against political party organs and tabloids. It was in 1995 that it was used for the first time against national newspapers in Sri Lanka, the government of Chandrika Bandaranaike Kumaratunga announcing that it would brook no non-sense from a press that nosed too much into the private lives of public officials, especially ministers and the President.

Serial cases of criminal defamation were later filed against a string of other editors, and even publishers, for publishing stories against the president and others in her government. At one point, five editors and two publishers were in court defending themselves under this law. Gone were civil suits and actions for damages; in came the state police and state prosecutors—and some judges whose promotions were in the hands of the all-powerful president, the virtual complainant in most of these actions. The 'chilling effect' syndrome was in place. The media was expected to fall in line.

From such draconian acts came good. The media did not take all this lying down. The disorganised band of individual editors who lived in a world of their own editorial departments banded together and an Editors' Guild was formed with a common cause for the first time. Publishers had their own concerns and formed their Newspaper Society. It took two more years for the informal contacts to materialise into a substantive resistance movement.

In late 1997, under a banner of 'Friends of the Media', they organised a seminar on criminal defamation; and by April 1998 an international seminar was arranged with the support of the Commonwealth Press Union, Article 19, the World Association of Newspapers, the International Press Institute, the Committee for the Protection of Journalists and the Media Institute of Southern Africa. From the deliberations was born the Colombo Declaration on Media Freedom and Social Responsibility, which was to be the roadmap for the Sri Lankan media with regard to media freedom and professional responsibility. At the forefront of the declaration was the call to repeal the criminal defamation laws of the country.

The three media unions campaigned tirelessly. In 2002—four years after the Colombo Declaration—the then parliamentary opposition got a mandate from the people to work in a French style co-habitation government with President Kumaratunga, who remained a lame duck still in office. In the meantime, all political parties had been lobbied and convinced that criminal defamation laws were archaic, unfair and undemocratic. So, when the new government introduced a bill to repeal criminal defamation laws from the statute books of Sri Lanka, including the dreaded Section 479 of the Penal Code, it received a rare unanimous vote in an otherwise fractured Parliament, including the vote of President Kumaratunga's party.

As a fair exchange, the media unions said they would introduce a self-regulatory mechanism to police themselves, much in line with what already existed in the Scandinavian countries, the UK and Southern Africa. This promise was fulfilled in October 2003, a year and a half later, with the setting up of the Press Complaints Commission of Sri Lanka (PCCSL), with a board of directors representing the three media unions (now four with the signing of the Colombo Declaration by the Sri Lanka Working Journalists Association, the country's largest union of journalists) and a Dispute Resolution Council (DRC) headed by a much-respected retired civil servant, a former Secretary General of Parliament (Clerk to the House) with 'connections' to both the government and the opposition. With four members representing the press and four members representing civil society and the Chairman, civil society representation had the majority. The PCCSL was to function under the Arbitration Act with a secretariat of complaints officers overlooking the three language media in the country, that is, Sinhala, Tamil and English.

They would first try to settle a reader complaint by way of conciliation, that is, forward the complaint to the newspaper and expect it to follow up, or mediate a settlement between the complainant and the editor in cases where the newspaper did not respond, and finally when other avenues did not succeed, send it to the DRC for arbitration and a decision. It was the first, and so far only, self-regulatory mechanism to be created in South Asia.

On the government's part, they agreed to give self-regulation a chance and therefore, without repealing the Press Council Law of 1973, made the council's tribunal hearing public complaints *functus*. No new appointments were made to the Press Council as it went into disuse, maintaining only a skeleton staff that would register newspapers annually, and very little else.

From its inception in 2003, the PCCSL had received over 1300 complaints up to the end of 2011. Some of the newspapers carry regular advertisements announcing that they abide by the PCCSL and that readers are welcome to seek redress by writing to the editor about any complaints they have, or where they find the editor is not responsive, to write direct to the PCCSL. However, the PCCSL reports that it is only during the periods when they launch short public awareness media campaigns that the number of complaints tends to increase.

One of the positive responses that the self-regulatory mechanism has evoked is that the hitherto existing reluctance on the part of editors to carry a right of reply for an aggrieved party has been shed and newspapers will now opt to give the reader a right of reply rather than await a communication from the PCCSL. This is a significant step forward in newspapers taking responsibility for what they publish, and the PCCSL can take the credit for this change in approach by editors.

The PCCSL is the body by which the Code of Professional Practice of the Editors' Guild of Sri Lanka is implemented. The code also stemmed from the Colombo Declaration of 1998. During the campaign for the abolition of criminal defamation, the two arguments raised against its removal were: (a) that public servants especially would not have recourse to the law if they were defamed by powerful newspapers because they would not have the financial clout to match the Newspaper Houses in civil actions and (b) that the newspapers did not have a code of ethics for themselves. If the PCCSL was the answer to the first argument, the Editors' Code was the answer to the second.

Not that there was no code in existence. There was one drafted by the government-run Press Council, but it was treated as a regulation under the law and was therefore part and parcel of the Press Council law itself. Almost nobody in active journalism in contemporary times had ever heard of it. It had not been circulated, only gazetted. It was lost in history, and in any event it was not entirely drafted by practitioners and so was unacceptable to the journalists of the day.

The Editors' Guild of Sri Lanka is a motley grouping. With editors from the state media and private media in its ranks, the sharp differences are both political and personal. And yet, they all sat down, and influenced very much by the UK Editors' Code, thrashed out a code of their own. It was an achievement to have it passed with a unanimous vote. This code was revised in 2007. Some Newspaper Houses provide a copy of the code with the contracts of new recruits to journalism who sign that they agree to abide by it.

The 2001–2004 period saw some encouraging signs of more meaningful media freedom. Prime Minister Ranil Wickremasinghe came from a family that was a shareholder of Lake House and might have been a journalist himself, if not for taking to politics. It was during his brief tenure that there was a glimmer of hope for reform. He set up a committee under his own chairmanship comprising media representatives to implement at least some of the provisions contained in the Colombo Declaration. A Parliamentary Select Committee was established under the distinguished chairmanship of one-time Foreign Minister Lakshman Kadirgamar, a former Oxford Union President and Honorary Master of the Inner Temple, to study the need to introduce a Contempt of Court Law. The Attorney General, Justice Secretary and Legal Draftsman were co-opted into another committee to draft a Freedom of Information Act along with media groups. The Contempt Law was in the making while a Freedom of Information Act was made and approved by Cabinet and only had to be presented to Parliament when President Kumaratunga dissolved Parliament before the government's full mandate had run its course. In the ensuing elections, the Wickremasinghe government was defeated and with it both these laws flew out of the window, not to be discussed by succeeding governments.

In that brief interlude between 2001 and 2004, there was a sense that press freedom might be in the air. But all that has been countered by the present regime, which has made it clear that it will hear nothing of a Right to Information Law (despite paying lip service to one) and has opted to revive the statutory Press Council that had been in disuse since 2003.

The government's official stance on a Freedom of Information Law is that they will bring in the law. This is a veiled admission that they agree that such a law is a proper part of a modern democracy. Over 100 countries have this law, and in South Asia, Sri Lanka remains a conspicuous exception. Yet it is a foregone conclusion that the government will not bring in such a law. A bid by an opposition legislator to introduce a Freedom of Information Law as a Private Member's motion proved futile. Without backing from the government benches, it was defeated as soon as it was tabled. Media organisations are the only ones actively agitating for this law. Civil Society groups are so emaciated that—barring a few—such laws are not on their agenda.

In respect of the Press Council, the government appointed party supporters as members of this council and announced that they too would now begin accepting public complaints. The country's main media organisations protested loudly. They said in public statements that the government that preached media freedom was bringing back into operation a defunct law that provides for the jailing of publishers and journalists. The government deftly ignored these protests and went ahead, except that the law itself stood in the way.

The Press Council Law states that the council 'shall' comprise the Director of Government Information (ex officio) and a chairman and four members appointed by the President. However, there is a proviso that two of the four members shall be chosen from a panel of names sent to the President by media unions. With none of the media unions sending in names despite requests to do so, the government and the Press Council were in a quandary. They continued to sit nevertheless and legal objections have been taken to their composition. The dispute is ongoing with at least one politically oriented newspaper editor having openly defied the council within its chambers, saying it was illegal and walking out. The Press Council, knowing very well it is on uncertain ground, has not taken any action. It has not been confident enough to begin contempt proceedings. There are indications that the council wants to amend the law to drop these inhibiting provisions, suggesting that the government, unable to win the confidence of the media, may now insist in enforcing the authority of the Press Council against their wishes. In the meantime, the media organisations are contemplating challenging the jurisdiction of the Press Council, but if they went to court, they would do so with great trepidation, not due to the law itself, but to a lack of confidence in the judiciary.

To say that the Colombo Declaration of 1998 marked a turning point in the media in Sri Lanka is not an overstatement. It galvanised the factional media unions into one cohesive body, uniting journalists and media activists to work in unison for the improvement of the profession. A Sri Lanka College of Journalism was set up for the first time, a teaching institution feeding the industry with diploma holders. With the financial assistance of helpful Scandinavian donors, and input from the industry, this 'holy trinity'—the Press Institute, the Press Complaints Commission and the College of Journalism—helps to serve the needs of the industry to a great extent.

The Current Period

In 2008, the Colombo Declaration was re-visited on its 10th anniversary. Another international symposium was held and the 1998 Declaration was examined and revised. Among the proclamations made in the 2008 Colombo Declaration was that the media organisations resolved inter alia to call for constitutional guarantees and show alarm at the restrictions on Freedom of Expression and the derogation of Fundamental Rights in times of Emergency; oppose censorship; call for the repeal of the Official Secrets Act and the introduction of a Right to Information Act; express concern over the cost of newsprint; recognise the Internet as an important space for deliberative democracy; urge the improvement of working conditions of journalists and recognise the need for journalism training.

In addition to this roadmap, the Press Institute is taking the lead in moves to professionalise journalism in Sri Lanka. It is of little use to fight for press freedom, teach journalism or practise ethics if the community at large does not recognise journalism as a profession. Today, the Organisation of Professional Associations (OPA) which is the umbrella organisation for professional bodies in Sri Lanka does not recognise journalism as a 'profession'. Their argument is that journalism does not have a 'piece of paper' (a paper qualification) that is awarded by a professional body. Journalists are therefore relegated to the status of carpenters and masons who have no such credentials. This non-recognition extends beyond the OPA and has a negative influence in the decision-making process of parents who are reluctant to encourage their children to take up journalism as a profession. The dangers inherent in practising this 'profession' in a country like Sri Lanka, especially in recent times, on relatively low salaries have not helped. Towards this end, the Press Institute has initiated discussions with local and foreign universities to engage in a partnership to conduct degree awarding courses and also with the National Council for the Training of Journalists in the UK to hold examinations for those within the industry.

The challenges to the media remain on many fronts. On the one hand, there is growing concern that there is a general deterioration in the quality of journalism. Investigative journalism is not much in vogue today. Hardly any new generation journalist knows shorthand and few would take grammar seriously. In fact, the emphasis is on flashy layout, bold headlines and innovative advertisements. The distinction between an accused being discharged and being acquitted is deemed a distinction without a difference, as is distinguishing between the Attorney General and the Solicitor General. Style books are out of style and fashion pages are in fashion. It's the gloss not the content.

While successive governments have largely concentrated their attention on the print media as their main foe, they have slowly but surely come to the realisation that the Internet is becoming more and more of a potent threat to their existence. While the age-old Press Council has been tasked with shepherding the print media, a Telecommunication Regulatory Commission is painstakingly at work to control the dozens of online sites that seem to have taken full advantage of the worldwide web. Unfortunately the vast majority of these websites with servers abroad have not taken advantage of the lack of laws to control them, as compared with the print media. One would have liked them to indulge in more investigative reportage and in-depth analysis of serious and controversial issues, exploiting this lacuna, rather than bask in scurrilous stories laced with malice.

The government has tried to block some of these sites and has now asked them to register, a move that has been challenged in court by those who value press freedom. The Supreme Court is also unsure of what to do. Many newspapers with online editions willingly complied with the 'request' by the government to register without bothering to even find out if such a 'request' was legal, an indication that they opted for the path of least resistance so that they could just get on with their business. On the television broadcast front, the government has announced plans for stations to convert their equipment from analogue to digital. The catch is not in this order, but the fact that the government will provide the antennas for the signals. Private stations unable to invest funds to put up their own antennas island-wide will rent out the government antennas, which also means that the government retains the control to blackout a station at any given time, citing, for example, a technical breakdown.

Gradually, the government is acquiring a lordly overview of the media scene. They have been careful not to be too ham-handed in their approach. They have 'permitted' the independent Sri Lanka Press Institute to function, but launched, almost as a competitor, a Media Development Centre with UNESCO funding to do exactly the same programmes the Press Institute is implementing. They 'permit' the Press Complaints Commission to police the media through self-regulation while policing it through the statutory Press Council. They 'allow' the College of Journalism to have training courses, in addition to setting up their own.

Most of the traditional media houses today have a direct stake in the politics of the country. The state media are in a class of their own. As far as the private media are concerned, many of them have directors or relatives in parliament representing opposition political parties, or who are directors of state-run agencies. They do not necessarily direct what must be published, nor what is to be left out, and the public at large has come to, by and large, accept these contradictions and conflicts of interest as a reality of life.

The one newspaper group which regularly reminded its readers that it was 'unbowed and unafraid' of the government was only found out when the Editor admitted under cross-examination in a court case that the newspaper had secretly accepted cash from an opposition political party. Unable to continue any further under the strain of unsettled bank loans, lack of advertising and a string of court cases, they were forced to capitulate when the government had a businessman who made a fast buck in the stock market under its watch buy them over. On the other hand, it has given ammunition to a plethora of websites to claim that the mainstream press in Sri Lanka has vested interests in the politics of the country and that they, the online media, are the true independent voices to be read and heard.

This could not be further from the truth. Some of these websites are funded by persons with political agendas, both locally and overseas, hiding behind the veil of anonymity and masquerading as independent news outlets. Worse still, they are elastic with the truth and no great respecters of accuracy. But the Sri Lankan public, or at least the public that have access to the Internet, smartphones and tablets, quench their thirst for news by visiting these sites, as one of them said, 'even if I know that some of it may not be entirely true'. It is info-entertainment at its best or worst. Much of what emanates from these websites is imaginative and creative. Untrammelled by the old laws of civil defamation, privacy or contempt that have long cramped the print media in particular, they have a field day in whetting the appetite of a politically conscious public with titillating copy. So much so, that at a National Conference on Self-Regulation recently, the Press Complaints Commission had one session with the provocative title 'New Media; a Licence to Slander', which no doubt drew the wrath of social media advocates, but had a ring of truth to it.

In the aftermath of the 30-year separatist insurgency that had a debilitating effect on the nation, the Government appointed a Lessons Learnt and Reconciliation Commission to find ways and means to rise from the ashes. One of the causes, they said, that had contributed to bad governance was the way governments had treated media freedom. They identified attacks on journalists and media institutions as one of the primary reasons for the erosion of democracy and the rise of lawlessness.

In the final years of a secessionist insurgency, which resulted in an estimated 70,000–100,000 deaths over the years, media practitioners, including editors, were at the receiving end of what is an open secret: hit squads unleashed by the military establishment on unarmed journalists and media institutions. It was the era of the notorious 'white van syndrome', named after the vehicles that the hit men travelled in.

To his credit, the incumbent President Mahinda Rajapaksa has been absolved by the media in general of complicity in those crimes. However, he seemed powerless to prevent the continuous forages of the military by day and by night, because his priority was to have them liquidate the separatist terrorists. On one occasion, he was quite shaken when he met editors soon after one of their colleagues had been killed. He remarked that 'this was like as if I have been attacked'. But there was nothing more he could do except to keep reassuring journalists that 'it won't happen again'. Regrettably, it did, over and over again.

Today, that fear psychosis is not all over. With the insurgency defeated, those who combined to unleash this state-sponsored terror have fallen out of favour with the government, while those separatist guerrillas who engaged in terrorising journalists have been killed. Those in the state who combined to attack journalists cannot identify the others for fear of incriminating themselves. Despite the formal inquiries, what happened to the targeted journalists in those harrowing years will never be known, nor the perpetrators brought to justice. Not a single perpetrator of these crimes has been seriously pursued. There are still some journalists who fled the country and are afraid to return, and some who went missing, whose whereabouts remain unknown, with their families fearing the worst. Attention has now turned to vociferous trade unionists, stubborn rights' activists, student leaders and persons seen as obstructionists to the government's agenda. The white van syndrome is not over; it has only shifted focus.

The President is a skilful politician who can disarm even his fiercest critics with reassuring words and friendly banter. He will provide hospitality to journalists, give loans for the purchase of cars and still remain hardnosed in giving concessions towards media freedom. The carrot can often be deadlier than the stick, even though it does not come with the threat of violence.

The future for the media in Sri Lanka is uncertain. On the one hand, the political opposition, on which an independent media often depends for support against an increasingly authoritarian government, and vice versa, is emasculated. The government, particularly the Presidency, is media savvy and understands how to play to the strengths and the weaknesses of those in the media. A recent survey commissioned by the Sri Lanka Press Institute has shown that in a mixed economy such as that prevailing in Sri Lanka today, where the government has a fairly large stake, 32 per cent of its advertising budget is channelled to the state media and a large chunk of the balance to media outlets that 'toe the line'.

In these circumstances, it becomes all the more difficult to convince the government that they are treading the wrong path; that media freedom is a sine qua non of a modern liberal democracy and has the backing of the silent majority in the country, especially in the big cities.

In March 2012, the United Nations Human Rights Council in Geneva passed a US-initiated resolution against Sri Lanka calling for, inter alia, greater media freedom. Often, advocates of media freedom rely on 'foreign intervention', especially when there is no backing from domestic political forces, to nudge governments into action. But it can also rebound. The incumbent government has cleverly turned the tables to say western powers are interfering in the internal affairs of Sri Lanka. Which country wants others to dictate to them? And, with that, local campaigns for media freedom, instead of getting a boost, face a setback as issues get clouded by extraneous factors.

'*Ohama Yan*' is an age-old Sinhala axiom which means 'Let's just go like this'. It stands for maintaining your course in the face of adversity and waiting to see what the future holds. It is a fairly accurate summary of the current state of play in Sri Lanka's media scene.

3

Minority Media at the Crossroads

Ameen Izzadeen

Introduction

Sri Lanka is a multi-ethnic, multi-religious country, although the ethnic mix is predominantly Sinhalese. The country is blessed by the teachings of four main religions: Buddhism, Hinduism, Christianity and Islam. However, ethno-religious differences unfortunately gave rise to mutual mistrust and dragged the country into a devastating armed conflict that lasted for three decades. As a result, moves aimed at forging a national identity—a Sri Lankan identity—fell by the wayside. Instead, the country saw the rise of ethno-nationalism—with ethnic groups more interested in protecting their own interests than building a national identity.

Even in post-civil-war Sri Lanka, attempts to bring about a Sri Lankan identity that will rise above petty ethnic differences have not yielded the desired results. In neighbouring India, which is ethnically much more diverse than Sri Lanka, many people have no problem in saying, 'I am an Indian first, then a Tamil, Malayali, Punjabi or Gujarati'. In Sri Lanka, the lack of progress in the creation of an over-arching national identity is largely because aspirations, issues and problems facing the people differ from community to community. These differences are also reflected in the media representing each community.

Concerns over poverty, weak rule of law, lack of good governance and democracy usually cut across all ethnic boundaries, but in the Tamil media, the importance of these issues is measured by their impact on the minority communities. Even in the Sinhala media, threats to democracy, good governance, the rule of law and even freedom of expression received lukewarm treatment at the height of the war, because the priority was the national security and national interest. This divided approach has weakened the media's role in Sri Lanka, especially in strengthening democracy.

One Country, Divided Media

When people in Sri Lanka woke up on 14 February 2012 instead of the joy usually associated with Valentine's Day, there was anger. Many of them woke up to the news that transport costs had been jacked up by 20 per cent following a sharp price hike in fuel. The previous day, 13 February, private bus operators staged a lightning strike, virtually paralysing the country.

Sinhala and English newspapers carried banner headlines and led off with the bus fare hike story. But most Tamil newspapers led with a different story—that of a news conference held at the US Embassy in Colombo the previous day. The US Assistant Secretary of State, Robert Blake, and the Under Secretary for Civilian Security, Democracy and Human Rights, Marie Otero, who addressed the news conference, had said the United States would back a resolution against Sri Lanka at the upcoming United Nations Human Rights Council (UNHRC) sessions. They also said that they were hopeful that the Sri Lanka government would implement a credible domestic mechanism to deal with allegations of human rights and humanitarian law violations, especially during the last stages of the war.

Veerakesari, Sri Lanka's oldest Tamil national daily, in its lead story gave weight to the announcement that Washington would support an anti-Sri Lanka resolution at the UNHRC sessions. The *Island*, an independent English language newspaper with pro-Sinhala nationalist credentials, also carried the Blake-Otero news conference, but it was not the lead. The lead story was about Iran's assurance to Sri Lanka on the supply of oil despite US sanctions. The bus strike and fare hike story was placed near the lead story. However, the *Island* news story on the US officials' news conference had no mention of the US decision to support the resolution against Sri Lanka. Its headline read: US Calls for Domestic Solution for HR Violations in SL. Sri Lanka's largest selling English daily newspaper, the state-run *Daily News*, did not carry the Blake-Otero story.

The same dramatic difference of emphasis was noticeable in the different media's coverage of the end of the 30-year separatist war. When the war ended on 19 May 2009, all Sinhala and English dailies devoted page after page the following day to report various aspects of the victory.

Scores of photographs filled the front and inside pages. The huge fonts on the front and inside pages were not only symbolic of the importance of the news being reported, but also an expression of jubilation. The *Divaina*, an independent daily which supported the government's military approach to solve the ethnic problem, led off on 20 May 2009 with the story on troops recovering the body of the Liberation Tigers of Tamil Eelam (LTTE) leader, Velupillai Prabhakaran. Pictures showed jubilant soldiers and people celebrating on the street. Inside page articles glorified President Mahinda Rajapaksa. One headline described Rajapaksa as king of Sri Lanka. There were no pictures of Tamils celebrating. They did not celebrate. A majority of the Tamils were in a quiet and sombre mood. Many felt that the victory the Sinhalese people were celebrating was a victory against the Tamils.

The *Divaina* also carried a front page editorial in which it praised Rajapaksa for not only bringing victory, but also for standing firm against the pressure from the international community—euphemistically the west—which wanted the military offensive stopped to protect the people trapped in the war zone. The paper took a racist swipe at David Miliband, the then British foreign secretary, who visited Sri Lanka during the last stages of the war and urged the Rajapaksa government to ensure the safety of hundreds of thousands of Tamil civilians trapped in the war zone. The paper's political cartoon depicted Rajapaksa carrying the carcass of a tiger by the tail.

In contrast, the Colombo-based Tamil weekly *Sudar Oli*—now a daily—in its 24 May edition—the first issue after the war had ended—carried articles that would not find a place in either Sinhala or English dailies. One article was headlined: '*Azhivil varalatru vetri kanum thetku*', meaning 'The south sees historic victory in carnage'. Dismissing the President's claim that the victory was not against the Tamil people, the writer argued the countrywide celebrations indicated it was a victory of the majority over the minority.

The paper carried pictures of the displaced Tamil people and highlighted their plight. Now that the war was over, the *Sudar Oli* editorial opined, a fair solution to the Tamil question was an illusion because 'the Sinhala racists believe that a solution to the Tamil problem was not necessary'. The editorial, though it expressed pessimism, called on the government to address the grievances of the Tamil people. Like the *Divaina* editorial, the *Sudar Oli* editorial was also critical of the international community, but for a different reason. The *Sudar Oli* blamed the international community for not doing enough to save the Tamil people.

On 19 May 2009, when the war officially ended, President Rajapaksa announced that the country had been reunited and there were no minorities in Sri Lanka. But the manner in which different newspapers in different languages covered the news shows that far from building a national identity after the war the media continue to sustain the ethnic divide.

The division of the media on ethnic lines was more acute during the 30-year war; so much so that ethnic prejudice was evident even in the coverage of the 2004 tsunami, the national calamity in which more than 34,000 Sri Lankans perished. The Colombo-based Sinhala and English media—print and electronic media alike—gave more space and time to stories from the Sinhala-dominated south and much less to the devastation in the north-east—the region that suffered the most in the 2004 Boxing Day catastrophe.

There are national newspapers in Sri Lanka in the country's three main languages—Sinhala, Tamil and English. However, some critics ask how the Tamil newspapers could use the term 'national' or '*thesiya*' to describe themselves when their focus is largely on issues affecting the Tamil people. To some degree, the criticism also applies to Sinhala and Sinhalese-owned media where there is little empathy for the Tamil grievances.

In their own defence, the Tamil national newspapers say if a newspaper is to be commercially viable, it should cater to the needs of its readership. If Sinhala language newspapers can focus their attention on matters concerning the Sinhala people—the majority in Sri Lanka—they ask why Tamil newspapers cannot give more weight to Tamil grievances and the problems the Tamil-speaking people are facing. Their argument is plausible. If the Tamil media do not have a national outlook in their reporting and are accused of doing little to promote the national identity, the Sinhala media also should face the same charge.

It is more difficult to generalise about the role of the English language national media. Some newspapers promote Sinhala nationalism while others have tried to promote a Sri Lankan identity, though an ethnic undercurrent is discernible, depending on the ownership of the media.

Against this backdrop, the Tamil language media are described as minority media, a description essentially based on the minority status of their ethnicity, though the Sinhala and English language media are not referred to as majority media. In Sri Lanka, the minority media can be further categorised as minority media controlled by a member(s) of the minority ethnic group and minority media controlled by a member(s) of the Sinhala community or the majority ethnic group. For instance, *Dinapathi* (a Tamil daily) and *Chinthamani* (a Tamil weekly) were owned by the Independent Newspapers Ltd, a newspaper group owned by a Sinhala family. This newspaper group, which also published Sinhala and English newspapers, wound up its business in the mid-1980s following financial losses. Wijeya Newspapers Ltd, publishers of the *Sunday Times, Daily Mirror, Lankadeepa* (Sinhala daily and weekly), also run a Tamil news website called Tamil Mirror. In addition to this, the state-run Lake House group publishes the Tamil newspaper *Thinakaran* (daily and weekly).

The vigour with which the Tamil media owned by the Tamils cover Tamil issues is lacking in the coverage of Tamil issues by the Tamil media owned either by the state or the Sinhalese. This is because the structure of identity differs from community to community. For the Sinhalese Buddhists, who comprise 70 per cent of the population, their Sinhala-Buddhist-ness is synonymous with their Sri Lankan-ness, but for most Tamils who make up 17 per cent of the population their ethnic identity often supersedes their national identity or their Sri Lankan-ness. In other words, their Tamil-Hindu-ness or Tamil-Christian-ness has difficulty in fitting into the groove of Sri Lankan-ness which they feel has been monopolised by the majority community. And for Sri Lanka's Muslims, the second largest minority group (9.7 per cent of the population), it is their religious identity that often comes to the fore, although they are a Tamil-speaking community. An ethno-centric outlook has come to stay in the minority communities partly because of past history and partly because of the lack of force in successive governments' measures aimed at developing an all-encompassing Sri Lankan national identity.

A Journey into History

There were no newspapers or printing presses when the Sinhala King, Dutugemunu (161 BC to 137 BC), defeated the Dravidian (Tamil) Chola King Elara. Details of this battle, which still evokes Sinhala triumphalism over the Tamils, were passed on from generation to generation until the monk Mahanama in the 5th century AD wrote the Mahawamsa or the Great Chronicle, considered one of the longest unbroken historical accounts of early Sri Lankan history. It has come in for criticism for its alleged ethnic prejudice in favour of the Sinhala-Buddhists.

The arrival of the printing press in the country in 1737 during the Dutch colonial period led to the de-monopolisation of the task of recording events for posterity. However, till about the mid-19th century, the practice of writing history, literary works and other messages on Ola leaves prevailed.

The early development of the print media in Sri Lanka had its origins in the spread of Christianity and the measures taken by the Sinhala-Buddhists and the Tamil-Hindus to resist it. This daunting task and the subsequent challenges faced by the Sinhalese, the Tamils and the Muslims defined the shape and tone of the media throughout its subsequent history.

To stem the tide of Christian publications and to counter the propaganda carried out by the pro-Christian Jaffna-based newspapers such as *Morning Star* (in English) and *Udaya Tharakai* (in Tamil), Hindu intellectuals such as Arumuga Nawalar published Tamil literary works such as *Kanda Puranam, Sethu Puranam, Thirukkural* and *Thirukkovaiyar* in the north.

In the latter half of the 19th century, the zeal to preserve Hinduism and Tamil culture saw the emergence of monthlies and weeklies, magazines and newspapers. Even the English publications printed in Jaffna devoted a few pages to Tamil. For instance, the *Literary Mirror* published in Jaffna by I.C.W. Kadirvelpillai had a Tamil language section.

In 1862, Kadirvelpillai launched the *Ceylon Patriot* to pose a challenge to the *Jaffna Freeman* launched by Nicholas Gold. *The Ceylon Patriot* styled on the lines of *the Indian Patriot* promoted Tamil patriotism against colonialism. The newspaper had a Tamil section called *Ilangabhimani* (Ceylon Patriot), which was very popular. In 1867, Legislative Council member A. Kanakaratnam bought the two rival newspapers and amalgamated them. The merger only strengthened *Ilangabhimani* and helped grow Tamil readership.

It is also worth mentioning here that even the Sinhala print media had their origins in the propagation of Christianity by the missionaries and in counter moves taken by Buddhist clergy and intellectuals.

In the early 20th century, the Tamil media, based largely in the north, gradually shifted their focus from matters of religion to matters of politics, against the backdrop of Tamil language revivalism. Similarly, Sinhala-Buddhist revivalism dominated politics in the south. Although Sinhala-Buddhist and Tamil-Hindu revivalism were largely in response to colonialist moves aimed at proselytising the local populace, they had a destructive as well as a constructive role in the shaping of a national Sri Lankan identity.

The Independence Struggle

The early 20th century witnessed a joint Sinhala–Tamil struggle for independence. The Jaffna Youth Congress, founded in 1924, was the first Sri Lanka youth group to fight for *Poorna Swaraj* or complete independence from the British. Inspired by the Indian National Congress and Mahatma Gandhi's non-violent approach, their movement was committed to secularism and worked together with Sinhala leaders. The Jaffna Youth Congress's patriotic fervour was such that they opposed the 1931 Donoughmore Reforms on the basis that they did not concede enough self-rule.

No narration about Sri Lanka's independent history is complete without the mention of brothers Sir Ponnambalam Ramanathan and Sir Ponnambalam Arunachalam. The two Tamil leaders, the former in particular, joined Sinhala leaders to spearhead the campaign for independence. But later, when the British colonial rulers introduced more political reforms, the Tamils began to feel insecure because these reforms naturally favoured the majority Sinhalese within a democratic structure. The Ponnambalam brothers felt they were being betrayed by the Sinhalese leaders. More blows to Sinhala–Tamil unity followed when the Tamil political leadership boycotted the State Council in 1936, accusing the Sinhalese leaders of manipulating the formula for choosing members of the board of ministers.

When new political reforms were being negotiated in the 1940s, the Tamil leadership demanded a 50-50 representation in the new legislature—50 per cent of the seats to be allocated to the majority Sinhalese and the rest to the minorities. However, Lord Soulbury, who was heading the reforms commission and who later became the Governor General, gave more weight to a multi-party system and universal suffrage, to the great disappointment of the Tamil leadership.

Throughout this period, a few Tamil papers, such as the Jaffna-based *Hindu Organ*, adequately highlighted both the growing political tension between the Tamils and the Sinhalese and the Tamil side of the story vis-à-vis the political reforms. The two main Colombo-based Tamil newspapers at the time reported the developments, but their coverage lacked the force with which the Jaffna-based media reported and interpreted the growing ethnic tension. These were the *Veerakesari* (1930 to date) founded by P.P.R. Subramaniam Chettiar, a wealthy journalist, who came from India, and the *Thinakaran* (1932 to date) owned by D.R. Wijewardene, a Sinhala stalwart who campaigned for the country's independence. This was a time when journalists, even Tamil journalists, enjoyed a greater degree of media freedom. There was no undue pressure from the colonial government on the independent media.

The years that followed Sri Lanka's independence in 1948 witnessed an escalation of the Tamil–Sinhala political conflict. The Sinhala political leaders' moves in the 1950s to declare Sinhala the official language, replacing English, and the Tamil leaders' resistance to such moves, together with their demand for a federal constitution that would guarantee devolution of power to the Tamil-majority regions of the north and the east, dominated the news in the Tamil media. Intermittent ethnic conflicts, and the government resettlement programmes, which the Tamil leadership and the Tamil media saw as Sinhala colonisation of the Tamil areas, also occupied a big space in the Tamil media. A significant development during this era was the setting up of Sri Lanka's only broadcasting station, Radio Ceylon, which later became the Sri Lanka Broadcasting Corporation. The state-owned radio with English, Sinhala and Tamil channels became the virtual mouthpiece of the government of the day.

Minority Media During the Civil War

The three decades from 1980 to 2009, during which the country saw a southern insurrection from 1988 to 1990 largely by the Sinhala youth and an armed separatist rebellion in the north and the east, were the worst years in Sri Lanka's journalistic history. It was during this period that, for the first time, a journalist was abducted and killed. Popular television journalist Richard de Zoysa was abducted from his Colombo home by a state-sponsored goon squad on 17 February 1990 and his body was found the next day on the beach south of Colombo. Scores of journalists went underground, while some fled the country. At least one editor—Vijitha Yapa of the *Sunday Times*—was forced to resign during the government's brutal crackdown on the southern insurgency. Though the insurrection, which was led by the Marxist Janatha Vimukthi Peramuna (JVP), ended in 1990, the practice of threatening, attacking, abducting and killing journalists by state and non-state actors did not. According to Journalists for Democracy in Sri Lanka, 43 journalists and media workers were killed between 2004 and 2010. Of these, 37 were Tamil, 5 Sinhalese and 1 Muslim.[1] Among the Sinhalese journalists killed was the *Sunday Leader*

Editor Lasantha Wickrematunge, who wrote his own obituary, wherein he held the government responsible for his death (he died on 8 January 2009 after an armed gang brutally attacked him inside a high security zone in a Colombo suburb).

With the Tamil issue taking a militaristic turn in 1983, the Tamil media faced pressure from the government and numerous militant groups. Tamil media editors and journalists received death threats from militant groups, particularly the LTTE, and also from military-backed groups such as the Eelam People's Democratic Party (EPDP) or the so-called Karuna group, an LTTE breakaway group led by its erstwhile eastern commander.

Laws Restricting Tamil Expression

If in the past, the Public Security Ordinance (PSO) and emergency regulations were invoked by governments to check the media and impose censorship, the period after 1983 saw the implementation of a reinforced Prevention of Terrorism Act (PTA). This piece of legislation was initially enacted in 1979 as a temporary law with a view to suppressing any recurrence of the JVP insurrection of 1971. But it was made permanent in 1982 to deal with the growing Tamil militancy. The provisions of the new version of the PTA, together with emergency regulations (under the PSO), were used to threaten journalists with arrest and also to gag the media. While the government was armed with the draconian laws, goon squads, which operated with the connivance or blessings of the powers-that-be, also held a gun at journalists' heads.

Journalist Dharmaratnam Sivaram, a well-respected Tamil journalist who wrote in English, told a lecture audience in Canada in 1999 that the bases for repressing the media and restricting the freedom of expression in Sri Lankan are ensconced in the country's constitution itself.[2]

In addition to the PSO, Sivaram saw the Sixth Amendment to the Constitution of Sri Lanka as one of the most repressive instruments against the exercise of freedom of expression. The Sixth Amendment prevents citizens of Sri Lanka from advocating separatism. But Sivaram saw it as an affront to the right to exercise one's views within a democratic framework. He said:

> The Sixth Amendment to Sri Lanka's constitution inserted as Article 157A hangs like the sword of Damocles over Tamil journalists. The threat of civic

disability, the forfeiture of property etc., for 16 years since the introduction of Sixth Amendment in 1983 has created a generation of Tamil journalists who, over the years, have taken it for granted that the freedom of expression is a concept that does not apply to them. The owners of mainstream Tamil media have contributed in no small measure to this state of affairs.

Government Advice and Self-censorship

In addition to draconian legislation, the editors, publishers, television and radio channel owners came to be lectured at regular meetings with the President of the country—a salient feature of the media policy of the incumbent President Mahinda Rajapaksa. At these meetings, the President would make a gentle but firm request for the editors and media bosses not to be the voice of the terrorists. Although it was not like Margaret Thatcher's requests to the media to black out the Irish Republican Army, Rajapaksa's gentle message was chilling enough for the Tamil editors and media bosses to impose self-censorship.

Sri Lanka's journalists were known to resort to self-censorship during the reign of terror that prevailed during the 1988–1990 southern insurrection and the various phases of the government's war against the LTTE. But the kind of self-censorship the Tamil media exercised during the last years of the separatist war stemmed from their own dilemma: they were caught between the proverbial devil and the deep blue sea. The LTTE regularly summoned Tamil editors for meetings at its headquarters in Kilinochchi in Sri Lanka's north and gave guidelines. Lost in this exercise was objectivity. If the Tamil media resorted to self-censorship out of fear, sections of the Sinhala and English newspapers cooperated with the government out of patriotism or their opposition to terrorism, just as the CNN did during the Iraq wars.[3]

In this dangerous clime, one newspaper in Jaffna shone but it shone like a shooting star and died. Run by Tamil human rights activists, the *Saturday Review* was born in 1982 and died in 1987, 3 months after its office was bombed. In this short period, the newspaper highlighted human rights violations by Sri Lankan troops and the separatist militants, though it supported the liberation struggle of the Tamil people. Its journalists were arrested and tortured. The newspaper was banned under the PSO. Even after the ban was lifted, the newspaper continued with its bold journalism but decided to wind up in the face of continued harassment and death threats.[4]

Sivaram, Sivaramya and Tissainayagam

As the space within which the journalists in Sri Lanka could operate became more and more dangerous and small, being a journalist with a commitment to objectivity was a recipe for disaster. For Tamil media personnel, whether they wrote in Tamil or English, writing about human rights violations by both sides of the conflict was an invitation for a bullet in the head. After the death of the *Saturday Review*, the need for a Tamil voice that could operate within this dangerous space was badly felt.

Dharmaratnam Sivaram, who later became the editor of the Tamilnet, filled this vacuum. A Gandhian-turned militant, Sivaram took to journalism after his group, the People's Liberation Organisation of Tamil Eelam, surrendered its weapons and entered the democratic process under a deal worked out by India and Sri Lanka. In 1988, he was introduced to journalism by Richard de Zoysa, the first journalist to be killed in Sri Lanka. Sivaram worked as a freelance *Inter Press Service* journalist. But it was after he joined the *Island* newspaper that he became popular. His columns, which he wrote under the nom de plume Taraki, gave the southern readers an insight into the Tamil militants' mind, their struggle and their aspirations. He knew not only the geography of the area where the battles were being fought, but also the socio-economic and political life of the people in the north and the east—the areas where the LTTE was strong. As a result, his articles were looked forward to by political leaders and military commanders. Sivaram knew the limits to which he was allowed to go in exercising his free speech, but often he would stretch the limits, earning the wrath of the government and even the LTTE.

Sivaram's Taraki column later appeared in the *Sunday Times* and the *Daily Mirror*. He wrote in Tamil for the *Veerakesari*. A headstrong journalist, he would express his displeasure when the editors who wanted to avoid unnecessary confrontations with the government changed a word or two. In 1997, Sivaram reorganised the Tamilnet and made it one of the most visited Sri Lankan news websites during the war period.

By 2006, when the peace process collapsed and the war resumed, Taraki's Tamilnet was seen to be overtly pro-LTTE. He was critical of the breakaway LTTE group or the Karuna group. In one of his columns, Sivaram alleged that Karuna had embezzled LTTE funds and floated a company in his wife's name. Karuna is today a Deputy Minister in the Mahinda Rajapaksa regime.

During his lecture tours of western capitals, Sivaram criticised the government and spoke in favour of the Tamil's right to self-determination.

Ultra-nationalist Sinhala politicians branded Sivaram a Tiger—meaning an LTTE member. His house was searched twice and he was once taken in by the police only to be released because he was too well known not only among the local readership, but also among the diplomatic corps. A fun-loving intellectual, Sivaram was abducted by a group of armed men who came in a white van when he was strolling towards a bus stand opposite a police station in Colombo after a drinking session with friends at a pub. It was 28 April 2005. The following day, his body was found in the high security zone around the parliament complex. Senior journalist D.B.S. Jeyaraj, whose columns are as much sought after as Taraki's had been, hinted in an article that Sivaram was killed by the Karuna group or Karuna himself.

The killing drew wide condemnation, especially from the international community. The government arrested a person, but the case remains unresolved.[5] Journalists and academics in Jaffna and the media personnel in the LTTE-controlled areas protested over Sivaram's killing. In the Sinhala-majority south, the Free Media Movement held a demonstration. But apart from this, there was very little protest in the south. Sivaram himself saw this division along ethnic lines in the journalistic fraternity. In a paper he presented to a seminar in Canada, Sivaram quoted B. Sivakumar, the editor of Tamil journal *Sarinihar*, published by the Movement for Inter-Racial Justice and Equality, as saying:

> The organisations in Colombo that are supposed to protect the rights of journalists do not come out in protest when Tamil media people are arrested or harassed. Or they put out carefully worded statements reluctantly. These are the very organisations that agitate against the state very vociferously when non-Tamil journalists are arrested or intimidated. This is due to a feeling among them that all Tamils may somehow be linked to the LTTE.[6]

Such apathy in the journalistic fraternity was seen in the case of the Tamil broadcast journalist Sivanathan Sivaramya. In May 2006, Sivaramya was arrested by the police on suspicion she was an LTTE suicide bomber. Ironically, the arrest was made at a UNESCO ceremony to mark World Press Freedom Day. Sivaramya pleaded that she was a journalist attached to the state-run Sri Lanka Broadcasting Corporation and she wanted to attend the ceremony, which was held at the Bandaranaike Memorial International Conference Hall. But the police accused her of trying to kill a senior minister. She was taken to the dreaded Terrorist Investigations Department for interrogation. The protest over Sivaramya's arrest in the local journalistic fraternity was only a whimper, but the international cry was loud enough to get her released on bail. She later filed a fundamental rights case and obtained redress.

Jayaprakash Tissainayagam was not as lucky as Sivaramya. But he was not as unfortunate as Sivaram to end up as a lifeless corpse. Tissainayagam was a journalist cum human rights activist. Unlike Sivaram, Tissainayagam's writing did not have a political slant. His commitment to human rights issues and his determination to end oppression were evident in his columns. Tissainayagam is ethnically Tamil, but wrote in English for national English newspapers. He started his journalistic career in 1987 at the *Sunday Times* newspaper. Later, he left the *Sunday Times* and edited the *North East Herald* magazine, for which he received funds from foreign Non-government Organisations (NGOs) committed to promote democracy and good governance.

When he realised that the kind of material that found space in his magazine could no longer be entertained due to the worsening situation vis-à-vis media freedom in the country after the war escalated, he wound up the magazine and resorted to web journalism. Months after launching a website, which he named Outreach, Tissainayagam was arrested. That was on 7 March 2008. The arrest took place following a raid on a printing press which operated from a building where Tissainayagam's Outreach office functioned. Months before his arrest, he began a weekly column for the *Sunday Times*. He was issued clear guidelines as to the limits within which he could express his views. This is because the newspaper did not want to be seen by the authorities as giving a platform to pro-LTTE views. He was told: 'Tamil issues yes, but not in a way that would help the LTTE's cause of separatism'.

While he was detained by the Terrorist Investigations Department, his house was raided and detectives found two old copies of the *North East Herald*. The articles in these issues had been written at a time when Tamil journalists like Tissainayagam believed that there was still some space to express Tamil opinion. No charges were brought against him for 6 months. As international pressure mounted on the government, police on 25 August 2008 took him to court. He was charged with writing to incite 'ethnic disharmony'. His was the first case where a journalist was charged under the draconian PTA.

In September 2009, the Colombo High Court found him guilty and sentenced him to 20 years rigorous imprisonment in a judgment that received worldwide criticism. Amnesty International in a statement denounced the judgment as a direct violation of Tissainayagam's right to freedom of expression and more broadly as an assault on press freedom in Sri Lanka. The organisation called for the immediate release of Tissainayagam and an end to the use of the PTA to silence peaceful dissent. He was subsequently offered a presidential pardon, which was seen as a move to placate the European Union which was at that time threatening to suspend special concessions granted to Sri Lanka under its general system of preferences plus programme.

While the Tissainayagam case drew international attention, with even US President Barack Obama citing him as an example of journalists being jailed for expressing their views, the media fraternity in Sri Lanka was divided. Many journalists in the Sinhala media adopted the view that the police were simply doing their duty and 'let the courts decide the case'. Once again the *Sarinihar* editor was proved right. Perhaps Tissainayagam was arrested at the wrong time—at a time when patriotism had replaced objectivity for a national cause.

Embedded Journalism

The last years of the war also saw the entry of embedded journalism into Sri Lanka's media. Embedded journalism, which proved highly controversial during the Iraq war, became a feature of the late stages of Sri Lanka's own war, when journalists from some newspaper and television groups embedded themselves with the army and covered the frontline in a way that pleased the military.

Meanwhile, journalists who refused to be embedded and who tried to be independent earned the wrath of the powers-that-be. The *Sunday Times* Defence Correspondent, Iqbal Athas, had to leave the country following a series of articles that highlighted alleged irregularities in military procurement, while the *Nation* Defence Correspondent, Keith Noyahr, was abducted and almost killed for critically commenting on the manner in which promotions were given in the military.

New Media

As governments during the civil war period tried to muzzle the traditional media with emergency regulations and other tough laws at their disposal, developments in information technology made their efforts somewhat meaningless. The emergence of web journalism offered the news-starved masses the other side of the story which the closely monitored traditional media could not give out of fear of adverse repercussions.

With the traditional Tamil media both in Colombo and Jaffna unable to give an objective account of what was taking place in the war-affected areas because of threats from both sides, news websites such as Tamilnet operating from overseas carried stories explaining the situation at the war front and the plight of the civilians trapped in the war zone. These Tamil websites gave more weight to separatist viewpoints—and the government and the military leadership branded them Tiger mouthpieces. The paradox, however, was that even the Colombo-based independent media would occasionally publish a Tamilnet account of the war situation, though the objective was to give credibility to a government claim or undermine the LTTE.

Besides the English language Tamilnet, which is funded by the Tamil Diaspora, there were other websites in Tamil. Chief among them was puthinam.com. This website, now defunct, gave graphic accounts of the civilian casualties during the last stages of the war. Many video clips, the website posted, showing the civilian plight at that time, were included in the award-winning Channel 4 documentary—Sri Lanka's Killing Fields.

To counter the challenge posed by the new media, the government also launched several websites. Among them, defence.lk, a website maintained by the Defence Ministry, occupied the number one position among all Sri Lanka-based websites on the Alexa ranking during the last stages of the war.[7] In addition, supporting the government's position was Asia Tribune, a website edited by a Tamil businessman, which carried stories critical of the LTTE.

Parallel to the web journalism, the electronic media also developed. The LTTE carried out its propaganda work effectively through its radio station 'the Voice of Tigers'—*Puligalinkural*—and its satellite television station 'National Tamil Television'. In Colombo, the government's liberal economic policy paved the way for more private radio channels in Sinhala, English and Tamil. But the Tamil channels—which were largely owned by the Sinhalese, except for the channels owned by the Maharaja group—were more than careful in their news coverage. They did not want to earn the wrath of the government and lose their broadcast licences, as happened to the ABC Radio Network in 2007 via a court order.

To counter the LTTE propaganda and reach the Tamil people, the state-run SLBC Tamil service started a special daily evening programme critical of the LTTE but in favour of the government ally, the EPDP, led by Minister Douglas Devananda.

But what is heartening to note is the emergence of the social media and citizen journalism that act as powerful tools in the dissemination of news. Unlike the 1983 anti-Tamil riots that triggered Sri Lanka's civil war, the June 2014 anti-Muslim riots took place in the full view of the social media. (Details are given later.) This made a big difference giving us the news as it happened and let Sri Lankan leaders know that the world was watching and any attempt at news blackouts would be futile.

The social media deals a powerful blow to government efforts at censorship and make meaningless the act of self-censorship which some newspapers adopt for fear of earning the wrath of the powers-that-be.

Minority Media after the War

The war officially ended on 19 May 2009. But it did not herald an end to the troubles the minority media in Sri Lanka had been facing. Although the LTTE has been eliminated, the threat from goons who are alleged to be sponsored by politicians from the ruling coalition persists. On 28 May 2011, two years after the war had ended, S. Kavitharan, a journalist attached to the Jaffna-based *Uthayan* newspaper, which was the sole media voice of the Tamils in the government-controlled areas of the north throughout the war period, was attacked by an unidentified gang.

Kavitharan and his media colleagues had come under constant attack from a pro-government paramilitary group which had warned them not to publish photographs or articles about LTTE leader Velupillai Prabhakaran. A month after the attack on Kavitharan, the newspaper's news editor G. Kuhanathan was brutally attacked by an unknown gang. Investigations into the attacks on the *Uthayan* journalists have seldom led to successful prosecutions.

The *Uthayan* newspaper, which is run by E. Saravanabhavan, who is a member of parliament for the main Tamil opposition party, the Tamil National Alliance (TNA), continued its journalistic duty and paid a heavy price. During the war years, its office was burnt. A leaked US embassy cable posted on the WikiLeaks website had quoted President Rajapaksa's brother Basil Rajapaksa as saying he had asked the Ministers Douglas Devananda and V. Muralitharan alias Karuna, a former LTTE commander who broke away from the group, to rein in their members, who had become a law unto themselves.[8] Rajapaksa's comments, according to the cable, came in response to a question from the then

US ambassador in Sri Lanka, Robert Blake, who later became Assistant Secretary of State in charge of South and Central Asia.

In February 2009, the *Uthayan*'s editor in chief, N. Vidyatharan, who also edited the sister paper, *Sudar Oli*, from Colombo, was arrested by security officers at a funeral parlour where he had come to pay respect to a dead relative. Many of those present knew it was another 'white van' abduction and feared they would never see him again. However, following international diplomatic pressure, the government admitted that he was in police custody.

Even after the end of the war, the *Uthayan* and other independent Tamil newspapers operated with the same kind of threat that existed during the war years. The situation persisted until the government ended the state of emergency in September 2011.

In the post-war, post-emergency period, the independent Tamil media have displayed a little more courage to write about matters affecting the Tamil-speaking people, who also include the Muslims of Sri Lanka, despite unofficial 'guidelines' issued to them at the President's regular meetings with editors and media bosses. At these meetings, the presidential grouse often is that the Tamil media carry news items detrimental to the sovereignty of the country or that they act as the mouthpiece of the TNA, the main Tamil political alliance representing the Tamil people in parliament. During the war years, the TNA, like the Tamil media, was careful not to antagonise the LTTE. But the party's policies drew attacks from ultra-nationalist Sinhala leaders who accused it of being a mere mouthpiece of the LTTE.

V. Thanabalasingham, editor of the Colombo-based Tamil daily *Thinakkural* told me in an interview in February 2012 that in the post-civil war era, the independent Tamil media were being accused of 'working for the Diaspora'. In post-war Sri Lanka, the word 'Diaspora' tends to be used by critics to denote overseas Sri Lankan Tamils, who work against the interest of the country. In other words, the Tamil Diaspora is depicted as an LTTE ghost. Thanabalasingham points out that in the post-war period, probably in deference to the 'unofficial' government guidelines, no mainstream Tamil media glorify the LTTE. 'It looks like it is the government which is in need of an LTTE. It wants a bogey to distract the people from the real issues such as economic hardships', he said. Thanabalasingham said that in post-war Sri Lanka, the minority media has a cardinal role to play in highlighting the real issues facing the Tamil-speaking people. One such issue he identifies is the presence of the military, which largely consists of the Sinhalese, in the traditional

Tamil areas. 'The militarization of civilian areas in the north has denied the traditional-minded Tamil people their right to privacy'.

The new-found courage with which the independent Tamil newspapers publish news is rarely seen in the Tamil electronic media. With the exception of the Shakthi television and radio channel, which are run by the Tamil-owned Maharaja Group, which also runs Sirasa, the popular Sinhala TV and radio channels, and the English language MTV, most Tamil independent radio channels, which are owned by Sinhala businessmen, are cautious when reporting Tamil issues or carrying opposition viewpoints. The state controls three Tamil national TV channels—Nethra, Vasantham and Vetri. Hence, for the 'other side of the story', the news hungry Tamils depend on Maharaja's Shakthi or satellite television channels beamed from Tamil Nadu in India or internet-based radio and television operated from Europe. However, satellite television is still a feature associated with city and urban life and yet to touch the villages.

While independent Tamil newspapers such as *Thinakkural, Sudar Oli, Udayan* and *Veerakesari* give prominence to issues such as the militarisation of Tamil areas, the rehabilitation of the displaced Tamil people and the need for a political solution to meet the aspirations of the Tamil people, the Sinhala newspapers, the Sinhalese-run English newspapers and the state-controlled Tamil media hail the military victory and highlight dangers posed to the territorial integrity and the sovereignty of the country. The Sinhala and Tamil media's reporting on allegations of human rights violations and war crimes committed by the security forces during the last stages of the war also differs. The minority Tamil independent media give more weight to the western nations' concerns over accountability, while the Sinhala media and the Sinhalese-controlled English media display shades of nationalism and seek to protect the troops and hit out at western nations for their call for accountability.

The polarisation of the media that was visible on the eve of Sri Lanka's independence and throughout the post-independence period in varying degrees continues to be a salient feature of the Sri Lankan media scene. Issues such as democracy, freedom of expression and the all-important spiralling cost of living took a back seat at the height of the war, but are gradually coming to the forefront in the post-war media. But, again, there is a difference in the manner in which they are presented in the Sinhala-dominated media and the Tamil media.

Thanabalasingham claims that the independent Tamil media highlight dangers to democracy in a much better way than the Sinhala media. Thanabalasingham's book *Oorukku Nallathu Solven* (I will tell the good to the country), an anthology of *Thinakkural* editorials written by him is a testament to his statement. But the objective is what makes the difference. In the introduction to the book, Professor Karthigesu Sivathambi says 'a Tamil daily in Sri Lanka has two vital functions: (a) it has to report all major national events and (b) it has to indicate how those events affect the Tamils/Tamil-speaking people. This attitude is the core of the independent Tamil media in Sri Lanka'. The Tamil journalists will defend this approach by saying that their news and editorials have to cater to their readership's taste and expectations; and that such an approach is vital for a newspaper or a media group to be commercially viable. Unfortunately, these ethno-centric media policies sustain ethnic divisions and do not contribute positively to the development of a national identity. Besides, such divisions weaken the media's power and their role in promoting or strengthening democracy. In this sense, media unity assumes utmost significance. Media unity does not merely mean the coming together of Sinhala, Tamil and Muslim journalists on World Press Freedom Day. It essentially means uniting for a purpose, the purpose being democracy promotion which includes ensuring full media freedom with responsibility, the independence of the judiciary, the effective functioning of the rule of law, transparency in governance and public accountability.

Such a media unity with a common purpose would emerge only after the Tamil political question is effectively addressed. A political solution based on meaningful devolution of power to the Tamil regions could enable the Tamil media to divert their energy to highlight national issues such as the state of the economy, media freedom and the lack of good governance—with the entire nation's interest at heart, instead of only the interest of the Tamil-speaking community.

But Sri Lankan media's coverage of the recent attacks on Muslims in June 2014 indicates that the country's divided media are drifting further away from a point of convergence. When mobs provoked by an extremist Buddhist monk went on the rampage in three southern towns of Aluthgama, Dharga Town and Beruwala, attacking Muslim houses and shops, some mainstream English and Sinhala newspapers downplayed the incident, or adopted a partial news blackout policy, in an apparent bid to prevent the reports from sparking further violence in other areas. If it was so, the editors should be commended for exercising 'social responsibility'. But civic rights groups and Muslim readers saw it as an attempt to cover up the atrocities of an extremist group and accused the newspapers of ethnic bias.

As the violence continued for days, it became impossible for these newspapers to downplay the incident. This was largely because of the dynamic role played by the social media with a worldwide reach in disseminating news with videos, photographs and texts. These newspapers began to publish reports and articles, but not without attracting criticism from civic actions groups and media watchers for 'biased coverage'. Days after the violence, a Sinhala daily and an English daily published several pictures that showed a few Sinhala houses that were damaged in the riots, but for reasons best known to them, they chose not to publish pictures of damaged houses and shops of the Muslims, who were the worst hit.

However, two English newspapers stood out for their independent coverage. The *Financial Times*, a daily which is circulated largely in Colombo, won kudos for its independent on-the-spot coverage of the riots while the *Sunday Times'* editorial that condemned religious extremism was widely hailed as well-timed and forthright.

Unlike the Sinhala and English newspapers, the Tamil media were more forceful in their coverage of the riots. Besides the daily lead story on the front pages, page after page in Tamil newspapers highlighted the Muslim suffering and carried opinion articles and photo-features on the riots with several analyses making comparisons between the 1983 anti-Tamil riots and 2014 anti-Muslim riots. The manner in which the Sinhala, Tamil and English newspapers covered the anti-Muslim riots once again shows that the media in Sri Lanka—with the exception of a few—are susceptible to ethnic politics, instead of being guided by objectivity. Needless to say, media unity remains elusive.

The Muslim Media

Parallel to the Tamil media, there exists a Muslim media in Sri Lanka. Its existence further confirms the division of the media along ethnic lines in Sri Lanka. The Muslims of Sri Lanka are largely a Tamil-speaking minority scattered all over the island. A large number of Muslims live in the country's Eastern Province. Thus, the language of the Muslim media is largely Tamil, though newspapers and magazines carrying the Muslim viewpoint are also published in Sinhala and English. Though a Tamil-speaking minority, the Muslims in Sri Lanka claim they are a separate community. Hence, their political aspirations, they insist, are different from those of the Tamils.

The beginning of the Muslim media in Sri Lanka is no different from the beginning of the Sinhala or Tamil media. Their main objective was to protect Muslim identity from Christian missionary influence. The early Muslims wrote Tamil using Arabic script. Books were handwritten in Arabic-Tamil or *Arwi* until the early 20th century. But with the inception of Tamil printing in the 19th century, the Muslims resorted to Tamil letters extensively in their publications. This was because the *Arwi* or Arabic-script presses were not available in the country. The first Muslim news magazine in Tamil was printed in 1873. It was named '*Puthinalankari*'—a name coined by joining *puthinam*, meaning news, and *alankari*, meaning beautiful woman. In its editorial, the editor justified the publication of the magazine in these words: 'Just as the other communities benefit from the newspapers, the Muslims also should benefit'.

Two years later, a Muslim weekly, *Shingai Warthamani*, came out. It was followed by a fortnightly *Shingai Nation*. Both these news magazines were printed in Singapore.

A significant publication that contributed immensely to the Muslim literary and political revival was Siddi Lebbe's *Muslim Nation* in Tamil. However, none of the Muslim magazines or newspapers that started in the late 19th century lasted for long.

In the 1930s, the Muslim readership was attracted to Tamil publications and since then, Tamil newspapers have been giving some voice and space to Muslim issues. Occasionally, a Muslim newspaper or magazine would hit the newsstands. Significant among them are the *Al-Hasanath* magazine, a publication of the Sri Lanka Jamath E Islam, and the *Al Islam* (in English), monthly. Both these low-circulation publications are more than 40 years old and they highlight Muslim domestic and international issues. Today, the Jamath E Islam also publishes *Prabodaya* in Sinhala, underscoring that the Muslim community's main concern is their religion rather than the Tamil language.

A significant development during the civil war years was the emergence of Tamil national newspapers with a Muslim slant. Giving voice to the Muslim political revivalism in the late 1980s, *Navamani* newspaper echoed the policies of the Sri Lanka Muslim Congress, a political party which derives its strength from the Muslim-dominant areas in the Eastern Province.

In the post-war era, the Express Newspapers Limited, the publisher of *Veerakesari*, Sri Lanka's oldest Tamil paper, started *Vidivelli*, a Tamil newspaper with a Muslim focus. Other national newspapers, such as

Thinakaran and *Thinakkural,* today devote a considerable amount of space to highlight Muslim issues and make an attempt to identify with the Muslim community.

However, Muslim politicians and activists complain that there exists an anti-Muslim bias in the Tamil-run Tamil media. For instance, they say the problems of the internally displaced Northern Muslims—who were the victims of the ethnic-cleansing policy of the LTTE during the war years—are not given the right exposure. The Muslims say that this antipathy stems from the Tamil community's desire to derive maximum benefit from the limited resources available for resettlement of the displaced Tamil people. Moreover, the Muslims charge that the villages from which Muslims were evicted by the LTTE are now being occupied by the Tamils. So where there is a conflict between the Tamils and the Muslims, the Tamil-run Tamil media are not impartial, Muslim activists claim.

However, the independent Tamil newspapers gave wide coverage to the Muslim suffering during the June 2014 Sinhala mob attacks on three Muslim-dominated southern towns. This may be because the Muslims formed a substantial segment of their readership or due to a common feeling of insecurity that binds the minorities together.

The Muslim issues which the Tamil-run Tamil media shun are published in the country's only Muslim-run Tamil newspaper—*Navamani.* But the inadequacy of this newspaper in drawing the attention of policymakers to such issues has made Muslim activists, politicians and community leaders turn towards the English language national newspapers. The *Sunday Times*, the *Sunday Leader,* the *Island* and *Ceylon Today*, have been giving some space to highlight Muslim issues. But such generosity is linked more to moves aimed at wooing the Muslim readership than to any concern for the Muslims' quest for justice. The Muslims—and the Tamils—form a substantial segment of the readership of English newspapers, 70 per cent of whose readership is in Colombo and the suburbs or areas where a large number of Muslims and Tamils live.

Conclusion

Sri Lanka's media scene is at the crossroads. There is a pressing need to close the gap between what the media are and what they should be. Such an exercise is necessary in the long-term interest of the country, democracy and the reconciliation process.

Although the state of emergency has been lifted, there is little guarantee that it will not be imposed again under the PSO. In the Tissainayagam case, the PTA emerged as an effective weapon to intimidate journalists. New regulations crop up regularly to stifle the Tamil media. One such regulation was promulgated in July 2014, preventing NGOs from organising workshops for journalists and holding media conferences. This came after extremist Sinhala mobs disrupted workshops for Tamil journalists. Transparency International which organised the workshops said, 'the journalists were labelled as LTTE agents because they are Tamils'.

Together with the PSO and the PTA, the absence of a Right to Information Act has added to the woes of journalists, especially the Tamil media journalists, although the constitution of the country recognises the freedom of expression as a fundamental right

Media unity is essential in the journalists' fight for the enactment of a Right to Information Act. Such an act will not only allow the journalists to do their duty in an environment free from threats and intimidation, but also ensure corruption-free, good governance.

Notes

1. See http://www.jdslanka.org/index.php/killed-media-workers (accessed December 2014). Other sources, such as the Committee to Protect Journalists (CPJ), offer more conservative estimates. CPJ estimates that 25 journalists have been killed since 1992 with the motivation in 6 cases unconfirmed. The balance of state and non-state responsibility for the high death rate among assassinated Sinhala, Tamil and Muslim journalists also needs to be taken into account in interpreting these figures.
2. Sivaram (1999).
3. Michaels (2003).
4. Arulvarathan (2006).
5. Jeyaraj (2008).
6. Sivaram (1999).
7. Alexa is the leading provider of free, global web statistics based on visits and other data. They maintain and update a table which helps one to know the popularity of a website within a country.
8. Colombo Telegraph (February 2012)

4

Journalism on the Front Line

Amal Jayasinghe

Journalism is a risky business in Sri Lanka. At the height of fighting between Tamil rebels and Indian troops deployed in the island's northeast, and a more vicious battle between Sri Lankan forces and Marxist Sinhalese militants elsewhere in the island, I personally had reason to fear that a death squad was after me in the capital Colombo. More than 23 years later, both wars have ended, but an undeclared war against the media has continued. Decades of inter-ethnic war and two rebellions since 1971 by mainly Sinhalese youth have ensured that the media has to contend with many deadly adversaries, and not just the state security apparatus. Nearly 20 journalists as well as employees of media organisations have been killed and many more wounded, intimidated or forced to seek refuge abroad.

Afghan Comparisons

In the early 1990, my bosses in the French news agency Agence France Presse (AFP) thought I might be safer in Afghanistan! At the time, the Afghan capital of Kabul was almost under siege and more than a dozen rockets would hit the city on a daily basis, leaving scores killed or wounded. The only airline to fly into the war zone, Ariana Afghan Airlines, would do a hair-raising cork-screw manoeuvre to land at Kabul airport where bombed wreckage of Russian-built planes could be seen from the air. Yet the Afghan war somehow appeared less fearsome than the need always to be looking over one's shoulder and living in constant fear of abduction and torture at home. Fellow journalists and a few diplomat friends who met at the only hang out in Kabul, the UN Staff House, would make light of the situation. 'If you hear a rocket, that's good. That means you are alive and probably can report the attack. But, if you don't hear it, well, you may not be able to report it.'

Shortly before I was sent to Afghanistan, the *Inter Press Service* journalist Richard de Zoysa had been abducted and eventually killed, probably by the same killer squad that visited my home in the same neighbourhood. I had never worked with Richard, but knew him professionally and socially. His mother was our family doctor who helped deliver our first child almost two years earlier—on Richard's birthday.

There had been many a theory about why he was killed. It might have been a reaction to the impact of his journalism, or his political activism with university students. It was clear that members of the police had a direct involvement and the authorities wanted him dead. The same authorities had been unhappy about AFP's reporting on the conflict. At a time when there was censorship, both direct and indirect, on the local media, our (AFP) reports were well picked up by foreign radio stations, particularly the Sinhalese language programme of Veritas Radio, which broadcasts from the Philippines. Given the time constraint, Veritas had brief reports on Sri Lanka and the authorities probably felt that their side was not reflected adequately.

The then Media Minister, A.J. Ranasinghe, had raised this with me. We could provide him with our reports which always provided the balance required by good journalism standards, but we had no control over how our reports were edited by our media subscribers. The same went for Sri Lanka's state media which selectively edited our reports to put us in a bad light with the militants. It can be argued that you must be doing your job well if you are criticised by both sides, but in Sri Lanka, a militarised–terrorised society awash with illegal weapons, it could not be dismissed lightly. That is why my bosses took the decision to post me to Afghanistan for a year rather than risk it in Sri Lanka.

Media and Government

The priorities in Sri Lanka shifted rapidly when the Indian Peace Keeping Force troops withdrew in March 1990. A ceasefire between the Tigers and President Premadasa was short-lived and fresh fighting erupted by June. The government was pre-occupied with renewed fighting in the island's north-east as well as terror attacks elsewhere. The Sinhalese militants had been crushed, but dissension was growing within the government. The then President Premadasa took over the media in a manner that had never been seen in the country. Knowing that viewers tended to switch channels when state television carried lengthy reports on him, the President ordered that even private news networks must simultaneously carry the state media news reports so that television audiences could not escape him. The crisis came to a head when President Premadasa faced an impeachment motion put forward by two of his senior ministers. But towards the end of 1991, the impeachment was dropped and a badly bruised Premadasa attempted cosmetic changes.

The mainstream media was so subdued that there was hardly any critical debate in the local media. President Premadasa refused to meet foreign journalists, but his senior aides put up a valiant effort to defend him. Premadasa was eventually assassinated in what is widely believed to have been a suicide bombing. When Premadasa's assassination was formally announced in parliament, I was surprised to see the reaction of ruling party legislators. The Sri Lankan culture is such that you do not speak ill of the dead, nor do you rejoice in the death of even an enemy, but as leftist legislator Vasudeva Nanayakkara told me at the time, Premadasa's death was an exception. He was seen as an autocratic ruler.

Premadasa's tight grip on the mainstream media had spawned a crop of clandestine underground news sheets. He was succeeded by his political lightweight Prime Minister, Dingiri Banda Wijetunga, who introduced reforms which meant these news outlets were in danger of going out of business. But the relatively free era under Wijetunga was short-lived. His successor as President was Chandrika Kumaratunga, whose campaign had been supported by media activists keen on a freedom of information act, though in power she proved a disappointment. Her honeymoon with the media ended very early into her tenure. Under President Kumaratunga, the state security unit came to be known and dreaded as a hit squad for which journalists were often the targets. Kumaratunga's personal bodyguard was held responsible for an organised attack on press photographers who were covering an opposition protest in Colombo and was fined by the Supreme Court.

Her successor, President Mahinda Rajapakse, came to power promising more media freedom and sweeping reforms, but the escalating fighting between security forces and Tamil rebels meant a bleak period for the press. It was clear that the administration would not tolerate any criticism of its military strategy or tactics.

In June 2008, the defence ministry fired its first salvo against journalists critical of its war against Tamil rebels, labelling them 'cowboy defence analysts' and 'enemies of the state'. In two commentaries published on its website, the ministry also railed against what it said was 'crap' being written about the battle against the Tamil Tigers. The controversial offensive, in which the Liberation Tigers of Tamil Eelam (LTTE) were eventually crushed, was 'no holds barred'. The ministry presented reporters with a stark choice of being either pro-government or pro-terrorist. It said some writers were damaging morale and warned that the ministry 'does not wish to entertain mere doomsayers who always try to undermine the soldiers' commitment'. It also warned it would take 'all necessary measures to stop this journalistic treachery against the country'. 'Those who commit such treachery should identify themselves with the LTTE rather than showing themselves as crusaders of media freedom', the ministry said on its website.

At the end of June 2008, a journalist was attacked and his car smashed as he travelled home after work. Seven months later, in January 2009, the high profile anti-establishment editor Lasantha Wickrematunge was killed as he drove to work.

Up till then, the government was in the habit of referring to Wickrematunge as living proof of press freedom. His death became a symbol for the suppression of free expression in Sri Lanka. Sri Lankan President Mahinda Rajapakse himself expressed outrage at the killing of Wickrematunge. The President argued that the assassination was aimed at marring the military gains the security forces had been making against Tamil Tiger rebels in the north of the island. But the country's opposition and media activists remained unimpressed.

In a recent editorial, the slain editor himself had seen it coming. Wickrematunge said reporters and private media institutions were being targeted partly because of the ineffectiveness of the country's main opposition. 'More and more, even as the opposition has fallen mute, independent media institutions have taken on the job of the opposition, serving as a mirror of public opinion', he said in a commentary. 'That is why more journalists have been attacked more in recent years than have opposition politicians', Wickrematunge said in the *Sunday Leader*.[1]

Wickrematunge had been editing the paper since founding it in 1994. The *Sunday Leader* did not support the government's war effort against Tamil rebels to the same wholehearted extent as the state media. An ethnic Sinhalese, the editor had been openly sceptical of military claims. His colleague Manik de Silva, Chief Editor of the privately run *Sunday Island*, noted that Wickrematunge was undoubtedly friendly with the

President at one time but had at other times been on the receiving end of angry presidential criticism on the phone. 'It would be unfair to blame the killing on Rajapakse', said de Silva. 'But there are various persons in the government with their own agendas and whether any such were party to the killing remains to be seen'.[2]

If the government had no complicity, it was a good opportunity to carry out a thorough investigation and expose the killers and clear its name. That is yet to happen. Six months before Wickrematunge's assassination, the Sri Lanka College of Journalism (SLCJ) had asked me to conduct a brain-storming session on journalists' safety at work: how to avoid getting beaten up, or worse. By that time, 12 journalists and media workers had been killed in Sri Lanka since 2005.

We invited local police, military and medical personnel to speak on safety and offer tips on how to keep safe. They all agreed that reporting is a very risky business in Sri Lanka, where the long ethnic conflict had created many dangers for reporters. Part of the problem for journalists, said one navy officer, Commander Mahesh Karunaratne, is that they do not know who their assailants are and how to deal with the danger. 'We at least know what the danger is' he told local photographers, cameramen and reporters. 'In your case, you don't know from where the threat originates and the worst thing is that you are not prepared'.[3] Despite all the trials and tribulations, my experience is that the vast majority of senior officers are not predators of the press. The authorities have done them an injustice by not exposing the few who give everyone a bad name.

This brings us to the question: Who can the journalists trust? Minority Tamil journalists have had even more problems than their Sinhalese colleagues. Racial profiling meant that the authorities often looked at them with even more suspicion. Tamil journalists say they were singled out for 'special' scrutiny at security checkpoints despite repeated official pronouncements that there is no discrimination. With the end of armed hostilities in May 2009, and the dismantling of many of the checkpoints set up around the capital city, the situation has in that respect somewhat improved.

Legal Position

The state of emergency has been a sword of Damocles for Sri Lankan journalists. The threat of prosecution had been used from the time it was introduced over 35 years ago but the first high profile prosecution was in

2008. The Tamil editor J.S. Tissainayagam was arrested in March 2008 for his articles in the *North East Herald* monthly magazine and accused of inciting people to violence and causing racial hatred. The prosecution was an ominous threat to the freedom of the media. In a highly controversial decision, Tissainayagam was sentenced to 20 years in jail by the High Court. Although he was granted a presidential pardon in May 2010, and the state of emergency was allowed to lapse in 2011, the authorities can still use the draconian provisions of the Prevention of Terrorism Act to arrest and detain suspects, including journalists

Political parties which championed the cause of the free press have often failed to deliver when they were returned to power. Given the Sri Lankan experience, it is difficult to expect that the current opposition would act any differently if they were to come to power. The main opposition party, the United National Party (UNP) had proposed a freedom of information act but failed to get this law through parliament when they were in power between December 2001 and February 2004.

However, the UNP administration in April 2002 announced the repeal of the criminal defamation provision that had been used by the state against several anti-establishment editors who were handed down jail terms which had been suspended for long periods. The Colombo High Court had sentenced Lasantha Wickrematunge, the Editor of the anti-government *Sunday Leader* newspaper, to two years imprisonment suspended for five years for an article he published in September 1995.

The editor of another weekly, Sinha Ratnatunga of the *Sunday Times*, was convicted on charges of criminally defaming the President in July 1997 and given a one-year jail term, suspended for seven years.

I may have narrowly escaped the criminal defamation law myself. It was a year after the law was repealed when Defence Minister Tilak Marapone threatened to sue me for LKR 500 million (USD 5.15 million). AFP had picked up and expanded on a local media report that the minister staged a ritual to exorcise evil spirits. The minister was angered by the report and wanted to sue, but he dropped the case. He lost his job less than a year later.

The repeal of the criminal defamation laws has not meant an easy time for the media in Sri Lanka. The UNP administration which abolished them had also promised to do away with the Press Council Act. The Press Council is a quasi-legal body with the power to muzzle the press. The Act allows the state to impose censorship and shut down media organisations. But the move to repeal the Act had not gone through parliament and the present government has once again revived the Press Council.

Foreign Versus Local Media

Sri Lankans are generally friendly and well disposed towards foreigners, but the fighting between government forces and separatist Tamil Tiger rebels appears to have encouraged a degree of xenophobia which is also reflected in the local media, particularly the hard-line nationalistic media. Many hard-line nationalists blame the west and the international media for supporting or siding with the Tamil Tiger separatists. Criticism of the west has been seen as a popular move, helpful in garnering the votes of the Sinhalese majority. Attacking the international media has become very much a part of that strategy.

Despite accusing the foreign media of bias, the Sri Lankan government had brought out several volumes of press clippings from the international press about the atrocities of the Tamil Tigers, especially the recruitment and use of child soldiers and the deployment of suicide bombers.

I have also noticed many times that when the mainstream Sri Lankan press found it difficult to publish news on controversial issues, they would choose to reproduce foreign media reports in the hope that they could 'shift the blame' to the international media if the authorities took exception to the reports. This is probably why there is a perception, at least among some bureaucrats, that the international media is only highlighting the negatives in the country. Some local newspapers have launched virulent attacks against foreign correspondents based in the capital Colombo as well as abroad. The polarisation in the country was also reflected in the media. However, some private media organisations and even some of the state-run outlets managed to maintain a commendable degree of objectivity in extremely difficult circumstances.

The government did not allow free access for the international media during the final stages of its battle against the Tamil Tigers. 'A war without witnesses' is how Sri Lanka's battle came to be known outside the country. This policy of keeping out the foreign press and consistently denying them access to the conflict zone has come to haunt the government as it grapples with allegations of war crimes and crimes against humanity.

The government's own Lessons Learnt and Reconciliation Commission (LLRC), which looked at the final stages of Sri Lanka's separatist war, heard that the policy of keeping the international media out of the conflict zones in the island's north-east may have been highly counterproductive. 'The government should ensure the freedom of movement of media personnel in the north and east, as it would help in the exchange of information contributing to the process of reconciliation', the LLRC said in its recommendations. It also called for Right to Information legislation. Sri Lanka is coming under intense international and local pressure to implement the LLRC recommendations. The government has set out an 'action plan', but it remains to be seen if it will have the courage to fully implement it.

When ruling party legislators met for a workshop and discussed public relations in March 2012 at the hill resort of Diyatalawa, lawmakers resolved that they would have better rapport with the international media. This appears to be an immediate response to allegations abroad that Sri Lanka is responsible for war crimes while crushing Tamil rebels. After repeatedly accusing Britain's Channel 4 of fabricating an 'execution video' showing alleged Sri Lankan troops executing Tamil prisoners, the Sri Lankan authorities have now begun probing the video. The LLRC too had called for credible investigations into allegations of excesses, but the general position of the authorities has been that the charges are false and the videos shown on Channel 4 are fabrications.

Professional Standards and Media Training

Journalism is not recognised as a profession in Sri Lanka, but the media industry took the first steps towards ensuring professional standards by introducing the Sri Lanka Press Institute (SLPI) 10 years ago.

The SLCJ which is under the SLPI umbrella has been conducting diploma courses and providing recruits to the media industry. However, with the escalation of attacks against journalists and the poor salaries offered, there appears to have been a decline in the number of youngsters keen to enrol for training. While there are many senior journalists who are thorough professionals, there has been a dearth of talent at entry and mid-levels.

As an independent member of the panel of jurists for Excellence in Journalism awards (organised by the Editors' Guild of Sri Lanka), I have noticed an appreciable improvement in the number of entries and the quality of published material. One of the areas where there is a visible improvement is photo journalism. Many appeared to have benefitted from exposure to the work of the best photographers across the world and have clearly demonstrated their skills as top press photographers. This could also be partly due to the mid-career training undertaken by the SLCJ as well as the healthy competition among print media outlets in the country.

While most of the newspapers in Sri Lanka have invested heavily in new technology, the amount of money they spend on training and refresher courses for their staff could be a small percentage of their total budget or none at all. The high cost of news print (sometimes the state uses taxes on news print as a tool to pressure the media) and stagnant advertising rates may not encourage spending on training, though I trust this is an area of concern for senior editors.

Closer cooperation and exchange programmes with international media organisations and training outfits could help the Sri Lankan media, which is making a transition from an era of conflict to peace and reconciliation after nearly four decades of ethnic bloodshed.

Foreign journalists posted to Sri Lanka as well as Sri Lankans working for the international media have often been trained to cope in hostile environments, but there are no such mechanisms for those in the local media. There have been no studies to identify post-traumatic stress disorder among Sri Lankan journalists who covered the conflict as well as the dreadful events following the December 2004 tsunami which claimed over 30,000 lives.

Following the end of the fighting in May 2009, Sri Lanka has been recording high economic growth rates and aims to double its gross domestic product (GDP) per capita income to 4,000 dollars by 2015, but the media industry may not have kept pace both in terms of increasing its audience and raising the economic circumstances of its employees.

Sri Lanka's media is basically divided into two camps: the state-run and the privately owned news outlets. Within the private media, there are competing and conflicting political and business interests which dictate their news agenda. However, to their credit they have largely supported the industry-run Press Institute and the College of Journalism. This is clearly an area where the entire Sri Lankan media can come together to improve the professional standards of their staff. I have noticed employees from all these media organisations applying for scholarships and learning opportunities abroad and this high level of participation should augur well for the industry.

New Challenges

With Sri Lanka's war against Tamil Tigers over, the battle lines have shifted overseas, as Colombo struggles to defend itself against charges of war crimes. This brings new challenges to the local and Colombo-based foreign media. The authorities had taken a dim view of any foreign journalist making a critical analysis of the final stages of the conflict and the blackballing of Britain's Channel 4 is a just one example.

Senior Sri Lankan diplomats privately agree that the government may have mishandled the post-war developments and a more accommodating stance would have actually helped Sri Lanka's cause. However, a report by Sri Lanka's own version of a war probe, the LLRC, has somewhat taken the pressure off the press. For the first time, the LLRC has acknowledged that civilians had been killed as a result of military action and called for an 'independent' probe into specific allegations of rights abuses.

The suppression of the mainstream media may have also backfired on the Sri Lankan state. With little or no space for dissent, alternate views have found a cosy niche on the Internet and spawned a crop of websites. Like the underground news-sheets during President Premadasa's rule, the dissident websites are having a good run. Attempts by the telecommunications regulator to block access to them from Sri Lankan Internet Service Providers have only boosted their popularity. Some of them have blurred the line between facts, comment and gossip. Unfortunately, that is a price the authorities must pay for not tolerating home-grown dissent.

Notes

1. http://www.thesundayleader.lk/2010/05/30/the-anaesthetic-of-familiarity/ (accessed on 26 May 2014).
2. http://web.archive.org/web/20090113201105/http://blogs.afp.com/ (accessed on 26 May 2014).
3. Views expressed at a Hostile Environment and Journalists' Safety course, at the SLPI, in Colombo, July 2008.

5

Women Journalists: Fighting the Good Fight

Namini Wijedasa

The story of women in Sri Lankan journalism is broadly a positive one. There are admittedly fewer practising female journalists or editors today than there are male ones. But the story extends beyond simple numbers. Sri Lankan women journalists have overcome social, cultural and workplace barriers to break significant ground in media.

One of the most difficult challenges remains that of balancing work and family. Journalism can offer flexibility that women in other professions do not have. But the very fact that it is 'unstructured' can also complicate family life. Developing stories cannot be put on hold while the needs of a child are met. And when deadlines loom—as can happen on an hourly, daily, weekly or monthly basis—great sacrifice in time, energy and focus is required. Compiling news reports or features also often necessitates travel, a difficult prerequisite for women with young offspring.

Scientifically gathered information about the contribution of women journalists through the years is scarce, if not completely unavailable. The most reliable recent research conducted on this subject is a rapid assessment by Social Indicator (SI), the survey research unit of the Centre for Policy Alternatives (CPA). Commissioned by the Sri Lanka Press Institute, it seeks to understand female participation in mainstream print and electronic media. The resultant report, released in July 2011, observes that:

> As there is no data available regarding the number of journalists in Sri Lanka over the years it is difficult to trace the progress or lack of participation of female journalists in the media industry. Looking at what they have observed over the years in the industry, the journalists

interviewed are of the opinion that the number of female journalists entering the media industry in Sri Lanka has significantly increased over the years.[1]

This paper is not a study on the numerical strength of female involvement in Sri Lankan media. Instead, it aspires to provide a snapshot of the challenges faced by women in print media in the conduct of their profession. In doing so, it will elaborate on some central themes from the SI-CPA survey. It will also draw from conversations I have conducted with colleagues and from my own experiences as a woman journalist.

The Pioneers

It is a known fact that Sri Lanka gave the world its first female prime minister in 1960. It is a lesser known detail that at least 15 years before Sirimavo Bandaranaike assumed this mantle Anne Abayasekara became the first ever female Sri Lankan staff journalist.[2] Women who worked in media before her—there were reportedly only a handful, although statistics are not available—were expatriates living in Sri Lanka. Among them was Leela Shukla, an Indian whose husband was posted in Colombo.

Anne was 17 years old when D.R. Wijewardene, Chairman and Managing Director of Associated Newspapers of Ceylon Ltd, or Lake House, interviewed her for a position. It was wartime, he warned her, and they had temporarily suspended the women's pages because of newsprint rationing. Not only were female journalists rare. It was an age during which newspaper bosses could still not envisage women taking on anything more than the women's or children's pages. Anne agreed to a clerical position on the premise that she could join the editorial staff when things returned to normal.

Anne joined Lake House in February 1943, working first in the General Office and then in the Secretary's Department. In 1947, Lake House resumed the women's pages in their newspapers and Leela Shukla was made editor. When she returned to India a few months later, Anne became editor of the women's pages of the *Ceylon Daily News* (CDN) and *Sunday Observer*. The 22-year-old was the first Sri Lankan woman to head these pages and the only woman in the editorial at the time. She was assigned to fill three pages in the CDN, a page in the *Sunday Observer* and the twice-weekly women's sections in the *Evening Observer*.[3]

Throughout the 1950s and 1960s, more women started joining the industry but the numbers were still very small.[4] The first Sri Lankan woman editor of a newspaper was Rita Sebastian. She rose to that rank in the former *Sunday Times* which was published by the now defunct Times of Ceylon Group. I remember a conversation I had with Rita as we sat watching the launch of the Sri Lanka Freedom Party's National Workers' Charter at the Old Parliament in 1995. I had joined the media as a trainee journalist only the previous year but Rita, already a heavyweight in the industry, spent the prelude to the ceremony strongly encouraging me to stay on in journalism. As a trailblazer, she clearly felt it her duty to see that women's participation in media continued to increase.[5]

Rita died the following year, in March 1996. In a tribute, *Sunday Times* (published by Wijeya Newspapers Ltd) described her as 'a pioneer woman journalist who broke several male bastions in the profession'. Rita was a Correspondent for the *Indian Express, Inter Press Service, Kyodo News Agency* and others. She wrote regularly for the new *Sunday Times* and her investigative, in-depth and on the spot reports, especially on ethnic issues, were widely read and appreciated. She also founded the Foreign Media Journalists' Organisation.[6]

Rita was a trendsetter in other ways. She was one of the first women to undertake war reporting and repeatedly travelled to the conflict zone.[7] She often risked her life to go across enemy lines into territory controlled by the Liberation Tigers of Tamil Eelam.[8]

It was not common then for women to cover the war from the frontlines. One reason might have been the reluctance of media institutions to shoulder the liability, responsibility or, indeed, the 'embarrassment' of having deployed a member of the 'weaker sex' on dangerous assignments (Rita was at the time a freelancer). Not only was the warfront male-dominated, it was exceedingly treacherous. There were also many layers of socio-cultural barriers to breach before a woman could take on such assignments.

The status quo two decades on is dramatically different, particularly in the field of English print media. Progress is also observed in Sinhala and, to a lesser extent, in Tamil newspapers. This will be explored in the next section.

No Holds Barred

The SI-CPA in the course of their research interviewed women journalists covering a broad range of areas at their institutions. This includes politics, news, entertainment, fashion and social issues. The study holds that:

> Contrary to the popular belief outside of the media industry that there are certain sections that are male dominated, such as news and politics, and that entertainment and features sections are female dominated—according to the journalists interviewed, there are no such divisions. The journalists say that they have the freedom to write outside of their assigned beats/areas and that none of them have been restricted by the institutions that they work for … unless it is an institution policy not to cover particular topics.[9]

This conclusion is an accurate reflection of my own experience. I did initially face some resistance when, in 1997, at the age of 21, I wanted to report from the frontlines. My bosses were afraid for my safety, reluctant to send a young woman to the north, unsure of my ability to handle the task and worried about having to answer to my parents in the event of an accident. The newspaper already had an established, male defence reporter. Once I convinced them to assign me, the defence ministry expressed concern. The job I had argued so hard to do was a three-day tour of the conflict areas—and nobody else had nominated women.[10]

After this first hurdle was overcome, however, every institution that I worked for encouraged and, wherever possible, facilitated my travel to the warfront. Several other women—mostly from English media, including electronic—were also reporting from conflict areas at the time. Within a few years, the only obstructions to female journalists covering the war were their own reservations and/or those of their families.

This trepidation extends not just to war reporting but to other fields, depending on the thinking of journalists and their parents/spouses/partners on what is or is not appropriate. There is a sense—particularly among young journalists who still depend heavily on their parents for resources and guidance—that certain stories are not safe for women to cover. From conversations with trainee female journalists, I have also gathered that, while their parents consent to them entering the profession, they then demand a degree of control over the stories or assignments they cover. It is not uncommon, however, for some of these journalists to move way from such control as they grow in experience.

The SI-CPA report notes:

> Drawing from their observations over the years, some of the senior journalists said that restrictions with regard to covering particular

topics, travelling out of town, are usually not imposed on journalists by the institution but by the individuals themselves. These self-imposed restrictions sometimes arise due to family or other obligations or even due to cultural and personal beliefs of each individual. 'For some, their hesitancy to work on certain assignments, travel or work late comes not from any personal experience but it is imbedded in them—it is part of culture' (said one senior journalist).

According to the testimony of one senior female journalist cited in the *Ceylon Today* newspaper of 8 March 2012,[11] it would appear more difficult for women in Tamil media to break through cultural and social norms. This journalist describes how, as a woman, it was hard enough to getting a job in a Tamil newspaper, let alone covering the war. Now a well-known Tamil blogger and photojournalist, she joined the media in 1993 at the age of 21. But she had to face 'exam after exam and several rounds of interviews' before she was hired. 'Journalism was considered a dangerous job, so they repeatedly asked if my family was ok with it', she is quoted as saying.

The report adds:

> Even so, the management had several stipulations to ensure her safety—she was not to write on controversial issues, she was not to go into the war zone, she had to be accompanied by a male photographer on all assignments, whether one was needed or not, and she was not to work late into the night.

But despite the opposition—and challenges—she reported regularly from the frontlines. Since the war ended, she has moved to covering issues such as the cultural lifestyles of the Tamils and still travels widely throughout former conflict areas. She started a popular blog in 2005.[12] She shifted from print media to radio, television and finally to the web and uses modern tools for journalism. She is also a keen photographer. She tells *Ceylon Today*: 'I had to contend with a lot of professional jealousy, especially when I took up my camera and went into the war zone. Senior photojournalists who had had no competition from women in their sphere were seriously put off. They had this almost unbelievable attitude of "Who are you—a woman and a Tamil—to come into this?" she recalls'.[13] In the end, she says, it was a 'burning zeal' for the profession that made her stick to it for 20 years, and counting.

The associate editor and a long time news editor of the widely circulated Sinhala language *Lankadeepa* newspaper—a woman—entered journalism in 1980 through the now defunct *Dawasa* newspaper. She remembers there being 'one or two' women in the field at the time. 'It was not a nine-to-five job and we had to travel around a lot', she said. 'Now, most of the work is done out of offices using modern tools but we didn't have fax, email, Internet or telephones. We didn't get vehicles from the workplace. We either took public transport or walked everywhere.'[14]

This editor says that women gradually joined the Sinhala media in greater numbers. And while she admits there were certain social and cultural expectations that they felt constrained to meet, these were not serious challenges if women 'knew their limits and behaved accordingly'. This might mean that women could not accept every invitation they were tendered, particularly to social events at night. It might also mean that they could not meet with contacts over alcoholic beverages. But she did not see these as obstructions to carving out a successful career in journalism. In fact, she claimed that her gender sometimes helped her gather information more efficiently and effectively because male officials, of whom there are a great many, were more receptive towards female journalists.[15]

Asked how a woman could achieve success in the Sinhala print media, this editor said:

> We must show that we can work like men. I didn't wait for anyone to assign me stories. I took the initiative and even did work that was not assigned to me. I did not let my inhibitions or fears prevent me from going to places that men went to. A good woman journalist will have to sacrifice far more than a male journalist.

That said, there still appears to be numerically more female journalists from the English media covering certain 'types' of stories—such as war, politics, crime and business—than there are from Tamil and Sinhala media. It would also seem that fewer women journalists from the Sinhala and Tamil media travel to outstation areas than do women journalists from the English media.

Work-Life Balance

One of the most difficult tasks for married women journalists, particularly those with children, remains the management of their multiple roles as career woman, daughter, wife and mother. The SI-CPA study holds that this is largely dependent on the individuals and how they distribute their work and other responsibilities.[16]

It must be emphasised at the outset that women journalists all over the world face these dilemmas. One British TV reporter recently described how, two months after giving birth, she was off to a new assignment as the BBC correspondent in Sri Lanka. She initially hid her pregnancy from her managers because she was fearful that she would never get another foreign posting after having a child.[17]

Juggling family and a career was admittedly more difficult for this journalist because she was a foreign correspondent, whose presence was required at hotspots within short notice. But the pressures are high for female journalists across the spectrum. Testimonies from women everywhere show that there is no easy answer. It is an often painful predicament for those who want to give journalism their best but find they cannot do so without demanding considerable sacrifice from their spouses and children.[18]

The SI-CPA study concluded that journalists who work at newspapers sometimes found it 'a bit difficult' to manage their duties due to their erratic and long working hours. However, journalists have said they did not find their multiple roles to be a barrier to their work; neither have they impeded them from progressing in their career. Some journalists say it is easier to handle work because more women have joined over the years and now offer increased support. For some, travelling out of Colombo is not always easy with many responsibilities at home 'but they say that they manage somehow'.[19]

Not surprisingly, married female journalists said the support of their husbands was crucial and that 'without open minded and supportive husbands, journalism is a difficult field to continue to be in'. But the study quotes a senior journalist working at a Sinhala paper as saying it is sometimes difficult to continue as a journalist once a woman is married or has children 'as their husbands prefer their wives to have more conventional jobs or to stay at home'. She feels that the level of acceptance for this kind of work among Sri Lankans is still low.[20]

The associate editor of *Lankadeepa* quoted earlier said women journalists are required to make considerable sacrifices to further their careers. But she said that it was much easier now for a woman to balance work and family than when she started out. This is due in no small measure to the many technological and communication advances that have made it possible for women to interact speedily and efficiently with contacts, colleagues and managers; to gather information from a variety of sources, including the Internet, and to relay the reports to their publishers while sitting at home or at any other location of their choice;

to communicate with experts and professionals around the country and the world without having to be in situ, etc.

The impact of new information technology has had a definitive impact on transforming media culture; as observed, 'both the creative and technical aspects of production have long been computerised and all major newspapers in the country have access to the internet. Inevitably, this has made media networking easier with all the added advantages'.[21]

Journalists who are mothers admit there are times when they feel guilty that they might be neglecting their children, or being unfair by them. As a mother of two young children, I regularly battle these demons. But like many other women journalists, I have made sweeping adjustments to my work routine to enable me to spend a 'decent' amount of time with the children.

This has limited my scope professionally. For instance, I don't work after hours and I don't travel as I used to. But it is a personal choice that all institutions I was employed at have supported. Bosses accepted from the outset that family obligations also have to be met and I have never been under pressure to give one up for the other. Colleagues, many of whom have children themselves, have been supportive and empathetic. This is also true of male colleagues.

Other women journalists I know have also made changes to their work patterns. Flexibility remains a key attraction, as observed also in the SI-CPA study. But adjustments are not always possible. The researchers interviewed one journalist with 20 years of experience who said after she had her first child, she stopped working and stayed at home. She subsequently had another baby and ended up taking off six years from journalism so that she could be at home with her children. After six years, she came back to her old job and has continued since. However, she had quite a few colleagues who stopped working completely after they got married or had children.[22]

More Women in Media

Despite there being considerable equality for women in the workplace, the number of female journalists in employment is small. The SI-CPA study, which is the most recent gauge of women's participation in journalism, found 192 female journalists working in 31 Sinhala, Tamil and English language newspapers as against 464 male journalists. It is difficult to measure the progress or lack of participation of female journalists in the media industry as data were not collected over the years. However, all the journalists interviewed by the research team said the number of women entering the media industry has increased significantly and that this was a positive development. Still, women who are full time/permanent staff make up only around one-third of the journalists in both the print and electronic media institutions that participated in the SI-CPA study. It concluded, therefore, that despite the rise in female student intake for journalism courses and an increase in the numbers of women journalists, the female participation in media in Sri Lanka is still less than that of their male counterparts.[23]

In short, the number of active female journalists is less than the number of active male journalists. But this is gradually changing, with more women entering—and remaining—in the field. Sri Lanka appears to share this characteristic with many other countries, particularly in South Asia. Across the Palk Strait, there is now much talk of the 'feminisation' of the Indian media. An article published in the *Weekend Leader* in November 2011 states that, 'there can be no denying that the presence of women has registered a sharp rise'. It quotes Ammu Joseph, Indian media watcher and member of the Network for Women in Media India, as saying: 'If it's just a question of numbers, one can certainly say that there is some evidence of such a phenomenon (feminisation) in India, especially in big cities and in sections of the English language media'.[24]

The Global Media Monitoring Project in its 2010 report '*Who Makes the News?*' monitored 1,365 newspapers, television and radio stations and Internet news sites all over the world. It found that for stories reported on television, radio and newspapers, 'since the year 2000 the percentage of stories reported by women compared to those reported by men has increased in all major topics except "science/health". Nonetheless, stories by male reporters continue to exceed those by female reporters in all topics'.[25]

Notwithstanding the rise in female participation, there is still not even a handful of female editors in Sri Lanka. Women are more likely to be found at other levels, such as deputy or assistant editor, news editor, features editor, investigations editor, business editor, etc. They can also be observed at lower decision-making strata (such as deputy news editor, deputy features editor, etc.). By no means, therefore, is the picture an equal one.

The SI-CPA study uses data from *Guide to Media 2011, Department of Government Information, Sri Lanka* to confirm this opinion. It concludes that the disparity in the numbers of males and females in decision-making/managerial positions is quite high in all three media.[26]

This appears to be a worldwide trend. The Washington-based International Women's Media Foundation's 2011 study *Global Report on the Status Women in the News Media* found that in the Asia and Oceana region (with a few exceptions), there are barely 13 per cent of women in senior management. The report said that in more than 500 companies throughout 60 countries, men occupy the vast majority of the management jobs and newsgathering positions in most nations included in the study. Of the top management jobs, 73 per cent are occupied by men compared to 27 per cent by women. Among the ranks of reporters, men hold nearly two-thirds of the jobs, compared to 36 per cent held by women. However, among senior professionals, women are nearing parity with 41 per cent of the newsgathering, editing and writing jobs.

The report said:

> The two-year study covering 170,000 people in the news media found a higher representation of women in both governance and top management within both Eastern Europe (33% and 43%, respectively) and Nordic Europe (36% and 37%, respectively), compared to other regions. In the Asia and Oceana region, women are barely 13% of those in senior management, but in some individual nations women exceed men at that level, e.g., in South Africa women are 79.5% of those in senior management. In Lithuania women dominate the reporting ranks of junior and senior professional levels (78.5% and 70.6%, respectively), and their representation is nearing parity in the middle and top management ranks. [27]

The SI-CPA study quotes journalists as saying that one of the main reasons for low female representation in top positions is that they 'do not continue working long enough to reach the decision-making/managerial levels'. It says this view is strongly held by those in Sinhala media (print and radio) as well as several journalists in English and Tamil media. 'As females have other roles to fulfil as mothers and wives, they stop working after a while or make a conscious decision not to progress beyond a certain point and this is seen as one of the main reasons why there are minimal numbers of females at decision making and managerial levels when compared to the male numbers', the report states. It also quotes a female editor as saying that the media industry is 'a boys' club', with particular reference to the Editors' Guild of Sri Lanka.[28]

In interviews with this writer, several other senior female journalists confirmed the view that women stopped themselves from taking top positions. Among them was Indrani Peiris, who felt that many women put their family obligations first and this made it difficult for them to take on the high-pressure, intensive role of editor. In this job, she said, 'you cannot expect to be home for Sinhala New Year, for Vesak and on Poya holidays. You have to work like a man if you want the positions men rise to'.[29]

The Elephant in the Room

Sexual harassment is a sensitive topic. It could also (from this writer's understanding of discussions with female colleagues) be a subjective matter. That is, the definition of what individuals consider to be harassment could differ. What some categorise as 'harmless flirting' could cause serious offence to others. It is also felt that there are different degrees of harassment, ranging from mild to severe. It is arguable whether some forms are more tolerable than others. However, it is clear that reactions to harassment vary greatly. Writing about sexual harassment—generalising it—therefore, is a complicated task.

The SI-CPA study says that, when asked about discrimination and harassment at their workplaces and in the line of their work, some journalists 'explained that they have experienced situations where they have been intimidated by men or faced situations where men have tried to take an upper hand in matters'. It has been this writer's personal experience that men, even within the field of journalism, are uneasy with and around women in leadership positions. There is a tendency, wherever possible, to undermine them, to dismiss their authority or influence and to relegate them to the rank of 'designation holder' minus the powers.

These challenges could be direct (like insubordination) or indirect. There could, for instance, be crude, gender-based jokes or comments cast. These could even be made without the knowledge of the woman editor or designation holder concerned. The idea is to make her an object of ridicule, thereby undermining her authority. The SI-CPA study quotes a journalist who handles news and politics as saying that it is very common for men in Sri Lanka to 'pass remarks and comments at women and it is best to ignore them while working'. Sexual innuendo and gender-based jibes and jokes are observed in varying degrees at many newspaper offices. Here, again, some women handle it better than others.

The SI-CPA research states also:

> When asked for their opinions specifically regarding harassment of a sexual nature, none of the journalists interviewed said that they have personally

faced such issues. However, almost every journalist interviewed was of the opinion that sexual harassment is prevalent in the industry.

This certainly points to a problem in the industry that has not been tackled. From interviews I did among female colleagues, it was learnt that the harassment could on occasion be serious enough to prompt resignation. One senior woman journalist told this writer that:

It is very much below the surface. And it depends on the place you work and the way you handle things. There are people who would like to help you. But if you take into consideration each and every case, it can become ugly for some people. Even senior reporters will find it hard to cope.

It is difficult to say how this situation will evolve in future. Some colleagues felt the difference today is that strong women are fighting back and influencing change. As one colleague put it, 'I feel the tough women handle it better. The weak ultimately give up'.

Ironically, there even exists a 'Charter of Gender Equality for Media and Journalism in Sri Lanka' launched in 2006.[30] It sets out the minimum standards, principles and actions needed to underpin gender equity in media in Sri Lanka and outlines a practical programme of action to support the achievement of equality in media workplaces, journalists' organisations and the media itself. Unfortunately, even this charter does not address the sexual harassment of female journalists in the workplace; that is, by their male colleagues. Despite all the advances women have made in the field of journalism in Sri Lanka, it is questionable whether they would ever achieve their full potential—and in larger numbers—as long as this scourge exists. Here, then, is the glass ceiling.

No Bed of Roses

The general situation for journalists—and journalism—in Sri Lanka, however, remains hugely challenging. In some ways, it is reflective of the general malaise that afflicts the country.

Some of these impediments were highlighted by this writer in a keynote speech delivered before the Annual General Meeting of the Citizens' Movement for Good Governance on 23 May 2012.[31]

In this writer's view, intolerance is the biggest hindrance to the practice of journalism in Sri Lanka under the regime of President Mahinda Rajapaksa.

Narrow mindedness and chauvinism have affected not only members of the government, but also media practitioners. The standards set at the top have filtered down and pervaded society at different levels.

Reporters without Borders (RSF) in a country update published on 12 March 2012[32] summarised the status quo in Sri Lanka thus:

> 2011 was marked by violence, threats and propaganda aimed at journalists and media defenders seen as government critics. Resorting to censorship and disinformation, authorities have blocked access to websites considered unfavourable to the government, claiming legal justifications.

The branding of critics, whoever they might be, remains a fundamental concern. Some examples are outlined in the RSF statement.[33] The oppressiveness of the government—and the modus operandi through which this oppression is exercised—has bred much self-censorship among journalists. The type of self-censorship could differ based on where a particular journalist works, who the owners of his newspaper are, who his editor is, etc. Different institutions require their journalists to lay off 'certain politicians' or 'certain issues', 'certain organisations' or 'certain lines'.[34]

The state media is entirely under the control of the government. There is no vestige of independence left in these institutions. This is largely because this regime (and many regimes before it) operates on the grossly questionable premise that when something is owned by the 'state' it is equivalent to being owned by the 'party' or 'alliance' in power.[35]

Writing in the *Sunday Leader* (its founding editor Lasantha Wickrematunge died in a daylight assassination in 2009 that is still being investigated), blogger and commentator, Indi Samarajiva, summarises the situation in this manner:

> There is independent media and the government is quite roundly criticised both online and off. … This does not, however, mean that expression is truly free. Sri Lankan repression of speech is more subtle, but still very real. I was recently in the office of the head of a large media company. Quite casually, he mentioned that they screen certain stories for political content and pull them if they think it would jeopardise the company. This essentially, is the nature of censorship in Sri Lanka today.[36]

In Samarajiva's words, 'The government has made it in the media's self-interest to practice self-censorship'.[37]

Samarajiva makes other observations: 'Today the government doesn't have to openly repress or attack media. The media is effectively tamed by a judicious combination of violence, prosecution, and politics.'[38]

The picture of media freedom painted by some media activists (particularly those based abroad) is excruciatingly grim. For instance, a movement called 'Sri Lanka Campaign' states on its website that Sri Lanka's media is in crisis.[39] It says: 'Since 2005, 34 journalists have been murdered, not a single murderer has been sent to prison, and up to 25 journalists a year are fleeing the country.'

High figures have often been quoted by international media to support the claim that Sri Lanka is a brutally violent place for journalists. The Committee to Protect Journalists (CPJ), however, has taken a more careful, substantiated position. It counts as 19 the number of journalists killed since 1992 for which motive has been confirmed and six for which motive remains unconfirmed.[40] These statistics are bad enough. In this writer's opinion, however, the problems facing Sri Lankan journalists are wider and deeper than numbers on a slate.[41] The International Federation for Journalists offers a good look at recent developments in a chapter on Sri Lanka in its report *'Free Speech in Peril: Press Freedom in South Asia 2010–2011'*.[42]

Meanwhile, impunity remains an overriding national problem. The CPJ ranks Sri Lanka fourth in its 2012 'impunity index' with 0.431 unsolved journalist murders per million inhabitants.[43] A press release states: 'In Sri Lanka, ranked fourth worst, authorities have failed to win convictions in the murders of nine journalists—all of whom reported critically about President Mahinda Rajapaksa's administration.'[44]

Having said all this, I also feel some media organisations/activists over-dramatise and exaggerate the situation on the ground. I cannot second guess their motives but I do believe this is counterproductive for Sri Lankan journalism in the long term. A western diplomat once commented to this writer that Sri Lanka is a curious and interesting mix when it comes to media. On the one hand, journalists operate under tremendous constraints. On the other hand, many still manage to write. Even without broaching 'taboo' issues, there is much critical opinion expressed in the media. The objective of this paper, however, is not to reconcile these contradictions.

Conclusion

As is the trend in most countries, the number of female journalists entering and practising the profession in Sri Lanka is rising. The number of female journalists holding the post of editor is markedly low but there is optimism for change as the obstacles in their path are, more often than not, self-created. There are also a higher number of women appointed to other senior editorial positions, who wield considerable influence over the running of these newspapers.

Inability to find equilibrium has caused promising women journalists to opt out or to 'take a break'. Some have stopped field reporting and limited themselves to desk jobs, such as sub-editing. Others depend heavily on the support of their spouses and extended family, with or without success. Women with less personal commitments continue to forge ahead in a manner that often matches or surpasses the performance of male colleagues. Together, they have enriched journalism with perspectives that an exclusively male workforce could never have produced.

Women are today actively working on news, business, political, investigative, human interest and features desks. They have also taken on the defence and crime rounds, although in much smaller numbers. They write editorials and op-eds and are assigned their own columns on topics of their choice. For the most part, there are also no restrictions on assignments. While women did not traditionally cover sports or work in the photography department, even these are no longer the exclusive domains of men. Editors usually (there may be exceptions) entrust work to journalists on the basis of their skills, capabilities and willingness to carry out that task—not on their gender. This is especially so in the English media.

In terms of the overall environment, however, women journalists face many of the same constraints that their male counterparts do. In particular, several female journalists have been threatened or intimidated.[45] Some have had to take special precautions during times of heightened risk. In October 2009, two female editors at the *Sunday Leader* newspaper—Frederica Jansz and Munza Mushtaq—received death threats.[46]

Granted, numerically fewer female journalists have been abducted, assassinated or have had to flee the country. But that is small respite indeed.

Notes

1. Sri Lanka Press Institute (2011).
2. Anne Abayasekara, interview conducted by this writer on 20 February 2012.
3. *Ibid.*
4. The earliest records I could find of women's participation in journalism go back to the 1940s and 1950s. Roshan Peiris was another pioneer who started at Lake House in

1953. Writing on occasion of her death in 2008 (http://sundaytimes.lk/080518/News/news0033.html [accessed in June 2013]), Rajitha Weerakoon, herself a senior features editor, described Roshan as being 'amongst a handful of women journalists of the so-called 'Golden Age' of Lake House in the early 1950s who braved the citadel to work with the impregnable bastion of male journalists such as Tarzie Vittachchi, Denzil Peiris and Mervyn De Silva'. 'It was a difficult task but Roshan, just as the rest of the determined and committed women journalists at the time such as Ranji Handy, Jean Pinto, Vijitha Fernando, Malini Balasingham, Sumana Saparamadu, Hema Gunawardene and Mallika Wanigasundera, took them on and set trends of the highest order', Rajitha observed. Roshan wrote on a range of topics including politics, arts, fashions, health and human interest. She rose to the position of features editor and acting editor of the *Sunday Observer* in the 1970s, an opportunity which Rajitha notes, 'perhaps did not come in the way of other women journalists at the time'.

5. Rita was seated beside this writer at the Old Parliament in 1995. The conversation took place while we were waiting for the then President, Chandrika Bandaranaike Kumaratunga, to arrive for the official launch of the National Workers' Charter. The main architect of the charter, which was never passed into law, was Mahinda Rajapaksa, who was elected President in November 2005.

6. http://www.sundaytimes.lk/960331/frontm.html#Pioneer (accessed in June 2013).

7. http://himalmag.com/component/content/article/2801-razia-bhatti-rita-sebastian.html (accessed in June 2013).

8. http://www.island.lk/2001/04/29/editoria.html (accessed in June 2013).

9. Sri Lanka Press Institute (2011), p. 36.

10. During this period, even women soldiers were deployed only at brigade headquarters (in areas where there was civilian movement) and not in smaller detachments. This made it difficult for the defence ministry official coordinating the visit to find accommodation or facilities for a female reporter. Consequently, in one 'operational area', arrangements were made for me to sleep in the residence of the local post-mistress which doubled up as the sub-post office.

11. Muttulingam (2012).

12. http://humanityashore.com/ (accessed in June 2013).

13. Muttulingam (2012).

14. Indrani Peiris, associate editor and long time news editor of Lankadeepa, interviewed by this writer in March 2012.

15. Indrani said society had been transformed considerably since her induction to journalism. Women not only had more freedom now, there were more opportunities for them to circulate and to mingle. It was, therefore, important for them to set limits for themselves to preserve their dignity and the dignity of the profession. While it was not different for men, society tended to be more judgemental of women.

16. Sri Lanka Press Institute (2011), p. 41.

17. Harrison (2012).

18. Weiss (2009).

19. Sri Lanka Press Institute (2011), p. 40.

20. *Ibid.*, pp. 40–41.

21. Kishali Pinto-Jayawardena (1988), p. 28.

22. Sri Lanka Press Institute (2011), p. 38.

23. *Ibid.*, p. 35.

24. http://www.theweekendleader.com/Success/788/media%E2%80%99s-distaff-side.html (accessed in June 2013).

25. Who Makes the News?, Global Media Monitoring Project, http://www.whomakesthenews. org/images/stories/restricted/highlights/highlights_en.pdf (accessed in June 2013).

26. Sri Lanka Press Institute (2011), p. 35.

27. Executive summary of the *2011 Global Report on the Status Women in the News Media*, International Women's Media Foundation, http://iwmf.org/pdfs/IWMF-Global-Report. pdf (accessed in June 2013).

28. Sri Lanka Press Institute (2011), p. 36.

29. This is also my experience. As a mother of two young children, despite being senior in the field, I restrict myself from taking on too much at the workplace as I feel I have obligations towards them. Even if I were offered a position that entailed a higher salary and more authority, I would not—at this point—accept it if it also involved more work and more responsibilities since this would hinder me from assisting with schoolwork, shuttling the children between classes, being relaxed enough to deal with their childhood dilemmas, etc.

30. 2006 Charter of Gender Equality for Media and Journalism in Sri Lanka, http://www.ifj. org/es/articles/2006-charter-of-gender-equality-for-media-and-journalism-in-sri-lanka (accessed in June 2013).

31. http://cimogg-srilanka.org/2012/05/pre-agm-keynote-address/ (accessed in June 2013), Keynote address delivered by Journalist Ms Namini Wijedasa on 23 May 2012 prior to the AGM of the CIMOGG held in the Auditorium of the Organisation of Professional Associations, Colombo.

32. http://en.rsf.org/sri-lanka-sri-lanka-12-03-2012,42068.html, Reporters with Borders. RSF said: 'The number of cases of physical attacks, death threats and imprisonment may have fallen in 2010 and 2011, but the authorities continue to prevent the media from enjoying real editorial freedom and many journalists are still in exile'. The organisation called on the government 'to accept constructive questions from civil society and to stop branding its critics as "conspirators" and "LTTE accomplices"'.

33. Reporters Without Borders (2012b).

34. In Sri Lanka today, the owner of a mainstream newspaper might not only be aligned with a particular political party; he is sometimes a parliamentary member of a political party, or related to a parliamentary member of a political party. The controlling shares of several newspapers are now held by close friends/business associates of the ruling Rajapaksa family. This happened through comparatively speedy takeovers facilitated by the government. Indeed, 'buying into' newspaper companies is a favourite tool of the regime as is 'buying over' individuals working in them.

35. This writer is personally aware that journalists in state media do not all blindly subscribe to the views or endorse the policies of the ruling regime. They are merely not permitted to express opposing or diverse opinions, even under the guise of balanced discussion or reporting. To do so would result in political victimisation, even loss of employment.

36. Samarajiva (2011).

37. De Alwis (2012).

38. Samarajiva (2011)

39. Sri Lanka Campaign, http://www.srilankacampaign.org/media-freedom.htm (accessed in June 2013).

40. Committee to Protect Journalists, http://cpj.org/killed/asia/sri-lanka/ (accessed in June 2013).

41. I have exercised my profession without serious threat or intimidation. But I will admit that I have always skirted the boundaries, pulling back and curbing my journalistic

instincts without going 'out of line' or 'over the line'. There are just some stories you don't touch and personalities you don't expose. Self-censorship is a norm.

42. International Federation of Journalists (2011), http://www.jdslanka.org/images/documents/ifj_report_2011_sri_lanka.pdf (accessed in June 2013).

43. *Getting Away with Murder*, Special Report, Committee to Protect Journalists, http://cpj.org/reports/2012/04/impunity-index-2012.php#more (accessed in June 2013). CPJ's annual Impunity Index, first published in 2008, identifies countries where journalists are murdered regularly and governments fail to solve the crimes. For this latest index, CPJ examined journalist murders that occurred from 1 January 2002 through 31 December 2011, and that remain unsolved. Only the 12 nations in the world with 5 or more unsolved cases are included on the index. Cases are considered unsolved when no convictions have been won.

44. *Getting Away with Murder*, Special Report, Committee to Protect Journalists, http://cpj.org/reports/2012/04/impunity-index-2012.php#more (accessed in June 2013). It also states: 'In recent months, government officials have issued brazen public threats of violence against their critics, an alarming development given that 60 per cent of Sri Lankan victims were known to have received threats before they were killed.'

45. http://www.amnesty.org/es/library/asset/ASA37/023/2009/es/7d32a357-bc67-41b1-afaa-c442fba98222/asa370232009en.pdf (accessed in June 2013), Amnesty International, Urgent Action Appeal.

46. Mandana Ismail, deputy editor of the *Sunday Leader*, interviewed by this writer in June 2012, said she received a death threat by post about a week before the 2010 presidential election. Frederica Jansz, the newspaper's editor, was sent a similar letter.

Part II

Electronic and New Media

6

The Political Economy of the Electronic Media

Tilak Jayaratne and Sarath Kellapotha

An Overall Perspective

Reflections on the Early Years

Electronic Media in the form of radio broadcasting was introduced to Sri Lanka as early as the 1920s by the British colonial rulers. Sri Lanka is credited with being the first country in South Asia to commence such a service, just a few years after radio was introduced in Europe. Although it has a long history, it was experimental and amateurish in its early days. The British rulers were said to have modelled these broadcasting stations along the lines of the British Broadcasting Corporation (BBC), but at no time did these traditions actually prevail. It was a government-run enterprise from its inauguration.

Until October 1949, radio broadcasting was governed by the Post and Telecommunication Department, except during World War II, when radio operations were fully controlled by the allied forces. In October 1949, a separate department was established for radio broadcasting and it began to function as Radio Ceylon. Following world trends, the radio was used mainly to inform (about government activities) and to entertain. Educational broadcasts too have a long tradition beginning from 1931.

After independence, the government (meaning the party in power) increasingly began to show interest in the power of broadcasting, first as a vehicle for publicity and gradually for propaganda. We argue that this government stance was the outcome of mainly three factors:

- The government did not have a proper media policy (either for print or broadcasting) and acted on the whims of its senior members and in reaction to events and trends.
- Civil society organisations often did not competently carry out their role in advocacy or agitating for policy reforms. These watchdogs were few and the majority of them were 'toothless' in their practical impact on reform.
- Internationally, in most of the developing world, the policy in place, if there was any, was that of government control on the Soviet model. The parties that came to power in independent Sri Lanka had a natural liking for that 'policy'. It was the model to emulate. Governments of the day argued that emerging economies and societies need 'positive coverage' which in practice was equated to 'propaganda'.

During the first two decades after independence, rulers, politicians, media practitioners, the civil society and the listening public—all alike seemed to accept the status quo and were not very keen to challenge or change the government monopoly. There was, however, some concern expressed over what was seen as 'cultural vulgarisation', principally in the content of the commercial service of the state radio, which was catering to popular taste. If a voice was raised, it was to 'implore' some sort of fairness from the government media. Alternatives were hardly the order of the day.

This position prevailed even after 'Radio Ceylon' was made a government corporation under the Sri Lanka Broadcasting Act of 1966, which established the Sri Lanka Broadcasting Corporation (SLBC). This change, according to some critiques, was just a change of appearances, which allowed government control in a more subtle manner.

However, a certain outcome of this change, entailing the proliferation of trade union activities, brought about the politicisation of the media institutions. The government in power had its own trade union, while the main opposition parties had theirs. These unions were concerned only about promotions (in most cases without minimum qualification, which ultimately led to deterioration in the quality of broadcasting) and other benefits for their membership. In addition to these pro-party unions, there existed a strong trade union branch of the Ceylon Mercantile Union, independent of party politics. None of these trade unions were unduly concerned about the role or media policy of the station and they did not attempt to influence its working. This situation, to some degree, still prevails in all state media institutions including Lake House, the state-owned print media house.

Insurgencies and Separatist Wars

Violence against the government and civil disturbances usually prompt the rulers to resort to the control of the media. The Sri Lankan experience, in this context, is not different. This shows that media behaviour and media policy cannot be isolated from political developments and should be analysed within their context.

The pre-1956 Sri Lankan society was comparatively free of violence, except for the *hartal* (strike) demonstrations and riots in 1953, which were organised to protest against the policies and actions of the incumbent government. After 1956, however, civil disturbances were frequent and violent, with a racist slant, and the government policy became increasingly slanted towards using the media to justify its actions. No forum was offered to aggrieved parties to present their case. These concerns did not seem to impact upon government policy on media. Emergency laws and regulations were sufficient to stifle opposing voices.

The uprising of the southern youth led by the Janatha Vimukthi Peramuna (JVP) in 1971 had a deeper impression on the media in an indirect way. In the wake of the insurgency, the communication system of the country was severely disrupted. The government of the day, caught unawares, suddenly found the state radio to be a reliable ally in communicating directly with the public. It was alleged that even the insurgents used the radio without the knowledge of the authorities to send coded messages to their cadres. Although this was never acknowledged officially, it alerted the rulers to the dangers of such a move. These developments impacted on media policy in two respects. First, politicians' attention was drawn to the vast potential of the electronic media. This awareness compelled them to use the state electronic media increasingly for their interests, so much so that it gradually became a propaganda organ for the ruling party. Second, the argument that if the radio stations fell into the hands of insurgents it would be catastrophic was put forward (though never in writing) by the government to refuse licences for community radio stations. By the time the second uprising of the JVP took place in the late 1980s, a different administration was ready to use the media even more effectively in its favour, having learned from the experiences that had befallen its predecessor.

The impact of the long separatist war waged by the Liberation Tigers of Tamil Eelam (LTTE) was wide ranging on every aspect of Sri Lankan life. What interests us here is how this conflict affected government and private sector media, the attitude of the government towards the media and how it shaped the media environment. Except for very short periods, emergency laws, which gave governments sweeping powers, were in place throughout the country after the 1971 JVP insurrection. The manner in which governments used these emergency regulations, not only to deal with the media and curb dissent but also to tackle its opponents, is now history. The separatist war, dubbed a 'battle against terrorism', gave governments the pretext to keep these draconian laws in existence. The war situation had a direct and indirect impact not only on media policy and media practice but on all the democratic structures of society. It is in this context that one must assess why attempts to free the media from government control and to establish an environment conducive to democratic media practice did not succeed.

Globally, it is said that multi-ethnic societies more frequently tend to fall victim to conflict than societies with greater ethnic homogeneity. In such vulnerable societies

> media can be manipulated in an effort to move a society toward conflict or toward non-democratic rule ... media can also contribute to conflict involuntarily. Such passive incitement to violence most frequently occurs when journalists have poor professional skills, when media culture is underdeveloped, or when there is little or no history of independent media.[1]

During three decades of ethnic strife in Sri Lanka, ample examples illustrating the above assertion can be found. The manner in which the media was used by the parties to the war and how media and media personnel were treated is well known. The war proved to be a good excuse for political rulers to move forward their agendas. This impacted upon the media scene with catastrophic results.

The two main parties adopted a 'Dr Jekyll and Mr Hyde' stance as far as the media was concerned. When in opposition, each would agitate and fight for media rights. Their manifestos set out the best possible policies towards the media and best possible treatment of media practitioners. However, after coming into power, the same parties would do their utmost to move away from their previous position. For them, the war provided a cover to carry on with subversive agendas that twisted the notion of democracy.

Both parties to the war not only used this front to conceal atrocities and deficiencies but also actively worked to promote conflict. Over the years, this became the 'standard' practice. The proliferation of private electronic media did not help to arrest this trend. Instead, the private media vied with each other and the government media to nurture and foster this new media culture. The tactics used were simple subversive strategies tried and tested in other war theatres and areas of conflict and included the following:

- The construction of fear by strategies such as: 'focus on past atrocities and a history of ethnic animosity; manipulation of myths, stereotypes and identities to dehumanise; overemphasis on certain grievances or inequities and a shift towards consistently negative reporting'.
- Discouraging and/or crushing dissent.
- Using 'national security' as the keyword to control and condemn.
- Convincing audiences that the conflict was inevitable. Creating a self-fulfilling prophecy.
- Discrediting alternatives to conflict: especially, peace attempts which were often labelled as acts of treason.
- Branding improvements to democratic structures such as media reforms and the like as de-stabilising factors designed to aid and abet the 'conspirators'.
- Condemning reports by international organisations, including UN agencies which highlighted human rights violations, including repressive measures against the media, and other undemocratic measures, as acts of intervention and interference in the 'domestic affairs' of a free and independent country.

Media practitioners themselves were caught up in this 'trap'. The few who refused to conform were branded as traitors or even terrorists and were dealt with accordingly. The 'culture' thus created was capable of being utilised to deal with 'any situation'. As has been observed, 'mass media reach not only peoples' homes, but also their minds, shaping their thoughts and sometimes their behaviour'.[2] The long-term effects of these developments are unfortunately still very much in evidence.

Freedom Regained and Freedom Lost

The two decades of the 1980s and 1990s saw significant changes, both negative and positive, in the media landscape. The first change was seen within the government radio itself. In the early 1980s, a form of 'community radio' was introduced as an extension of the SLBC, especially to cater to the settlers under the gigantic Mahaweli Project. This, however, did not bring about radical changes in content and approach or structure and was never a trendsetter. In the early 1980s, with a new government adopting new approaches and policies, Sri Lanka like most other third world countries was caught in a whirl of liberalisation. This brought about many socio-economic and cultural changes, including policy changes regarding the electronic media. Television was introduced to the country. Towards the end of the decade, the government decided to issue radio broadcast licences to the corporate sector. Thus, for the first time in Sri Lanka's history, private radios appeared on the landscape.

Apart from the escalating violence in the north and east, the 1990s started comparatively peacefully, following the widespread violence and destruction of 1988/1989, during the quashing of the second JVP rebellion by the United National Party (UNP) government. The UNP's newly elected President, Ranasinghe Premadasa, was firm in his dealings with his own government and with other organisations, institutions and persons in the society at large. However, as violence again escalated, repressive measures were taken against the media. This period, as the international media watchdog Article XIX (Article19) pointed out at the time, was 'marked by a lack of freedom of expression and the violation of so many other related human rights. There have also been many examples of individual efforts to stand up for such rights. Some, like the broadcaster Richard de Zoysa, paid with their lives for speaking out against intolerance and human rights abuses; others endured threats and intimidation or sought refuge abroad'.[3] With the demise of President Premadasa, this tight control imposed by the government over Sri Lankan society was loosened somewhat.

A few private radio stations and a couple of TV stations were operative during the early part of the 1990s although they were not allowed to broadcast news, including stories pertaining to Sri Lanka in foreign TV newscasts. But this 'plurality' did not bring about a democratisation of the media or seriously affect the monopolistic status of the state sector broadcast media. The rise and fall of the 'New Education Service' (NES) of the SLBC demonstrate the frame of mind of the rulers and the atmosphere of the period.

A Case Study: The New Education Service

One of the authors of this study, Tilak Jayaratne, was centrally involved in the development of NES and this is his account of how the new service emerged and developed.

During the period leading up to the 1994 general election, there had been a general feeling of relaxation in all spheres of the country. The government of the day headed by the interim President, D.B. Wijetunga, sensed this imminent change and took the first steps. With an ongoing large-scale civil war, it was futile to expect the government to relax all controls. But certain 'spaces' began to appear where the activists could work to bring about more democratic changes. The media was one such sphere.

The advent of private broadcast stations brought about a new media culture and practices unfamiliar to existing media consumers. This 'unfamiliarity' was often interpreted as a vulgarisation or debasement of the age-old culture and became the main source of opposition to new stations. These new stations did not seem to have a clear broadcast policy and the time spent on the struggle to obtain a broadcast licence would have been, most probably, more than the time spent on planning the broadcasts. Their programmes, in the initial stages, looked alien and coarse at best. The criticisms appeared valid to the authorities.

As a result of lobbyists' action, the Wijetunga government came up with an idea to establish a new service of the SLBC which could be utilised to mitigate the ill effects of private media 'vulgarisation'. The concept was promoted by the then Minister of Education, W.J.M. Lokubandara, who volunteered to find the funds necessary for such an enterprise. The task was entrusted to the new chairman of the SLBC who took a personal interest in it. It was decided that the Education Service of the SLBC would be used for the purpose. Initial discussions were held with the senior broadcasters of the service, which was thought to be the best to handle such an assignment. However, though a very broad idea of the proposed service was presented, it was not clearly or precisely defined. What is 'culture'? Can anyone 'save' it? As the controller of the service, it became my responsibility to look into all the aspects of the new service. The positive factor, however, was that we were never given guidelines or instructions on how to set up the new service and what the form or shape it should take. There were huge challenges considering the structural controls and procedures that existed at SLBC and the media environment of the country. The 'freedom' thus afforded was probably the most significant factor that allowed us to overcome the challenges.

The first task was to take stock of the resources at hand. The technology and equipment were quite inadequate but the main worry was the personnel. The serving staff had been so attached to SLBC traditions for so long, it was considered impossible to change their ways or thinking. The next option was to employ new hands. Thus, 18 young men and women were recruited as 'communicators'. They included several university graduates who had offered media as a subject but their knowledge was shown to be insufficient for the task. This reflected the state of media education at university level. These recruits were given an orientation exposing them to media theories and practices in circulation globally. In addition, they were given practical training in basic production skills.

The next phase was the planning and designing of the new service. The strategy employed was to work as a goal-oriented, not task-oriented, group, combining talents and providing innovative solutions to unfamiliar problems. This group process, with a participatory approach in planning a broadcast, was a wholly new strategy employed for the first—and so far the only time. Thus, democratic values were incorporated from the planning process up to the production and presentation stage. The new service set out with a clear vision: to help people to fulfil their unmet needs and to offer them a platform for free expression. During the period it was operative, despite a multitude of pressures, the NES did not deviate from its original mission and did not compromise its principles.[4]

The NES was inaugurated in June 1994 during President D.B. Wijetunga's regime. His successor, Chandrika Kumaratunga, after leading her Peoples' Alliance (PA) to victory in the parliamentary elections of August 1994, ending the 17-year rule of the UNP, was elected President in November with a landslide victory. Her rise to power was on a manifesto that promised to end corruption and terror and re-establish democratic rule. High on her agenda was the pledge to do away with censorship and to free the media from government control. Many media organisations and activists openly and actively supported her candidature. To be fair to the newly elected President, she commenced well in this task. Private channels were allowed to broadcast their own news bulletins. Four committees were set up that made wide-ranging and seemingly far-reaching recommendations for media reforms. However, Article XIX, while welcoming the priority that the new government appeared to attach to restoring press freedom and the right to information, warned that:

> the legacy of the past is a heavy one and the new government faces many obstacles as a result. Systematic censorship, which permeated government institutions and led to a culture of self-censorship within Sri Lankan society, will be difficult to eradicate. The government needs to demonstrate real strength of purpose and determination if it is to carry through successfully its programme to bring Sri Lanka to the position where it can be counted a full, open and flourishing democracy, one which pays due respect to the rights of all Sri Lankans.[5]

These words proved to be prophetic. Tilak Jayaratne recalls that as soon as the new government assumed its duties, PA trade unionists and party supporters took over from their UNP counterparts at SLBC. They hailed NES as an emancipated service and under the pretext of expounding the new media policy of the government made arrangements to broadcast some NES programmes over the other services of the SLBC, branding them as model programmes to be emulated. Their motive, however, was not the promotion of freedom or quality. The programmes they selected were critical of the previous regime. But as soon as dissent was allowed to be expressed regarding the new government's actions, the tide turned. The 'reverse journey' began when a programme while on air was arbitrarily stopped half way by a new 'boss man'. As controller of the service, Tilak Jayaratne was interdicted and sent home. It was a pointer to things to come.

But the episode did not end on a defeatist note. A regular listener who had also participated in the discussions on the programme went before the Supreme Court alleging that his fundamental right to free speech and expression had been violated by this abrupt and arbitrary stoppage of the broadcast. The court issued a landmark judgment that dealt specifically with rights of the broadcast media in the case of Wimal Fernando v. SLBC.[6]

The SLBC argued that staff of the disputed programme were using it to air their own views and claimed that the contents of the programme exposed them to civil and criminal defamation. In a strong judgment that dealt extensively with the rights of broadcast media, the Supreme Court refused to accept these reasons as adequate for stopping the programme. The court could find nothing defamatory in the content of the disputed programmes. On the contrary, it found that the topics discussed were all of tremendous public interest. Significantly, the court referred to observations made by the Supreme Court of India in Secretary, Ministry of Information v. the Cricket Association of Bengal (1995) which declared that: 'Broadcasting media by its very nature is different from the press. Airwaves are public property. … It is the obligation of the State that they are used for the public good.'[7] Notwithstanding this clear call from the judiciary, the NES was never allowed to broadcast again in its original form or intent.

The PA Government's About-turn

It did not take long for the new government to show its true intentions and hidden agendas. The government presented the 'Sri Lanka Broadcasting Authority Bill' (SLBAB) in the Government Gazette on 21 March 1997, seeking the establishment of a regulatory authority for the broadcast media and a number of content restrictions for broadcasters. It was placed on the Order Paper of Parliament on 10 April 1997. Within days, 15 individual petitions challenging the constitutionality of the bill were lodged with the Supreme Court of Sri Lanka. In adjudicating on these petitions, the Supreme Court held that 'distinguishing between different classes of persons was acceptable, but only where a rational basis for the differentiation existed'. No such basis had been suggested by the government in this case and so the bill was held to be discriminatory. In making this ruling, the court quoted extensively from Article XIX's 'Broadcasting Freedom—International Standards and Guidelines' which calls for a single regulatory body for the broadcast media.[8]

The court then went on to hold that limited frequency availability meant that the regulation of broadcasting, both for technical and certain other reasons, for example, to prevent monopolies, was legitimate. Such regulation, however, was only consistent with the constitutional guarantee of freedom of expression if the regulatory authority was independent of government. The composition of the board and members' lack of security of tenure coupled with the broad regulatory powers of the minister, meant that the authority lacked the requisite independence. The court noted significant differences in this respect between the SLBAB and its Indian, South African and American counterparts.

Toby Mendel, Head of Law Programme, Article 19, in his analysis of this important decision asserts that it lays down the following important principles:

- Good reasons are required to justify different rules for public and private broadcasters;
- Bodies with regulatory powers over the media must be independent of government;
- Regulations simply issued by a minister do not qualify as 'provided for by law';
- Broad, general or vague restrictions on freedom of expression are unacceptable.[9]

The above decisions on Sri Lanka's electronic media suggest that court action could be sought to challenge undemocratic actions on the part of a government.[10] But while court decisions could force the rulers to desist from adopting regulations or taking the 'legal path' to control the media and curb freedom of expression and other democratic rights, the government had other ways of responding in situations like these. In a speech broadcast on radio and TV, President Kumaratunga said:

For the past five years, the media attacked me. During this election the media made various degrading allegations against me. I was not shaken up by this. I tolerated this. We cannot allow media freedom to be misused. The people have a right. They pay for the newspaper. They pay for the TV. I had confidence that the people will not be misled and therefore tolerated it. But in the future I am not going to be gentle. ... We also haven't chased any UNP-ers from state media institutions. During the recent polls, they worked against us. We'll see to that later.[11]

If President Chandrika Kumaratunga's first term began amidst hopes of restoring democratic rights including media freedom, the second term spelled despair as she began increasingly to use the repressive powers of the executive presidency. Censorship, lifted in 1994, was reintroduced in 1998 and remained in place during the following years. The escalation of the separatist war provided the perfect cover for the continuance of emergency regulations which enabled the government to use suppressive or even tyrannical measures against those accused of being agitators and dissidents—and in the eyes of the government, the media and media practitioners fell into that category.

Eventually, the government appointed a 23-member Parliamentary Select Committee to draw up a 'Legislative and Regulatory Framework for the Media' using a 'bipartisan approach'. The committee sought 'submissions and representations from individuals and organisations'. Minister of Media at that time, Mangala Samaraweera, headed the committee.

In 1998, a symposium on Media Freedom and Social Responsibility was jointly organised by the Sri Lanka Working Journalists Association (SLWJA), the Free Media Movement, the Editor's Guild of Sri Lanka and the Newspaper Association of Sri Lanka together with the World Association of Newspapers and the Centre for Policy Alternatives. An outcome of the symposium was the drafting of the Colombo Declaration on Media Freedom and Social Responsibility,[12] which included a series of proposals meant mainly for the Sri Lankan state. The points particularly relevant to the electronic media are as follows:

1 Public Broadcasting Service

All state-funded and managed broadcasting services in Sri Lanka should be converted to publicly owned bodies and not subject to any form of state control.

Values of public broadcasting should be safeguarded by ensuring that the governing bodies of the broadcasting authority should have a balanced and independent composition.

2 An Independent Broadcasting Authority

There should be an independent broadcasting authority which is genuinely independent of any form of governmental or non-governmental pressure to oversee the implementation of the broadcasting policy, and be responsible for the licensing of community radio, public and private broadcasting, including technical aspects. The legislation should specifically state the public's right to receive information and opinion on matters of public interest, and specifically state the principle of maintaining a fair balance of alternative points of view. The selection process for the members of this body must be such as to ensure it is not dominated by any political group.

3 Community Radio and Television

A policy for the development of community radio and television should be set out in law. A regulatory authority should ensure that at least 50 per cent of the programming should be within the declared aims of the community service.

Media and Government: A See-Saw Phase

When the UNP, led by Ranil Wickremasinghe, won the 2001 December general elections, a new and politically interesting situation arose in the country where the executive president belonged to one party and the power in the parliament to another. In the parliamentary election, though the UNP alliance won only 109 seats out of 225, Ranil Wickremasinghe was able to form a new government and was sworn in as the Prime Minister of Sri Lanka on 9 December 2001. This marked the initiation of an abrasive relationship between the Executive President and the newly elected Prime Minister.

Wickremasinghe, by then a veteran politician, knew he could not gain any leverage from the president who did not want to share power. His strategy appeared to be to consolidate the power he derived from the voters to withstand any 'attack' by the president. He believed that 'investment in peace makes sound political and economic sense for both Sri Lanka and its partners abroad' for he thought 'growth in Sri Lanka will be good for everyone'. In his address to the UN General Assembly on 18 September 2002, he claimed a clear national mandate to end the conflict in the north-east and welcomed international support for the peace process. He looked forward to re-establishing Sri Lanka as 'an investment-friendly country with an efficient bureaucracy and a thriving private sector'.[13]

The area of media policy and law reform was one of the 'areas' he chose in which to implement changes. According to Bradman Weerakoon, the PM's secretary at the time, regarding structure and mechanisms relating to the media, 'there were three specific areas on which Wickremasinghe acted very fast after the elections'.[14] The first was to establish a legislative framework for the media. Following a series of regular meetings with editors, he got passed through parliament legislation which was of extreme value for the creation of a conducive media environment and would match the highest standards required of a free media. This legislation was to cover the concept of freedom of expression, to amend the existing law regarding criminal defamation which acted as a constraint to the free expression of views, to set up a press complaints commission to replace a moribund press council and to establish a press institute which would set, from within, standards for journalists to follow, and update their training.

The second approach was to establish a fully equipped and staffed government media centre. This was on the premise that the press was not going to be curbed again with emergency regulations, which had censored the press effectively for long periods. Since a virtually free press was going to be stimulated, Wickremasinghe felt that a strong mechanism should be in place for the propagation of the government's own position. The third idea was to work towards a gradual broad basing of the state owned media.[15]

Some of these plans were implemented promptly. For instance, the Press Council was made defunct following an unwritten bona fide contract between the political parties represented in parliament and the media organisations representing publishers, editors, working journalists and media activists to introduce, promote and support a self-regulatory mechanism in place of the statutory Press Council. The Press Complaints Commission of Sri Lanka was thereby established in 2003 with a Dispute Resolution Council comprising a majority of non-media representatives, chaired by Mr Sam Wijesinha, to settle disputes between the public and the press under the Arbitration Act No. 11 of 1995.

Nonetheless, the prime minister's plans came to an abrupt end. On 4 November 2003, when he was in Washington for a meeting with President Bush about a free trade agreement with the USA, the President launched her first strike. Using presidential powers, she prorogued parliament and took over the Ministry of Defence, the Ministry of Interior and the Ministry of Mass Communications, which ran the government media institutions—two TV stations with all island coverage, the radio broadcasting station and Lake House with its daily English, Sinhala and Tamil newspapers. Elections were held on 2 April 2004 and the President's coalition won the election with the JVP in a new political formation.[16] This marked the demise of Ranil Wickremasinghe's Media Reform programme.

Wickremasinghe's actions marked a deviation from what had been the common practice of politicians who come to power making many promises and forget them wholesale overnight. His policy may have been shaped by the unique political situation and possibly by a determination to do better than his predecessors. His maternal grandfather was the founder of Associated Newspapers of Ceylon—commonly known as Lake House—and his own father, Esmond Wickremasinghe, was one-time boss of Lake House.[17] He was known to be committed to democracy and liberal ideals. However, he could be fiercely critical of journalists. The Free Media Movement on one occasion expressed its disappointment at the attitude of 'intolerance and animosity' displayed by him towards a *Daily Mirror* reporter'[18]. His criticism of Uvindu Kurukulasuriya, one-time convener of Free Media and Director of the Sri Lanka Press Institute and his tussle with the Sirasa media group also cast legitimate doubt on the genuineness of his intentions towards the media.

Media Freedoms under the Rajapaksa Regime

Perhaps, there is no other leader of Sri Lanka since independence (not even President Ranasinghe Premadasa) who has been criticised so vehemently in regard to media repression as President Mahinda Rajapaksa. The circumstances, under which he assumed power in 2005, will help, to a certain degree at least, to explain his strategies.

In the path towards Mahinda Rajapaksa's ascendancy to the office of the Executive Presidency, his appointment as the opposition leader in March 2002 was a significant stepping stone. He was not the automatic choice of the party and the nomination for the premiership was not handed to him on a silver platter. Other names, not his, were floated as strong contenders. Nonetheless, following the victory of the United People's Freedom Alliance in the elections of 2 April 2004, President Kumaratunga appointed Mahinda Rajapaksa to the post of Prime Minister, despite the opposition of the JVP, her coalition partners. Many in the party and the country, especially the Buddhist clergy headed by the Chief *Sanghanayakas* (head prelates), welcomed this move.[19]

Subsequently, in July 2005, Kumaratunga was forced to accept Rajapaksa as her successor and the party's presidential candidate. Although what went on behind the scenes was not well known, this was how the *Asian Tribune*, Colombo, in its issue of 28 July 2005, reported the situation:

> Speculation that President Chandrika Kumaratunga would nominate her brother to succeed her ended yesterday when a ten-member committee of the ruling party nominated Prime Minister Mahinda Rajapaksa as the next presidential candidate. Anura Bandaranaike, whose face was plastered all over the city recently as the most suitable candidate for the presidency, was given the second prize of the prime ministerial seat. Mahinda Rajapaksa's nomination will end the in-fighting within the ruling party. With his nomination, the race for the presidency will begin in earnest.[20]

But the in-fighting continued. President Kumaratunga attended only seven propaganda meetings for this election and a section of the PA ministers shunned Rajapaksa's campaign. Rajapaksa was not well supported by the urban middle-class elite. However, he received support from the Buddhist clergy and a wide range of political parties in his bid to win the elections. The JVP and JHU and 28 other political organisations figured prominently in the presidential campaign. According to an article in the *Island* newspaper:

> 'Mr Mahinda Rajapaksa won the Presidential election held on 17 November 2005. He was able to achieve success because of his personal qualities: patience, determination, equanimity, courage, valour, amiability and simplicity. They are of course Buddhist values'.[21]

His struggle for power did not end with the presidential election victory. Within the party, Kumaratunga was not ready to relinquish her power nor did she want to accept his victory. But compared to the UNP leader, he received the unqualified sympathy if not the support of the majority of Sinhala-Buddhists. Even those who may not have voted for him grudgingly acknowledged his Sinhala-Buddhist leadership. This faith or trust led Rajapaksa to play along with the tide and turned his image from a 'showy' southern politician to a pious, mature Buddhist national leader. According to political commentator Kusal Perera, it was his party that groomed him for this role:

> Mahinda to begin with could never leave the grooming of the SLFP that fixed him body and soul with the Sinhala Buddhist thinking. He for sure feels secure peddling this slogan to be among the 'Giruwa Paththuwa' voters.

Therefore, even after spearheading a successful human rights campaign, as Kusal Perera observed, 'he opted to be the 'Southern Sinhala Leader' with his widely publicised 'Sri Rohana Jana Ranjana' honour, received from the Malwatte Chapter'.[22] As the Colombo-centric elite of the country sometimes openly, sometimes inconspicuously, did not admit him to their fold, Rajapaksa gradually and quite naturally drifted more towards his 'son-of-the-soil' role. A salient feature in his ascendancy to power has been his willingness to accommodate anyone and everyone and his ability to attract the support of a broad spectrum of groups with widely different ideologies.

Nevertheless, there was a cause that unified them all: the war. This became the rallying point. Even the members of parliament who crossed over from the UNP justified their action by claiming they wanted to strengthen the hand of the president in his war effort. For the most part, the media, both print and broadcast, readily joined the cause. They were travelling together towards the same destination. In the present day, the war has ended but the legacy of the war remains. Rajapaksa's attitude towards the media and media practice in the country is fundamentally shaped by these dispositions. An example to illustrate this point can be found in his presidential election manifesto of 2005 entitled *Mahinda Chinthana*. This manifesto states that:

> The freedom of the media could be truly established only if the living conditions of the media personnel are raised. In order to ensure the independence of media personnel:
>
> - Computers will be provided to every media personnel duty free.
> - All accepted news reporters will be given a duty free motor cycle.
> - The Chief Editors of recognised print and electronic media institutions will be provided vehicles duty free.
> - An Ombudsman will be appointed with full authority to solve their problems and steps will be taken to provide scholarships to the more creative journalists serving the state and private media.
> - A system to evaluate the capacities of the media personnel annually will be introduced. A special state award ceremony will be organised for the

media. Facilities will be provided to media personnel to build their own homes and a retirement gratuity scheme will be provided for the benefit of the retired media personnel.

All Sri Lankan politicians in power, irrespective of the party they belong to, use the word 'responsible' in respect of the media to imply that the media should be controlled (not regulated) on the pretext that the media act 'irresponsibly'. If one carefully reads the section on Information and Mass Media in the Mahinda Chinthana policy, the manner in which the word 'responsible' is used gives an indication about the intentions of its authors. As regards free expression and media rights, what President Mahinda Rajapaksa did or failed to do are well documented and will be discussed in the succeeding section.

These references to political events aim to elucidate the real significance of the actions of political players. For example, it may appear, taken out of context, that Ranil Wickremasinghe was the only leader to work towards the freedom of expression and independence of the press, whereas Mahinda Rajapaksa may look like the worst culprit in that regard. Wickremasinghe initiated reforms in respect of media freedom during his short stint as the 17th Prime Minister of Sri Lanka in 2001–2002. It was a unique situation where the all-powerful executive president belonged to a party which was traditionally opposed to the prime minister's political group. In the same way, President Mahinda Rajapaksa's actions—or inaction—should be judged against the backdrop of his struggle to come to the top in politics in the face of opposition from the elitist sections of civil society, the ethnic conflict, international pressure, especially from western countries, and the growing nationalism that he nurtured amongst Sinhala Buddhists.

Country at the Crossroads

The following excerpt from a report on Sri Lanka by Freedom House, a prominent international democracy monitoring organisation, illustrates the attitude of the Mahinda Rajapaksa government towards media freedoms during the last years of the war:

> Over the last four years, the human rights and governance situation in Sri Lanka has deteriorated sharply. Much of the decline can be attributed to the government's extensive use of force against the Liberation Tigers of Tamil Eelam (LTTE) rebel group. However, the country has also suffered

from the current administration's increasingly hostile attitude toward critical or dissenting views among journalists, politicians, and civil society. The president and three of his brothers, all of whom hold government positions, currently make all critical decisions and control public spending. ... They have increasingly exercised this power to intimidate the media and opposition figures.

Media independence and freedom have been seriously undermined since the 2004 national elections. ... In recent years, journalists who report on sensitive issues like corruption, human rights abuses, and military strategy, have been subject to harassment, intimidation, and, increasingly, physical attacks; a total of 34 journalists have been murdered since 2004. Between mid-2008 and mid-2009 alone, 11 Sri Lankan journalists were forced to flee the country. ... Moreover, the police have failed to make an arrest or identify suspects in most of these cases. In the 2009 Impunity Index, compiled by the Committee to Protect Journalists, Sri Lanka ranked fourth out of 14 countries in which journalists are killed regularly, with at least nine journalist murders in the 1999–2008 period currently unsolved.

[P]rivate news outlets that are seen as critical of the government have faced increased harassment and attacks. For example, Leader Publications, publisher of the Sunday Leader and Morning Leader, was the target of an arson attack in 2007, and the Sirasa TV studio complex was nearly destroyed by armed men in January 2009. Several private outlets have closed down due to this climate of fear and violence, while others, such as the Standard Newspaper Group, have been driven out of business by government financial pressure. As a result, the availability of objective, independent sources of information in the country has drastically diminished, and the government line has dominated reporting since the last phase of the war began in 2006.

Past governments have used highly restrictive slander and libel laws to prevent media criticism of public officials. Because of the inefficiency of the court system, slander or libel suits are invariably dragged out over several years, increasing the cost to the targeted media organisation. The laws, which favour plaintiffs, contribute to media self-censorship, particularly on national security issues, corruption, and human rights abuses.[23]

An earlier EU report of October 2009 underlined many similar concerns.[24] Since the end of the war, the situation has improved in some respects, though severe restrictions remain. A UN report published in July 2010 explained: Notwithstanding the end of the conflict, restrictions on media independence and freedom are reported to persist, including restricted access to certain regions of the country. Despite a reduction in the number of high-profile attacks on media professionals since June 2009, concerns continue to be voiced in relation to journalists, publishers and other media personnel, who report critically on sensitive matters. A variety of reports indicate that such journalists could be subject to intimidation, harassment, physical attacks, arbitrary detention and disappearances. Politically motivated abductions are still reported and are alleged not to be effectively investigated or prosecuted. Credible reports also indicate that several prominent journalists have fled Sri Lanka in the last 18 months.[25]

The International Federation of Journalists' (IFJ) report on Press Freedom for 2010–2011 saw the media in Sri Lanka as 'struggling for a conducive environment for independent reporting after a tumultuous few years'. They reported that overtly 2011 was a period of relative calm. Overall, the situation improved from what it was during the final phase of the war and the immediate aftermath of the 2010 presidential election. No murders of journalists were reported and there was a decline in the number of recorded attacks on journalists, though several incidents were reported.

The report said that in the final years of the war, journalists, local and foreign, were barred from the north, unless they were part of a government entourage or embedded with the army, making it impossible for independent reportage from these areas. That situation had improved but the reporting climate was 'in no way conducive to assertive journalism'. The report said 'there are still high levels of anxiety and journalists continue to look over their shoulders and to curtail their comments and reports. A major factor contributing to this sense of unease is the government's failure to conduct proper investigations into any of the attacks against media persons and institutions, which has helped foster a climate of impunity and indifference'. The IFJ report highlighted an insecure environment for journalists, drastic reprisals for media that do not toe the line, an active restriction of space for critical reportage, and self-censorship by journalists. In an update for 2012, the IFJ described media freedoms as a 'neglected dimension of post-war politics'.[26]

In 2008, Reporters without Borders ranked Sri Lanka 165th amongst 173 countries in its annual Worldwide Press Freedom Index. The next year, the country was ranked 162nd, and in 2010, following the end of the war, 158th. In 2011/2012, it slipped back to 163rd. The exact manner in which these rankings are decided, however, may be legitimately questioned.

Free Speech in Peril

The substance of the argument presented here can be summarised in a few key points.

- Although the broadcast media was introduced to Sri Lanka quite early by the British, the traditions of radio in Britain did not take root in this country, nor did a local tradition develop. Thus, the broadcast media remained a tool for state propaganda and after broad basing, became a source of income for the corporate class. Even though a few public service broadcasting characteristics could be evidenced, it was mostly top-down propagandist stuff. Community Radio in Sri Lanka is a misnomer, as the stations are not owned, managed and run by the community. On the corporate channels, a focus on 'entertainment' is maintained at the expense of 'information and education'.

- As in the case of democratic ideals, concepts like independence of the media and freedom of expression remained alien to the Sri Lankan society. For the most part, governments, politicians, the intelligentsia and civil society[27] did not take steps to popularise these principles. The vast majority of the public remain blissfully unaware of their rights as well as their responsibilities

- From the British colonial period onwards, all governments, irrespective of party differences, took direct and indirect measures to control the media and stifle free expression. There may have been slight differences in the degree of abuse under different regimes but these dissimilarities were the result of circumstances rather than commitment.

- Media personnel generally lacked the competencies associated with broadcast professionalism. For most it was a job rather than a profession, which they found attractive not because of the income they derived (which was satisfactory enough) but for the fame and 'status' it brought them. Most were recognised as announcers, news anchors, programmers, entertainers or as 'broadcasters', and were satisfied with that identity. Professionals in other fields, the intelligentsia and the academics, were interested in their 'acquaintance' rather than the development of professionalism in broadcasting and broadcasting standards. A few stood out, no doubt. But that was mostly due to their inborn talents, their own personal efforts and perseverance.

- Broadcast training was haphazard. Early broadcast practitioners hardly received training and even afterwards it was a case of 'some training was better than no training at all'. Veterans became the role models for the new comers to emulate, resulting in what media people label 'generation losses'.

- The SLBC Training Institute did help in some ways but that was more in the form of skills development rather than providing all-round quality training with a theoretical base. The 'training institute' was known amongst the employees of SLBC as 'Siberia'. When governments changed, it was the place to send the prominent sympathisers of the defeated party. Those who were sent either tried their hands at 'training' or became mere 'passengers'.

- Foreign training and scholarships were irregular and were employed more to cater for 'perceived needs' rather than 'felt needs'. Political affiliations and internal politics played a big role in the selection process and the scholarships were used more as 'reward' or 'bait'. Some individuals did benefit from foreign training and were able to put that knowledge to good use. But even those who were keen to acquire new knowledge or skills hardly got the opportunity when they came back to share their experience or practice what was learnt.

- The portrayal of Sri Lankan rulers in both local and foreign media has tended to present one ruler as better than the other. However, an analysis of their actions reveals that all governments irrespective of the person at the helm tried to intimidate media practitioners and muffle free expression. In the early days, it was more a case of omission rather than commission. Later, with the rulers resorting to new tactics, methods of repression became more oppressive and direct. At the same time, with the proliferation of media, the coverage given to these tactics became more extensive (perhaps disproportionately so), giving the impression that anti-democratic actions themselves had increased.

Socio-cultural Dimensions of the Problem

If we are to understand the violence that is prevalent in the society today, the aggressive suppression of democratic ideals and practice, we have to examine recent undemocratic events and actions. Why do people tolerate brazen violations of human rights? Why do people, especially in a country professing Buddhist principles of *ahimsa* and tolerance, prefer to look the other way when a person who fought for their rights is killed openly?

Finding answers to these questions will prove to be valuable to those who seek solutions to the problems and issues related to good governance, the rule of law, accountability, transparency and other fundamental democratic ideals. Such an understanding is most valuable for those who strive to study mass media and its practice in the country. Inadequate knowledge of local conditions, or what the 'masses' themselves think, is a failing of most mass media research/study attempts. Basil Fernando of the Asian Human Rights Commission (AHRC) relevantly asked whether it is possible to protect and promote human rights without a thorough scrutiny of society and culture in Sri Lanka?

> The experience in Sri Lanka shows that despite increase in the number of legal enactments on human rights and quite a lot of programs for education on such rights, the country's human rights problems are increasing. There has not been a significant improvement either in the civil or the economic rights spheres. Any serious attempt at promotion and protection of human rights must be accompanied by an effort to understand the root causes for the existence of such a situation.[28]

He goes on to identify non-acceptance of equality, tolerance of violence, extra-judicial killings, culture of impunity, belief that the pursuit of justice may lead to further trouble, indifference towards the weakest in society, professionals' long-standing cultural habit of exploiting the ignorance and the backwardness of the poorest sections of society, failure to grant right to information and freedom of expression, as some of the human rights issues that afflict the contemporary Sri Lankan society. Hence, he asserts that:

> the cultural foundations of human rights violations need to be scrutinised if the root causes of human rights violations are to be grasped. Without such a grasp, no deep transformation is possible, and any human rights project will remain a cosmetic exercise as it is often accused of being. If it is to become a dynamic movement capable of unleashing the inner energies of people to pursue its aims, the shadowy side of society and culture should come within the scrutiny of human rights practitioners.[29]

Professor Sasanka Perera has framed the discussion in the following manner:

> It is reasonable to argue that the best option for Asian societies in general and Sri Lanka in particular, would not be to articulate human rights concerns within a paradigm of tradition and convention but within a clear paradigm of modernity and universality which would nevertheless not be hostile to historical memory.[30]

We believe that restrictions and impediments to media practice and violations of media rights should be weighed and analysed in the context of these considerations. It may be true that these infringements and contraventions of the law have accelerated and increased in the recent past. But, as shown above, these happenings are not, or at least not only, the outcome of policies and actions of any individual leaders, for leaders are themselves the products of the same society as others, with a shared culture, shared patterns of behaviours and interactions.

This is not to say that those who commit 'crimes' should go unpunished and the people should bear the brunt of the consequences of unpunished crimes without protest. However, merely grumbling and looking the other way or voting 'failed' political leaders out of office in the hope that the new incumbent will deliver the goods are both strategies which have failed. This is an aspect that should be taken into serious consideration by those who fight at the risk of their lives for democratic rights. It is not that people reject the concept of 'democracy'. Democracy continues to be the preferred ideology and by far the most preferred political arrangement. The difference is in the way they go about it. While electoral democracy had enabled almost all citizens to stake a claim in the process of governance, it has failed to 'root' democratic ideals.

Ownership Patterns in the Sri Lankan Media

State or Private Ownership?

The crucial relationship between the role of the media in society and media ownership is succinctly summarised in the following observation:

> The availability of information and its accessibility is central to the functioning of contemporary democracies and in modern economies and societies in general. It is vital to the ability of constituencies to make informed political and economic decisions during voting and when making economic decisions.[31]

Although little comprehensive empirical and theoretical study exists on the issue, the relationship between media ownership and economics, and the media's role in society, affords substantive material for active public and policy debate. As Robert W. McChesney explains in his book, *The Political Economy of Media: Enduring Issues, Emerging Dilemmas*:

> political economy of media is a field that endeavors to connect how media and communication systems are shaped by ownership, market structures, commercial support, technologies, labor practices, and government policies. The political economy of media then links the media and communication systems to how both economic and political systems work, and social power is exercised, in society.[32]

The central question for political economists is whether, on balance, the media system serves to promote or undermine democratic institutions and practices. The media has definitely and radically changed the way we work, play and communicate. As in the case of other countries, the Sri Lankan media is owned by a few companies and organisations. Given their wealth and their shrewd donations into the political process, the advocates for the public interest are in far too short supply. In the context of the reach and influence of electronic media in the country, who owns these media, what is delivered over them and, fundamentally, in whose interest they work are critical issues. Are the media a force for social justice or for oligarchy? And equipped with that knowledge, what are the options for citizens to address the situation? Ultimately, will the political economy of the media be a critical exercise, committed to enhancing democracy?

In its early years, the BBC, in support of maintaining a publicly subsidised monopoly of radio and television in Britain, expounded the idea that state-regulated public ownership can expose the public to less biased, more complete, and more accurate information than it could obtain with private ownership. This argument was, subsequently, repeated in many developing countries. The public interest theory predicts that the consequence of public ownership is more economic and political freedom, and better social outcomes.

In contrast, the public choice theory holds that a government-owned or publicly owned media outlet would distort and manipulate information to entrench the incumbent politicians, preclude voters and consumers from making informed decisions, and ultimately undermine both democracy and markets. Because private and independent media supply alternative views to the public, they enable individuals to choose amongst political candidates, goods and securities—with less fear of abuse by unscrupulous politicians, producers and promoters. It is obvious that the two theories have distinct implications for both the determinants and the consequences of media ownership.

Ownership Structures[33]

Radio Broadcasts

Before the liberalisation of the 1980s, there was only one broadcasting station in Sri Lanka. Radio Ceylon had been a government department until it was made a public corporation in 1966 under the name SLBC, though this did not materially change the level of government involvement. SLBC operates radio broadcasts in all three national languages viz. Sinhala, Tamil and English. It has two components: a national service with no commercial content and a commercial service. Its commercial broadcasts were popular both in Sri Lanka and in India in the 1950s and 1960s. Catering to new trends, the SLBC started an FM channel—City FM—in 1989.

With its three regional stations, several community radios and its external services, SLBC has the most diverse network of stations in the country. Lakhanda, which was started by SLBC in 1996 in the face of growing commercial competition and later transferred to the Independent Television Network (ITN), is another government-run FM radio station. However, these state radio channels, even Lakhanda, have been gradually losing audiences to the expanding commercial radio sector. Before 2000, apart from the state-run radio stations, there were some 10 commercial stations in operation. By mid-2011, according to the Ministry of Mass Media and Information website, the number had risen to 59 radio channels owned by both state and private sector institutions.[34]

The first private radio station to go on air in Sri Lanka was TNL Radio, which started broadcasting in April 1993. The other pioneer station was FM99, since renamed Shree FM, which was set up in 1992 by Colombo Communications Ltd, with Livy Wijemanne, a former chairman of the SLBC, at the helm. It began broadcasting in June 1993. Colombo Communications also have an English channel, E FM, (originally Capital Radio) and a music channel, Ran FM. The company was taken over in 1998 by a local business with jewellery interests, EAP Edirisinghe Holdings Ltd, which also owns two TV channels, Swarnavahini and ETV, and is one of the country's leading media groups. Equally successful and more diversified is the Maharajah group, a largely Tamil business conglomerate with TV and radio interests. It started three successful radio channels in the 1990s: Yes FM in English, Sirasa FM in Sinhala, Shakthi FM in Tamil. Y FM, a youth radio channel, was added in 2005. The Maharajah group also has three TV channels: Sirasa TV, Shakthi TV and MTV Sports. A third major group is the Asia Broadcasting Corporation (ABC), which now claims to have the largest radio network in Sri Lanka. This includes Hiru FM, a long-established Sinhala channel, Sooriyan FM, a leading Tamil channel, Gold FM and Sun FM, two music channels, and Shaa FM, a youth channel. ABC is owned by Rayynor Silva, whose brother, the controversial MP, Duminda Silva, crossed over to the ruling alliance in late 2007, following the suspension of ABC's licence. ABC also runs Hiru TV, an up and coming Sinhala language channel. It took over three radio stations from the UK-based Sunrise Radio group and has since expanded its operations considerably.

In the commercial radio sector, a number of recent entrants have also made an impact. These include Neth FM, owned by Asset Radio Broadcasting, a business with close links to the government; Derana FM, owned by Power House Ltd, part of a business conglomerate, which also provides advertising services to the ruling party; and Buddhist FM, which is broadcast with its sister TV channel from the Sri Sambodhi Viharaya in Gregory's Road, Colombo. Buddhist FM and Neth FM pioneered more regular religious programmes on prime time radio, a trend which became more marked at the height of the war when the government was working to galvanise Sinhala opinion.

According to industry sources, by 2013, the state-run SLBC Sinhala radio service and the ITN station, Lakhanda, were attracting relatively small audiences compared to their commercial competitors. Sirasa FM, long the market leader, was also facing stiff competition from Hiru FM and Neth FM, with Shree FM giving ground to the same stations. The state Tamil radio services, ITN's Vasantham FM and SLBC's Thesiya FM, were also lagging well behind their commercial competitors, Shakthi FM and Sooriyan FM. It was not clear why the government was permitting a decline in the effectiveness of its own radio channels but it seemed to be relying instead on pro-government commercial channels and more extensive use of mobile phone messaging.

Apart from these domestic radio stations, several international broadcasters operate radio stations in Sri Lanka or use local stations for their broadcasts. These include: BBC Sandeshaya and BBC Tamilosai— the BBC's Sinhala and Tamil services; China Radio International's

Sinhala Service; Germany's Deutsche Welle; Lihinimedia of Canada; the International Broadcasting Bureau from the USA; NHK World Network of Japan and Vishna Vani of India.

TV Broadcasts

Interestingly, television was introduced in 1979 to Sri Lanka as a private venture. This was made possible because of the political links that local partners had with the government rather than because of a policy decision. This TV channel called ITN was converted to a government-owned business undertaking just three months after its inauguration—again not a policy decision but to help the local partner out of an impasse. It was later brought under the Sri Lanka Rupavahini Act of 1982 along with the newly created Sri Lanka Rupavahini Corporation. After assuming power in 1977, J.R. Jayewardene's government decided to utilise the funds, which had been set aside by the German government to start TV, to expand medium wave radio transmissions. Later, the government took a firm decision to start a national state-run TV station, initially as an educational broadcast, with Japanese aid. In December 1992, after the government allowed private TV broadcasts, the Maharaja group launched MTV in collaboration with Singapore Telecommunications Limited. The group added two other channels, Sirasa TV and Shakthi TV, in Sinhala and Tamil, in 1998. Swarnavahini TV was launched by the Edirisinghe group in 1997. Since then, especially after 2000, we have seen a proliferation of private TV networks in the island. By mid-2012, there were 23 Sri Lankan terrestrial channels and 18 local satellite or cable channels. But apart from one or two channels, such as Derana TV and Hiru TV and the niche Carlton Sports Network, few of these new entrants were making any substantial impact.

In the field of television, unlike in radio, the government-owned channels, Rupavahini and ITN, have continued to maintain substantial audiences and to attract solid advertising revenues. According to industry sources, in mid-2013, they had more than 30 per cent of the market between them and higher ratings than any other channels. Their old commercial rivals, Sirasa and Swarnavahini, were also maintaining a healthy market position. But they had not overtaken the state-run channels. In television, the entry costs of providing terrestrial coverage are much higher than in radio and many of the best transmitter sites have already been taken. But ministerial control of licensing procedures is the other critical factor. Without ample funding and ministerial support, relative newcomers find it difficult to break into the market. In 2013, the ruling party's dominance of politics and of the airwaves was reflected in the fact that TNL, the TV and radio enterprise owned by the family of the leader of the opposition, was not making a major impact, despite its political affiliation. The allocation of a sports channel licence to interests close to the President's family (and the channel's success in winning rights to coverage of Sri Lankan cricket and other sporting fixtures) was another manifestation of government, if not family control, of licensing procedures.

Ownership Issues

Until the liberalisation of the 1980s, the electronic media in the country was the sole property of the government—or rather the political party in power. The radio was used to present the government point of view, government propaganda and image building of the ruling party and its leaders. Dissent was not allowed and in some cases, the media was used to vilify and even harass opponents. The practitioners themselves did not see anything wrong in the use of the media in this manner as they considered themselves bound by the law to serve the government. This state of affairs was not dissimilar to the situation in many third world countries where democratic ways of life were yet to take root. In 1977, the UNP led by J.R. Jayawardene came to power when ideas of economic liberalisation were being popularised all over the world. Partial or full privatisation of government institutions and assets, greater labour market flexibility, lower tax rates for businesses, less restriction on both domestic and foreign capital and open markets were its main characteristics. Jayawardena opted for a 'free economy' mainly to attract foreign investments and not because he was 'liberal' in his approach or ideas. Other spheres of public life in the country were tightly controlled. The media fell into that category, although it was during his regime that community radios and regional broadcasting stations commenced. The opposition was muffled in more ways than one. In such an atmosphere, it is idealistic to expect concepts like 'freedom of expression', 'uninhibited marketplace of ideas', 'diversity and plurality' to flourish. His successor was even more direct in his approach. Therefore, the granting of broadcast licences to a few supportive private companies did not really amount to an 'act of liberalisation'.

After the defeat of the UNP in 1994, with a new government in place, radio and TV channels began to proliferate. Taken at its face value, this development may appear to have been an attempt to fill the 'airwaves' with many diverse and competing voices. However, all the owners were from the corporate or elitist class. Even the so-called community radios were owned by the state-run SLBC. Thus, instead of providing unprecedented diversity in broadcast media in the country, this 'diversification of ownership' in reality only allowed a handful of companies to operate, seeking to minimise competition and maximise corporate profits rather than maximise competition and promote the public interest. Obtaining a licence to broadcast was not an easy task. Although it is hard to collect statistics regarding the number of applications made for licences and the number granted, we are personally aware of several instances where the receipt of the applications for broadcast licences was not even acknowledged. The licensing process was dependent largely on the goodwill of the minister concerned. Later on, it was made necessary to renew these licences annually, making it more dependent on the minister. In addition, the government could stop broadcasts whenever it wanted. Thus, the private media institutions were constantly under pressure to 'keep the government happy'. After all, who would want to lose their broadcast licence after investing a huge amount of money? Therefore, they took care not to condemn or confront the government. The slightest deviation from the practice was quickly dealt with in ways that the government thought appropriate, as ABC and Sirasa, and later Siyatha, found out the hard way.

This may give the impression that the private radio and TV stations in the country would be willing to join the struggle to re-establish and nurture democratic rights and liberties, if it were not for the 'sword of Damocles' of government control that hung over them. While admitting that government control is a deterrent, we believe that the private sector electronic media have an agenda which is commercial, economic and even political. Sirasa TV is a case in point. This is a hypothesis based on long-term observations, which needs to be examined in depth through formal research.

Because of this concentration of private media in the hands of a few companies (which invariably have other business interests as well), content provision, packaging and distribution have also 'become a standardised production and marketing process in which the messages communicated are constrained and directed in both quantity and quality to meet the economic imperatives of that process'.[35] The media has become such a powerful device of political propaganda not only because of government influence and malpractice, but also because the private sector media watering down and censoring news sources for private gain. Their concern is not with accurately reporting the news, but with manipulating media consumers for their own benefit.

Thus, it is obvious that in Sri Lanka the mainstream electronic media is not as free or independent as it should be, and there is no room for community or other alternative media. The state media, which has island-wide coverage and a large audience of listeners and viewers, is in the clutches of the party in power. The so-called 'private media' are owned by a few companies—several of them 'family enterprises'—which are worried only about profits and commercial gains. Thus, the act of granting licences to the private sector has not resulted in broad basing the electronic media of the country.

After more than 60 years of independence, it is clear that governments will not, on their own, seek to create an environment conducive to the exercise of free democratic rights, including freedom of expression. Deliberate about-turns and a plethora of 'wasted opportunities' leave no doubts whatsoever in our minds. The government will not willingly or readily slacken its grip on the media: Media freedom can be won only through a dedicated and focused struggle.

Private broadcasting institutions do offer a platform for media rights agitations and appear to be in favour of abolishing rules and regulations that allow government to control over them. Nevertheless, it is not clear that they are really interested in having a free and independent media in the country. With 'the spread and intensification of commercialisation and the decline of public broadcasting, the erosion of the 'public service' ethos in journalism, the growth and consolidation of the advertising industry and the development of communication technology spurred by business demand, the trend is towards the consolidation of 'corporate power' in the field of broadcasting. The private sector broadcasters are either frightened into submission by the government or worried about their investment in 'serving a democratic society, where a diversity of views is vital to shaping informed opinions'. The ruse they often adopt is to 'repackage government spin and pass it off as journalism'.

A content analysis of the broadcast media would definitely reveal that the realities of the ordinary world that Sri Lankans inhabit are shunned by both state and private media. The dominant discourse in the society—that of the elitists—is being presented by the media and the masses are forced to accept it as a discourse relevant to them. The state-run media often gloss over widespread social and economic difficulties and problems and focus on government 'spin'. The private media vie with each other to stage fake 'reality' shows instead of showing the unacceptable and unbearable reality of the lives of the people. Personal shortcomings and natural disasters are, for them, easily marketable commodities!

One could argue that if the people were to own the media, it could provide a base, a platform for stabilising democratic rights through media interventions. Community radio could have provided such a space. Sadly, community radios in Sri Lanka do not belong to the community but to the state—the classic violator of democratic rights.

Two American broadcasters have commented that 'the onrush of digital convergence and broadband access in the workplaces and homes of America is radically changing the way we work, play, and communicate. Fiber-to-the-premise (FTTP) from the regional Bells, Voice over IP (VoIP) telephony, bundled services from cable companies, and increased capacity in satellite and wireless technologies will transform the platforms on which we communicate. Who owns these platforms, what is delivered over them, and, fundamentally, in whose interest they work are critical issues before us now'.[36] Is it too early for us to anticipate a similar scenario in terms of the media in Sri Lanka? Certainly, we can agree with these writers that 'a blow against media ownership consolidation—now or in future—will have far-reaching implications, as critical information gains exposure to a caring, active public. Instead of fake reality TV, maybe the media will start to cover the reality of people struggling to get by and of the victories that happen every day in our communities, and in strife-torn regions around the globe'.[37]

When people obtain information, they are empowered. Therefore, it is imperative to ensure that the airwaves are open for more of that by removing ownership obstacles to free expression. As we all know, democracy relies on a vibrant media with many voices. As such, a fresh look at the entire media ownership framework in the country is necessary to encourage diversity of ideas and voices.

Media Rights

Reflections on International Pressures

Let us consider a report which evaluates the role of the international community:

A number of international organisations actively contribute towards improving the media situation in Sri Lanka by acting as watchdogs for media freedom and the freedom of expression, lobbying the government, conducting programmes for training and capacity building of journalists and media personnel and supporting civil society organisations working in the area. Organisations such as International Freedom of Expression Exchange (IFEX) and Reporters Sans Frontieres (RSF) working with local organisations such as the Free Media Movement, provide global news alerts on violations of freedom of expression and restrictions on media freedom, highlighting attacks on journalists, use of censorship and other restrictive laws, taking information on violations to a global forum and lobbying the government for action, investigation and redress.[38]

Tracing the happenings after the end of war and the emergent culture of impunity, it has been maintained that if international pressure can be applied properly and adequately, the prevailing situation could be changed. Judging from actions in the past, this line of argument has limitations both in the execution and outcome. International organisations, including the global press, have not been silent. But governments are not easily restrained. For example, the EU's move to restrict trade concessions under its Generalised System of Preferences failed to rein in the government of Sri Lanka. On the contrary, the danger is that in Sri Lanka, external pressure helps government espouse 'conspiracy theories' to seek popular support. Here, we are trying to establish two points: one is that 'international pressure' alone will not be able to stop the blatant violations of media and other human rights by the government. Certainly, international pressure is needed and it helps. There is no doubt about it. But this alone cannot change the situation. It has to be combined with other meaningful strategies. Otherwise, it may bring about a negative effect. The second point is that one should approach the revelations in world media with caution and prudence to arrive at a more level-headed and realistic picture.

Our concern here is not international politics, government diplomacy and the like, but to help readers to better understand the media situation in post-war Sri Lanka. The path to democracy in Sri Lanka, as in so many post-colonial countries, has not been simple, smooth or systematic. It has contained so many ups and downs, diversions, pitfalls and potholes and even roadblocks. Democracy as practised here may be quite a distance from the ideal and is definitely different from the experience of others. Even Freedom House recognises that 'cultural differences, diverse national interests and varying levels of economic development and human rights may limit the volume of news flows within a country'.[39] Although there is a global debate over the validity of this hypothesis, it is worth bearing in mind before arriving at conclusions about the situation in Sri Lanka.

The political scientist and media columnist, Gnana Moonesinghe, has pointed out that 'in the globalised world, territorial borders have lost their rigidity and weight since there is a convergence of concerns by the entire international community on the political, military, economic and social contours of all countries in a more intrusive manner'.[40]

But some countries, who take an interest in the affairs of other nation states, may have hidden agendas other than the proclaimed intention of protecting human rights and enriching democratic traditions. Analysis of experiences worldwide during the past few decades shows that global politics play a major hand in these interventions. An in-depth study of the current wave of 'peoples' revolutions' would reveal such schema. If we take the Sri Lankan situation, the Rajapaksa government's slant towards countries like China, Russia and Iran has surely riled the west headed by the USA which expresses concerns about 'human rights and democracy'. If this realpolitik changes, perhaps the west may not be as keen as now to intervene in bringing back 'normalcy' to Sri Lanka. Our premise is based on the fact that in the past, when the governments of Sri Lanka maintained friendly ties with the west, there were no such vigorous 'human rights and democracy' campaigns, even though there was no shortage of human rights violations.

A specialist in democratic governance has suggested some restrictions on such international interventions:

> Most industrialised countries have elaborate programs for promoting democracy beyond their own borders. This intervention into the internal political affairs of other countries at times poses serious problems. In my eyes, international democracy promotion is justifiable only as long as it occurs in close cooperation and upon explicit invitation of relevant political forces of the host country, and is limited to legitimate methods.[41]

There is no rule to say that all those who want to see a democratic rule in Sri Lanka which recognises and promotes pluralism in media, freedom of expression and other human rights, should act in unison and make concerted efforts to that effect. It is conceded that such a scenario is too optimistic, impracticable and unfeasible. Even when people or organisations share the same views, such an exercise may not be possible as strategies are bound to differ. Sometimes this diversity of action may prove to be beneficial because even if some strategies fail, others might bring the desired result. On the other hand, if these different strategies contradict each other and even go counter to each other, then the very objective they desire to achieve may not be accomplished. And doubts begin to appear about the intent.

A recent case in point is the Galle Literary Festival of 2011. At the instigation of Journalists for Democracy in Sri Lanka (JDS), international media freedom group RSF called on authors to boycott the festival because of the country's poor human rights record. But this action brought them criticism from the sorts of people they usually defend from repressive regimes.[42] As human rights activist, Sunila Abeysekara, wrote in a personal letter to a leading signatory of the RSF/JDS appeal[43]: 'It is extremely disappointing to find those who defend media freedom in Sri Lanka playing a role in depriving us of an opportunity to express ourselves, and our desire for a democratic and peaceful environment in which to live and work, with a broader community from outside the country.'

Government Action

Successive governments have had their own interests in manipulating and controlling the media. These actions have taken the form of direct interventions such as formulating regulations and laws, takeovers, direct censorship, sealing and closing down of media institutions, intimidation, arrests and jailing, abductions, causing bodily harm to and even killing of media personnel. In fact, the editor of the *Sunday Leader*, the late Lasantha Wickrematunge, reflected in his posthumously published editorial that 'indeed, murder has become the primary tool whereby the state seeks to control the organs of liberty'.[44] Indirect tactics, like 'buying' or favouring, vilifications, causing fear and other subtle methods, to force media personnel into submission, compliance and/or self-censorship, are also used.

In pragmatic terms, licensing procedure is a lethal weapon in the hands of an authoritarian government, which uses it to control, obtain allegiance and compliance from the private broadcasters. Although the state monopoly over radio and television ended in 1992, broadcasting licences are still issued by the Ministry of Media. However, it is no secret that, like in other matters, the ultimate power of decision lies with the President. There is no declared or established basis for granting new licences or renewing existing ones, which is entirely at the minister's discretion. The Telecommunications Regulatory Commission of Sri Lanka wields authority in spectrum management. This 'power' has being used and is being used by the government to directly and indirectly control the content, activities and policies of radio and TV channels of the country.

The suspension and the restoration of the broadcast licence of the ABC is a classic example to illustrate the point. As US Department of state report says:

> On October 26, 2007, the Ministry of Information suspended the license of five private FM radio stations, which belonged to the Asia Broadcasting Corporation (ABC), after domestic media outlets incorrectly reported an LTTE attack. The radio network apologised for the inaccuracy but the government did not reinstate ABC's broadcasting license, although other media sources also aired the inaccurate report. On November 1, the Supreme Court rejected a petition to lift the suspension of the broadcasting license and charged ABC with contempt of court for technical inaccuracies in its petition. However, a resolution seemed likely after Duminda Silva, the brother of the broadcast licensee, a provincial politician, agreed to 'crossover' to the ruling Sri Lanka Freedom Party. ABC Networks appeared poised to regain its broadcasting licenses and indicated it planned to recommence broadcasting in January 2008.[45]

In mid-April 2008, barely six months after the crossover, the licences of ABC were restored. This 'process' (if one can call it such) is in sharp contrast to the procedures advocated by Article XIX. It advocates that 'the process for obtaining a broadcasting licence should be set out clearly and precisely in law. The process should be fair and transparent, include clear time limits within which decisions must be made and allow for effective public input and an opportunity for the applicant to be heard'.[46]

Direct Interventions and Legal Manoeuvrings

Direct actions are many and are reported in the international media more frequently and more vividly than in the Sri Lankan media. We distinguish two broad periods in the post-independence era, with 1970 as the dividing line between them.

The pre-1970 period was comparatively 'calm' as far as government interventions in the broadcast media were concerned. There was only one broadcast media institution: the state radio. It was directly under the control of the government in power. Nobody, including its media personnel, expected it to be free. But the post-1970 period was quite eventful. Perhaps it was the SLFP-Marxist alliance under Prime Minister Sirimavo Bandaranaike that set the tone. The sealing and subsequent closure of the Davasa group of newspapers and the takeover of Lake House group of papers stand out. The politicisation of the state radio and direct control of content heightened. The suppression of opposition views and the intolerance of dissent came to the fore. The politicians began to call the shots and to control, tame and even destroy all media that did not fall in line. The harassment of media people increased—not only those who refused to bow down, but also those neutral practitioners whom they thought useless. This trend, which began from the early 1970s, continues unabated, and on a very high note unparalleled in the history of the media in the country. During the 1960s and 1970s, the dominant discourse on the media was influenced by the 'Soviet model', which, according to Professor Wimal Dissanayake, 'focuses on the role of the state in shaping media activities as well as media policies'.[47] It is of note that Sri Lanka was ruled for 12 years by the SLFP, which was described as 'socialist' by party sympathisers and the opposition as well. In the post-independence era, during the formative years, this 'socialist' influence weighed heavily on media policy. Even the conversion of state radio to a public corporation from a government department was seen, as mentioned earlier, as a step to exercise more government control. It was the order of the day. The government was convinced that it had the final say on all matters including the media.

The Director of the AHRC, Basil Fernando, identifies six themes which, in his opinion, lie at the heart of the current situation of abysmal lawlessness in Sri Lanka: the lost meaning of legality; the predominance of the security apparatus; the disappearance of truth through propaganda; the extraordinary concentration of power in the hands of the executive president (termed 'the superman controller'); destroyed public institutions and the zero status of citizens.[48]

Fernando goes on to describe the impact that years of conflict have exerted on the propagation and dissemination of truth in Sri Lanka. He says 'equal in strategic importance to the struggle for control over territory during the conflict was the struggle for control over information. The military and the LTTE both vied to cast their polarised propagandistic perspectives as the single version of the truth'.[49]

The state has learned to excel at creating and controlling a single, official version of the truth. Society, for its part, has largely accepted the state's self-anointed role as arbiter of truth and falsehood. Fernando observes that: 'Those who run the media also usually comply with demands to reproduce and disseminate government propaganda. Those who do not comply are threatened'.[50]

The International Bar Association's Human Rights Institute, which highlights issues of international concern to the public, the media and the legal community, notes that the media has reached this point, in part, through years of intimidation and harassment. As a result of these dynamics, there is a general level of societal disinterest in truth itself. When the truth is so cynically manipulated, Fernando explains, 'people cease expecting to know the truth of anything'.[51] As a result, government spokespeople automatically deny any allegations of human rights violations, knowing that no one will come forward to speak what they know, either out of fear or out of a sense of sheer futility. Many observers cite the dwindling critical voices in the media, the legal profession and Sri Lankan civil society in general as a key factor in the degeneration of the rule of law in Sri Lanka. Certain policy decisions at far broader levels, too, are also influenced by security concerns. These include the government's media reform policy.[52]

Sri Lankan law contains many restrictions on the content of what may be published or broadcast that go beyond what are acceptable limitations on freedom of expression. The Prevention of Terrorism Act, a draconian law separate from the emergency measures, remains in force. In the now lapsed emergency regulations, as Article XIX[53] points out, no distinction whatsoever was made between information which might genuinely threaten national security (and which could legitimately be restricted by law) and information which should properly be placed in the public domain. The regulations were phrased far too broadly and in contravention of international standards on freedom of expression and national security. In addition, they were applied in practice in an arbitrary manner.

Although the emergency regulations appeared to impose a blanket ban on publishing news on the subjects listed, in practice all such items had to be submitted for approval, prior to publication, to the official censor, the Competent Authority on Censorship, a civilian official appointed by the government. With the approval of this official censor, or with the censor's alterations incorporated into the text, such items could then, in fact, be published; without such approval, their publication was unlawful.

In addition to these legal restrictions, governments exercise control of the media through a range of other subtle tactics. The IFJ wrote in its report for 2010–2011:

> An insidious threat to media freedom which is emerging in Sri Lanka is the increasing number of media houses coming under government control through political manoeuvrings. Media owners have become government MPs or ministers, and editors have become close affiliates

of powerful ministers. Licences for television and radio are given to political allies, and as a result, a large number are government controlled by proxy. The situation has led to policy and content slanted in favour of the government.[54]

Governments sometimes adopt tactics which may seem quite innocuous but which are in truth disguised tactics to control the media. One such step was to do away with the annual radio and television licence fees. President Chandrika Kumaratunga, as the Finance Minister, announced this measure in the annual budget and it became effective from January 2000. Supposedly, it was a relief measure and no doubt many in the country accepted it as such. But it meant the government lost a considerable amount of revenue and it was not a relief that the ordinary man had cried for. It has been suggested that this measure was taken to relieve the government media of its public service broadcast obligation, since licence holders enjoy certain rights, as was established in the *Wimal Fernando v. SLBC* case.[55]

Role of Media Practitioners, Rights Groups and Media Organisations

Media practitioners' organisations, lobbyists, pressure and advocacy groups, and watchdog organisations in Sri Lanka appear to outsiders to constitute a vibrant, energetic, knowledgeable and even fearless body of individuals who are committed to win back and stabilise basic democratic rights, including freedom of expression. Their integrity or genuineness of purpose was never in doubt, although there may be some who tend to accuse them of political leanings. However, the structure of the groups and their effectiveness in safeguarding freedom of expression and achieving media and public reforms need to be examined.

Structure of the Groups

There are several well-established and active media organisations in the country. The most well-known groups are almost entirely based in the capital city and may be accepted as national level media organisations.

Their membership consists of journalists and a few freelancers. The following are the most active and have formed an alliance: SLWJA, IFEX member Free Media Movement, South Asian Free Media Association, Sri Lanka Muslim Media Forum (SLMMF), Sri Lanka Tamil Journalists' Association, Journalists Against Suppression and Federation of Media Employees Trade Union (FMETU).

Although they work very closely on many issues, a few are professional trade union organisations and some serve specific ethnic constituencies. Some have affiliations with world media organisations. Although broadcast media personnel are allowed to join, these organisations are still dominated to some extent by print media practitioners. Over the years, these major bodies have emerged as champions of freedom of expression and other basic democratic rights, resorting to lobbying, agitating and intervening. They work to improve the lot of their membership, even providing training to improve professionalism.

In the provinces, local media organisations are mainly associations of local correspondents of the mainstream media. Their main concerns are the redress of grievances and the welfare of the membership. Media reforms do not seem to be a priority.

Mobilisation of Public Support

Journalists in Sri Lankan society are generally looked upon as a special small community with many privileges. Because of the nature of their work and their close links with the politicians and other power brokers, some media personnel themselves wield power to a certain extent. The politicians, knowing the value of their services, afford 'favours' to their friends in the profession. Each side does not want to lose the goodwill of the other.

For the public, however, it is the talent, skill and popularity of these journalists which counts the most and not their role as champions of democratic rights of the people of this country. Radio and TV broadcasters like the late Ravi John and the late Premakeerthi de Alwis can be cited as good examples. Both were respected and loved by their audiences for their versatility as broadcasters and were even considered 'radicals' as presenters. But they never sought to bring about changes to the 'system' and never used their popularity to mobilise public support for democratic media rights.

This close relationship between the politician and the journalist may have prevented media personnel from seeking support elsewhere for their cause, even after they organised themselves into associations and unions.

Strategies Employed

Critical social movements are the key to revitalising democracy today and the struggle for communication rights is one of the most important democratising struggles of the current era. In this sense, we can use media democratisation as the criterion to assess the work of these groupings. Media democratisation means media-oriented activism that expands the range of voices accessed through the media, builds an egalitarian and participatory public sphere, promotes the values and practices of sustainable democracy and offsets the political and economic inequalities found elsewhere in the social system. We propose to employ this criterion in assessing the work and strategies of the dominant Sri Lankan activist groups in the democratisation of the media in the country.

In their early phase, these organisations were interested mainly in the welfare and occupational rights of the membership. This becomes evident when one examines their 'manifestos'. A summary of the objectives of three major organisations illustrates this point:

The FMETU, which is an alliance of six trade unions in the state sector media, claims to be the largest and most active non-partisan organisation of journalists, with a membership of nearly 2,200. It accepts the Ministry for Media and Information as the official body that governs matters relating to the media and asserts that despite the many political and financial constraints faced by the federation, it is doing its very best to assist and equip its members with educational programmes and workshops at different levels to meet the many challenges of today.

The SLWJA, established by a Parliament Act in 1987, has a membership of over 1,200. Its goals include standing up for rights of expression and free media, the protection of the rights and the dignity of journalists, the enhancement of their professionalism and their welfare facilities and the improvement of the media in Sri Lanka.

The SLMMF started in 1995 and has over 500 members. Its stated mission is to bring together Muslims who are involved in the print and electronic media and those who are involved in the communication industry in educating, imparting knowledge and training of media personnel in the country.

These stated objectives show their main focus and concern is for the welfare and improvement of the status of their members rather than to agitate for the cause of the media.

Efficacy of Media Strategies

Efforts to rally the support of the media personnel, intellectuals, academia, civil rights groups and other interested parties for formulating policies and media reform have been quite successful at one level. Problems have been discussed; different aspects have been explored; diverse views have been aired and plans have been drawn up. The magnitude of the exercise made relevant parties take notice. The international community was impressed and ready to help. Sadly, the journey ended there.

When dealing with the authorities, the approach that critics have followed is one of cooperation rather than confrontation in the belief that it stands a better chance of success. Thus, they have thought it wise to work closely with political parties who appear to be genuinely committed to bring about changes and reforms that would establish a free media culture. However, none of the governments that came into power (except perhaps during Ranil Wickremasinghe's brief stint as PM) kept their promises regarding media freedom. Not only that, governments reneged on their promises and began to crush media freedom, leaving those who supported them out in the cold.

The main strategies adopted by these media groups have failed to bring about substantial results as far as the media environment in the country and media reforms are concerned. If at all, the situation has worsened gradually and significantly in spite of their 'interventions'. The important question for the researcher is: Why did these efforts lack the force to make rulers listen? There are several reasons.

First, the lack of an independent media in the country paradoxically contributed to the unsuccessfulness of the strategy. There was little reason for governments to feel apprehensive of a handful of journalists when they were confident that the media institutions they worked in could be manipulated or subjugated. Once again, this is an issue linked to media ownership. This strategy only invited personal danger for those few who were instrumental in keeping these activist organisations going in spite of pressure from several quarters. Secondly, as a consequence of the above policy of 'going it alone', these organisations hardly attempted to organise or harness 'people's power'. They never took meaningful steps to sensitise or educate the masses on matters concerning media and other democratic rights. Thus, the debate did not become a public discourse. The masses were reduced to mere spectators who were made to watch the two sides (government and media organisations) battle it out.

The occasion when 'Sirasa' TV 'took on' an offending minister is an example. Sirasa TV sent a crew of two to cover the opening of the second phase of the flyover at Thorana Junction in Kelaniya, near Colombo. Minister Mervyn Silva was known for his aggressive attitude towards the media and during the filming his bodyguards had assaulted the correspondent Thushara Saliya Ranawaka and video cameramen Waruna Sampath and seized their cameras. Now, obviously this was an act to be condemned. It was part of a worrying trend that has become almost entrenched in our society. However, Sirasa TV took it upon itself to chastise the minister and challenged him through its news bulletins, saying that Sirasa will not 'give in' until the minister 'backs down'. Another instance was their 'running battle' with the JVP. On both occasions, public support was neither solicited nor obtained.

In short, the media practice prevalent in the country has not made the masses feel that the media community is a part of the larger society. On the contrary, it is considered an elitist group which brandishes and exerts power on its own behalf.

Media and Elections

The election period is undoubtedly an ideal time to assess and judge the quality of media practice in a country, for, more often than not, the hidden agendas, prejudices, biases and other bad practices come to the fore during this phase. As it is supposed that the role of the media is to provide adequate information with regard to political parties, policies, candidates and the election process itself to enable the voter to make an informed choice, the significance of the media is amplified during elections. Nevertheless, in many countries in Asia, free elections are themselves a new phenomenon; and across most of the globe the central role of the media in elections is a very recent development. Because of this peculiar position, the media in these countries—more so the broadcast media—struggle to find suitable strategies for election coverage. We have made studies of three elections in Sri Lanka—the 2004 parliamentary elections and the 2005 and 2010 presidential elections—and have reached the following conclusions:

- Although elections are held both regularly and frequently, the Sri Lankan media institutions appear unaware of their role in providing fair and unbiased information to support informed decision making by voters.
- Apart from commercial and propagandist intentions, the media do not appear to be interested in professional and systematic election coverage.
- Most importantly, the media—very noticeably the state media—demonstrated a callous disregard for the country's election laws and the guidelines issued by the Election Commissioner.
- The journalists in both sectors did not demonstrate the will, the skills or the commitment to provide fair and balanced election coverage.
- While they may be constrained by institutional decisions and internal policies, it is regrettable that media practitioners completely overlook social responsibility in content generation.
- Journalists brought into their election coverage the inherent bad practices associated with their regular/daily coverage.

Broadcasting Training and Practice

As stated earlier, broadcast media started in Sri Lanka with state radio. Pioneer broadcasters were not afforded training. At the time, the art of radio was just emerging and, as in other spheres, broadcasters looked to the west for inspiration. The presentation styles, content, formats, program ideas and even the names of programmes were copied directly from England and America. However, after independence, there was no means or perhaps no need to follow new trends in broadcasting forms, which elsewhere were becoming progressively more listener-centred. The radio station was a part of government and was run like a government department. There was no vision or guidance to formulate broadcast policy. With time, skills may have developed but 'broadcast media theories' failed to penetrate the hierarchal façade. Seniors trained their juniors on the job and the cycle continued. Private sector radio began mostly with recruits from the state radio.

When TV came, it was case of déjà vu. Those who had influence managed to crossover to TV from radio. It was the radio traditions that they took with them. Formats, programme types and even the programme names and artistes were from radio. There was a slight difference, though. Unlike in the early days of radio, a fair number of TV staff were sent abroad for training. But they were mostly engineering and technical staff. Thus, there was hardly any change in 'thinking'.

Coupled with this lack of exposure to media theories and concepts was the fact that many recruits to the sector, including the occasional university graduates, failed to acquaint themselves with modern knowledge, including democratic rights and principles. This deficiency was quite visible in the practice of both state and private sector radio and TV broadcasting in the country, though there are a few individual exceptions.

In our wish to reflect upon the practice of journalism in a detached and objective manner, we have selected the following yardsticks not only because we feel they are best suited for a general analysis of this nature, but also mainly because they conform to our belief (and that of many others like us) that 'the primary purpose of journalism is to provide citizens with the information they need to be free and self-governing'.[56]

Journalism's first obligation is to the truth and its first loyalty is to citizens.

Even if broadcasters in Sri Lanka are aware of these two guiding principles, in practice, adherence to these principles is very poorly displayed. As far as state radio and TV is concerned, it is the propaganda of the government in power. Broadcasters attached to government radio and TV often present facts selectively. The performance of the private sector broadcasters is no better. As one of the present authors observed in a previous study of media behaviour, 'the Sri Lankan media, irrespective of their ownership differences, are fond of creating propaganda for the parties or groups they prefer'.[57] Thus, the state broadcast media consider the citizens mere recipients of their propaganda, while private sector broadcasters see them as consumers of their 'products'. Both have their loyalties elsewhere.

Its essence is a discipline of verification.

Verification separates journalism from entertainment, propaganda, fiction and art. It is verification that helps towards the journalistic process of seeking the truth in the news that reporters cover. In the mêlée to be the 'first with the news' in the highly commercialised environment of the broadcast media of the country, this has become an unnecessary inconvenience to practitioners. The myth or the misconception of some broadcast journalists is that citizens want infotainment; short stories with no substance. Lack of proper media education, laziness, bias and haughtiness may be other contributory factors. Thus, a diversity of views, balance and different angles to the story are lost and the listener/viewer is presented with a lopsided view.

Its practitioners must maintain an independence from those they cover. It must serve as an independent monitor of power.

The nature of the profession is such that journalists are in constant contact with those who wield power: the politicians, corporate bosses, the elite, celebrities, academics, civil society leaders and the like. Being a comparatively new media in the country, first the radio and then the TV broadcasters began to realise the extent of that power.

This position, born out of unwritten mutual understanding, is valued by both parties and hence is a position that they mutually strive to maintain. Thus, independence is not sought and their first loyalty gradually goes to those they cover. This situation results in several malpractices and the truth suffers. Dissent is resented, and only the voice or the point of view of those they cover is presented. Broadcasters no longer become free and independent themselves and thus are unable to provide citizens with the information they need to be free and self-governing. They lose the capacity to serve as watchdogs over those whose power and position most affects citizens.

It must provide a forum for public criticism and compromise.

The news media are considered to be 'the common carriers of public discussion' and the media also 'should strive to fairly represent the varied viewpoints and interests in society, and to place them in context rather than highlight only the conflicting fringes of debate'. It can be argued that attempts are being made (especially after the proliferation of private radio and TV channels in the country) to offer the public a forum for debate and discussion.

Apart from the Mahaweli Community Radio programme types, the first *genuine* attempt at this was made by the short-lived NES of the SLBC. There were other efforts by both state and private broadcasts to 'give voice to the people'. But as studies show, these were mostly programmes with hidden agendas. For state broadcasters, they were a means to win back dissatisfied audiences, while for the private broadcast media they constituted smart new packaging to attract more audiences. This may have two possible causes. Either the broadcasters are not aware of these theoretical approaches and as such not competent to handle the task. Or else, they are not allowed to go further than the distance they have been allowed to travel. Our personal experiences compel us to suspect both.

It must strive to make the significant interesting and relevant.

Journalism is storytelling with a purpose and is a balancing act. It must balance what readers know they want with what they cannot anticipate but need. In short, it must strive to make the significant interesting and relevant. The effectiveness of a piece of journalism is measured by how much it engages its audience and enlightens it. The broadcast media in Sri Lanka from the early days have taken it upon themselves to 'educate' or teach their audiences. It is with good intentions they do it and at times their programmes are helpful and meaningful. However, it is they who make the decisions. They seldom bother to find out the concerns and the needs of the audiences. This leads them to preach and teach. This may be the outcome of the top-down approach that exists. The deficits in applying this principle of journalism do not seem to spring from compulsion but are rather due to ignorance and the attitudes which journalists adopt, which could be rectified by a proper media education and training.

It must keep the news comprehensive and proportional.

This is the mostly disregarded, ignored or forgotten principle of journalism by Sri Lankan broadcasters. This again is mostly the result of ignorance, insensitivity and unfamiliarity rather than lack of independence and freedom on the part of the broadcasters. Time, resources, space, skills are other contributory factors. Kovach and Rosenstiel argue that 'journalism is our modern cartography. It creates a map for citizens to navigate society. ... [A]s with any map, journalism's value depends on its completeness and proportionality'.[58] Thinking of journalism as map-making helps us see that proportion and comprehensiveness are keys to accuracy; and that news should be accurate, fair, balanced, citizen-focused and credible.

Its practitioners must be allowed to exercise their personal conscience.

This principle is about the moral and ethical obligations of the journalist. Every journalist must have a personal sense of ethics and responsibility.

When we look at the broadcast media—both state and private—it is no secret that there is hardly any commitment or compulsion amongst practitioners to fulfil these obligations. Of course, one cannot expect broadcasters to be self-sacrificing when no such tradition or culture exists in other professions in the country. On the other hand, if you are a professional you have to conform to professional standards. It is with pride we note that there were and there are broadcasters who are prepared to sacrifice their lives even in the exercise of their personal conscience. But these types are extremely rare and almost non-existent in the state sector. Very few refuse to take the easier route. That explains why the majority opt for self-censorship. An equal number is prepared to toe the line or even go beyond that. Neutrals usually keep mum. Thus, we have a very obedient, compliant set of broadcasters in the country.

Observations and Suggestions

We have made some observations and comments in the relevant sections. We now put forward certain recommendations which cover a broad set of issues rather than particular concerns. We believe that laws that seek to regulate are not necessary (except to regulate the allocation of broadcast spectrum as it is a scarce resource) to promote a free, independent and pluralistic media regime. Self-regulation is adequate. It is the absence of laws that denotes a free and independent environment. Many western countries do not have such laws. Furthermore, in some Asian countries, though the constitutions of the country guarantee certain rights, the rulers still manage to 'choke the press', indicating there are other dimensions to the issue. However, we begin with a law that is indispensible.

Right to Information

This piece of legislation seems to have met with *balagiridosha* (always tomorrow, not today). *Sri Lanka Brief* reported on 4 July 2011 that the previous week the President had 'categorically told newspaper editors that a law to protect the people's right to information was unnecessary'.[59] This follows the move by the government to defeat a draft bill to this effect presented to parliament by the deputy leader of the opposition UNP, Karu Jayasuriya MP. Earlier, they tried to dissuade Jayasuriya by promising to present a bill of their own. However, the president's statement, we feel, should not deter efforts to get this very important law passed. It only signals that more concerted efforts are necessary. In this regard, we urge that the path taken by the citizens' movements in neighbouring India be followed, however, hard and arduous it is.

Broadcast Media

Although the broadcast media in Sri Lanka has a long history, the way it has evolved over the years has paved the way for a government stranglehold over both radio and TV. This is because the legal framework currently in existence with regard to radio and television broadcasting gives the government in power a considerable influence and even control over broadcasting carried out not only by the state sector, but also by the private radio or television stations.

As has been suggested by many individuals and by national and international organisations, such as Article XIX, we propose the establishment of an independent broadcasting authority completely free of direct and indirect government (and corporate) control to ensure meaningful independence for state sector broadcast organisations so that they can fulfil their public service functions freely. Such a move would pave the way to resolve concerns linked with ownership and licensing.

The authority would also free the private broadcast media from the shackles of the corporate bosses and promote the healthy competition that could be expected to ensure better fare for the listeners and viewers. We know that when jargon like 'authority', 'board', 'commission', is employed, it sends jitters through the spines of free media advocates. But as Reinhard Keune, President of the Intergovernmental Council of UNESCO's International Programme for the Development of Communication rightly points out, such a body 'needs to comprise all important groups of society, government and opposition, employers and trade unions, men and women, representatives of different religious denominations, ethnic groups and minorities of all kinds. Only such a wide and heterogeneous composition can guarantee the necessary distance from government and help effectively in insuring the whole board against becoming a prey to one or two dominant groups'.[60]

A free and independent licensing body will also help the proliferation of a community broadcast media movement. Notwithstanding certain limitations, there are many advantages of a genuine community broadcast media for South Asian countries such as Sri Lanka. If we are to consider media as cartographers, we are confident that the community broadcast media would be able to cover many more locations in geographical, topical, demographical/communal, political, social, economic, cultural, linguistic and gender maps.

We believe that the 'Tholangamuwa Charter'[61] is a good starting point for media reforms, as it is a cooperative effort of Sri Lankan media who have an adequate knowledge of the ground situation. The Charter stands 'for a democratic and pluralist media culture and social and professional rights for media and journalism in Sri Lanka'. It believes that 'fair, balanced and independent media is essential to good governance' and it asserts that 'a professional media with a responsibility to the public interest, independent of government or partisan influence and interference, is a vital part of the series of checks and balances central to democracy'.

We particularly endorse the following:

1.5 Journalism and media policy in Sri Lanka must be guided by the following principles:

- That media, whatever the mode of dissemination, are independent, tolerant and reflect diversity of opinion enabling full democratic exchange within and amongst all communities, whether based on geography, ethnic origins, religious belief or language.
- That laws defend and protect the citizens' rights to freedom of information and the right to know.
- That there is respect for decent working and professional conditions, through legally enforceable employment rights and appropriate regulations that guarantee editorial independence and recognition of the profession of journalism.

2.4 Responsibility for ethical conduct in journalism rests with media professionals who should be responsible for drawing up codes of ethical conduct and who should establish credible and accountable systems of self-regulation.

2.5 There should be no legislation beyond the general law that interferes in matters that are the responsibility of working journalists: namely, the gathering, preparation, selection and transmission of information. Freedom of expression, press freedom and freedom of association should be guaranteed in law in accordance with international standards.

2.6 In addition, media policy should encourage the adoption of internal editorial statutes and other provisions safeguarding the independence of journalists in all Sri Lankan media.

3.6 Public service values in the media should be respected in all state-owned media. Urgent reform of the state media sector is needed with the following objectives:

- To remove all forms of direct political control over the public service media.

- To create a framework for the administration of public service media, in line with international standards, through ethical, accountable and financially transparent structures.

- To support editorial self-regulation by journalists and media professionals that will promote editorial independence and high standards of accuracy, reliability and quality in information services.

4.2 There should be openness and transparency in the business and social affairs of all media enterprises including full public disclosure of political affiliations and ownership information.

4.3 Representatives of the media and the workforce should agree an action plan to promote the economic and social development of Sri Lankan media, including the provincial media, and improvements in working conditions through collective agreements.

Broadcast reforms are not the responsibility or liability of a single party or section. It is a combined and collaborative effort of all the stake holders, needing judgment, patience, sensitivity, tact and thoughtfulness and above all time. Conflicts of interest are bound to arise and those should be resolved carefully without deviating from the purpose. Although Sri Lanka is credited with a western type representative democracy, where people elect their representatives and have regular elections, the system is flawed. Thus, western models of agitation—lobbying, protests, demonstrations and even recourse to the law—may not achieve the same results. From a pragmatic point of view, different strategies and approaches have to be mapped and adopted. This conclusion may seem highly contentious to an outsider but it is the lesson we have to learn from the democracy that has been practised in the country for so many years. It is a tough task but the only way to achieve results is through awareness and education, including media education.

Notes

1. Frohardt and Temin (2007).
2. Metzl (1997).
3. Nissan (1994).
4. Personal reflections by Tilak Jayaratne.
5. Personal reflections by Tilak Jayaratne (p. 4).
6. [1996] 1 Sri LR 157.
7. Personal reflections by Tilak Jayaratne.
8. Supreme Court Determination 1/97–15/97.
9. Mendel (2001).
10. Judicial interventions attempting to restore freedom of expression and media freedoms are discussed in Chapter 8 by Kishali Pinto-Jayawardena and Gehan Gunatilleke.
11. President Chandrika Kumaratunga over state radio and TV, 3 January 2000, as reported on the website http://www.sangam.org/NEWSEXTRA/CBKonTVJan00.htm.
12. Colombo Declaration on Media Freedom and Social Responsibility, 1998. Sections 9 and 10
13. http://www.undemocracy.com/generalassembly_57/meeting_15
14. Weerakoon was a senior civil servant who held many high-ranking posts and served six Prime Ministers and three Presidents of Sri Lanka.
15. Weerakoon (2004).
16. *Ibid.*
17. *Ibid.*
18. Free Media Movement (2008).
19. Official web-site of Mahinda Rajapaksa (2004).
20. http://www.asiantribune.com/news/2005/07/28/presidential-race-begins-mahinda-Rajapaksa-people%E2%80% 99s-alliance-candidate (accessed in August 2014).
21. http://infolanka.asia/opinion/sri-lanka/mahindarajapaksa-the-statesman (accessed in August 2014). Reproducing an article by Nihal P. Jayathunga appearing in 'The Island'.
22. Kusal Perera, in his blog '*My Thoughts*', posted on 22 July 2005. This article remained unpublished.
23. Freedom House, Countries at the Crossroads (2010).
24. Report on the findings of the investigation with respect to the effective implementation of certain human rights conventions in Sri Lanka (2009)—Commission of the European Communities. Brussels, 19 October 2009, pp. 26 and 75.
25. UNHCR Eligibility Guidelines for Assessing the International Protection Needs of Asylum-Seekers from Sri Lanka, United Nations High Commissioner for Refugees (UNHCR), 5 July 2010.
26. Free Speech in Peril. Press Freedom in South Asia 2010–2011. Ninth Annual IFJ Press Freedom Report for South Asia 2010–2011, May 2011, http://asiapacific.ifj.org/assets/docs/043/219/7bb382b-82afadb.pdf (accessed in August 2014); see also IFJ Situation Report 2012 Sri Lanka :Media Freedom a Neglected Dimension of Post-War Politics, http://asiapacific.ifj.org/assets/docs/080/019/c8ddf50-b0e8d13.pdf (accessed in August 2014).
27. Used here and elsewhere in the paper to denote the so-called 'intermediary institutions' such as professional associations, religious groups, labour unions, citizen advocacy

organisations that give voice to various sectors of society and are supposed to enrich public participation in democracies.

28. Fernando (1997).
29. *Ibid.*
30. Perera (1997).
31. Begoyan (2007).
32. McChesney (2008).
33. This section on Ownership Structures was updated by Sarath Kellapotha and David Page in late 2013 for the publication of the book.
34. Accessed on 29 June 2011.
35. Melody (1978).
36. Goodman and Goodman (2004, 2005).
37. *Ibid.*
38. A Study of Media in Sri Lanka (2005) A Report by the Centre for Policy Alternatives (CPA) and International Media Support (IMA) Copenhagen K, Denmark.
39. Freedom House (2011a).
40. Gnana Moonesinghe, freelance writer and author, has worked with SIDA and Marga. The quotation is from her article Small Country Diplomacy, in ground views, 23 March 2011, http://groundviews.org/2011/03/23/small-country-diplomacy/.
41. Democracy, Democratization and the Challenges of Sustaining and Promoting Democratic Governance, Paper Presented by Dr Ronald Meinardus at the Democratic Pacific Assembly (DPA) Taipei, Taiwan, 12–25 August 2004, http://www.fnf.org.ph/liberallibrary/democracy-democratization.htm.
42. Sumathy and Thiruvarangan (2011).
43. *Ground Views*, 24 January 2011.
44. *Sunday Leader*, 11 January 2009.
45. Sri Lanka Country Reports on Human Rights Practices (2007) Released by the Bureau of Democracy, Human Rights, and Labor, United States Department of State, 11 March 2008.
46. Article XIX—'Access to the Airwaves' Section 5 (2002).
47. See interview with Prof. Wimal Dissanayake, 10 March 2011.
48. Fernando (2010).
49. *Ibid.*
50. Fernando (2010).
51. *Ibid.*
52. *Ibid.*
53. Article XIX Report (1997).
54. International Federation of Journalists' (IFJ), Ninth Annual Press Freedom Report for South Asia 2010–2011.
55. [1996] 1 SLR 157.
56. Kovach and Rosenstiel (2001).
57. Jayaratne (2005).
58. Kovach and Rosenstiel (2001).
59. http://www.srilankabrief.org/2011/07/law-to-protect-right-to-information-is.html#more (accessed on 16 July 2011).
60. Keune (2010).
61. See http://www.unesco.org/new/fileadmin/MULTIMEDIA/HQ/CI/2.%20Tholangamuwa%20Declaration.pdf (accessed in August 2014).

7

New Media, Old Mindsets

*Nalaka Gunawardene**

Introduction

> The communications revolution … carries with it a promise that is, in the
> same instant, both exciting and frightening. Which of these alternative
> 'futures' we realise will depend on how responsibly the human race is
> able to face its obligations to its fellows.

Sir Arthur C. Clarke (1917–2008), who was Sri Lanka's most prominent
foreign resident for half a century, offered this caution in an essay written
on the eve of the new millennium.[1]

Clarke was well aware of the wider societal, cultural and political
implications of new information and communications technologies
(ICTs). Having first proposed (in 1945) the concept of geosynchronous
communications satellites for worldwide telecommunications and
broadcasting, he then chronicled and critiqued the gradual rise of
today's information society during the second half of the 20th century.
His perspectives are relevant as Sri Lanka grapples with policy, legal and
regulatory challenges arising from the rapidly evolving new media—
especially mobile telephony (introduced in 1989) and the Internet (1995).

This is not the first time that Lankan society has confronted a new and
transformative communications technology. The most notable recent

---

* This essay was originally written in late 2012, but was updated with the latest
telecommunications and social media-related statistics in October 2013. It is written strictly
in the author's personal capacity as a science writer, technology columnist and new media
practitioner. Its analysis and opinions do not in any manner reflect those of any companies
or organisations he is associated with. He can be reached at http://nalakagunawardene.com.

example is the introduction of television broadcasting (1979) and the dawn of trans-boundary satellite television over Asia during the 1990s. Many global level developments in ICT and mass media have historically taken time—years or decades—to arrive in Sri Lanka. In 2009, I compiled a rough chronology covering the key media and telecom developments during the past two centuries. This is given in the annexure.[2]

This chronology raises some interesting questions. For example, while fixed telephone and AM radio services were introduced in Sri Lanka within a few years of their market introduction elsewhere in the world, FM radio and TV broadcasting took several decades to arrive. How and why this happened is open to speculation by media scholars and cultural researchers.

But what is clear from this chronology is that the 'time lag' between global and local has been steadily shortening. Where mobile telephony and Internet are concerned, the global rollout has been especially rapid. With economic and information globalisation gathering pace, Sri Lanka has been receiving 'new waves' of media/telecom innovations faster since the mid-1980s. This is both good and bad news. On the positive side, a developing country like Sri Lanka—now a lower- middle-income country (with a per capita GDP of USD 2923 in 2012)—is no longer such a 'laggard' when adopting newer ICTs and media. However, it also means that Sri Lanka must confront the policy, law and regulatory challenges of ICTs without having the time or opportunity to study how other comparable economies and societies respond to them. The scope for experimentation and innovation still exists. So does the room to make policy blunders or wrong technology choices with costly results.

Internet and Mobile Telephones in Sri Lanka: A Brief History

The privately owned Oriental Telephone Company introduced telephony in Ceylon in 1881, but the government took over the service in 1896. The Department of Posts and Telecommunications operated and self-regulated the state telecommunications monopoly for the next eight decades.

Reforms started when the postal and telecom functions were separated in 1980, and gathered momentum in 1991 when the department was turned into a government-owned corporation called Sri Lanka Telecom. The office of the Director General of Telecommunications was set up as the regulatory body (renamed in 1996 as Telecommunication Regulatory Commission of Sri Lanka, or TRCSL). Allowing local and foreign private companies to enter the telecom market led to a rapid modernisation of services, accompanied by a phenomenal expansion of service both in quantity and quality.

It was this deregulation of the telecommunications sector that paved the way for the introduction of mobile phones and commercial Internet services. Sri Lanka was the first country in South Asia to introduce mobile telephony as well as commercial Internet services. Although some limited Internet and email facilities were available in academic institutions from 1984, commercial Internet services became available to private subscribers only in April 1995, when Lanka Internet Services Limited started operations.

Internet and Telephone Access: Current Trends

The growth in telephones and expansion of Internet use are closely linked. Connecting to the Internet, done through dial-up facilities with limited bandwidth and speeds for much of the first decade, is now possible via broadband of varying speeds and quality.

According to the TRCSL, the official collector and collator of telecom industry data, the total number of fixed phones went up from 121,388 subscribers in 1990 to 2,795,688 by June 2013. The number of mobile subscriptions, which was just 2,644 in 1992 (3 years after mobile services were introduced), reached 19,533,274 by June 2013.

This means that there are now more phone connections—when fixed and mobile are taken together—than people in Sri Lanka (which counted a total of 20,277,597 people in March 2012 during the latest census of population). The island's telephone density exceeded 100 in 2010, and had reached 116.9 phone connections per 100 persons by 2012.[3]

The number of Internet connections and users is a bit harder to ascertain precisely because it is a constantly growing market. TRCSL reported, by the end of June 2013, a total of 437,725 fixed Internet subscriptions and 1,037,901 mobile Internet subscriptions (the latter used

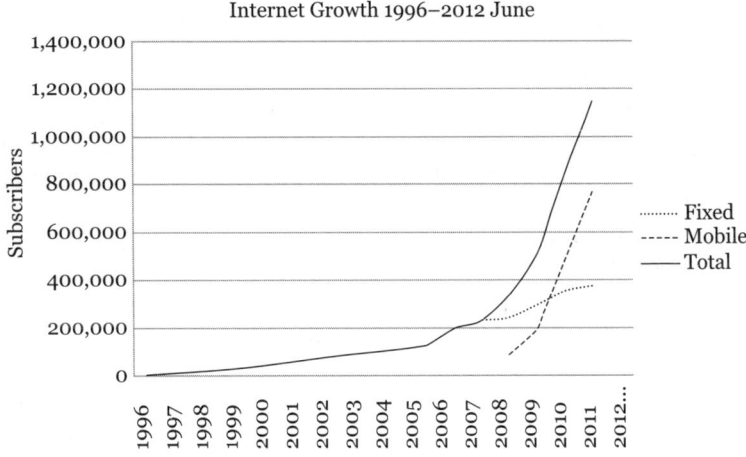

Internet Growth 1996–2012 June

Growth in Officially Known Internet Subscriptions in Sri Lanka

Source: TRCSL website. http://www.trc.gov.lk/information/statistics.html

via mobile devices such as laptops, smart phones, iPads, etc.).[4] Together, this came to just under 1.5 million Internet subscriptions.

Determining the number of Internet users is open to interpretation: many fixed subscriptions—in offices, homes and cybercafés—have multiple users while mobile Internet accounts are less likely to be shared. If we assume an average 3 users per subscription, whether fixed or mobile, the number of Internet users could be in the range of 4.5 million (or 22 per cent of the population).

The International Telecommunications Union (ITU), the UN agency that tracks information society indicators and issues worldwide, estimated 18.3 per cent of Sri Lanka's total population used the Internet by the end of 2012.[5]

Other analysts cite different figures. The latest number given by the Internet World Stats website for Sri Lanka is 3,222,200 Internet users by June 2012, which lists ITU as its source. A less reliable figure used by some data trackers is the number of Facebook users in a country. Internet World Stats cited this number for Sri Lanka as 1,515,720 by December 2012.[6]

These raw numbers represent only part of a much larger and dynamic picture. The telecom services market, user types and profiles as well as socio-cultural and economic impacts of Internet use have all evolved during 18 years of commercial Internet connectivity. While the constraints of connectivity and affordability have eased off in recent years, and Internet is no longer an urban or elite monopoly, there still exist some urban–rural disparities, as well as limitations in local language (Sinhala and Tamil) fonts and applications.

According to LIRNEasia, an Asian regional ICT think tank anchored in Colombo, Sri Lanka's recent increase in broadband use is primarily due to the high rate of adoption of third generation (3G) mobile technologies such as HSPA and HSPA+ dongles and associated SIM cards.

'This trend is typical of Sri Lanka and other South Asian countries which do not have access to widespread copper last mile connectivity, and therefore are reliant on wireless networks to increase access, be it simple voice or broadband. Several factors have contributed to Sri Lanka's success in connecting its citizenry to the internet via mobile broadband', says a LIRNEasia study titled *Broadband in Sri Lanka: Glass Half Full or Half Empty?* (2011).[7]

The study, the most recent assessment of broadband Internet in Sri Lanka available in the public domain, added: 'However, having reached this stage, Sri Lanka needs to overcome several challenges if it is continue on its early success and make broadband a truly mass-market product instead of the niche popularity it still enjoys.'

'High quality broadband is still a major problem in Sri Lanka', says Helani Galpaya, Chief Operating Officer of LIRNEasia and principal author of the study. 'A key challenge is that of bringing a product of adequate quality to consumers. Budget broadband/budget telecom models mean low cost and therefore low prices. But they also mean low quality.'

Part of the reason is advertising which promises broadband speeds that are theoretically possible, but not in reality. But a bigger issue is in the infrastructure, especially bottlenecks in international connectivity due to high prices.

Lankan Media Online

The mainstream print and broadcast media in Sri Lanka started engaging the Internet as an additional publishing medium from the early days. In September 1995, the state-owned Associated Newspapers of Ceylon Limited (Lake House) was the first to introduce web editions of their flagship daily and Sunday newspapers.[8] Wijeya Newspapers Limited followed with web editions of their English newspapers in April 1996, and was also the first to produce a web edition of a Sinhala newspaper one year later.[9]

Radio and TV broadcasters were slower to get online, partly due to the serious limitations of bandwidth during the early, dial-up years. As bandwidth improved and more people connected to the web, this situation changed gradually. Today, most stations have their own websites for audience engagement and many offer live audio or video streaming. This has enabled the large number of overseas Lankans (estimated to be at least 1.5 million) to maintain stronger cultural links with their home country. In fact, the growing significance of diaspora economics has inspired a few online media offerings particularly tailored for that audience.

The past few years have seen the emergence of entirely web-based news services that have no direct print or broadcast counterpart. Some, like Lanka Business Online, make a clear distinction between news and commentary.[10] Others have blurred this separation, and have become platforms for expressing dissent and discussing contentious topics in a manner no longer possible in any print or broadcast media in Sri Lanka. A few of these, such as Colombo Telegraph, are operated by Lankan journalists living in self-imposed exile.[11]

The dominant business model of Lankan news and current affairs websites, irrespective of their content, is based on advertising revenue. Attempts to introduce subscription-based services, supported by pay walls, have so far failed.

Legal and Regulatory Framework

Sri Lanka has a multitude of laws and regulations related to telecommunications, information technology, digital intellectual property and mass media. These have evolved over time and lack coherence to address media and technology convergence.

Sri Lanka's Constitution, under Article 14 (1)(a), guarantees the right to freedom of speech, expression and publishing. But this right is subject to various restrictions including public morality and national security. In addition, there is no specific provision that recognises access to the Internet as a fundamental right, or guarantees online freedom of expression.

The Supreme Court has recognised in past judgements the 'indispensability' of freedom of expression to the 'operation of a democratic system' and the importance of wide dissemination from 'diverse and antagonistic sources'. However, the court has not yet had the opportunity to consider the applicability of existing freedom of expression guarantees to the Internet.

Despite many years of advocacy and several false starts, there is no Right to Information (RTI) law. It seems unlikely that any will be introduced soon. The secretary to the Ministry of Mass Media and Information publicly declared in July 2012 that the government will not be introducing the RTI legislation 'because it would compromise the country's national security'. This statement was condemned by journalists' associations and media freedom groups.[12]

Thus, the Internet users in Sri Lanka operate within a restrictive framework. Some restrictions arise from specific laws and regulations while others stem from seemingly arbitrary decisions made by the executive branch of government. These curb the basic freedoms as well as retard the evolution of a pluralistic information society.

Sri Lanka's IT laws per se are focused more on combating computer crimes and intellectual property rights violations. Information contained within computers is admissible in civil and criminal judicial proceedings. Some laws make it an offence to report on or publish official secrets, information about parliament that may undermine its work, malicious content and any content that could be considered an incitement to violence or cause disharmony.[13]

As in most such situations, much depends on definitions and interpretations. 'As a result, online content that can be deemed an incitement to ethnic and religious violence, or poses a threat to national security, runs the risk of restriction and/or criminalization', notes the *Freedom On the Net 2012* Sri Lanka Report, compiled by Freedom House in the USA.[14]

The watchdog group has assessed Sri Lanka's Freedom on the Net Status as 'Partly Free'. The report says that while the country has not blocked any web 2.0 applications (such as YouTube, Twitter, Facebook), there have been attempts to regulate content critical of the government. It also cites some arrests of bloggers and other ICT users.[15]

The report further notes:

> Despite recognition of the Internet's value and impact on economic growth, the military campaign against the Liberation Tigers of Tamil Eelam (LTTE, or Tamil Tigers)—which ended in May 2009—hindered adequate investment in the ICT sector and expansion of the internet across the country. Furthermore, the empowering impact of the Internet in Sri Lanka has been undermined by the government's efforts to arbitrarily block, filter, and regulate online content that provides dissenting views and reportage on sensitive political issues.

Another global advocacy group, Reporters Without Borders (RSF), has also expressed similar concerns about Sri Lanka's restrictions on Internet freedoms. They noted in March 2012: '2011 was marked by violence, threats and propaganda aimed at journalists and media defenders seen as government critics. Resorting to censorship and disinformation, authorities have blocked access to websites considered unfavourable to the government, claiming legal justifications.'[16]

Digital Content Filtering, Blocking and Web Censorship

Broader Context, Local and Global

Curbs on digital content generation and dissemination need to be seen in the broader context of freedom of expression in Sri Lanka. Threats to Internet freedoms take place in a society that has experienced many acts of harassment, intimidation and violence against independent media, intellectuals and other dissenting voices.

The Centre for Policy Alternatives (CPA), an independent think tank based in Colombo, argues that the murder and abduction of journalists, censorship, intimidation and tolerance of a culture of impunity, continue to directly impact on media freedom and also represent a threat to the freedom of expression online.[17]

These trends in Sri Lanka should also be viewed against the backdrop of global developments. Around the world, governments of all political persuasion are finding it a challenge to balance freedom of expression online with protecting societies from probable and perceived threats.

The use of blocking and filtering technologies without the provision of a legitimate reason is also a violation of Article 19 of the International Covenant on Civil and Political Rights. This was highlighted by Frank La Rue, the United Nations Special Rapporteur on Freedom of Opinion and Expression, in his path-breaking Report to the General Assembly in 2011 on the right to freedom of opinion and expression exercised through the Internet. As he noted, if 'the specific conditions that justify blocking are not established in law, or are provided by law but in an overly broad and vague manner' content risks 'being blocked arbitrarily and excessively'.[18]

He further noted that, even where justification is provided, 'blocking measures constitute an unnecessary or disproportionate means to achieve the purported aim, as they are often not sufficiently targeted'.[19]

Sri Lanka's Growing Web Restrictions

Restrictions on mobile phone use and web content access commenced during the final phase of Sri Lanka's civil war, originally citing reasons of national security. Content producers and users, though not fully convinced, lived with an unknown and undisclosed level of such content control. Worryingly, some of these still continue, over four years after the war ended.

The first documented blocking of access to a website within Sri Lanka occurred in June 2007, when TamilNet, a news website, was blocked by all major Internet Service Providers (ISPs) on the orders of the government.[20] Since then, there have been many instances where access to websites has been blocked by local ISPs apparently acting under governmental instruction.

Beginning 2007, CPA, RSF and other watchdog groups have chronicled many instances of arbitrary blocks on websites being accessed from within Sri Lanka. These monitors have discerned that many such blocked websites report or discuss human rights violations, corruption in state agencies and other governance-related issues. Although there is no formal censorship in Sri Lanka, they claim that this is tantamount to unofficial and ad hoc censorship of web-based content that is critical of policies and actions of the government and ruling coalition.

In 2008, the President ordered the telecom regulator, TRCSL, to block access to adult entertainment websites, and in June 2009 in response to an application put forward by the Inspector General of Police, the Colombo Magistrates Court ordered TRCSL to block access to several pornographic websites.

These measures were introduced and promoted in the name of safeguarding children from exposure to pornography. While that objective was certainly laudable, concerns were raised on the methodology and efficacy of such content filtering—and whether the coverage could easily extend to filtering political dissent as well.

As Sanjana Hattotuwa, editor of the online journal *Groundviews*, wrote in March 2009: 'I certainly agree with the fact that we need to protect our children from pornography, but it does not really tell us how it is going to do this. It is an incredible technical challenge to do this. It could also be pornography today but the same technology can be used to create what is called the Great Firewall of China.'[21]

Absence of Enabling Laws

The executive has engaged in such activity without specific legal provisions to do so. CPA says that 'almost all attempts by the government to block web content have been extra-legal, circumventing the minimum requirement of judicial intervention and based on arbitrary orders issued by government authorities'.

In the most comprehensive report on Internet freedom in Sri Lanka, released in November 2011, CPA noted:

> The directives of national security and arbitrary judgements by government officials on what constitutes the national interest and public morality have been manipulated to stifle dissent and block web content that is considered offensive. The situation is compounded by a legislative framework with broad provisions that allow for civil liberties to be trumped in favour of national security provisions and regulatory standards that demand neither an independent regulatory commission nor transparent administrative practices and adequate protection of data and privacy.[22]

The report offers a sound analysis of the prevailing national security laws and general laws that are cited and used for restricting freedom of expression and dissent, both in established print and broadcast media and in new media.

Registration of News Websites

In November 2011, the Department of Information issued a press release requiring all 'websites carrying any content relating to Sri Lanka or the people of Sri Lanka ... uploaded from Sri Lanka or elsewhere' to 'register' for 'accreditation'. The registration authority was the Ministry of Mass Media and Information.

The immediate reason for this was cited as some individuals (including politicians and entertainment industry figures) being maligned and defamed by certain websites.

This was once again a public demonstration of the befuddled mindset of officials handling information- and communication-related policy and regulation. For example, did this cover only web-based news services, or even private individuals engaged in blogging about local issues of their interest? Even if a mandatory registration was introduced, how could it be enforced in practice especially for content generators based outside Sri Lanka?

The vague and overbroad nature of this measure was pointed out by civil society groups and activists. In a statement issued shortly afterwards, they noted:

Concerns about defamation and the right to privacy notwithstanding, the government has failed to provide a legitimate rationale for the registration process consistent with the values of a democratic society or international standards on permissible legal restrictions on the freedom of expression. While under the law of Sri Lanka there is ample scope for legal redress in case of defamation or an invasion of privacy, the measures the Ministry has taken so far are also inappropriate and disproportionate to its stated aim of ensuring online media ethics.[23]

In December 2011, the operator of a website who had challenged the blocking of his site through a fundamental rights petition in the Supreme Court agreed to a settlement with TRCSL and other state institutions. In return for lifting the block on that website, the settlement required compliance with several terms and conditions that included the immediate registration with the TRCSL and the Ministry of Mass Media and Information.[24]

By late 2012, some news and current websites had registered with the Department of Information, while others had declined to do so.

Intermediary Liability

Freedom House in its latest country report says that any legal requirement for ISPs to comply with requests from TRCSL to block websites is based either on political pressure, or specific licence conditions. The latter is difficult to confirm, it says, given the lack of transparency in telecom licensing.[25]

This report has also brought into sharp focus the role and liabilities of communication service providers or intermediaries: the ISPs and mobile telecom operators who have always conformed to the government's arbitrary requests for blocking and filtering of web content, shutting down SMS services[26], and during the last stages the war, cutting off entire telephony services to hundreds of thousands of people in some areas.[27]

Apart from the pornographic websites specifically mentioned in judicially sanctioned blocking, there is no other list of websites whose access is blocked by ISPs in Sri Lanka. Even in a competitive telecom market, ISPs and mobile operators disregard individual consumers' rights to the service they pay for. This aspect has received little attention from consumer activists who are mostly preoccupied with adulterated goods or financial scams.

Post-connectivity Challenges of the Information Society

Sri Lanka is slowly but surely evolving into an information society. The policy dilemmas and contentious debates outlined above are only part of that process.

Connectivity and basic access issues dominated the public discourse during the first dozen years after the introduction of Internet services. As these ease off across socio-economic groups and the urban–rural disparities gradually recede, we now face a more complex and nuanced set of challenges.

These post-connectivity challenges include the following:

Improving IT Literacy and Web Literacy

Measuring computer literacy is not based on precise methodologies and much depends on definitions. Different figures have been cited on how many among Sri Lanka's 20.2 million people have computer literacy.

The Household Income and Expenditure Survey 2009/2010 carried out by the Department of Census and Statistics revealed that 12.5 per cent of Lankan homes have a computer.[28] The same department, in a separate survey on computer awareness and literacy in 2009, assessed that 20.3 per cent of people (aged 5–69) had the ability to use a computer on their own.[29]

There are geographical, income and educational factors that determine this skill which also has many levels. With over a million smart phones in use, all of which are Internet-enabled, web browsing skills are increasingly common. But no systematic survey of such skills has been done, so insights remain anecdotal.

The government is implementing, through its ICT agency (ICTA), a five-pronged strategy that encompasses 'building information infrastructure and an enabling environment; developing ICT human resources; modernising government and delivering citizen services; leveraging ICT for economic and social development and promoting Sri Lanka as an ICT destination'.[30] ICTA also says that the government aims to provide 'diverse and unrestricted sources of information and means of communication' to all citizens.[31]

Technical Standardisation

Both Sinhala and Tamil languages have their own distinctive alphabets whose fonts are very different from roman characters. Developing and disseminating content in local languages across different platforms and applications remains a challenge.

While Tamil content developers have been able to benefit from substantial technical innovation in southern India, their Sinhala language counterparts have had to localise entirely on their own. Because the state did not facilitate a standardisation process during the first decade, multiple Sinhala font systems developed in isolation have been marketed and adopted with no inter-operability.

The belated adoption of a Unicode Sinhala font, the international standard for non-Latin scripts, has helped. But retrospective conversion of existing, mutually exclusive applications remains a formidable challenge.[32]

Privacy and Data Protection

While the right to privacy is protected in specific instances in Sri Lanka's legal system, there is no right to privacy under the Constitution of Sri Lanka. There are also no laws to protect general information gathering and handling, whether electronic or otherwise.

There are also concerns about the extent to which the data and privacy of customers are protected by mobile phone companies and ISPs: The circumstances under which telecom companies can intercept customers' private communications are not clearly spelt out.

Another issue is telecom companies allowing certain political parties and candidates access to mobile phone numbers for sending out campaign text messages en masse. This occurred during the 2010 presidential and parliamentary elections, with operators claiming that the directive came from the TRCSL.

Cyber Surveillance

The Telecommunications Act No. 25 of 1991 (amended in 1996) and the Computer Crimes Act No. 24 of 2007 provide limited protection to Internet users from surveillance and other forms of intercepting communications. However, both the Acts contain provisions that allow law enforcement agencies and relevant ministers to intercept communications without any apparent restrictions or guidelines on their exercise of this power.

Activists and international watchdog groups have expressed concern about possible Chinese technical assistance for web surveillance in Sri Lanka, especially in view of the increasing involvement of Chinese telecom giants, ZTE and Huawei.

Sanjana Hattotuwa wrote in February 2012:

> The communications network infrastructure in question connects us all, irrespective of any kind of party political, ethnic or other identity and geo-physical based divide. It is the DNA of our country, and determines how we engage with domestic challenges as well as global opportunities. It may be only of concern to a few today, but the implications of possible network intrusions, that can go undetected for years and the full scope of which may never be accurately known, affects us all.[33]

Nexus Between Established Media and New Media

Although most print and broadcast media organisations have developed their own websites, and some have also started reaching out on key social media platforms (notably Facebook and Twitter), they have yet to tap the potential of the new media in the full process of information gathering, processing and dissemination.

These limitations stem not so much from a lack of technology or human resources as from a fundamental lack of understanding of the nature and dynamics of the new media. Many media groups—at both management and editorial levels—are stuck in an analogue-era mindset that views new media merely as another 'extension' of their print or broadcast output. They have yet to re-orient themselves to the new realities that have also flummoxed their counterparts in many other parts of the world.

Some acknowledgement of this new media reality was made on the 10th anniversary of the Colombo Declaration on Media Freedom and Social Responsibility in 2008.[34] Whereas the original declaration in 1998 contained no mention of the Internet and web-based media, its reiteration a decade later included the following new sections:

> 10.3 Internet: One of the most significant developments in the last ten years has been the growth of the Internet, which has resulted in the democratization of media and encouraged the emergence of non-professional journalists in the form of bloggers etc. We acknowledge the contribution of bloggers towards the promotion of free speech and democratic media. We also recognize that bloggers are as susceptible to controls by the state and misuse of their work as traditional print and broadcast media. We take this opportunity to commit our support to responsible bloggers and other new media practitioners, and hope to work with them in solidarity towards establishing a convergent media which is strong and independent.

> 10.4 We specifically call on the government to recognize the internet as an important space for deliberative democracy, and extend to it all such policies as would enhance the space of free speech on the Internet, and to avoid all policies of banning, blocking, or censoring websites without reasonable grounds. There is now a convergence between the traditional print media and the internet, with a number of newspapers being accessed through the internet, and we would strongly urge that all the privileges and protections sought in this declaration be extended to the web editions of newspapers.[35]

Despite this, the established media organisations still adopt an ambivalent attitude towards entirely web-based news services and citizen journalists and other web-based new media initiatives promoting the public interest.

With or without the mainstream media's endorsement, citizen journalism thrives in Sri Lanka. Close to 1,500 local bloggers are syndicated by one popular aggregator named Kottu.[36] Other services, and a loose alliance of Sinhala language bloggers, have seen numbers and activity grow.

Without the trappings and inertia of the more institutionalised media, citizen journalists are quick to adopt new communication tools and platforms. This is especially evident at times of national distress. For example, some of the first images of the devastating flooding that engulfed nearly half of Sri Lanka in January and February 2011 were posted on Facebook. Tweets with vital updates came from grassroots organisations like Sarvodaya, who leveraged Twitter and Facebook to raise awareness and solicit flood relief donations. The mainstream media, in contrast, struggled to cover this diverse and rapidly evolving story and failed to use new digital tools to communicate information in a user-friendly manner.

As I noted in a commentary at the time:

> Our cyber-illiterate editors, who have repeatedly shown their inability to lead, must either follow their digitally-savvy younger colleagues—or just get out of the way! To survive the new media tsunami, media managers must come to terms with the new reality of collaborative, user-involved news generation and consumption. Business as usual is not an option.[37]

Public Perceptions of Internet-based New Media

Even after 18 years of commercial Internet services, Lankan society at large is still uneasy with the medium despite its increasing economic, educational and other applications. This, in turn, has policy and regulatory implications.

During the early years of connectivity, from 1995 to 2000, the Internet was widely seen as an elite medium used by the English-educated, urban middle class—and even in this socio-economic group, it was the younger persons typically under 40 years who engaged it. During the past decade, as detailed earlier, access has improved substantially. There has also been a steady growth in locally relevant content in local languages.

Despite this, the Lankan public has a love–hate relationship with the web. This probably stems from several factors, inter alia:

- a general suspicion of all new forms of communication;
- a deeper distrust of technology and forces of globalisation;
- deliberate vilification of the web by certain activist and political groups and
- distorted coverage of new media issues in the mainstream media that magnifies negative social and cultural effects.

As new media becomes more relevant to the island's culture, economics and politics, these and other factors need to be studied in depth.

Unfortunately, such intellectual leadership has not been evident among a majority of Lankan academics and researchers: many have avoided probing the confluence of ICT, society and culture while some have even helped reinforce popular myths and misconceptions about new media. I had a glimpse of this during 'National Media Summit 2012' organised by the island's oldest mass communication department at the University of Kelaniya in May 2012.[38]

This event was attended by academics and researchers on journalism and mass communication from several universities. From my own engagement as a speaker, it was evident that they are either oblivious—or indifferent—to the various policy dilemmas, regulatory challenges and balancing of interests that new media proliferation requires of a society and its government. Instead, their attention seemed exclusively focused on the adverse social and cultural impacts of Internet and mobile phones and the need to 'control' these media supposedly in the public interest.

Part of the confusion—alarmingly common among many policy makers, opinion leaders in Sri Lanka—arises from a fundamental lack of understanding of the nuances and dynamics of the new media landscape.

For example, many conflate private communications online (e.g., *via* Facebook) with the open, public-access online content (e.g., blogs) and public access content that performs public media functions (e.g., news websites). Similarly, the critical need for common technical standards (to ensure inter-operability) is misinterpreted by some as a justification for government-imposed content monitoring and censorship.

A convergent medium like the Internet poses challenges to policy makers and law makers. Trends like Citizen Journalism, user-generated content, privacy and RTI are often discussed in abstract terms in Lankan mainstream media or academic circles without focusing on the options and choices policy makers have when confronted with rapidly evolving new media.

Sri Lanka's 'Other Digital Divide'

Sri Lanka's last two decades of experience in adopting the newer technologies of mobile phones and Internet provide useful insights into how a highly conservative—and according to some, semi-feudal—Lankan society is struggling to come to terms with modernity as a whole.

Researchers and promoters of new media have found considerable scepticism, cynicism and resistance from old mindsets that still dominate many areas of political, cultural and academic activity.

Such negativity is not necessarily confined to 'Digital Immigrants', or those who started using digital technologies in their adult lives. Deep-rooted suspicions about these ICTs are also found among some 'Digital Natives', young persons raised in an increasingly digital world.[39]

I call this the 'Other Digital Divide'—a successor to the better known divide created by disparities in access and/or affordability. As basic connectivity issues have eased out, a new gulf has appeared inside the minds of some users of devices and services. This might be the result of insularity and insecurity nurtured by conspiracy theorists and sections of the media.

This essay was not intended to investigate such contentious—albeit intriguing—issues of cultural identity and technological anthropology raised by this collision of different worlds and worldviews. We must acknowledge, however, the larger picture against which policy makers, law reformers, researchers and activists have to promote the public interest in a country where that very notion has been under siege for at least three decades.

The Bigger Picture: Social and Political Context

Many negative reactions to new media proliferation in Sri Lanka stem from a deeper disorientation in society. To repeat a key question I have raised in recent public forums: Is there sufficient public and societal demand for ideals such as freedom of expression, Rule of Law, RTI, transparency (in state and corporate sectors) and overall good governance? If not, why?

In my view, many researchers, journalists and activists have not paid sufficient attention to this 'demand' side of the freedom equation even as they work hard—and under many pressures—to increase the 'supply' of basic freedoms and other public goods. Public demand cannot simply be presumed.

For sure, we cannot apply a strict economic analysis of supply and demand here. At the same time, why do the products of investigative journalism, civil society advocacy and human rights advocacy seem to elicit such limited enthusiasm from a largely apathetic Lankan public today?

One explanation is that three decades of civil war have left behind some unhealthy legacies where public information and communication are concerned. For much of that time, successive governments asked the Lankan public to tolerate the curtailment of civil liberties under Emergency Regulations. In the interests of counterterrorism, we lived with various restrictions on information flows.

Over time, these restrictions created an entire generation that does not know what normalcy is. The public administration system became used to excessive controls and the withholding of public information citing the catch-all cause of national security. Law enforcement agencies were granted wide powers with limited judicial oversight. The mass media became increasingly uncritical and submissive so as to prove their 'patriotic' credentials. Professional bodies also muted their criticism of authority.

The Lankan war officially ended in May 2009, but more than three years later, the dominant mentality of a National Security State still casts a long and formidable shadow over much of the island's polity, society and processes of governance. The prevailing logic seems to be that anyone who questions authority—let alone confronts it—is an 'enemy of the state'.

Does this, in turn, inhibit the 'demand' side for basic freedoms and other public goods in a country that is still struggling to achieve a really post-conflict society? Uncomfortable though this question is, it needs to be confronted.

Conclusion: A Choice of Futures

We can react to the emerging information society in two different ways.

One choice is to view the status quo with alarm and despair over the gradual loss of privacy, death of anonymity and the feared rise of Big Brother like scenarios.

The other choice is to be cautiously optimistic and hopeful. The always-connected, networked modern world presents many new opportunities to promote the public interest.

I far prefer the latter. Even when the current situation is not too promising, we can and must reflect on these issues in aspirational terms.

At the same time, let us not forget Marshall McLuhan's caution decades ago: 'The price of eternal vigilance is indifference.'

Annexure

Information and communications technologies in Sri Lanka: A brief chronology: 1832–2012

Mass Media Type or Communications Technology	Public/Commercial Introduction in the World	Sri Lanka's Commercial/ Public Adoption
Modern newspapers printed with movable type	France & The Netherlands, Early 17th century	*Colombo Journal*, 1832
Fixed telephone services	The Telephone Company, UK, 1879	Oriental Telephone Company, 1881
AM radio broadcasting	The Netherlands, 1919 USA & UK, 1922	Colombo Radio, December 1925
FM radio broadcasting	USA, 1937	SLBC's City FM, November 1989
Terrestrial television broadcasting	USA, 1929	ITN, April 1979
Mobile telephone services (commercially available)	NET, Japan, 1979	Celltel, 1989
Email only Internet (academics only)	MAILBOX, MIT, 1965 ARPANET, 1973	LEARN, 1990
Commercial Internet connectivity (dial-up)	Late 1980s	Lanka Internet Services, 1995
Broadband Internet connectivity	Cable modem service by Rogers Communications, Canada, 1996	Sri Lanka Telecom ADSL, 2002
3G mobile telephony	NTT DoCoMo, Japan, October 2001	Dialog Telekom, 2006

Principal Sources: Wikipedia entries for various ICTs, and *Handbook of the Media in Asia*, Shelton Gunaratne (ed.), SAGE, 2000.
Note that the dates used refer not to their invention, but the market introduction of a new communications technology or media.

Notes

1. Clarke (1999).
2. Originally included in keynote speech by Nalaka Gunawardene at the Sri Lanka launch of *Asia Media Report 2009* at Galle Face Hotel, Colombo, 4 August 2009.
3. Annual Report 2012, Central Bank of Sri Lanka, available at: http://www.cbsl.gov.lk/ pics_n_docs/10_pub/_docs/efr/annual_report/AR2012/English/7_Chapter_03.pdf (accessed on 25 October 2013).

4. Latest available industry data, TRCSL website, http://www.trc.gov.lk/information/statistics.html (accessed on 25 October 2013).

5. Measuring the Information Society 2013 Report, released by ITU in October 2013; http://www.itu.int/en/ITU-D/Statistics/Pages/publications/mis2013.aspx (accessed on 31 August 2012).

6. http://www.internetworldstats.com/asia.htm#lk (accessed on 31 August 2012) and http://www.internetworldstats.com/asia/lk.htm (accessed on 31 August 2012).

7. www.infodev.org/en/Publication.1113.html (accessed on 31 August 2012).

8. The first web edition of *Daily News* was published on 4 September 1995 and *The Sunday Observer* went online for the first time on 10 September 1995; http://www.academia.edu/4378630/Internet_in_Sri_Lanka_The_First_Five_Years_book_chapter_written_in_late_2000 (accessed on 31 August 2012).

9. *Lankadeepa*, www.lankadeepa.lk (accessed on 31 August 2012), which started its web edition on 15 April 1997.

10. http://www.lbo.lk/aboutus.php (accessed on 31 August 2012).

11. http://www.colombotelegraph.com (accessed on 31 August 2012).

12. http://www.sundaytimes.lk/120805/news/information-ministry-secs-comment-draws-fire-from-media-associations-8001.html (accessed on 31 August 2012).

13. Official Secrets Act No. 32 of 1955; Parliament (Powers and Privileges) (Amendment) of 1997; and Prevention of Terrorism (Temporary Provisions) Act No. 48 of 1979.

14. Freedom on the Net 2012 Report, Sri Lanka section, available at: http://www.freedomhouse.org/report/freedom-net/2012/sri-lanka#_ftn1 (accessed on 25 September 2012).

15. *Ibid.*

16. Reporters Without Borders (2012a).

17. Freedom of Expression on the Internet in Sri Lanka, Centre for Policy Alternatives, Colombo. November 2011. http://cpalanka.org/wp-content/uploads/2011/11/FOE-REPORT-NOV-2011-FINAL-CPA.pdf (accessed on 8 September 2012).

18. Report of the Special Rapporteur to the General Assembly on the right to freedom of opinion and expression exercised through the Internet, May 2011; http://www2.ohchr.org/english/bodies/hrcouncil/docs/17session/A.HRC.17.27_en.pdf (accessed on 8 September 2012).

19. *Ibid.*

20. Tamilnet blocked in Sri Lanka, BBC Sinhala.com; http://www.bbc.co.uk/sinhala/news/story/2007/06/070620_tamilnet.shtml (accessed on 8 September 2012).

21. http://ict4peace.wordpress.com/2009/03/14/revisiting-the-colombo-media-declaration-rough-transcript-of-presentation/ (accessed on 8 September 2012).

22. *Ibid.*, p. 17

23. Arbitrary blocking and registration of websites: the continuing violation of freedom of expression on the Internet. Civil society statement issued on 9 November 2011; http://www.sacw.net/article2383.html (accessed on 8 September 2012).

24. http://www.freedomhouse.org/report/freedom-net/2012/sri-lanka#_ftn20 (accessed on 8 September 2012).

25. *Ibid.*, p. 14.

26. http://lirneasia.net/2008/02/the-great-firewall-of-china-and-its-sri-lanka-equivalent/ (accessed on 31 August 2012).

27. Over 200,000 in Jaffna deprived of phone service now for two months. LIRNEasia, 30 October 2006; http://lirneasia.net/2006/10/over-200000-in-jaffna-deprived-of-phone-service-now-for-two-months/ (accessed on 31 August 2012).

28. http://www.statistics.gov.lk/HIES/HIES2009_10FinalReport.pdf (accessed on 31 August 2012).
29. http://www.statistics.gov.lk/Newsletters/Publication1%28Computer%20litalary%29. pdf (accessed on 31 August 2012).
30. ICT Agency website, http://www.icta.lk/en/programmes.html (accessed on 31 August 2012).
31. ICTA Nenasala website, http://www.nanasala.lk (accessed on 31 August 2012).
32. Guide to creating Sinhala and Tamil Unicode fonts, ICT Agency. November 2010; http://www.icta.lk/attachments/1090_Guide%20to%20creating%20Sinhala%20&%20 Tamil%20Unicode%20fonts.pdf (accessed on 31 August 2012).
33. Are Chinese Telecoms acting as the ears for the Sri Lankan government? Sanjana Hattotuwa, Groundviews.org, 16 February 2012; http://groundviews.org/2012/02/16/ are-chinese-telecoms-acting-as-the-ears-for-the-sri-lankan-government/ (accessed on 25 September 2012).
34. The original declaration, adopted in 1998 and signed by the Sri Lanka Working Journalists Association, Free Media Movement, Newspaper Society of Sri Lanka, Editors' Guild of Sri Lanka, is at: http://cpalanka.org/wp-content/uploads/2007/8/ Colombo_Declaration.pdf (accessed on 25 September 2012).
35. Full text at: http://ict4peace.wordpress.com/2009/03/18/full-text-colombo-declaration-on-media-freedom-and-social-responsibility-october-2008/ (accessed on 25 September 2012).
36. http://www.kottu.org/ (accessed on 25 September 2012).
37. Drowning in media indifference, by Nalaka Gunawardene, Himal Southasian, March 2011; http://www.himalmag.com/component/content/article/4293-drowning-in-media-indifference.html (accessed on 25 September 2012).
38. http://nalakagunawardene.com/2012/05/25/new-media-old-minds-a-bridge-too-far/ (accessed on 25 September 2012).
39. For a detailed exploration of these concepts in relation to new media and mainstream media in Sri Lanka, see 'Confessions of a Digital Immigrant', Groundviews.org, 21 November 2009; http://groundviews.org/2009/11/21/confessions-of-a-digital-immigrant/.

Part III

Legal and Institutional Reforms

8

One Step Forward, Many Steps Back: Media Law Reform Examined

Kishali Pinto-Jayawardena and Gehan Gunatilleke

Introduction

> Our liberty depends on the freedom of the press, and that cannot be limited without being lost.

> —*Thomas Jefferson (1743–1826)*

> [T]he press, once thought of as an antidote to established power, is more likely to reinforce it, because access to the press—that is the mass media—is distributed as unequally as are other forms of power. It is not, of course, that the less powerful never speak in the mass media or that their doings are never reported or never sympathetically. But the deck is stacked against them, because the press is itself a formidable power in our society, allied intimately (although not simply), with other formidable powers.

> —Lichtenberg, J. ed. (1990) *Democracy and the Mass Media.*
> Cambridge University Press (pp. 102–105).

The emergence, growth and (what appears to be now) the notable regression of media freedoms and media independence in Sri Lanka has had a chequered history. Given proud traditions of competent and skilled journalism in the early years following independence and much vaunted high literacy rates of the reading public, the flame of media independence in Sri Lanka should have burned brightly and strong. Yet, this flame has spluttered and flickered, gathering strength only rarely and weakening to a veritable pinpoint of wavering light during the past decade in particular. State violence generated as a result of conflict in the north and east due to the armed struggle carried on by the Liberation Tigers of Tamil Eelam until active fighting ended in May 2009, as well as the brief (in comparison) but equally violent insurrections in the south by predominantly Sinhalese youth militants in the 1970s and 1980s, have framed the theory and practice of media law and policy in Sri Lanka. Amidst deepening hostility between the state and the private media, journalists and editors have been threatened, intimidated and in some notable cases, have died in the pursuit of their profession and at the hands of state as well as non-state actors.

The very Constitution and subordinate laws have been used to compel media obedience to state agendas. Such extreme violence has been directed deliberately at the suppression of freedoms of expression, opinion and information within the confines of a relatively small media industry, as compared to its giant counterparts elsewhere in South Asia.

Familiar questions of media law reform and excessive government regulation inevitably dominate the discussion. In some respects, these law reform questions have resonance elsewhere in the world; in the United Kingdom for example, a 1992 lament that 'it is none the less regrettable that so much of (prevalent laws) should impinge on public interest reporting and so little of it work to eradicate discreditable press practices'[1] still remains true to a large extent today. Closer to home and despite laws governing the issue, neighbouring India still grapples with thorny questions of contempt being utilised as a weapon to restrain information regarding the due functioning of the judiciary. Right to information (RTI) activists and media personnel have been targeted and sometimes even killed in pursuit of their fight for a less corrupt society.

Ideally, Sri Lanka's post-war years should have heralded the opening up of a vibrant media culture with all its potential to aid reconciliation between communities. Instead, almost the converse has occurred; stifled and effectively 'chilled' by an over-mighty state and with traditional constitutional checks and balances against abuse of power negated to a large extent, Sri Lanka's media has struggled to retain its integrity and independence. Practices of self-censorship have become common, posing an even greater threat to the credibility of the media than overt government censorship. Strong tensions between state media and the private media have continued with the state media (broadcast as well as print) being wholly appropriated by the government of the day. Meanwhile, there has been increased soul searching within the media industry and the wider public space as to how independent the private media can really profess to be in the context of not only government but also corporate challenges to the independence of the editorial room.

This analysis of issues relevant to media policy and law reform in Sri Lanka is primarily focussed on the print media, and is conducted from three distinct perspectives: legal, institutional and educational. The objective is to examine the broad framework within which the Sri Lankan print media functions, in order to better understand where reform is most needed, and how such reform could be best achieved. We begin by discussing some of the salient features of the media industry in Sri Lanka, thereby broadly defining the media landscape in the country.

Next, the chapter deals with previous reform efforts by both state and civil society actors, again with the focus on print media, but incorporating electronic media reforms whenever appropriate as highlighting broader points of discussion. The intention of detailing such efforts is to contextualise the current status of the Sri Lankan media and define the approximate stages of its development. In Sri Lanka, the troubling development is that the media law reform process appears almost to have come to a standstill and the battle is now on to retain even the little freedoms that the media had won following long and crucial struggles in the past. Threats and intimidation of journalists, unresolved killings and disappearances continue to haunt the media, stifling robust reporting and 'chilling' free expression, paradoxically in the post-war years.

The analysis also attempts to interrogate sensitive questions of editorial independence from government and management, the nature of free media activism, interactions between the academic teaching of media studies and professional courses, the explosion of web based media, as well as the way forward in law and industry reforms.

The objective is to move the debate from an exclusive focus on the excesses of authoritarian governments (tempting as this may be in the current context), to a broader look at the very nature of the media industry itself, its successes and challenges. The objective is not to limit the discussion to matters of theory and analytical interest but to fuse the theoretical analysis with practical observations not only by media practitioners themselves but also by the public at large.

Where the way forward for Sri Lanka's media is concerned, the link between these reform efforts and the overall democratic structure of governance is unquestionable. There is an imperative need to restore rights of speech and expression along with a plethora of concomitant rights through a combination of committed media groups and civil society. However, it remains an overriding responsibility of the media itself to drive this process. In the alternative, there is little doubt that the Sri Lankan media, once hailed as among the best in South Asia, will be driven to the ground, an immediate victim of its own loss of public credibility.

An Overview of the Media Industry in Sri Lanka

The Nature of the Media Landscape

The media landscape in Sri Lanka is reasonably well developed, though perhaps less sophisticated in comparison with India. This landscape is founded upon a long and established culture of harnessing the media for social debate and commentary.

The current Sri Lankan media comprises a wide range of providers both in the print and electronic sectors and has thus evolved into a fairly diverse industry. Recent circulation figures of newsprint are quite impressive, with a circulation of 493,000 copies for daily newspapers, and 720,000 for Sunday newspapers. This circulation amounts to approximately 25 copies of dailies and 36 copies for Sunday papers per 1000 inhabitants.[2] Readership figures are in fact six times higher than circulation figures, at least for the main dailies,[3] which suggest that on average, six people read every newspaper purchased. Radio and television is also well distributed in Sri Lanka, though less so in rural areas.[4]

Based on such statistics, it appears that Sri Lanka possesses a society with abundant and diverse information and with advanced levels of literacy and reasonably sophisticated reading habits. No firm up to date figures are available in respect of the overall circulation in regard to the Sri Lankan print media.[5]

Generally, it is encouraging to note that the 2008–2009 global recession affected the South Asian media (including the Sri Lankan media) to a lesser extent than the Western media. A recent study by PricewaterhouseCoopers revealed that revenues from print advertising plunged 47 per cent in the hard-hit North American market, while the outlook for Europe, Middle East and Africa remained 'tepid'.[6] Yet Asia's newspaper advertising is expected to steadily rise 3.1 per cent annually throughout the period

2010–2014.[7] The adverse impact of the global recession on Sri Lanka has accordingly been less noticeable.

Despite these reasonable levels of sophistication and economic resilience, the notion of an 'independent media' in Sri Lanka requires further reflection.[8] A closer look at the media institutions from their inception reveals that there were 'ideological and material interests behind the operation of these bodies'.[9] Hence, Sri Lanka may still be a far distance away from establishing a truly 'independent' media. This question will be interrogated further during the course of this analysis.

Meanwhile, a growing phenomenon during the recent decade in particular has been the emergence of 'new media' and the proliferation of news websites that have flourished whereas freedoms of the media have drastically declined in respect of the mainstream. On the one hand, the 'website culture' has provided badly needed space for the circulation of news and opinion without repercussions for individual journalists or publishing houses. On the other hand, unrestrained by the law[10] or by effective self-regulation,[11] gossip and slander masquerade as 'news' on some of these websites.[12] In the context of the consistent suppressing of conventional news gathering by the intimidation, threatening and killing of journalists, these developments have been unfortunate but hardly surprising.

In this section, we discuss some of the broader developments that have taken place in the media industry in Sri Lanka with specific attention being paid to the print media. Two issues may be of particular importance: first, the diversification of the Sri Lankan media and second, the tension between the state and private media.

Diversification of the Sri Lankan Media

The Sri Lankan print media was initially very much the elite preserve of a few individuals who 'dominated both media and politics'.[13] The advent of a vibrant print media in Sri Lanka was largely due to private entrepreneurship. The Wijewardene dynasty could be linked to all three of the country's largest and most powerful media institutions, namely the Lake House, the Upali Group and Wijeya Newspapers.[14] Since the state monopolies on radio and television broadcasting were broken in 1984 and 1992, respectively,[15] private investments increased and added to the diversity of Sri Lankan electronic media channels. Additionally, the public—albeit mostly the English-speaking public—has had reasonable access to international services, such as BBC World and CNN, due to the recent emergence of satellite and cable providers. These developments have collectively established a highly diversified media in Sri Lanka and have placed a broad range of media content at the consumer's disposal.

Where language diversification is concerned, it has been suggested that the new generation of Sinhala newspapers marked two significant milestones in the Sri Lankan media. First, it 'identified the nation's rapid economic growth and the need for the Sinhalese to be in touch with the 'news' to keep abreast of these developments'.[16] Second, the emergence of the new Sinhala newspapers 'marked an ideological awakening of the Sinhalese that suggested the centrality of media as the fourth estate [sic]'.[17] These developments appeared to have amplified the role of the press as a 'fourth estate', thereby transforming the media from being a mere tool of politicians to an institution and powerbase in its own right.[18] The role played by the Sinhala 'alternative' press (exemplified by the *Ravaya* and *Yukthiya*), in the 1980s in combating the governments of the day under Presidents J.R. Jayawardene and Ranasinghe Premadasa, also emphasised the 'vernacular' media's coming into its own as a significant opinion maker capable of generating informed public debate and even bringing down governments.

Concurrently, the Tamil-speaking community also began to harness 'the new-found potential and mass penetration of the press to reach a wider audience'.[19] For decades, various revivalist groups and smaller socio-political actors controlled the Tamil press, though three national newspapers developed by professional newspaper producers eventually began to dominate the sector. These included the *Virakesari*, a journal launched by a group of Colombo-based Indian Tamil traders, the *Illakeswari*, a Jaffna-based newspaper that was particularly popular with the Tamil literati and the *Thinakaran*, which was a newspaper launched by D.R. Wijewardene himself as part of a rapidly advancing newspaper empire.[20] It has been suggested that 'while *Thinakaran* became one of the leading newspapers in the country in a very short time, the paper failed to develop its own personality, remaining conservative and predominantly anti-socialist under Wijewardene's shadow'.[21] In later years, the Tamil media too expanded, with papers such as the *Uthayan*, *Sudar Oli*, *Yal Thinakkural* and *Valampuri*, some of which were restricted in their circulation to the Northern peninsula and inevitably operated under heavy restrictions of the military during the long years of conflict. Journalists working at these newspapers remained singularly susceptible to intimidation and threats as would be discussed later on in this chapter.

The diversification of the media industry also extends to the nature of journalists employed in the field. Recent estimates indicate that approximately 4,000 journalists work in Sri Lanka's media sector. While around 2000 of them are employed full time by media organisations, the rest function as correspondents or freelancers.[22] Journalists working in the provinces in particular function mostly on a part-time basis.[23]

Thus, the Sri Lankan media remains a complex industry with numerous stakeholders holding multiple, and often divergent interests. These interests have framed industry responses to specific issues of media reform, including revision of the constitutional, legal and regulatory framework; improvement of professional standards amongst journalists; journalists' pay and working conditions; institutional and structural shortcomings within media institutions; safety of media personnel and problems faced by the media industry owing to external economic factors, such as the high cost of newsprint and limitations in advertising budgets.

Quite apart from the sheer weight of government intimidation, the sheer diversity of these interests may perhaps explain why past media reform efforts have been either ineffective or have lost momentum. In the recent decade, editors and publishers have banded together to advance collective positions on matters that are crucial to the Sri Lankan media but the road to collective action has been complex in the face of coercive divide and rule policies pursued by powerful governments. Effective trade unions safeguarding the interests of journalists and with lobbying power both at industry and at government levels have been largely absent. In their place are journalists' associations which were never very cohesive in their approaches and in any event, lost even whatever cohesiveness they possessed as a result of sustained and effective government attacks. Understanding these interests—the driving forces behind media stakeholders—is key to effective sustainable reform in future.

State versus Private Media

The state media in Sri Lanka is generally perceived as a tool of propaganda in the hands of the government. However, the manner in which private media players enforce their political/corporate agendas on their publishing houses has become a legitimate topic of discussion particularly during the recent decade. Moreover, the relationship between the state media and the private media has heavily impacted on the nature and direction of media reform. Undeniably, the existing power structure, in which the state possesses an almost indomitable advantage, is central to the process of designing and strategising future interventions for reform.

Elmqvist and Bastian (2006) observe that regardless of the political party in power at the time, '[a] significant section of media in Sri Lanka is controlled by the state, and there is a tendency by the regime in power to use state owned media for its own political ends'.[24] Yet this feature of 'interest groups influencing media content' is not restricted to state media. Both in terms of print and electronic media, it appears to be fairly obvious that both state and private media groups have certain interests as owners—be they economic, social or political interests.[25] These controlling interests, even in the private sector, tend to be sympathetic to different political groups or parties, thereby causing the politicisation of the private media as well.[26] This is a point of view that appears to find immediate resonance across the wide range of media practitioners, academics and civil society members interviewed for the purpose of this study[27] who lamented in general that the content of a newspaper appears to be determined by the management in an increasing number of cases and not by individual editors.[28]

Newspapers espousing political views may be a common phenomenon, as many news organisations in the developed world, and particularly in the United States, are fairly transparent about their political leanings. For example in the USA, Fox News Channel has unambiguously represented the views of American conservatism, mainly espoused by the Republican Party, while CNN has often revealed its liberal preferences, which is more in line with the ideology of the Democratic Party.

In Sri Lanka, even though newspaper groups in the country have always had powerful links to political parties either in the government or in the opposition, a relatively recent trend has been the covert control of private newspaper groups by investors with direct links (either personal or financial) to the government.[29] There has been no systematic review of the relationship between media ownership and political interest groups in Sri Lanka.

The status of the electronic media in this respect requires a brief mention at this point of time. Historically, Sri Lanka opted to follow the British model of retaining government control over broadcasting rights, which led to a virtual state monopoly on radio.[30] This was in complete contrast to countries such as the USA and Australia, which enjoyed free-market broadcasting. This state monopoly was eventually broken in the early 1990s when several privately owned radio stations began broadcasting. In 2005,

16 radio stations were in operation, of which private companies owned 12.[31] Furthermore, recent statistics reveal that these privately owned radio stations have succeeded in capturing a significant market share, thereby effectively breaking the government's hold over broadcasting.[32]

However, certain factors that ensure ultimate governmental control over the media still prevail today. First, Sri Lanka's private broadcasters have limited transmission capabilities, broadcasting only on the FM band, while the Sri Lanka Broadcasting Corporation (SLBC), by comparison, broadcasts island wide on medium wave, short wave and FM bands. Second, the licensing of radio frequencies remains under state control. Despite these restrictions, it has been observed that the SLBC is rapidly losing ground in metropolitan areas where its channels compete directly with private channels.[33]

Unlike radio, the first venture into television broadcasting was facilitated not by state authorities, but by private entrepreneurship.[34] The first television station, Independent Television Network (ITN) was initially launched with the support of the then ruling United National Party Government. However, ITN's 'independence' was short-lived, as within a few months, the J.R. Jayewardene government decided to appropriate the station, perhaps prompted by 'the well-known potency of the impact of television'[35] and perhaps also prompted by personal interactions with the owners of ITN. Two years later, the Sri Lankan Government established the Sri Lankan Rupavahini Corporation (SLRC), a second state-operated station, established under the Sri Lanka Rupavahini Corporation Act.[36] This well-resourced television station, popularly known as 'Rupavahini', was built with the assistance of the Japanese Government. The station soon became the dominant television station 'relegating ITN to the position of a minor station with limited reach'.[37] The state monopoly over television remained until 1992, when the government allowed private investors to enter the field under the control and supervision of the SLRC. By 1998, six private channels were in operation. These included Maharaja Television, later known as 'MTV', its Sinhala counterpart Sirasa, Swarnavahini and ETV, both owned by the EAP Edirisinghe Group of companies, TNL and Dynavision,[38] later rechristened 'Art TV'.

A recent survey carried out by a non-governmental organisation depicts the overall penetration of state and private television stations. The findings are summarised in Table 8.1.[39]

Based on these findings, it appears that similar to the power dynamics concerning radio broadcasting, the arrival of new commercial and better-financed television enterprises has not displaced the ultimate control of

Table 8.1

Audience reach of Sri Lanka's state and private television stations

Station	Percentage of Respondents Reached (%)
Rupavahini	97.0
ITN	92.2
Channel Eye	84.7
Swarnavahini	80.3
Sirasa	77.7
TNL	65.2
MTV and Shakthi	51.3
ETV	29.6
Dynavision	25.3

the state. State television still enjoys a privileged position, as the state remains in control of allocating television transmission frequencies and transmission licenses. Moreover, the state media holds a significant advantage over private media by retaining those frequencies with the widest coverage.[40]

Media Law Reform

Introductory Remarks

State policy relating to media law reform in Sri Lanka has often been dictated by expediency and the inevitable bargaining that goes on between the media industry bodies and a particular government in power. Hence, state policy has commonly lacked consistency and durability; manifestoes of political parties while competing for votes from the electorate, boast of grand promises of media liberalism that are seldom adhered to when in government. Significant obstacles to media professionalism in Sri Lanka, posed by archaic and outdated legal and regulatory fetters which adversely impact on the independence of the media,[41] have remained largely unaddressed. The need for a thorough reform process is clear regardless of whether the media institutions are state owned or privately owned.[42]

This section begins by discussing the current constitutional/legal framework applicable to the media in Sri Lanka. Next, constitutional reforms and certain past reform initiatives undertaken by numerous stakeholders are analysed. The section also highlights the various challenges faced by reformers, thereby uncovering some of the key barriers to improving the current system. It is noted at the outset that perhaps the most significant achievement to the credit of the Sri Lankan media during the last decade or so has been the abolition of criminal defamation provisions in the penal law as well as in the 1973 Press Council law. In contrast, media reform initiatives towards codifying the law on contempt of court and on enacting an RTI have been attended with less success.

In terms of the 1978 Constitution (hereafter the Constitution), Article 14(1)(a) declares that every citizen is entitled to 'the freedom of speech and expression including publication'. Certain restrictions are, however, imposed under Article 15(2) of the Constitution, which states: 'The exercise and operation of the fundamental right declared and recognised by Article 14(1)(a) shall be subject to such restrictions as may be prescribed by law in the interests of racial and religious harmony or in relation to parliamentary privilege, contempt of court, defamation or incitement to an offence'. Article 14(1)(a) is also subject to the general restrictions on fundamental rights imposed by Article 15(7) of the Constitution.[43] Moreover, the Sixth Amendment to the Constitution imposes a total ban on the advocacy of secession from the Sri Lankan state.[44]

The legal framework pertaining to media freedom is further defined by a series of legislative provisions. Section 120 of the Penal Code[45] provides for a broad definition of 'sedition' as an offence and is 'interpreted in a very loose manner for the purpose of suppressing the expression of views [against] those with governmental or bureaucratic power'.[46] The Public Performance Ordinance[47] regulates public performances and requires approval from a Public Performances Board under the Ministry of Defence prior to any public performances or public display.[48] The Official Secrets Act[49] restricts the communication of any official secret to the media and is believed to lead to self-censorship.[50] It has been observed that such restrictions could mean that matters that should be open to debate, such as corruption, may not always reach the public domain.[51] Furthermore, the Prevention of Terrorism Act[52] and Emergency Regulations under the Public Security Ordinance[53] provide for far-reaching restrictions to be imposed on the freedom of speech and expression. Even at times when one or the other of these two 'emergency' laws has not been in force, the threat of their implementation at virtually a moment's notice has been daunting.

In sum, the constitutional and legislative framework pertaining to media freedom in Sri Lanka operates on two levels. First, the constitutional framework provides for certain basic liberties with standard restrictions, barring perhaps the inappropriate inclusion of parliamentary privilege as a basis for limiting rights under Article 14(1)(a). Second, a deeper analysis of the surrounding legislative framework, which complements the Constitution, reveals that considerable powers have been afforded to the state to impose limitations on the freedom of speech and expression generally, and on media freedom specifically. Thus, the state has a variety of legal mechanisms at its disposal to curtail media freedom.

Moreover, this framework has been interpreted and made operational by the Sri Lankan state in an illiberal fashion. This approach has led to a distinct practice of restricting the media, which mere legislative reform may not necessarily remedy. The business of media reform does not merely concern the amendment of legal provisions. Rather, reform measures raise fundamental questions about the media culture in Sri Lanka. Thus, reform must involve an integrated and holistic process of reforming not only the legal framework, but also the institutional and educational frameworks pertaining to the media together with subversive state practices. The following sections, which discuss the success rate of past reform initiatives, clearly establish the veracity of this claim.

The R.K.W. Goonesekere Committee Report

The Report of the Committee to Advise on the Reform of Laws Affecting Media Freedom and Freedom of Expression, popularly known as 'the R.K.W. Goonesekere Committee Report', was in many ways the genesis of media reform initiatives in Sri Lanka. This comprehensive report examined virtually every aspect of the media and presented a host of recommendations, which established the foundation for reform efforts to follow. Notably, despite the lapse of 15 years, key recommendations presented in the report remain unimplemented today.

The mandate of the Committee was to:

> Study all existing legislation and regulations affecting media freedom, freedom of expression and the public's right to information, with a view to identifying the areas which need to be rescinded, amended or reformed in order to ensure media freedom, freedom of expression and the public's right to information; and to make recommendations as to the amendments

and/or repeal of existing legislation as well as new legislation required to strengthen media freedom in general and to ensure freedom of expression and the public's right to information.[54]

One of the primary conclusions reached by the Committee was on the inadequacy of the constitutional guarantees in respect of the freedom of speech and expression. The Committee recommended that the provisions of the Sri Lankan Constitution be rephrased to reflect the wording of Articles 18 and 19 of the International Covenant on Civil and Political Rights (ICCPR), and in particular, to include the freedom of information.[55] It was also recommended that the broad restrictions on free speech and expression under the Constitution be altered to ensure that the constitutional framework is consistent with Sri Lanka's international obligations. More specifically, the Committee insisted that all restrictions imposed on free speech and expression by the Constitution be 'necessary, in a democratic society'.[56]

The Committee was of the view that provisions of the Penal Code that dealt with criminal defamation should be repealed, as 'despite the several defences it allows, the possibility of such prosecution can discourage criticism of government ministers and policies or expression of political dissent'.[57] Moreover, the Committee strongly emphasised the need to exclude parliamentary privilege altogether as a ground for restricting media freedom, as 'neither Parliament nor its members require any protection from defamation over and above that enjoyed by ordinary citizens'.[58] The Committee was also one of the first to recommend a comprehensive law on contempt of court. It observed that in view of the 'perils faced by the media' when engaging in its duty to keep the public informed, there should be a Contempt of Court Act that clearly restricts the concept of contempt to 'the publication of [an] abusive or scurrilous comment about a judge as a judge, or of an imputation of impropriety or of corrupt bias, or attack on his integrity as a judge'.[59]

It was recommended that a Freedom of Information law be enacted, which makes a clear commitment to the general principle of open government. Moreover, the Committee stressed inter alia the importance of specifically listing the types of information that could be withheld; indicating the duration of secrecy; and providing for appeal to an independent authority when information is withheld.[60] As discussed below, the framework suggested by the Committee in 1996 remained the benchmark that most future advocates of the RTI aspired to reach through their respective proposals to the government.

Apart from these fundamental recommendations, the Committee also made several pertinent suggestions, many of which continue to be relevant today. The Committee observed that the absence of protection in respect of confidentiality of sources in Sri Lanka was a 'serious impediment to investigative journalism and the exposure of public scandals and wrongdoing'.[61] Hence, the Committee recommended that the right of journalists not to be compelled to disclose their sources of information should be guaranteed by law.[62] Moreover, the Committee proposed that certain crucial reforms be introduced to better ensure the independence of the media. Such proposals included the establishment of an independent broadcasting authority to regulate the granting of broadcasting licences, and a 'Media Council' to function as an independent body to inquire into complaints from members of the public against newspapers and radio and television stations.[63]

Reviewing Media Reform Since 1996

Since the R.K.W. Goonesekere Committee Report, a number of key initiatives have been placed on the reform agenda. In this section, the successes and failures of some of these initiatives are examined and assessed. These include attempts at constitutional reforms as well. Early advocates of media reform appear to have focused mainly on legal reform, seeking inter alia independent regulatory mechanisms, better laws on contempt of court and defamation and a specific Freedom of Information Act. A majority of these initiatives have yet to achieve their goals. Subsequently, the reform agenda of the media industry turned inwards, seeking improvements in media standards, professionalism and ethics. Such efforts met with far more success, as institutions such as the Press Complaints Commission were set up and a new code of conduct received widespread recognition. However, despite major advances on the institutional front, some operational problems such as the lack of resources continued to persist.

Finally, educational reforms were undertaken. Reformers seem to have realised—fairly late in the day—that the media faces a more fundamental challenge in terms of competences and skills, which has deeply affected the quality of the profession. Moreover, grand progress on the legal and institutional fronts may be pointless if the forerunners of the profession are incapable of making best use of the space provided to them. This educational aspect of the reform agenda is perhaps the least developed and requires a separate analysis altogether. The following review will only address the legal and institutional reforms introduced over the past two decades.

1 Constitutional Reforms

In one of the few major (but unsuccessful) attempts to reform Article 14(1)(a) and its relevant restrictions, the Constitution Bill of August 2000, which was never enacted into law,[64] stated as follows:

Article 16(1)

Every person is entitled to the freedom of speech and expression including publication and this right shall include the freedom to express opinions and to seek, receive and impart information and ideas either orally, in writing, in print, in the form of art or through any other medium.

This draft constitution formulation was far more satisfactory than Article 14(1)(a) of the current Constitution. Article 14(1)(a) is fundamentally defective in the manner in which it limits itself to 'citizens' as evidenced by the contrasting rulings given by the Supreme Court on the question as to whether a company and its shareholders can avail themselves of this right to come before the court on free speech issues.[65] In contrast, the international formulations, including the Article 19 of the ICCPR pointedly state the right as being available to 'everyone', which stipulation has been interpreted by regional tribunals to apply to legal as well as juristic persons.[66] In that sense, draft Article 16(1) of the Constitution Bill is preferable as far as Sri Lanka is concerned.

The proposed Article 16(1) has modeled itself closely on the wording of Article 19 of the ICCPR, excepting only the fact that it has preferred to omit the freedom to 'hold' opinions, as opposed to the freedom to 'express' opinions, in the definition of the right to free speech itself.

This omission deserves closer study both in terms of the international formulations as well as the applicable Sri Lankan jurisprudence. It is interesting in this context that framers of both Article 19 of the ICCPR and Article 10 of the European Convention on Human Rights (ECHR) had thought it fit to include the right to hold opinions within the substantive content of the right to free speech. This has been specifically interpreted to protect more than simply expression in the sense of public communication of ideas. On the contrary, it has been held applicable on the basis of the holding of individual opinion, such as when the state refuses to recruit applicants to civil servant posts because of their extremist political opinions.[67] In such instances, it has been decided that there is a violation of the right to expression and to hold opinion as well as the obvious right to non-discrimination.

The omission of the right to hold opinions in the substantive right of freedom of speech, in the currently applicable Article 14(1)(a) of Sri Lanka's Constitution, led to judicial creativity in linking the freedom to hold opinions with the RTI. Earlier pronouncements of the Supreme Court had held that an RTI existed within the right of free speech.

In *Fernando v. Sri Lanka Broadcasting Corporation*,[68] the court held that the right to hold opinions (as subsumed in the RTI) is a corollary of the freedom of thought guaranteed by Article 10 of the Sri Lankan Constitution and properly belonged there, rather than within the ambit of the right to freedom of speech in Article 14(1)(a).

This reasoning intertwining the right of information with the right of thought, conscience and religion was further developed in a determination of the Supreme Court in 1997[69] when a bill put forward by the government sought to set up a regulatory authority that was given the power to issue and refuse licences to private broadcasters. The bill was determined as unconstitutional on the basis that it held real potential for the arbitrary suppression of freedom of thought and speech. Not only did it seek to establish a body that was under executive fiat to an unacceptable degree, but also it gave an overly wide discretion with regard to decisions on licences.

Conceptually, the bringing in of the right to hold opinions/information under the right to freedom of thought may be innovative. However, explicitly engaging the right to freedom of information/freedom to hold and express opinions in the context of the right to freedom of speech (as indeed, has been the practice with regard to the ICCPR and the ECHR) will yield a richer interpretation of that right. Therefore, if at an appropriate time, national debate in Sri Lanka returns to a consideration of the appropriate constitutional framework in guaranteeing freedom of expression and information, such a constitutional provision should therefore comprise two parts: the first providing for the freedom to hold opinions and the second providing for the right to speech and information, with the restrictions necessarily applying to the second only.

It is also important that a constitutionally secured RTI should encompass the duty on the part of government authorities to provide information to an applicant. Such an inclusion should not prompt fears that confidential information or secrets impacting on national security could be entered through the back door. As evidenced in the jurisprudence of the European Court relating to Article 10 in the ECHR which is of persuasive value for Sri Lanka, the right to receive information has been specifically ruled to exclude the right to compel the state to reveal secret information.

> The right to receive information basically prohibits a Government from restricting a person from receiving information that others may wish or may be willing to impart to him. Article 10 does not, in circumstances such as those of the present case, confer on the individual a right of access to a register containing information on his personal position, not does it embody an obligation on the Government to impart such information to an individual.[70]

It is, however, different if disclosure is requested in a general sense and in the public interest. It is difficult to see how any objection could be sustained in that particular context.

In so far as restrictions on the substantive right are concerned, the range of restrictions provided for by Article 15(2) and (7) of the Constitution is clearly unacceptable in their width and substance. Article 16(2) of the Constitution Bill declared that:

> Any restrictions shall not be placed on the right declared and recognised by this Article other than such restrictions prescribed by law as are necessary in a democratic society in the interests of national security, public order, the protection of public health or morality, racial and religious harmony or in relation to parliamentary privilege, contempt of court, defamation or incitement of an offence or for the purpose of securing recognition and respect for the rights and freedoms of others.

The Sri Lankan courts, by careful balancing of the right and concomitant restrictions, have subsumed the European test of proportionality in relation to declaring any restrictions legitimate.[71] The explicit embodying of this proportionality test in Draft Article 16(2) is sensible. It contains the strict three-part test laid down by the European Court that the restrictions must be provided for by law; that the law must be accessible and 'formulated with sufficient precision to enable the citizen to regulate his conduct'; that it must then pursue one of the exclusive list of legitimate aims; and most importantly, must be found necessary to secure the legitimate aim. Restrictions must therefore serve a pressing social need, the reasons given to justify them must be relevant and sufficient and they must be proportionate to the legitimate aim pursued.

Yet, this draft Article's retaining of the long list of grounds on which freedom of speech could be restricted appears to be contrary to international law norms and is also cumbersome in its application. This objection relates particularly to the retention of parliamentary privilege as a ground for restricting free speech. Parliamentary privilege applies only to the privileges of parliamentarians within the precincts of the House, in relation to which they are accorded special powers. Such privileges should not be applied as a general ground of restriction with regard to freedom of speech of individuals. None of the international or regional covenants include parliamentary privilege as a ground for restricting freedom of speech. Its retention in Draft Article 16(1) and in any further revisiting of the formulation of restrictions on the constitutional right to freedom of expression is problematic.[72]

2 Media Declarations, the Media Charter and the National Media Policy

In or around 1998, several organisations directly linked to the media industry began to focus their attention among other issues on the legal and regulatory framework within which the media operates; on a code of ethics; and on the social responsibility of journalists. These objectives and priorities formed the basis of the Colombo Declaration on Media Freedom and Social Responsibility. The first of such declarations was adopted at a symposium on Media Freedom and Social Responsibility jointly organised by the Sri Lanka Working Journalists Association, the Free Media Movement (FMM), the Editors Guild, the Newspaper Association of Sri Lanka, the World Association of Newspapers and the Centre for Policy Alternatives (CPA).

The declaration covered a number of important issues requiring immediate attention, including constitutional and legislative provisions for media freedom; the impact of Emergency Regulations on media freedom; necessary reforms for a public broadcasting service and industry-specific issues, such as the high cost of newsprint. The declaration also included a section on the 'Responsibilities of Media Institutions and Personnel' and a Voluntary Code of Ethics, which stipulated guidelines for the conduct of journalists. Crucially, the declaration brought three of the main stakeholders in the media industry, namely, FMM, the Editors Guild and the Newspaper Society together to address some of the key issues faced by the Sri Lankan media.[73] These institutions have diverse and often contradictory agendas and interests.[74] FMM, for instance, is a network of journalists committed to campaigning on issues of media freedom and rights of journalists. The Editors Guild comprises editors of the leading mainstream newspapers. The Newspaper Society is an association of newspaper owners. Thus, as Elmqvist and Bastian (2006) observe, 'the conditions in the media and problems faced by the journalist profession have brought [these institutions] together'.[75]

Despite these positive attributes and certain attempts by the United National Front (UNF) Government of 2002 to give effect to some of the principles contained in the declaration,[76] there has been a distinct lack of initiative on the part of the state to respond to the main concerns of the industry.[77]

Subsequently, key media institutions came together in Tholangamuwa in September 2005 to adopt a Media Charter (also referred to as the 'Tholangamuwa Declaration'). The institutions involved were the Federation of Media Employees Trade Unions, the Sri Lanka Working Journalists Association, Sri Lanka Tamil Media Alliance, Sri Lanka Muslim Media Forum and FMM. The charter was ultimately finalised at a conference facilitated by CPA and the International Federation of Journalists and succeeded in gaining the support of 29 organisations representing regional journalists.[78] The charter declares:

> A professional media with a responsibility to the public interest, independent of government or partisan influence and interference, is a vital part of the series of checks and balances central to democracy. ... There needs to develop a strong and democratic public service culture within the news media so that it reflects the richness of society, serves the whole community independent of commercial, partisan or government interests and provides a plurality of voices from across the spectrum of society in Sri Lanka.[79]

The charter highlights certain 'Fundamental Principles', such as respect for truth, pluralism, diversity and human rights, and thereafter lists certain key commitments that ought to be undertaken in respect of editorial freedom, media pluralism, social dialogue and the rights of journalists. Interestingly, the charter also contains a 'Practical Program for Follow-up Actions', which lists certain key measures to be undertaken by representatives of the media during the 6 months to follow. These key measures included engaging in discussions with the Press Complaints Commission of Sri Lanka with the aim of strengthening the Sri Lankan code of ethics and building support and commitment among journalists for the code; launching a broad-based campaign to promote genuine public service media and seeking a charter on ethical election reporting with editors and publishers.[80] While the follow-up plan received some attention, the campaign—like many of its nature—lost momentum later.

In 2006, several media organisations including FMM, the Editors Guild and the Newspaper Society[81] issued the Weligama Declaration on the Role of Media for National Unity. This unique policy document adopted a self-critical approach to media reform, a feature that was perhaps less visible in other declarations. The declaration acknowledged that the media 'plays a significant role in nurturing social and cultural attitudes and political values ... and enabling public discourse'.[82] Hence, there was a consensus that the media played a crucial role in fostering national unity. It was further agreed that 'a self-critical approach by the media as well as constructive criticism of the media by the intellectual community will help the media profession and industry play a more positive role'.[83] One of the crucial recommendations made by the signatories to the declaration was that there should be 'regular, focused consultation among media practitioners on various important aspects of the national issues in order to build a common professional discourse'.[84] The responsibility to carry out such recommendations was cast not only on media professionals, but also on the industry ownership.

A stark contrast may be observed between policy initiatives put forward by the media and civil society actors and the policies formulated by the government. In 2007, the Ministry of Mass Media and Information released a National Media Policy. The policy is incredibly brief and for the most part consists of 'instructions to, or standards for, the media rather than policy statements as such to guide government action in this area'.[85] This is evident in the section on 'Media Freedom and Right to Access Information'.[86] While the drafting of a Freedom of Information law would be the natural course to take to ensure the right to access information, there was nothing in the policy to suggest that the government intended to pass such a law.[87] Moreover, the policy articulates a commitment to '[e]nsure that the media would not in any manner harm the Sri Lankan National identity and [to] prevent any person or community being subject to contempt, insult, disgrace or hate by the media'.[88] It has been observed that the focus once again is on the responsibility of the media, rather than on the government's role in balancing media freedom with the protection of other social interests.[89] Hence, the National Media Policy of 2007 appears to be merely another disingenuous governmental gesture, which ultimately does very little to address the major issues plaguing the Sri Lankan media.

However, some interesting ideas were presented in the policy in relation to 'Media Development'. The policy promises the creation of a new theoretical and institutional framework to introduce digital technology for electronic media; the establishment of a 'Media City' to present all media services from one focal point; the establishment of a 'Media Authority' to streamline media performance and ensure quality standards and the establishment of a 'Media Development Council' to 'recognise and identify the challenges, problems and new trends [in the media] and to formulate methodologies to cope with those [*sic*]'.[90] While such plans may look 'media friendly' at first blush, they remain largely underdeveloped, which ultimately justifies scepticism over their implementation.

In October 2008, a revised declaration on Media Freedom and Social Responsibility was issued by the Sri Lanka Working Journalists Association, FMM, the Newspaper Society and the Editors Guild. The 2008 declaration was adopted following an international symposium held that month to commemorate the 10th anniversary of the previous Colombo Declaration on Media Freedom and Social Responsibility.[91] The symposium held 10 interactive sessions on key issues faced by the Sri Lankan media, including press freedom, self-regulation, contempt of court, restrictions under emergency law and the RTI.

The signatories to the revised declaration noted that apart from certain limited positive developments, little had been done to implement the proposals previously set out in 1998.[92] Hence the signatories were compelled to reiterate the main concerns that the media industry had raised during the decade since the 1998 declaration. Such concerns would be discussed individually and in greater detail in the following sections.

3 Independent Broadcasting Authority

Media activists have continually lobbied for an independent broadcasting authority and have specifically called for the repeal of Section 44 of the Sri Lanka Broadcasting Authority Act,[93] which empowers the minister to issue licences for the establishment and maintenance of private broadcasting stations. Moreover, Section 44(4), which confers extensive powers on the minister to make regulations governing the functioning of such stations both in terms of their composition and the nature of programmes,[94] has also been severely criticised as facilitating excessive state control over the media. Hence, interest groups have actively pursued the establishment of an independent broadcasting authority to regulate the granting of licences to private broadcasters, thereby ensuring that the Sri Lankan media enjoys procedural as well as substantive freedom from state control.[95]

In April 1997, the Chandrika Kumaratunga government controversially tabled in Parliament a bill to establish a new broadcasting authority, which, instead of liberalising the media sector, would have considerably extended governmental control over the broadcasting media.[96] The bill stipulated that the proposed authority be directly appointed by the minister responsible for media, and further empowered the minister to issue guidelines in respect of the operation of stations via state-issued licences. Thus, the proposed authority would have fallen well short of being 'independent' of the government. The bill also contained absolutely no safeguards nor procedural mechanisms to ensure that non-partisan and competent people would be appointed to the authority. Moreover, it afforded the minister the power to dictate policy and programme content in a manner that would have 'rendered the electronic media completely vulnerable to the whims and fancies of politicians and any partisan interests they might represent'.[97]

The bill, described by the media advocacy body, the FMM as 'draconian',[98] was tabled in Parliament hastily and surreptitiously,[99] possibly to avoid review by the Supreme Court.[100] However, the FMM along with several other media organisations and private radio and television companies responded rapidly, filing between them a total of 15 petitions in the Supreme Court. The petitioners sought to challenge the constitutionality of the bill. The several petitions objected inter alia to the 'excessive political interference in the proposed authority [and] the severe controls which would be imposed on the freedom of operation of the industry'.[101]

The Supreme Court's ruling against the entire bill is a seminal judgment and a reflection of the independence of the judiciary during that period. Expounding on the proper role of the media in society and the regulatory role of the state, the court observed:

> Having regard to the limited availability of frequencies, and taking account of the fact that only a limited number of persons can be permitted to use the frequencies, it is essential that there should be a grip on the dynamic aspects of broadcasting to prevent monopolistic domination of the field either by the government or by a few, if the competing interests of the various sections of the public are to be adequately served. If the fundamental rights of freedom of thought and expression are to be fostered, there must be an adequate coverage of public issues and an ample play for the free and fair competition of opposing views.[102]

The court further held that while a certain margin of appreciation must be afforded to the state in matters of licensing, the principle of pluralism must be safeguarded to 'ensure that freedom of thought and expression may not only survive but thrive and flourish vigorously'.[103] The court also commented on the role of mass media in society, and accordingly observed that 'without free political discussion, no education, so essential for the proper functioning of the process of popular government is possible'.[104] Moreover, it was held that the role of the electronic media is not limited to the formation of political opinion, but also involves 'satisfying other public needs, including intellectual, spiritual and emotional needs, [which] ought not to be ignored or underrated'.[105] It has been observed that the court's implicit recognition of the representational role of the mass communication system is laudable, as the media had often been inadequately described as merely a provider of information to the public.[106] The court may therefore be commended for appreciating the media's role in presenting competing interests in a free and fair manner:

> In a situation in which at least two kinds of competing interests have reached the level of violent political conflict—i.e. the ethnic conflict and the class conflict reflected in the JVP insurgencies—can anyone doubt the importance of the media's role in this regard?[107]

Since the 1997 ruling, successive governments have stalled on the process of establishing an independent broadcasting authority. In 2012, however, the Ministry of Mass Media and Information launched a new project to establish a 'National Broadcasting Authority'.[108] The project is still at a nascent stage; hence, the actual level of independence afforded to the authority remains to be seen.

4 Contempt of Court

Owing to considerable ambiguity in the law as well as the occasional (judicial) misuse of the doctrine, several attempts have been made to reform the law on contempt of court.

Case law in relation to contempt of court has generally proceeded along conservative lines.[109] However, contempt was rarely used to stifle freedom of expression as a matter of common usage until the period of the Sarath Silva Court (1999–2009). This was best evidenced in 2003, where the then Chief Justice Sarath N. Silva clashed with members of the minor judiciary, who alleged that they had been unfairly dismissed from service without a proper hearing and on political grounds.[110] Subsequently, the heads of certain media institutions, that reported the dispute and published or broadcast interviews with the concerned judges, were sent letters by the Registrar of the Supreme Court warning them that contempt of court charges may be instituted against them.[111] Strong protests were issued by FMM in response to these letters. Moreover, the media institutions concerned immediately responded to the letters of the Registrar, arguing that mere reportage of facts concerning a dispute of public importance could not constitute contempt of court.[112]

Though no significant developments took place in respect of this issue thereafter, the incident reflected a wider judicial tendency of intimidating[113] the media and constraining the reporting of vital matters with regard to the independence of the judiciary.[114] The incident 'illustrated the imprecise nature of contempt of court in Sri Lanka'.[115] It seems that the current uncertainty is further exacerbated by conservative judicial attitudes towards the issue of contempt.[116] Such attitudes have undoubtedly enhanced the need for immediate legislative reform.[117]

Sri Lanka has witnessed several attempts to draft a comprehensive Contempt of Court Act. In April 2000, the Editors Guild submitted proposals to the Law Commission of Sri Lanka urging the Commission to undertake legal and regulatory reform including the drafting of a Contempt of Court Act. Moreover, an All-Party Select Committee was subsequently appointed to study the need to codify the law on contempt of court.[118] However, due to the sudden dissolution of Parliament for political exigencies by the then President Chandrika Kumaratunga in late 2003, the said Parliamentary Select Committee also lapsed thereafter. Despite considerable work done by the Committee during its sittings, its term was not renewed at the next parliamentary sessions.

In 2006, the Bar Association of Sri Lanka (BASL) requested a special Committee[119] to draft a Contempt of Court law. After several deliberations, a draft Contempt of Court law was finalised and approved by the Bar Council on 25 February 2006. It was thereafter forwarded to the government by the Bar Association. However, there has been no progress since then.

More recently, a draft Contempt of Court law prepared by the Law Commission of Sri Lanka received fairly wide circulation, indicating that some progress had been made in this regard. The Law Commission observed that '[t]oo harsh a law on contempt can act as a barrier to the development of a healthy and vibrant jurisprudence. Ideally a legal system should encourage both spontaneous and reflective criticism of judgments while preserving the sanctity and dignity of the courts and ensuring the smooth and effective administration of justice'.[120]

The BASL draft law reflected principles commonly accepted in the modern law of contempt.[121] These principles include the standard that 'contempt should only be found if the impugned act is of such a nature that it substantially interferes or tends substantially to interfere with the due course of justice in active proceedings'[122]:

> [A] fair and accurate report of legal proceedings held in public, published contemporaneously and in good faith should not amount to contempt of court as much as an abridged or condensed report of the same, published contemporaneously and in good faith, provided it gives a correct and just impression of the proceedings. The defence of innocent publication or distribution should also be made available.[123]

Accordingly, the draft law permits honest and accurate publications of reports[124] of court proceedings and stipulates that the 'publication of court proceedings that tend to interfere with the course of justice shall not amount to contempt where the publication was made in good faith and the publisher was not aware that such proceedings were pending in a court'.[125] Moreover, the law prevents the courts from prohibiting the publication of the report of any court proceeding except where there is a substantial risk or prejudice to the administration of justice.[126] Crucially, the draft law stipulates that fair and bona fide commentary on a judgment of a court would not amount to contempt.[127] Thus, the scope for fair and reasonable criticism of judicial decision making was accepted as fundamental to the proposed legislative framework.[128] The judicial thinking captured in the reflection below was the basic premise of this draft.

> This is the first case, so far as I know, where this court has been called on to consider an allegation of contempt against itself. It is a jurisdiction which undoubtedly belongs to us, but which we will most sparingly exercise, more particularly as we ourselves have an interest in the matter.
>
> Let me say at once that we will never use this jurisdiction as a means to uphold our own dignity. That must rest on surer foundations. Nor will we use it to suppress those who speak against us. We do not fear criticism, nor do we resent it. For there is something far more important at stake: it is no less than freedom of speech itself.[129]

Similar to the UK Contempt of Court Act of 1981, some of the other draft laws on contempt of court, such as the BASL draft, specifically afforded protection against disclosure of sources. This protection was, however, omitted in the Law Commission draft. The BASL draft recognised inter alia that no court may require a person to disclose a confidential source, nor would such a person refusing to divulge a source be guilty of contempt of court, nor may any adverse inferences be drawn against such a person. The only acceptable exception to this framework was when it could be established that such disclosure was necessary in a democratic society in the interests of justice, national security or for the prevention of disorder or crime.[130]

This clause was deemed necessary because the legal position in Sri Lanka on compulsion of journalists to disclose sources is highly ambiguous, as various judges have sought to interpret this area of law differently. For example, two criminal defamation indictments were concurrently filed against the Editors of the *Sunday Times* and the *Lakbima* Newspapers over the publication of an incorrect news item about Former President Chandrika Kumaratunga. In the *Sunday Times* case, the High Court Judge, Upali de Z. Gunawardene chose to draw an adverse inference against the Editor for refusing to disclose his source. By contrast, in the *Lakbima* case, High Court Judge Tilakawardane took a contrary view and held that a journalist should not be compelled to disclose his source of information. For separate reasons, the *Sunday Times* Editor was convicted and the *Lakbima* Editor acquitted. However, as discussed later in this chapter, with the repeal of criminal defamation laws in the country, the matter was never properly heard in appeal, leaving the issue of disclosure of sources largely unresolved.[131]

Despite the extensive efforts of reformers to introduce a Contempt of Court Act, the initiative continues to be filibustered at the legislative level. Section 105(3) of the Constitution empowers the Supreme Court and Court of Appeal to punish for contempt of itself and also empowers the Court of Appeal to punish for contempt of the High Courts, tribunals and other institutions. Article 136(1) of the Constitution confers power on the Supreme Court to make rules regulating generally the practice and procedure of the court. Article 136 (1)(b) decrees that the Supreme Court has power to make rules as to the proceedings in the Supreme Court and the Court of Appeal in the exercise of the several jurisdictions conferred on such courts by the Constitution (which would therefore include the power to charge for contempt of court as envisaged in Article 105(3) of the Constitution. Up to now, no such rules have been prescribed by the Supreme Court and the court's power remains unfettered in this regard. As illustrated in the preceding analysis, such power has also been used arbitrarily on occasion. Meanwhile, the statutory provision regulating the trial of offences for contempt of court is found in Chapter LXV of the Civil Procedure Code (CPC). Section 792 of the Code states that the procedure detailed in Chapter LXV is to be followed in 'all' courts (emphasis added).

The Law Commission has pertinently observed that, the Supreme Court 'appears to have followed a different procedure to that prescribed on subordinate courts'.[132] For example, a court is required under the CPC to issue summons on the alleged contemnor. However, the practice in the Supreme Court has instead been to issue a rule *nisi* on the alleged contemnor. The Law Commission rightly observes that this practice is without any statutory basis whatsoever.[133] As questions over the independence of the Supreme Court continue to be raised today, the space for reporting and commenting on judicial proceedings could significantly diminish. In this context, the need for immediate legislative reform[134] becomes even more acute.[135]

A further interesting question arises as to whether a constitutional amendment is required to stipulate rules of procedure and of substance in regard to contempt of court as applicable to the superior courts of record in Sri Lanka. It is an accepted premise that an ordinary statute cannot impose limitations on constitutional provisions that are widely phrased. Views may be advanced in support or in opposition to this argument. But there is considerable force in urging that, in the spirit of a constitutional philosophy which enhances the rights of individuals rather than restricts them, an ordinary law may suffice to prescribe the parameters within which the law of contempt could be exercised by all courts.[136]

5 Parliamentary Privilege

Recent reform in the area of parliamentary privilege has ensured that at least some space for reporting on parliamentary debates is afforded to journalists.

An important step towards liberalising this aspect of the law took place in September 1997, when on the initiative of then Minister of media, posts and telecommunication, Mangala Samaraweera, Parliament repealed the 1978 Amendment to the Parliament (Powers and Privileges) Act.[137] The 1978 Amendment had given Parliament concurrent power with the Supreme Court to punish offenders in respect of breaches of privilege specified in Part A of the Schedule of the Act. The Amendment had long served to restrain the media in reporting and commenting on the work of Parliament.[138] While not many media personnel were actually punished under these provisions, there were numerous attempts and threats made by Members of Parliament to prosecute-specific journalists or media personnel on issues of parliamentary privilege.[139] The Amendment of 1980,[140] which some have described as 'equally undesirable'[141] continues to be in operation. The said amendment penalises the wilful publishing of any report of any debate or proceeding in Parliament containing words or statements after the Speaker has ordered such words or statements to be expunged from the official report of the Hansard. Thus, the amendment significantly affects the right to free speech and expression including publication of the press, and appears to permit irresponsible Members of Parliament to evade accountability for statements made on the floor.[142]

In 2002, the then government promised to amend the Privileges Act to allow the media to cover proceedings of meetings held by the Committee on Public Enterprise (COPE). This was on the initiative of the COPE itself which requested media coverage given the public interest nature of the activities that it was engaging in, most importantly, the monitoring and interrogating of state institutions for corruption. However, this promise was not carried through.

Parliamentary privilege was subjected to scrutiny in *De Silva and Others v. Jeyaraj Fernandopulle and Others*.[143] In this case, a majority Bench of the Supreme Court held that remarks made by an MP in Parliament could be used against him to controvert sworn statement made in an affidavit to court.

The conclusions and recommendations of the R.K.W. Goonesekere Committee in respect of parliamentary privilege continue to be applicable today. The Committee concluded that the constitutional provisions that made 'parliamentary privilege' a ground for restricting free speech and media freedom was wholly inconsistent with Sri Lanka's obligations under international law.[144] This undesirable framework is yet to be remedied, and hence requires the immediate attention of present-day reformers.[145]

6 *The Broad-basing of Lake House*

Following the initial proliferation of privately owned print media institutions, the government in 1973 passed the Associated Newspapers of Ceylon (Special Provisions) Law[146] changing the status of one of the leading media institutions in the country: the Lake House Group. The law effectively placed the group directly under the control of the state. However, the takeover was subject to a specific undertaking: to broad base the newspapers and gradually divest the majority of the shares acquired by the Public Trustee to the public.[147] The intention of such a plan was ultimately to create a 'publicly owned' media.[148]

Since the law was passed, no such broad-basing was carried out. Some attempts at reform were put in motion in mid-1995, when a Committee appointed by the People's Alliance Government recommended that Lake House shares be 'redistributed in a manner that would ensure the creation of a broad-based democratic newspaper company with the widest possible citizens' participation'.[149] The report published by the Committee marked the first cogent attempt to address the problem.[150] However, these recommendations were never given effect.[151] Instead, 'the Lake House Group became subject to a callous manipulation of its resources, its Chairmen routinely changed upon every shift of political power and its journalists coerced into following the party political line in their work'.[152] At present, the newspapers published by Lake House have displayed unbridled partiality towards the government.[153] Thus, the notion of broad-basing the state media appears to have fallen by the wayside.[154]

7 Criminal Defamation

Throughout the late 20th century and early 2000s, a potent threat was posed to the non-state media in the form of criminal defamation indictments filed arbitrarily at the instance of the Attorney General due to political pressure. The constant threat of suits by political factors contributed heavily to the curtailment of media freedom during this period. The predicament was further exacerbated when certain procedural safeguards against arbitrary and politically motivated prosecutions were done away with in 1980 in what was undoubtedly a political exercise.[155] The resulting framework encouraged a spate of prosecutions against editors and journalists by successive governments.[156] In the entire history of the law of criminal defamation, only one prosecution had been instituted by a private individual.[157]

Following the filing of several criminal defamation indictments against editors of the private media seen to be hostile to the Chandrika Kumaratunga administration, several media associations and lobby groups began extensively lobbying for the repeal of the law on criminal defamation from the late 1990s. The campaigners emphasised that erring media professionals should be sanctioned under the civil law and not under the criminal law.[158] After nearly a decade of campaigning, the repeal of the provisions on criminal defamation on 18 June 2002 was no doubt 'a notable event in media history in Sri Lanka'.[159]

As a consequence of these much-anticipated reforms, many pending criminal defamation cases were withdrawn.[160] One particularly interesting case concerned the criminal defamation charges filed against the Editor of the *Sunday Times*.[161] The Editor was convicted of criminally defaming President Chandrika Kumaratunga under both the Penal Code and the then Press Council Law, a finding later affirmed by the Court of Appeal.[162] The case itself provided critical leverage to the campaign against the law on criminal defamation. Following repeal of the criminal defamation provisions, the Editor was discharged from all proceedings and the conviction was set aside.

However, as has been observed, this was on condition that the newspaper agreed to 'publish a statement in the newspaper wherein the Editor accepted responsibility for the impugned publication as Editor, reiterated that there was no malicious intent whatsoever on the part of the writer, the newspaper or himself in wanting to defame the President and regretted the publication of the said erroneous excerpt'.[163]

Though no doubt timely, these reforms were also a reflection of the prevailing political situation and not necessarily a success story for which media and civil society actors could take sole credit. The distinction between efforts to repeal the law on criminal defamation and other reform efforts, such as those on contempt of court, parliamentary privilege or freedom of information, is that the political circumstances at the time favoured swift reforms in respect of criminal defamation.

Following the UNF victory at the parliamentary elections of 2002, a precarious political arrangement prevailed, in which the UNF cabinet, controlled by Prime Minister Ranil Wickremasinghe, was compelled to 'cohabit' with President Chandrika Kumaratunga. The President's overt attempts to control and manipulate the media largely motivated the UNF Government to expedite media reform. One of the least complicated of such reform initiatives was the repeal of the criminal defamation law.

While other similar initiatives were in the pipeline during the short UNF rule, the change of government in 2004 restored the status quo and governmental apathy if not outright hostility towards media reform once again became the norm.

8 Freedom of Information

The need for a sound legal framework that ensures public access to vital information has been greatly emphasised in recent times,[164] perhaps due to the culture of secrecy prevalent in most state departments and ministries.[165] The RTI stems from a broader notion of holding the state accountable for its actions and ensuring transparency. Hence, freedom of information legislation is necessary to guarantee access to data held by the state and ultimately strengthen democratic institutions. In the absence of such statutory protection, the government could use a variety of excuses such as 'national security' or 'the prevention of terrorism' to hide information from the public. It has been often said that 'the arguments that are proffered—security and terrorism—are … weak and somewhat dishonest and jingoistic'.[166]

One analyst has compared the situation in Sri Lanka in the following manner:

> In Sri Lanka, unlike in India, we have a politicised public service. … In Sri Lanka, unlike in India, we do not have the possibility of judicial review of legislation. So once a law is passed even if the law is inconsistent with the Constitution it cannot be challenged in the courts. … [W]e have a lot of laws in place that were passed in British colonial times in a completely different political context which are very anti right to information and which cannot be challenged because of the absence of judicial review of legislation. So again, that is another difference between Sri Lanka and India.[167]

The archaic nature of the current Establishments Code of Sri Lanka is particularly relevant, with a portion of the Code specifically stating that:

> No information even when confined to statement of fact should be given where its publication may embarrass the government, as a whole or any government department, or officer. In cases of doubt the Minister concerned should be consulted.[168]

This analysis reveals a serious need for specific legislation to be enacted to ensure freedom of information in Sri Lanka. In response to this dire need, there have been numerous attempts to draft a Freedom of Information law, most notably under the UNF Government of 2002–2004. During this time, a draft was formulated by a committee of senior government officials with the input of civil society and the media, and subsequently approved by the Cabinet. However, its enactment was 'stymied' by the dissolution of Parliament in April 2004, and since then, 'has been delayed due to the lack of political will on the part of post-April 2004 Governments'.[169]

The Law Commission of Sri Lanka was also previously responsible for a draft law, which sought to give statutory recognition to a judicially acknowledged principle that the freedom of speech and expression carries with it an implicit right of a person to secure relevant information.[170] A later revised version of the Law Commission draft accorded access to official information in the possession, custody or control of a public authority to citizens of Sri Lanka.[171] A 'public authority' is defined to include ministries of government, departments, public corporations, higher educational institutions, local authorities, companies in which the government has a majority shareholding, any department or other authority established by a Provincial Council and anybody or office established under the Constitution other than the Parliament and the Cabinet of Ministers.[172]

Moreover, the bill provides for the establishment of a Freedom of Information Commission vested with the power of monitoring the implementation of the bill.[173] The Commission also functions as an appellate body to which appeals may be made against decisions denying access to information.[174] The main criticism against the Law Commission draft is that the grounds for denial of information were too broad and, most notably, included parliamentary privilege.[175] The Law Commission draft remains one of the numerous reform initiatives that failed to see fruition.

Prior to the 2010 General Election, then Minister of Justice and Law Reform, Milinda Moragoda, initiated efforts to resurrect the debate on the RTI. These efforts resulted in the circulation of yet another draft Freedom of Information Bill. The 2010 draft was a slightly improved version of the previous Law Commission draft, as it excluded parliamentary privilege as a ground for denial of information.[176] However, several issues of concern still remained unaddressed. For instance, Section 5(1)(c) of the bill permits information to be denied in respect of instances where 'the information consists of memoranda or letters within a public authority or between one public authority and another', which may be too wide a ground for denial.

Moreover, unlike the Law Commission draft, the 2010 draft lacked the right of appeal to the Supreme Court as the third and final tier of appeal against arbitrary denials of information. Finally, the provisions for protecting whistle-blowers appeared to be insufficient, as Section 37 of the draft only provided protection in terms of 'official information which is permitted to be released or disclosed on a request submitted under [the] Act'.[177] Internationally recognised standards in respect of whistle-blower provisions require that persons should be protected from prosecution for disclosing not merely 'official information' but 'any information', so long as the whistle-blower acted in good faith, and in the reasonable belief that the information was substantially true, and that such information disclosed evidence of wrongdoing or a serious threat to the health or safety of any citizen or to the environment.

As a result of more recent political developments, the agenda for introducing a RTI law once again appears to have lost momentum.

Ironically, the state agenda during the last decade has moved in the opposite direction, as the current administration has sought to tighten secrecy laws even further and resolutely refused to support even a private member's bill to enact an RTI for Sri Lanka, going so far as defeating the motion on a vote to conclusively establish its opposition to the very idea.[178] In this context, the struggle for the RTI in India is instructive as a comparative example. There, the fight for the RTI has been a grass-roots movement strongly connected with the life and livelihood of the people. This recognition that the RTI is a matter of life and livelihood has ensured the continued fight to attain that right, despite the obstacles that RTI activists have had to encounter. The Right to Information Act of 2005 has been effectively implemented in recent years and the deaths of some RTI advocates in trying to ensure the effective working of its provisions have not deterred its proponents. Success stories which have benefited the people who fought for it abound.[179] The strong conviction of those who fought for an Indian RTI law has resulted not only in ensuring the enactment of a statute, but also its effective enforcement powers. In the light of these comparative illustrations, it is instructive to consider whether the movement in Sri Lanka towards ensuring a good RTI law should re-envision itself as a social movement of the public for the attainment of meaningful rights of ordinary people as contrasted to a purely media-driven initiative.

Despite several failed attempts to enact an RTI law in Sri Lanka, there may be some value in discussing the main issues of concern raised by the several media and civil society groups involved in the campaign for such a law. There is certainly a need for the stakeholders involved to reach broad consensus on the principles that should underlie a draft bill.[180] The following principles have been listed as crucial in this regard:

Standard as to maximum disclosure: The Act should establish a presumption in favour of disclosure on the part of all public bodies and should prevail over existing laws restricting information. [...]

Standard [regarding the] obligation to publish ... should be imposed on ministries and public authorities to make public records and information of a particular kind coming under its purview within certain stipulated time periods. The duty to give reasons for decisions should be automatic and not upon request. [...]

[...]

Standard as to exceptions: Access to official information should be subject only to narrow and clearly drawn exceptions (particularly with regard to national security), which would be subject to a substantial harm test and a public interest override.

Standard [regarding the] processes to facilitate access: Requests for information should be processed fairly and rapidly and there should be independent review of refusals which allows appeal to a Freedom of Information Commission and finally to the appellate court. [...]

[...]

Standard [regarding] protection for whistleblowers: There should be provision [...] which from legal, administrative or employment related gives protection to individuals sanction for releasing information on wrongdoing.[181]

Moreover, it is important that the media itself plays a pro-active role in promoting the RTI. It has been previously observed that the role of the media tends to vary from case to case.[182] For example, while the media took up controversial issues such as the *Galle Face Green Case*,[183] 'there was reluctance to devote space to regular monitoring'.[184]

Furthermore, the media has displayed a distinct lack of interest in systematically pursuing information in respect of much larger projects, such as the Southern Expressway Project.[185] This inconsistency may contribute to the current lack of momentum in reform efforts. If the media consistently highlights actual examples of vital information being withheld from the public, the practical value of a Freedom of Information law may become clearer. Hence, the current campaign, which has thus far relied mainly on abstract principles, may benefit greatly by the infusion of a more experiential dimension.

Judicial Responses to Media Issues

While legislative and institutional reforms have been prioritised in the various reform initiatives discussed above, there may be some value in examining the manner in which the Sri Lankan judiciary has responded to some of those identical issues.

The Supreme Court, through its jurisprudence over the past two decades, has extensively dealt with the scope and content of Article 14(1) (a).[186] As observed previously, M.D.H. Fernando J., in the standard-setting case of *Wimal Fernando v. SLBC*, insisted that this constitutional provision not be interpreted narrowly.[187] Justice Fernando observed:

Not only does [Article 14(1)(a)] include every form of expression, but its protection may be invoked in combination with other express guarantees (such as the right to equality [...]) and it extends to and includes implied guarantees 'necessary to make the express guarantees fully meaningful' [...] Thus it may include the right to obtain and record information, and that may be by means of oral interviews [...], publications [...], tape-recordings [...], photographs, and the like; and, arguably, it may even extend to a privilege not to be compelled to disclose sources of information, if that privilege is necessary to make the right to information 'fully meaningful'. Likewise, other rights may be needed to make the actual exercise of the freedom of speech effective: rights in respect of venues, amplifying devices, etc.[188]

The ruling in *Wimal Fernando's Case* has further significance, since the court suggested—albeit obiter dicta—that if a mere listener had complained instead of a participatory listener, the rights violation would have arisen under Article 10 of the Constitution, which guarantees the freedom of thought. This view was most probably based on the reasoning that 'information is the staple food of thought, and that the RTI is a corollary of the freedom of thought guaranteed by Article 10'[189] Jayaratne et al. comment that the specific reason for the court to draw such a distinction between Article 10 and 14 was that Article 14(1)(a) could be restricted by law on a number of grounds stipulated in Articles 15(2) and 15(7).[190] By contrast, Article 10 embodies a 'near absolute right', which could be amended only through approval by no less than two-thirds of the Members of Parliament, as well as by the people through a referendum.[191] This dictum is crucial, as it appears to establish—or at least intimate the existence of—a stronger RTI than could be inferred from Article 14(1)(a) which is not of an entrenched character like Article 10. However, since the case did not deal directly with Article 10, this jurisprudential matter remains largely unresolved and thus requires further judicial scrutiny.

The court in *Environmental Foundation Ltd v. Urban Development Authority of Sri Lanka and Others (the Galle Face Green Case)*[192] also made a contribution to the jurisprudence on the RTI. The petitioner in this case sought to compel the Urban Development Authority to issue a copy of the lease agreement it had signed with a private developer for the purpose of establishing an entertainment centre at the Galle Face Green in Colombo. The then Chief Justice, Sarath N. Silva, was of the view that for the right to expression to be meaningful and effective, a person has an 'implicit right' to secure relevant information from a public authority in respect of a matter in the public domain. Pertinently however, it may be said that this was simply a case where the particular public interest in the matter outweighed the confidentiality that attached to affairs of state and official communications. Broad reliance on this ruling as a general principle therefore cannot be manifested.[193]

The general attitude of judges towards media issues and the freedom of speech and expression including publication has tended to fluctuate over the past three decades. The Sri Lankan courts appear to have avoided acknowledging the pre-eminent rights of any one stakeholder or institution and have preferred to adjudicate on issues on a case-by-case basis. During the late 1990s and early 2000s, the free speech jurisprudence in the country saw notable instances where the courts were quick to uphold the rights of ordinary citizens. Important examples of the court's keenness to uphold free speech and the freedom of expression include cases in which the right of individuals to disseminate leaflets critical of the government to the public,[194] the right of teenage students to dissent,[195] the right of citizens to participate in noise protests,[196] the right to freedom of speech of a participatory listener to a radio broadcast programme[197] and the right to exercise one's vote[198] have all been upheld. Moreover, judges have tended to be sympathetic towards the claims of journalists where the government has engaged in opprobrious acts such as the banning of a press, seizure of copies of newspapers[199] or assault of media personnel in the line of duty.[200]

However, despite acknowledging the role of the media as 'watchdog' or the 'fourth estate', the courts have been overcautious in respect of specific claims of journalistic privilege.[201] The Sri Lankan Supreme Court articulated the following view in the case of *Victor Ivan v. Sarath Silva, Attorney General*:

> The freedom of the press is not a distinct fundamental right but is part of the freedom of speech and expression including publication which Article 14(1)(a) has entrenched for everyone alike. It surely does allow the pen of the journalist to be used as a mighty sword to rip open the facades that hide misconduct and corruption but it is a two edged weapon which he (she) must wield with care not to wound the innocent while exposing the guilty.[202]

As observed in the Law and Society Trust's Annual Review of the State of Human Rights in Sri Lanka in 2000,[203] the courts seems to have rejected the position that a free press is 'not merely a neutral vehicle for the balanced discussion of diverse ideas...but instead, an organised expert scrutiny of government'[204] which needs particular protection.[205] It is observed that such protection ought to be over and above the general protection given to the right to free speech.[206] This advanced form of protection, however, has not been acknowledged in any case thus far.

As mentioned earlier, in the absence of a definitive legislative framework on contempt of court, judicial attitudes in respect of contempt have remained largely conservative.[207] For instance, in *Hewamanne v. Manik De Silva*,[208] the majority of a five-judge bench of the Supreme Court was of the view that 'the law of contempt of court which had hitherto existed would operate untrammelled by the fundamental right of freedom of speech and expression contained in Article 14'.[209] The respondents in the case—the Editor, owner, printer and publisher of the *Daily News* Newspapers—were charged with contempt of court in respect of a news item which called into question the integrity of two judges including Justice K.C.E. de Alwis over his recommendation to impose civil disabilities on Felix Dias Bandaranaike. The majority opined that there was no unfettered right to publish judicial and particularly parliamentary proceedings,[210] and accordingly confirmed the Rule issued against the respondents—though for mitigating reasons, the court ultimately discharged them. A similar conservatism may be observed in respect of the court's treatment of comments on pending proceedings.[211] Judicial attitudes on the sub-judice rule have been strongly critiqued,[212] particularly given that cases in Sri Lanka could drag on for interminable lengths of time. Thus, it has been argued that the sub-judice rule may in fact seriously impede discussions on matters of public interest.[213] In the area of censorship, the Supreme Court has been equally conservative, as would be discussed later on in this chapter.

The above survey demonstrates that reformers cannot—and indeed should not—expect the judiciary to be the vehicle of change. While litigation may be a strong strategic tool at the disposal of reformers, sole reliance on litigation could doom campaigns to certain failure. Fortunately, reform efforts in Sri Lanka have rightly focused on alternative strategies to litigation, including collective advocacy, institutional improvement and educational reform.

Notes

1. Robertson and Nicol (1992), p. xvii.
2. World Association of Newspapers (2006), p. 406.
3. *Ibid.*, p. 407, 8ba.
4. The Centre for Policy Alternatives (CPA) and International Media Support (IMS) (2005).
5. Circulation figures of daily and weekend newspapers calculated as at 2005 are contained in the CPA/IMS publication: *A Study of Media in Sri Lanka (Excluding the North and*

East) but these figures are contested by the publishing houses concerned and for that reason are not cited here.

6. Lanka Business Online (2007a)
7. *Ibid.*
8. See discussion, *infra.*
9. Elmqvist and Bastian (2006), at p. 10. The authors comment: 'Hence, during the colonial period, the interests of the plantation capital, indigenous capital, independence movement and vernacular intelligentsia have played an important role in the development of the newspaper. These currents have transformed themselves into political and nationalist interests in the post-colonial period'.
10. Laws, legislation and policy reforms have been justifiably critiqued as lagging behind technology and innovation. The inability to address rapidly changing technological advancements has been identified as the main reason for laws to be behind technology. 'Cyber squatting' or registration of a domain name with a trademark of someone else provides a good example of how legislation failed in regulating cyber issues. Furthermore, the legislative or judicial measures are capable of controlling the physical layer but not the content layer of the new media. For some pertinent perspectives on this issue, see *National Conference on Self-Regulation: Speeches and Interactive Sessions* (September 2011), Press Complaints Commission of Sri Lanka (PCCSL) (hereafter National Conference on Self Regulation [2011]) Session on the Internet: A Licence to Slander? at pp. 46–47 (presentation made by Jayantha Fernando, Attorney-at-Law).
11. 'The Code of Practice of the Editors' Guild of Sri Lanka addresses the online publications of the print media. But the effectiveness of this Code has not been measured in the industry as Sri Lanka does not have organisations such as the Internet Watchdog Foundation in the UK where internet service providers and the content hosting providers are compelled to remove any publication which is contrary to the codes of practice. ('notice and take down procedure')' *National Conference on Self-Regulation* (2011), Session on the Internet: A Licence to Slander?, pp. 46–47 (presentation made by Jayantha Fernando, Attorney-at-Law). 'Regulating the new media even by way of self-regulation has been resisted based on the contention that the success of the Internet is inherent in its free nature which facilitates innovation. The attempt to regulate content as opposed to regulation at an engineering level would be superfluous as the ability of the new media to ensure a solid audience would be based on the accuracy of the information provided by such media. The inability to provide accurate information would result in the audience being diverted to other sources readily available on the web'. National Conference on Self-Regulation (2011) Session on the Internet: A Licence to Slander?, pp. 54–55 (interactive session based on the presentation made by Nalaka Gunewardene, science writer and columnist).
12. 'The imperative need to organise web managers to form an association and to have a self-regulatory mechanism has been advocated by the SLPI and PCCSL for the last couple of years' (Imran Furkan, CEO of the Sri Lanka Press Institute, interviewed on 9 February 2012). Furthermore, as our interviews disclosed, the recent government initiative to ban five websites has been viewed as an impractical measure by most of the stakeholders in the media industry. This decision has been criticised for its lack of coherence, the inherent misunderstanding of the nature of new media as seen in such measures, the difficulty of enforcement and the existence of alternative pathways to view those banned websites which effectively increases the popularity of the banned websites.

13. Brady (2005), p. 2.
14. *Ibid.*, at p. 3. Lake House was taken over by the government in 1973. Currently, two major English daily/weekly newspapers (*The Sunday Island*/*Island* published by the Upali group and the *Sunday Times*/*Daily Mirror* published by Wijeya Newspapers) originate from the Wijewardene dynasty. More recent publishing houses include the *Lakbima* group, the Ceylon Today group as well as the Nation newspapers group, all with direct political or financial links to politicians in the government or in the opposition.
15. Nohrstedt et al. (2002), pp. 10–12.
16. Brady (2005), p. 5. The author refers to an interesting observation contained in the *Lak Mini Pahana* on 1 June 1978: 'In the same manner foreign traders come to know about matters pertaining to trade through English newspapers, so should the Sinhala traders through Sinhala newspapers'.
17. *Ibid.*
18. *Ibid.*
19. *Ibid.*, p. 6.
20. *Ibid.*
21. Muthulingam (1997), at pp. 181–192. Also see Brady (2005), p. 7.
22. CPA and IMS, p. 15.
23. *Ibid.*
24. Elmqvist and Bastian (2006), p. 11.
25. 'The notion of independent media has been identified as an ideological concept rather than a realistic conception as both state and private media reflect the views and interests of the owners/publishers/investors. The close affiliation of the media houses with the government and the opposition has been reflective in the views presented by such media houses' (Bandula Padmakumara, Chairman, Lake House (state news media group), interviewed on 8 January 2011).
26. The comparatively small nature of the media industry in Sri Lanka has led to highly polarised and politicised debates with unfortunate consequences to the overall health and vitality of the industry.
27. The relationship between profit and the necessity to prove political loyalties to the establishment may become complex in these situations. As Hiniduma Sunil Senevi, senior lecturer in media and mass communications in the Department of Languages, Sabaragamuwa University emphasised, when interviewed on 1 June 2012, 'Normally, the profit motive is the foremost aim when operating a media establishment. However, in Sri Lanka, the reality has become different and perhaps more perverted. Here, the extent of politicisation is so great that profit may sometimes be sacrificed for the fulfilment of the political agendas of a particular media house, be it print or electronic'.
28. The question of editorial independence should be seen in context. As opined by two prominent publishers, Ranjit Wijewardene (Publisher, Wijeya Newspapers, interviewed on 21 February 2012 and Kumar Nadesan (Publisher, Express Newspapers, interviewed on 20 February 2012), it is the editor who generally decides the content of news but the publisher may resort to intervening in a rare case. Generally, disputes are resolved through compromise as otherwise the working relationship will become intolerable. There is a wide degree of mutual trust and this process cannot be reduced to hard and fast rules.
29. Dr Devanesan Nesiah (retired senior civil servant, member of PCCSL interviewed on 21 February 2012).

30. Brady (2005), p. 9.
31. CPA and IMS (2005).
32. See Brady (2005), at p. 9. Commenting on the 2005 CPA-IMS Study, the author observes: 'The study also suggests the private radio stations have been successful in capturing a significant segment of the audience share, with the Sinhala language stations Sri FM owned by the Edirisinghe group and Sirasa owned by Maharaja Broadcasting recording a 22.62% and 18.67% share, respectively, in 2003. Meanwhile, the SLBC's national service Swadeshiya Sevaya, the regional transmissions—Rajarata and Ruhuna, and the modernised replacement of the SLBC Velada Seyaya commercial service—Pavana, have recorded only a mere 16.09% which includes a 10.35% share enjoyed by Swadeshiya Sevaya. Meanwhile the SLBC's Tamil service Thendral recorded 3.77%, while the Asian Broadcasting Corporation's Soorian and the Maharaja owned Shakthi Tamil stations both rated higher with Soorian capturing 4.25% of the audience share and Shakthi reaching 11.21%'.
33. *Ibid.*, p. 9.
34. Brady (2005), p. 12.
35. *Ibid.*
36. Act No. 6 of 1982.
37. Brady (2005), p. 13.
38. *Ibid.*
39. CPA and IMS (2005).
40. Brady (2005), at p. 13. The author notes: 'Even early in Sri Lanka's television history with only a transmitting station on Mount Pidurutalagala and two sub-transmitting stations in Kandy and Kokavil (the latter destroyed by the LTTE in July 1990), SLRC was able to provide its services to 84% of the population'.
41. Hiniduma Sunil Senevi (1 June 2012).
42. Elmqvist and Bastian (2006), p. 11.
43. Article15(7) declares: 'The exercise and operation of all the fundamental rights declared and recognised by Articles 12, 13(1), 13(2) and 14 shall be subject to such restrictions as may be prescribed by law in the interests of national security, public order and the protection of public health or morality, or for the purpose of securing due recognition and respect for the rights and freedoms of others, or of meeting the just requirements of the general welfare of a democratic society. For the purposes of this paragraph 'law' includes regulations made under the law for the time being relating to public security'.
44. See Gunasekera (1998), p.105.
45. Ordinance No. 2 of 1883.
46. Gunasekera (1998), p. 105.
47. Ordinance No. 7 of 1912.
48. Gunasekera (1998), p. 105.
49. Act No. 32 of 1955.
50. See Section 7 of the Act. According to Section 27 of the Act, 'official secret' means: 'any secret official code word, countersign or password; any particulars or information relating to a prohibited place or anything therein; any information of any description whatsoever relating to any arm of the armed forces or to any implements of war maintained for use in the service of the Republic or to any equipment, organisation or establishment intended to be or capable of being used for the purposes of the defence of Sri Lanka; and any information of any description whatsoever relating directly or indirectly to the defences of Sri Lanka'. Also see Bolin (2006), at p. 9.

51. Bolin (2006), p. 9.
52. Act No. 30 of 1981.
53. Ordinance No. 25 of 1947.
54. Report of the Committee to Advise on the Reform of Laws Affecting Media Freedom and Freedom of Expression (R.K.W. Goonesekere Committee Report) (1996), p.1.
55. *Ibid.* at pp. 4–5. Also see the International Covenant on Civil and Political Rights, GA res. 2200A (XXI), 21 UN GAOR Supp. (No. 16) at p.52, UN Doc. A/6316 (1966); 999 UNTS 171; 6 ILM 368 (1967), Article18 and Article 19.
56. R.K.W. Goonesekere Committee Report (1996), p. 6.
57. *Ibid.*, p. 12.
58. *Ibid.*, p. 14.
59. *Ibid.*, p. 16.
60. *Ibid.*, pp. 27–28.
61. *Ibid.*, p. 47.
62. *Ibid.*
63. *Ibid.*, pp. 49–51.
64. The Constitution Bill of 2000 (hereafter the Constitution Bill), was based on a text of Devolution Proposals submitted by the People's Alliance when that party formed the government in 1995, which proposals were concretised for the first time in 1997. Discussed thereafter for over four years, these reforms were included in a Constitutional Bill which provoked a near constitutional crisis in the mid-2000 when it was hurriedly gazetted as an urgent bill and referred overnight to the Supreme Court by President Kumaratunga prior to presentation in Parliament. Citizens' groups, members of the clergy and the opposition opposed this attempt on the basis that, though some provisions of the Bill had been put before the people, the country remained unaware of the Constitution Bill in its entirety, as formulated in the final draft. When the draft became public, the fact that its Transitional Provisions contained troublesome clauses permitting President Kumaratunga to assume the powers of a ceremonial head of state as well as that of a cabinet style Prime Minister (as envisaged in the Bill) for the remainder of her presidential term (i.e., for a period of six years from December 1999) led to a storm of protests. Although legal challenges to its constitutionality failed in the Supreme Court, extreme public agitation against the Constitution Bill resulted in the government withdrawing it from parliament. However, the Bill still remains the most substantive reform document in existence.
65. *Fernando v. Liyanage* (SC 1161/82 and 134/82), when the Supreme Court in ruling that a company is not a 'citizen', took away the right of media companies and their shareholders to come before the court on free speech issues, affirmed in *Neville Fernando and Others v. Liyanage and Others*, [1983] 2 SRI LR 214, where the court unequivocally held that a company, not being a citizen, cannot complain of infringement of fundamental rights and that its shareholders too cannot complain of a violation since they have not suffered any distinct and separate injury such as to entitle them to allege infringement of their fundamental rights. However, see *Visuvalingam and others v. Liyanage and others*, [1983] 2 SRI LR 311. A more recent precedent is *Environmental Foundation Ltd v. Urban Development Authority of Sri Lanka and Others (the Galle Face Green Case)*, SC (F.R.) Application 47/2004, S.C. Minutes 28.11.2005, discussed more fully in the succeeding analysis.
66. *Autronic AG v. Switzerland* (1990), 12 EHRR, 485.
67. *Glasenapp v. Germany*, 1986 EHHR, 25, and *Leander v Sweden*, 1987, 9 EHRR, 433.

218 KISHALI PINTO-JAYAWARDENA AND GEHAN GUNATILLEKE

68. [1996] 1 Sri L.R. 157.
69. *In Re The Broadcasting Authority Bill*, S.D. No 1/97–15/97, delivered on 5 May 1997.
70. *Leander v. Sweden*, 1987, 9 EHHR, 433 at para 74. See also *Gaskin v. UK* (1989) 12 EHHR, 36.
71. *Joseph Perera v. The Attorney-General* [1992] 1 SLR 199, also *Palihenage Don Saranapala v. S.A.D.B.R. Solanga Arachchi, Senior Superintendent of Police, Police Headquarters, Colombo 1 and Others*, SC Application No: 470/96, SC Minutes of 17/07/1997.
72. See the Report of the RKW Goonesekere Committee on Reform of the Legislative Framework Relating to the Media in Sri Lanka which suggested that parliamentary privilege be abolished as a ground of restriction of free speech in the Constitution.
73. Elmqvist and Bastian (2006), p. 11.
74. *Ibid.*
75. *Ibid.*
76. For example, the UNF Government established the Prime Ministerial Committee on Media Law Reforms in 2003 with a view to introducing much-needed reforms within the media sector.
77. Elmqvist and Bastian (2006), p. 11.
78. Media Charter for a Democratic and Pluralist Media Culture and Social and Professional Rights for Media and Pluralism in Sri Lanka (September 2005).
79. *Ibid.*
80. *Ibid.*
81. Other signatories included: the Sri Lanka Working Journalists Association, the Federation of Media Employees Trade Unions, the Sri Lanka Muslim Media Forum, the Sri Lanka Tamil Media Forum, the Sri Lanka Photo Journalists' Association, the Sri Lanka Environment Journalists' Association and the South Asia Free Media Association.
82. Weligama Declaration on the Role of Media for National Unity (2006).
83. *Ibid.*
84. *Ibid.*
85. See Article XIX and the Centre for Policy Alternatives (CPA) (2007a).
86. Ministry of Mass Media and Information (2007).
87. Article XIX and CPA (2007a).
88. Ministry of Mass Media and Information (2007).
89. Article XIX and CPA (2007a).
90. Ministry of Mass Media and Information (2007).
91. See *10th Anniversary of the Colombo Declaration on Media Freedom and Social Responsibility—International Symposium: Speeches and Interactive Sessions* (October 2008), Sri Lanka Press Council (SLPI), hereafter *10th Anniversary of the Colombo Declaration 2008*.
92. The signatories observed that since the 1998 Declaration, the only positive developments were the abolition of criminal defamation provisions in the law, the repeal of the 1978 amendment to the Parliamentary Powers and Privileges Act, and the establishment of the Sri Lanka Press Institute, the Press Complaints Commission and the Sri Lanka College of Journalism. See Colombo Declaration on Media Freedom and Social Responsibility (October 2008). Recommendations as proposed in the Colombo Declaration (1998) in relation to repeal/update of the existing archaic media laws must be identified as an immediate action point by the government as it has been almost 14 years since the initial recommendation [vide interview with I. Furkan, 9 February 2012].
93. Act No. 5 of 1974.

94. Pinto-Jayawardena (2003), at p.15. The Minister is empowered to make regulations in respect of 'the control and supervision of programmes by such stations, the prohibition, regulation or control of the ownership of private broadcasting stations by prescribed persons or classes of persons, the regulation or control of the transfer of shares in companies holding licences for private broadcasting stations and for the regulation of fees to be charges for such licences.

95. *Ibid.*

96. Gunasekera (1998), p. 108.

97. *Ibid.*, p. 110.

98. Free Media Movement Statement in the Sunday Observer 14 April 1997. Also see Gunasekera (1998), p. 109.

99. Despite assurances that any proposals for a Broadcasting Authority would be published as a White Paper to enable public discussion prior to any legislation being tabled, the Government of Sri Lanka, without warning or notice, tabled the Bill in parliament just prior to the lengthy New Year holidays in April. This made it incredibly difficult for interested parties to critically examine the Bill or challenge its constitutionality. See Gunasekera (1998), p. 113.

100. Article 121(1) of the Constitution of Sri Lanka states: 'The jurisdiction of the Supreme Court to ordinarily determine any such question as aforesaid may be invoked by the President by a written reference addressed to the Chief Justice, or by any citizen by a petition in writing addressed to the Supreme Court. Such reference shall be made, or such petition shall be filed, within one week of the Bill being placed on the Order Paper of the Parliament, and a copy thereof shall at the same time be delivered to the Speaker. In this paragraph 'citizen' includes a body, whether incorporated or unincorporated, if not less than three-fourths of the members of such a body are citizens'.

101. Gunasekera (1998), p. 109.

102. *Athukorale and Others v. The Attorney General (Sri Lanka Broadcasting Authority Case)* [1997] 2 BHRC 610.

103. *Ibid.*

104. *Ibid.*

105. *Ibid.*

106. Gunasekera (1998), p. 112.

107. *Ibid.*

108. Ministry of Mass Media & Information (2011).

109. *In the Matter of a Rule on De Souza* 18, NLR, 41; *In Re Hulugalle*, 39, NLR, 294.In *Hewamanne v. Manik de Silva and Another* (1983 1 SLR 1), the impugned publication contained an account based on the Order Paper under the heading 'FDB's Pleadings Prepared in Judge's Chambers' and 'Select Committee Probe of Mr K.C.E. de Alwis's Representations'. The publication stated that a resolution was to be moved in parliament appointing a Select Committee to probe into representations made by a former appellate court judge that a court ruling disentitling him to continue as a member of a Special Presidential Commission was biased. Subsequently, parliament upstaged the Supreme Court decision that the publication amounted to contempt by enacting parliament (Powers and Privileges) Amendment Act No 25 of 1984, which stipulated that the publication of any extract of any paper published by order of parliament, bona fide and without malice, would not amount to contempt of court. Even more troublingly, *In Re Garuminige Tillekeratne* (1991 1 SLR 134) was an instance where a provincial

correspondent of a Sinhala paper, the 'Divaina', sent a report of a speech made by a Member of Parliament in the opposition at a time when the presidential election petition was being heard, in which the latter said that 'the petition had already been proved and if the petitioner did not win her case, it would be the end of justice in Sri Lanka.' Contempt of court was found inter alia on the basis that the publication *might or was likely* to result in prejudice to the pending hearing of the presidential election petition, inferring that the judges had already made up their minds and thus possibly deterring potential witnesses from giving evidence.

110. Pinto-Jayawardena (2003), at p. 9. Two judges, respectively, the President and the Secretary of the Judicial Services Association alleged also, in petitions filed in court, that they had been prevented from holding the Annual General Meeting of the Association. This, they contended, was due to arbitrary and coercive actions of the Chief Justice who wanted to prevent them from holding positions in the Association because they had opposed him in the past on the basis that his behaviour was not conducive to the honour and dignity of the office.

111. *Ibid.*, p. 9.

112. *Ibid.*

113. 'The tendency of intimidation has further resulted in direct and indirect self-censorship by the journalists who have been forced to exercise caution and constant vigilance' (Chandra Jayaratne, Former Head, Chamber of Commerce and prominent member of civil society interviewed on 4 March 2012).

114. *Ibid.*

115. *Ibid.*

116. See discussion, *supra* at 101.

117. 'The misuse of power and the arbitrary exercise of discretion by judges in exercising the power to punish for contempt is primarily why there is pressure in certain countries for enactment of a codified contempt of court law rather than relying on the general practice of the balancing of different interests by the judiciary'. *10th Anniversary of the Colombo Declaration (2008)* Session on Contempt of Court—The Need for a Law on Contempt of Court at pp. 59–60 (presentation by Justice Michael Francis Saldanha, Retired Chief Justice, State of Karnataka, India).

118. 'This initiative was welcomed by journalists as a timely initiative to ensure that both the judiciary and the media personnel are informed as to the scope and applicability of the law relating to Contempt of Court' (K. Janaranjana, senior journalist, Ravaya Newspaper, interviewed on 4 January 2011).

119. Constituted by President of the Bar Association, the late Mr Desmond Fernando, President's Counsel, the Committee was chaired by Dr J. de Almeida Guneratne, President's Counsel, and comprised attorneys J.C. Weliamuna and Kishali Pinto-Jayawardena.

120. Law Commission of Sri Lanka, *Contempt of Court Law: Explanation*, available at http://www.lawcomdept.gov.lk/info_English/index.asp-xp=723&xi=1129.htm (accessed on 16 January 2011).

121. Pinto-Jayawardena (2003), p. 10.

122. *Ibid.* The author comments: 'A publication made as or as part of a discussion in good faith of public affairs or other matters of general public interest should not amount to contempt of court if the risk of impediment or prejudice to particular legal proceedings is merely incidental to the discussion'.

123. *Ibid.*, p. 11.

124. As per the views expressed by some of the media personnel, mere amendments to existing laws would not be sufficient, as a proper balance in this regard would be arrived at only by bringing forth a generation of professional court reporters who are capable of producing accurate, professional and reliable reviews and reports [vide interview with B. Padmakumara, 8 January 2011].

125. See Draft Contempt of Court Law, available at: http://www.lawcomdept.gov.lk/info_English/index.aspxp=723&xi=1129.htm (accessed on 16 January 2011).

126. *Ibid.*

127. *Ibid.*

128. Explaining further, a senior journalist expressed the view that judicial power as a part of the sovereignty of the state derives from the people and therefore rests with the people. The obligation of the judiciary towards the taxpayers and the right of the citizenry to engage in fair and reasonable criticism must not be hindered by the identification of the judiciary as a prohibited zone [vide interview with K. Janaranjana, 4 January 2011].

129. *R V Metropolitan Police Commissioner ex parte Blackburn* (No. 2) 1968, QB 150.

130. *Ibid.*

131. For a discussion of the two cases, see *10th Anniversary of the Colombo Declaration (2008)* Session on Contempt of Court—The Need for a Law on Contempt of Court, at p. 58 (panel presentation by Kishali Pinto-Jayawardena).

132. Law Commission of Sri Lanka (2011).

133. *Ibid.*

134. Such legislative reform would have to reflect a positive recognition of the pluralistic nature of Sri Lankan society. *10th Anniversary of the Colombo Declaration (2008)* Session on Contempt of Court—The Need for a Law on Contempt of Court at p. 54 (presentation by Justice of the Supreme Court, Shiranee Thilakawardane).

135. However, press freedoms have been questioned by some as attempting to grant special privileges to journalists, as for example, the opinions expressed by Chairman of the Sri Lanka Press Council, W. Dayaratne, PC (interviewed on 5 April 2012). A more nuanced response to this complex question emphasised the importance of professionals and civil society to engage in open and transparent debate on national issues including freedoms of the press as situated within independent judicial systems and regulatory institutions (vide interview with C. Jayaratne, 4 March 2012).

136. For a comprehensive discussion on the subject, see Pinto-Jayawardena and De Guneratne (2004).

137. Act No.21 of 1953.

138. Gunasekera (1998), *op. cit.*, at p.105. Earlier, exclusive jurisdiction had been vested in the Supreme Court in this respect. The 1978 amendment had been strongly critiqued on the basis that parliament should not be empowered to sit as a court and impose punishments of imprisonment or fine and its repeal was welcomed at that time.

139. Gunasekera (1998), p. 105.

140. Act No.17 of 1980.

141. Pinto-Jayawardena (2003), p. 11.

142. *Ibid.*, pp. 11–12.

143. 1996 1 SLR 22.

144. See R.K.W. Goonesekere Committee Report (1996), pp. 13–14.

145. 'Laws relating to parliamentary privileges pose problems to the professionalism of the media in Sri Lanka as they put journalists reporting on proceedings of the House under vague and arbitrary restrictions which impact on the public right to know' (Sukumar

Rockwood, CEO of the Press Complaints Commission of Sri Lanka interviewed on 14 February 2012).

146. Law No. 28 of 1973. See Asian Media Information and Communication Centre, *Mass Media Laws and Regulations in Sri Lanka* (compiled by N. Selvakumaran and Rohan Edrisinga with a commentary by Sinha Ratnatunga and Kishali Pinto-Jayawardena, 1998) where at p.6 the following observation is made: 'In an act meant to teach a lesson to the management of ACL (Lake House) that had been traditionally allied against leftist parties, 75% of the shares of ANCL were vested in the Public Trustee on behalf of the government. ANCL became the media voice of the United Front government. Later governments continued to hold onto this one-time national press institution, reducing it to an unashamedly blatant propagandist of the policies of whatever party in power. This was amidst a clear flouting of the ANCL law itself which specifically stated that the vesting in the Public Trustee was to be transitory and that there would be an eventual broad-basing of ownership'.

147. *Ibid.*, Section 5.

148. 'The idea of publicly owned media has been gladly received by the different stakeholders of the industry. A proper mechanism free of ulterior motives would ensure meaningful broad-basing of the state owned media. Furthermore, it may be opportune to suggest that even the privately-owned media must allow the public to own at least one-third of the shares of such media houses' [A.C. Visvalingam, retired senior professional and President, Citizens Movement for Good Governance (CIMOGG) interviewed on 13 April 2012—views expressed in personal capacity].

149. Pinto-Jayawardena (2003), p. 14.

150. *Ibid.*, at pp. 3, 14. The Committee considered the fact that the election manifestoes of the major political parties in the country had pledged to broad-base the Lake House Group, subject to the condition that no single person or group could own more than a quarter of the divested shares. However, the government ultimately disregarded the Committee's report.

151. 'The broad-basing of state media (i.e., Lake House) as recommended by Colombo Declaration (2008) has not yet been implemented by the successive governments' [vide interview with S. Rockwood, 14 February 2012].

152. Pinto-Jayawardena (2003), pp. 3, 14.

153. 'It would be necessary to ensure genuine broad-basing of state media as there are many pseudo broad-based media institutions which are effectively managed and controlled by proxies and lackeys' [vide interview with C. Jayaratne, 4 March 2012].

154. 'State media institutions such as Lake House need to be broad-based in order to be held accountable to public opinion, given that public funds are being used in the maintenance of this institution' [vide interview with I. Furkan, 9 February 2012, and S. Rockwood, 14 February 2012].

155. The earlier framework under the Criminal Procedure Code included the requirement that proceedings must first originate in the Magistrate's Court with the written sanction of the Attorney General pursuant to an investigation by the police, after obtaining the authority of the Magistrate. However, Amending Act No. 52 of 1980 did away with this framework by introducing Sections 135 (6) and 393(7) to the prevailing provisions of the Criminal Procedure Code. This effectively countered a ruling by the Court of Appeal in *R.P. Wijesiriv. The Attorney General* [1980] 2 Sri L.R. 317, to the effect that the Attorney General had no power to send a direct indictment to the High Court in a criminal defamation prosecution without lawful investigation by the police

and preliminary inquiry by the Magistrate. The case involved an indictment against a Member of Parliament for criminally defaming then President J.R. Jayawardene, which was issued directly by the Attorney General to the High Court.

156. Pinto-Jayawardena (2003), p. 5.
157. *Ibid.*
158. *Ibid.*
159. *Ibid.* The then United National Front Government presented Penal Code Amendment Act No.12 of 2002, repealing Chapter 19 of the Penal Code and making consequential procedural amendments to Section 135 (f) of the Criminal Procedure Code. Moreover, Parliament repealed Section 118 of the Penal Code, which penalised attempts by contumacious or insulting words or signs, to bring the President into contempt. In addition, the Press Council Amendment Act No.13 of 2002 repealed the provisions relating to criminal defamation contained in the Press Council Law No. 5 of 1973.
160. The editor of *Lakbima* newspaper, Bandula Padm.akumara was acquitted on 6 February 1998 of the charge of alleged defamation of President Chandrika Kumaratunga in an article published on 19 February 1995. The contents of the article in *Lakbima* were similar to the article that was published in the *Sunday Times*.
161. *The Democratic Socialist Republic of Sri Lankav. Sinha Tissa Migara Ratnatunge,* High Court Case No. 7397/95.
162. The indictment was filed on two counts under the Penal Code and the Press Council Law over the publication of an item in a gossip column titled 'Anura; Sootin says courting days are here'. In an issue where words such as 'Epicurean' and 'in the heat of the silent night' which the defence argued were mere journalese in a trivial report while the prosecution maintained that the publication had harmed the reputation of President Chandrika Kumaratunga.
163. Pinto-Jayawardena (2003), p. 7.
164. The importance of the right to information was echoed by almost all the media-related personnel interviewed during the research conducted in relation to this chapter, including those heading or involved in state media institutions.
165. The immediate relevance of an RTI law extends to far more than the media industry encompassing therein the ordinary citizen's right to know. 'The relevance of right to information in the light of multipurpose development projects involved with public funds is clear. One example was the Hambantota Port project. Except for the secrecy surrounding the project, which is a common concern regarding all major projects in Sri Lanka, there have been several issues which should have been discussed and debated prior to the commencement of the project. Questions regarding the presence of a rock of substantial dimension being revealed by the original geological investigations carried out at Hambantota, potential market for the services that the Hambantota Harbour was geared to provide, calculation of the cash flow for the repayment of the loan, adequacy of infrastructure, etc. were few issues which warranted such discussion' [vide interview with. A.C. Visvalingam, 13 April 2012].
166. Asoka (2010).
167. 10th Anniversary of the Colombo Declaration (2008) Session on The Right to Information—A Fundamental Right of the Citizen, at p.119 (presentation by Rohan Edrisinha, Lecturer, Faculty of Law, University of Colombo). See further, Pinto-Jayawardena (2003), at p. 8. One example of this phenomenon is when in 2000 the Cabinet announced that it would implement Section 3 of Chapter XXXI of Volume 1 and Section 6 of Chapter XLVII of Volume 2 of the Establishments Code, which

prohibited public officials from disclosing any information to the media. The author recounts that this move 'led to jittery public servants refusing to release information of any kind to the media, including even refusing to confirm or deny information already in the hands of journalists, giving initials of public servants and giving statistical information without the sanction of the Secretary of the Ministry'.

168. *Ibid.*
169. Pinto-Jayawardena (2008), p. 15.
170. Law Commission of Sri Lanka (2010).
171. See Section 2 of Draft Bill, available at: http://www.lawcomdept.gov.lk/info_English/index.asp-xp=723&xi=808.htm (accessed on 15 January 2011).
172. *Ibid.* Section 36.
173. *Ibid.* Section 10.
174. *Ibid.* Sections 13(c) and 29.
175. See Law Commission of Sri Lanka (2010). As discussed earlier, the wholesale exclusion of parliamentary privilege from the framework for restricting the freedom of speech and expression has been a longstanding recommendation, which dates back to the R.K.W. Goonesekere Committee Report. See R.K.W. Goonesekere Committee Report (1996), pp. 13–14.
176. See Section 5 of Draft Freedom of Information Act (2010).
177. *Ibid.* Section 37.
178. There appears to be no discernible rationale put forward by the government as to why it refuses to enact an RTI law, leading one to the unfortunate conclusion that the predominant reason would be to keep government actions secluded from public scrutiny, particularly in the light of wide scale corruption being alleged in the post war development process.
179. 10th Anniversary of the Colombo Declaration (2008) Session on Right to Information—A Fundamental Right of the Citizen, pp. 112–117 (presentation by Nandani Sahai, Director, Media Information and Communication Centre, India).
180. The difficulty faced by the minority communities due to the non-recognition of the right to information has been a major concern. Consequently, minority communities have not been able to express their views and they have been unable to raise questions for which they would prefer to obtain answers from the authorities [vide interview with K. Nadesan, 20 February 2012].
181. Pinto-Jayawardena (2003), pp. 8–9.
182. See The Access Initiative (TAI) (2007).
183. See *Environmental Foundation Ltd v.Urban Development Authority of Sri Lanka and Others* SC (F.R.) Application 47/2004, S.C. Minutes 28.11.2005. The case involved the right to information regarding an agreement between the UDA and a private company to establish an entertainment centre at the Galle Face Green in Colombo.
184. See TAI Report (2007)
185. According to one view, right to information should not be considered as a concern regarding the day-to-day functioning of journalists, but rather as an issue which demonstrates a lacuna in the general law of the country [vide interview with K. Janaranjana, 4 January 2011].
186. Jayaratne et al. (2005), p. 18.
187. *Wimal Fernando v. Sri Lanka Broadcasting Corporation*, [1996] (1) Sri L.R. 157.
188. *Ibid.*, p. 179.
189. *Ibid.* Also see Jayaratne et al. (2005), p. 19.

190. Jayaratne et al. (2005), p. 19.
191. *Ibid.*
192. SC (F.R.) Application 47/2004, S.C. Minutes 28.11.2005.
193. Pinto-Jayawardena (2009).
194. *Ratnasara Thero v. Udugampola* [1983] 1 Sri L.R. 461.
195. *Ekanayake v. Herath Banda* SC Application 25/91, S.C. Minutes, 30 October 1996.
196. *Amaratunga v. Sirimal and Others* [1993] 1 Sri L.R. 264.
197. *Fernando v. SLBC and Others* [1996] 1 Sri L.R. 157.
198. *Karunatilleka and Another v. Dayananda, Commissioner of Elections and Others* [1999] 1 Sri L.R. 157.
199. *Deshapriya and Another v. Municipal Council, Nuwara Eliya and Others* [1995] 1 Sri L.R. 362.
200. *Sumith Jayantha Dias v. Reggie Ranatunge, Deputy Minister of Transport* [1999] 2 Sri L.R. 8.
201. See *Sri Lanka Broadcasting Authority Case* [1997] 2 BHRC 610); *Fernando v. The SLBC and Others* [1996] 1 Sri L.R. 157; *Sunila Abeysekera v. The Competent Authority and Others*, SC Application No 994/99, decided on 15 May 2000.
202. *Victor Ivan v. Sarath Silva, Attorney General* [1998] 1 Sri LR, 340 at 347.
203. Pinto-Jayawardena (2000).
204. See Francis (1986), cited in Pinto-Jayawardena (2003), p. 1.
205. Pinto-Jayawardena (2003), at p. 1. It was further observed that in the USA, 'even with an explicit 'free press' clause and with ringing judgements in favour of unrestricted freedom of expression and an unfettered press, acrimonious debate still continues as to whether the media can claim special privileges as an institution'. However, it was conceded that regardless of such vociferous debate, 'a substantially favourable constitutional law of the press prevails in that jurisdiction and journalists have found the attitudes of the Supreme Court to be a useful barometer of the social and political status of journalism'.
206. *Ibid.*
207. Pinto-Jayawardena (2003), p. 10.
208. [1983] 1 Sri L.R. 1.
209. *Ibid.*, p. 13 (per Wanasundera J.).
210. *Ibid.*, p. 68 (per Wanasundera J.).
211. See for example, *In Re Garuminige Tillekeratne* [1991] 1 Sri L.R 134. In this case, a provincial correspondent of a Sinhala paper, the 'Divaina', sent a report of a speech made by a Member of Parliament in the opposition at a time when a presidential election petition was being heard. The said MP was reported to have said: 'The petition had already been proved and if the petitioner did not win her case, it would be the end of justice in Sri Lanka.' Contempt of court was found inter alia on the basis that the publication 'might or was likely' to result in prejudice to the pending hearing of the presidential election petition, inferring that the judges had already made up their minds and thus possibly deterring potential witnesses from giving evidence.
212. See Kadirgamar (1992–1993); de Silva (1992–1993). Citing the two OPA Journal articles, it is observed that the decision in the *Garumunige Case* was criticised primarily because 'it did not take into account the need to demonstrate a 'substantial likelihood of prejudice' and in fact, accorded too much importance to what was essentially, a political statement' [vide Pinto-Jayawardena (2003), p. 10].
213. Pinto-Jayawardena (2003), p. 10.

9

Why a Right to Information Act Is an Urgent Necessity

Jayantha de Almeida Guneratne

Introduction

The concept of fundamental rights has different meanings. In the UK, they may be classified as rights based in the Common Law. They include, for instance, a person's right of access to the courts[1] and the right controlled by a government legal officer to invoke the aid of courts for the enforcement of the criminal law.[2] Fundamental rights also include those rights enshrined in the European Convention on Human Rights and Fundamental Freedoms, which in the UK are incorporated in to the law by the Human Rights Act of 1998.

By comparison, Sri Lanka's constitution has a Fundamental Rights Chapter which can be enforced by the courts. It incorporates the right to equality[3] and to freedom of speech and expression including publication.[4] This has been judicially held to imply a right to information, but only in limited situations.[5]

There are other rights in English law—such as the right to justice, liberty and property—which have been recognised and upheld in Sri Lanka.[6] However, as was observed by the current Sri Lankan Court of Appeal, English Law principles would continue to apply so long as they have not been modified by the statute law of the country. Subject to these qualifications, the English Law principles in the realm of Public Law continue to guide Sri Lankan courts, which place extensive reliance on English decisions as precedents.

Against this background, how should media freedom and rights fit into the existing constitutional cum legal framework of Sri Lanka? In the absence of a freedom of information Act similar to India's,[7] how should our appellate courts approach the issue? Are there any relevant judicial precedents? These are the issues this chapter proposes to examine in regard to media rights in general and journalists' rights in specific contexts. Sri Lankan governments in the past decade or more have failed and/or refused to enact a Freedom of Information Act. The Free Media Movement and the Editors' Guild[8] have both lobbied for such a law. The Law Commission of Sri Lanka has been in favour as well,[9] notwithstanding the alleged shortcomings of its own initiatives.[10]

Are Media Rights Fundamental Rights?

English Judicial Precedents

R. v. Home Secretary ex parte Brind[11] was concerned with the imposition of certain restrictions by the Secretary of State on broadcasting corporations.

Responding to this cardinal issue, the court had laid down the following principles which may be discerned as follows:

(1) Even when the executive is given apparently unlimited discretion in exercising a power conferred on it, the courts may review the exercise of that discretion if it is found to infringe fundamental human rights.

(2) However, the primary judgment (as decreed by parliament) must be conceded as to whether the public interest justifies restrictions by the executive in the exercise of its discretion.

(3) The courts are entitled to exercise a secondary judgment by asking whether an agent of the state[12] could reasonably make that primary judgment on the material before him.[13] This principle of reasonableness lies at the heart of the judicial interpretation of fundamental rights.[14]

Investigative Journalism

Under the UK law, it has been held that the government's wide powers of administrative discretion do not allow for the obstruction of prisoners' correspondence or interviews with journalists and others for the purpose of challenging the justice of their convictions. It is held to be a part of their right to access to justice that they should have access to investigative journalism. Miscarriages of justice have often been exposed in this way. Although the courts had held that the right was restricted for that purpose only,[15] the legal ruling in effect invalidated a government policy that journalists must undertake not to use the information professionally. The issue involved was investigative journalism, and therefore media freedom. The highest British court in effect upheld media freedom as being a basic or fundamental right, bringing into play 'a presumption of general application operating as a constitutional principle'.[16]

The judgment has a special impact on the Sri Lankan situation, given the significance of the constitution of Sri Lanka. In a nation such as the UK, which historically has come to acknowledge the Sovereignty of Parliament, the judiciary has nevertheless ascribed to itself the power of review of administrative discretion where media freedoms have been involved.

How should the Sri Lankan administration approach the issue of investigative journalism and media freedom?

The Constitutional Framework in Sri Lanka

The Relevant Constitutional Provisions

Clearly the predominant characteristic of the Sri Lankan constitution is the concept of People's Sovereignty. This includes inter alia that 'the fundamental rights which are by the constitution declared and recognised shall not be abridged, restricted or denied save in the manner and to the extent hereinafter provided'.

These fundamental rights include 'the freedom of speech and expression including publication'.[17] This constitutional right has been judicially expanded, as will be discussed in this chapter.[18]

These freedoms may be limited by law in the interests of national security, public order and the protection of public health or morality, or for the purpose of securing due recognition and respect for the rights and freedoms of others.

The wording of the constitution indicates that, when parliament enacts a statute or the president issues, a regulation under the Public Security

Ordinance,[19] both the legislature and the executive must be found to have reasonably exercised primary judgment as to the manner in which the right in issue is required to be 'abridged, restricted or denied'. If not, are not the courts (exercising a secondary judgment) obliged to review the executive judgment?[20]

As noted above, the courts in the UK have assumed the power of review, deriving a constitutional basis therefore from the concept of Common Law. In contrast, the Sri Lankan courts, both the minor and the higher judiciary including the Supreme (apex) Court, derive their power from a written constitution and statutes. Given the fact that the Supreme Court is vested with the sole jurisdiction to interpret the constitution,[21] the Supreme Court may claim to be on an even higher footing. The concept of the sovereign power of the people[22] is entrenched in the constitution[23] (as interpreted by the court).

Judicial precedents in Sri Lanka may be examined at this point in the context of Article 14(1) of the constitution. We may ask the question whether despite the absence of a Freedom of Information Act, the Supreme Court could still recognise the right to investigative journalism and media freedom as a basic, fundamental right.

Wickremanayake v. The State[24]: A Restrictive Judicial Interpretation on the Scope of Article 14(1)(a)

This case involved a parliamentary bill which was challenged for its constitutionality, where the petitioner had contended that, the provisions of the bill, inter alia, contravened Article 14(1)(a). The Supreme Court held that the proposed bill fell within the provisions of Article 15, 'which sets out the manner and extent in respect of restrictions that can be placed on fundamental rights'[25] and that the bill was not unconstitutional on these or other grounds.[26]

Visuvalingam and Others v. Liyanage and Others[27]

In this case, an appeal was made against an order promulgated under the terms of emergency regulations (ER) declared under the Public Security Ordinance.[28] The order was that: (a) No person shall print, publish or distribute or in any way be concerned in the printing, publication or distribution of the newspaper '*Saturday Review*' for one month from the date of the order and (b) that the printing press in which the said newspaper was printed shall, for a period of one month from the date of the order, not be used for any purpose whatsoever.

Implications of the Supreme Court Ruling

In reflecting on the propositions contained in the court's ruling, the principles relating to media freedom as a fundamental right may be construed as follows:

The Rule

Freedom of speech and expression logically includes freedom of the press, as a democratic initiative to propagate a diversity of views and ideas and the right of free and general discussion of all public matters, including matters not palatable to the government.

Qualification to the Rule

Should a newspaper publication highlight the atrocities and excesses of the police and the armed forces in a context of unsettled conditions, powers exercised by the state under ERs in arresting such an ensuing situation cannot be regarded as unreasonable. In referring to 'unsettled conditions' (during a state of declared emergency), the court shows a clear distinction in its possible approach to the closing down of a press during an emergency as opposed to normal times.[29]

The reference to editorial policy must be regarded as a decree issued to editors of newspapers to maintain a balance in exercising media freedom, particularly when the security of the country and its people are at stake.

Consequently, media freedom cannot be accepted as an absolute right or freedom. It is submitted that that aspect of the ruling addresses not only the media freedom which the court acknowledged as a right (though not absolute), but also the attendant issues relating to media responsibility or accountability.

In referring to emergency situations, this aspect of the ruling provides a jurisprudential framework for reflection as follows:

First, courts would be willing to give the executive sufficient leeway in dealing with an emergency situation, thereby implying that such leeway may not be afforded to the executive in normal times.

This has important implication for the debate on the exercise of media freedoms during ordinary times.

Second, if a distinction in approach is to be adopted between 'emergency situations' and 'normal times', then it becomes necessary for the courts to determine as to whether 'an emergency situation' exists.[30]

The Supreme Court Decision in Fernando v. SLBC[31]

The state-run SLBC had a new education service or non-formal education programme (NFEP) dealing with a wide range of topics, such as human rights, ethnicity, sociology, politics, current affairs, etc. It was planned to cover a long period with a regular schedule of programmes. Participation in a programme included staff, invited experts and also listeners. The petitioner who was a regular listener complained that while a telephone interview with a minister was in process, the broadcast was abruptly stopped and the programme (NFEP) was discontinued and the person in charge removed. Petitioner complained of violation of Article 14(1)(a).

This important issue had arisen in consequence of the submissions made by the Attorney General on behalf of the respondents. He had contended that the NFEP was stopped for good reasons—constraints of money, time and equipment, possibility of being sued for defamation, irrelevancy of content, complaints by the public. But he had made the submission that (the petitioner being) a listener might have been able to complain that his freedom of speech had been infringed if the broadcast had been stopped by a third party but not if the broadcaster itself had caused the stoppage.[32]

The court reflected that the submission seemed to concede a fundamental right to a mere listener.[33]

The court then posed the question: '...whether (where a third party stopped the broadcast) if the broadcaster itself did not complain of the infringement, a listener had an independent right to receive information which would entitle him to complain of that stoppage?'[34]

The Attorney General hesitated to concede such a right. The court then proceeded to consider whether a (mere) participatory listener could be declared as having freedom albeit not only to expression, but also to a right to receive information.

The court held thus: 'The criticisms were not something irrelevant, but related to matters connected to the success of the NFEP'.

The court's reasoning may be summarised as follows:

(1) The respondent (i.e., the Sri Lanka Attorney General) had not averred that criticisms contained in the programmes were untrue or exaggerated, and therefore it must be presumed that what was said was factually correct.

(2) The criticisms were restrained in language and balanced in content in that, while the Chairman of the SLBC was commended for his positive response, subordinates who failed to comply with orders from the top were criticised.

(3) The respondents had not averred that these issues should have been raised internally and even if that had not been done, such default at most would have justified a reprimand to the officer concerned but not to the stoppage of the whole NFEP.

(4) As to its right to stifle criticism of its own broadcasts, it is well to remember that the media asserts, and does not hesitate to exercise, the right to criticise public institutions and persons holding public office, while of course such criticism must be deplored when it is without justification.

(5) The government's media policy was intended to encourage criticism in the public interest to expose shortcomings in the context of which, as required by the right to equality, the media itself is not immune from justifiable criticism, internally and externally.

The court observed: 'The three complaints constituting (allegedly) public discontent with the NEFP were to the effect that, while media freedom was necessary, yet there should be some limit to criticisms of the Government, the SLBC and high officers'.[35]

Reflections on the Findings of the Court

A number of principles are clear from the court's ruling in this case:

(1) The facts (as alleged) must be presumed where the state authorities fail to aver the contrary.

(2) Expressions (language) used must be restrained, balanced and justified.

(3) Subject to the above, Article 14(1)(a) is not to be interpreted narrowly but broadly, to include every form of expression for the protection of which it may be invoked, in combination with other express guarantees, such as the right to equality.

(4) Thus, the court is seen not to hold that the freedom of expression necessarily encompasses an implied right to information as a fundamental right. This is explicit in the ruling which includes the words: 'I doubt, however, that it includes the right to information *simpliciter*',[36] such a right being thus restricted to a participatory listener of a state sponsored media programme.

It is submitted that, notwithstanding a right to information, the court was prepared to acknowledge to a participatory listener, nevertheless, the apex court is seen to be constrained in holding that Article 14(1)(a) which guarantees freedom of information includes the right to information as a general right.

Consequently, the Supreme Court ruling may be construed as a decision that went thus far and no further in regard to the existence of a right to information within the framework of the constitution, thus emphasising the need for legislation recognising such a right.

The Decision in Leader Publication (Pvt.) Ltd v. Ariya Rubasinghe and Others[37]

This was a case where the Competent Authority, appointed under ER, made an order prohibiting a publisher, printer and proprietor of newspapers from distributing its newspaper for a period and further had directed the Inspector General of Police to take possession of the said Company's printing press and its premises.

The petition of the company was allowed by the court.[38]

The upshot of the decision was to restore the freedom of the press, where the judge directed the Inspector General of Police to restore forthwith the petitioner's possession of the printing press, etc.[39]

A printing press and its publications depend on what they gather from communication with the public. The closure of a printing press has the effect of denying such communication. From that perspective, the ruling by implication upholds the right to information through investigative journalism as a fundamental right of expression under the constitution.

It is not, however, recognised as a basic fundamental right to every citizen, being limited to a participatory listener[40] and to a printing press whose closure is ordered without legal competence or authority.[41]

Need for a Freedom of Information Act

The Supreme Court Determination in the Sri Lanka Broadcasting Authority Bill

The Ceylon Broadcasting Corporation Act[42] had established the Ceylon Broadcasting Corporation[43] for the purpose of radio broadcasting and to exercise, supervise and control programmes broadcast by it. Section 3 of the Act required it to satisfy itself in regard to several requirements in doing so.

Likewise, the Sri Lanka Rupavahini Corporation Act[44] established the Sri Lanka Rupavahini Corporation[45] for the purpose of carrying on television broadcasting and casting on it functions and duties in similar terms to that of the SLBC.

The Sri Lanka Broadcasting Authority Bill (1997) sought to establish an authority to regulate the establishment and maintenance of broadcasting stations to provide for the issue of licences for that purpose. Clauses in the bill sought to empower the authority to impose such terms and conditions on licences issued by it in regard to both radio broadcasting as well as television broadcasting. Consequently, amendments were sought to be made to both the SLBC Act (1966) and the SLRC Act (1982).

Fifteen citizens including incorporated bodies challenged and attacked the bill for lack of constitutional validity on several grounds.

The Supreme Court ruled that some provisions in the bill were inconsistent with those of the existing provisions of the SLBC Act and the SLRC Act. The court examined the provisions of the bill in the light of the maxims *leges posteriores priores contrarias abrogant*[46] and *generalia specialibus non-derogant.*[47] The court determined that several clauses of the bill had the effect of enabling the authority to supervise, direct and control the content of the programmes to be broadcast via radio as well as television. They were therefore inconsistent with the provisions of the SLBC Act and the SLRC Act. But the result left intact the two corporations' right merely to satisfy themselves in regard to the content of their respective broadcasts.

Impact on Other Radio or Television Broadcasting

Having held so, the Supreme Court determined that, 'if the proposed Bill is enacted, other radio or television broadcasters will not have the privilege of self-regulation enjoyed by the SLBC and SLRC concerning the content of their programmes; for they are to be, in that respect, subject to the supervision, direction and control of the proposed Authority sought to be established by the Bill'.[48]

Consequently, the court proceeded to hold that the bill contained discriminatory provisions as between the SLBC and SLRC, on the one hand, and other radio and television broadcasters, on the other, in enabling the proposed authority to impose different standards for the issue of licences to them and the content of their programmes.[49] Accordingly, the court determined that the said provisions in the bill were inconsistent with Article 12(1) of the constitution and cannot become part of the law of Sri Lanka unless they are passed by a special majority in terms of Article 84 of the constitution.[50]

Responsibility of a Broadcasting Licensing Authority for the Allocation of Frequencies and Other Technical Aspects of Broadcasting

This section considers the bearing of International Covenants on the responsibility of Broadcast Licensing authorities. We cite a publication of the international non-governmental organisation Article XIX, entitled 'Article XIX on the subject of Broadcasting Freedom—International Standards and Guidelines'. In it, the importance of uniform standards for public and private broadcasting, administered by an independent,[51] single authority, is underlined. This was specially referred to by the court in its decision. Article XIX lays emphasis on the need to achieve 'pluralism' for the sake of promoting freedom of thought. The US Supreme Court had also spoken of:

> the 'evils to be prevented'. These were not the censorship of the press merely, but any action of government might prevent free and general discussion of public matters, which seemed absolutely essential to prepare the people for the intelligent exercise of their rights as citizens.[52]

Nevertheless, the court, having regard to the purpose of the bill, viz: to provide for the establishment of a body to regulate the establishment and maintenance of broadcasting stations and to provide for the issue of licences for the purpose,[53] rejected the petitioner's challenge to the bill. The court did not endorse the contention that any attempt to regulate broadcasting by a system of licensing would deprive broadcasters of their fundamental rights of freedom of speech and expression.[54]

However, the court ruled that the composition of the Board of Directors and the Minister's involvement with the proposed authority went against the need for an independent regulatory body. It amounted to creating an authority which is 'no more than an arm of the government', the court said. Moreover, the court determined that such lack of independence had the potential to open the door to interference with a licensee's right of publication in the public interest and the right of the public to balanced programmes, taking account of the diverse nature and interests of the population.

Further, the court determined that, in addition to the lack of independence of the authority proposed to be created under the bill, the minister's unbridled power to make regulations could interfere with the presentation of programmes. It would thereby undermine the principle of fairness which is at the heart of responsible broadcasting. Similarly, it would interfere with commercial advertisements and thereby interfere with and or/infringe the right of the public to have information to enable them to make independent judgments.

The court ultimately determined that several clauses contained in the proposed bill are inconsistent with Article 10 and 14(1)(a) of the constitution and in terms of Article 83 of the constitution required to be passed by a special majority of parliament and approved by the people in a referendum.[55]

Judicial Observations Noted by the Court

The previous sections have assessed the impact of decisions of the Sri Lankan Supreme Court on issues of free expression. At this point, it may be appropriate to refer to earlier judicial observations noted by the court that:

(1) The right to information (the staple food of thought) could be seriously jeopardised unjustifiably because the constitution does not permit it.[56]

(2) The basic assumption in a democratic polity is that the government shall be based on the consent of the governed. This implies not only that the consent shall be free, but also that it shall be grounded on adequate information and aided by the widest possible dissemination of information.[57]

(3) The freedom to form public opinion, which plays a crucial role in modern democracy, demands the condition of virtually unobstructed access to and diffusion of ideas viz: the right to know and the right to hear.[58]

(4) The dissemination of ideas can accomplish nothing if otherwise willing addressees are not free to receive and consider them.[59]

(5) The US Supreme Court has said that it was now well established that the constitution protects the right to receive information and ideas.[60]

To summarise the current position in Sri Lanka:

(1) The citations made by the Sri Lankan Supreme Court leave no doubt that there is a need to recognise the right to information in a democratic system.

(2) Although the US constitution recognises the right to information,[61] the constitution of Sri Lanka does not (at least expressly).

(3) Although the right to information is recognised through constitutional or statutory provision in many countries, including India and the United States,[61] the constitution of Sri Lanka does not (at least expressly). This is explicit from the observation made by court thus:

> the right to freedom of speech and expression includes the freedom to hold opinions and to receive and impart information and ideas without interference by public authority.[62]

(4) As such rights carry with them duties and responsibilities, they may be subjected in their exercise to some restrictions such as those contained in Article 15(2)[63] and in Article 15(7).[64]

(5) In as much as a regulation to be passed by a minister such as those contemplated by the proposed Sri Lanka Broadcasting Authority Bill (1997) did not fall into those restricted categories, clauses in issue in the proposed bill violated rights, including the right to information. This prompted the court to hold that, as a whole, the proposed bill was inconsistent with Article 10 as well, for the freedom of thought was at the core of other rights such as expression, speech, publication and information.

(6) Finally, it would follow from the reasoning and approach of the Supreme Court that, if one has freedom to think, one must have the right to express oneself through speech and publication. And for one to publish, there must be in turn the right to receive information. The logical connection cannot be denied.[65]

Some General Reflections and Conclusions

In surveying the existing state of the law in relation to the right to information, the following question may be posed. Given the fact that the constitution of Sri Lanka does not expressly recognise the right to information, could the Supreme Court in the context of the constitution have recognised such a right?

Wickramanayake v. The State[66] clearly adopted a restrictive interpretation of Article 14(1)(a) which guarantees the freedom of expression, thus shutting out any argument extending the scope of that article to other such articles in Article 14 and to a general constitutional right to information.

In *Visuvalingam and others v. Liyanage and others*[67] principles on media freedom as propounded in that decision reveal that freedom of speech and expression was taken to include the freedom of the press, subject to responsible editorial policy. This placed the emphasis on media accountability. This salutary aspect of the right to investigative journalism was not even touched upon, apart from the fact that the court emphatically held that during emergency times it would be a mere 'hands off' policy with regard to any claim based on media freedom. The right to information even as a token right was not discussed.

The decision in Fernando[68] demonstrates the laborious process of reasoning that the court had to get involved in, in recognising an implied right to information contained in the right to expression. But that too was in the special facts and circumstances of that case, such a right being recognised as a restricted right confined to a listener of a state-authorised programme.

Moreover, the court doubted that Article 14(1) includes the right to information *simpliciter.*[69] The decision in *Leader Publication (Pvt) Ltd*[70] may be viewed as a ruling that restores the freedom of the press and an implied right to information through investigative journalism but limited to a printing press whose closure had been ordered without legal competence or authority. *Environmental Foundation Ltd*[71] stands revealed as a decision that indeed upheld the right to information in the public interest but only where the state authorities deny disclosure of information which they admit as being in their possession. *Joseph Perera's case*,[72] while carrying illuminating dicta suggesting the need for a right to information in a democratic system, was slow to declare such a right.

Finally, the Supreme Court determination in the *Sri Lanka Broadcasting Authority Bill*[73] appears to have come the closest to recognising a right to information. Yet it left room for two interpretations. The broader interpretation no doubt favours the inclusion of a right to information in the light of Article 10 read with Article 14(1)(a). The narrower interpretation would restrict that right to publication to 'balanced programmes'. The right of a licensee to balanced programmes in the public interest was narrowed further, in the context of the right of the public contained in the bill to information in commercial contexts.

Yet another aspect needs reflection at this point. Progressive as the judicial exposition in the said determination was, the judicial thinking and advancement was in the context of a parliamentary bill for determination of its constitutional validity. Thus, the same would not be good enough for the public's right to balanced programmes or to information even in commercial contexts. The public would only be able to claim such a right if it were conferred by legislation.

Limits to Judicial Activism

India has in its statute book a Right to Information Law.[74] So has the USA.[75] These are two jurisdictions that have no doubt influenced the Sri Lankan judicial jurisprudence on account of the fact that both have written constitutions like Sri Lanka. This is perhaps the reason why English precedents have not been preferentially adhered to. The task for American Judges in particular has been made that much easier for the US constitution explicitly recognises the freedom of the press.

In contrast, the Sri Lankan Court has had to grapple within the narrow confines of Article 14(1) relating to the freedom of expression, stretching its judicial initiatives to the maximum in recognising a right to information in limited areas as demonstrated in this chapter.

It is common knowledge in the country that there have been attempts in the recent past to enact a Right to Information Act for Sri Lanka, which have proved to be abortive. Consequently, it is submitted as a fervent hope that the government of Sri Lanka of the day be sensitive to the need for such an enactment in the name of good governance and the Rule of Law and enact such a law with such riders as may be necessary in the interest of national or public security.

Until a Right to Information Act is contained in the statute book of Sri Lanka, if not a Constitutional Amendment expressly recognising the right to information, the civic expectation of the body politic of the Sri Lanka nation that the country is committed to basic democratic values will remain unfulfilled.

Notes

1. See *R v Lord Chancellor*, ex p Witham [1998] QB 575.
2. See Observations in *Gouriet v. Union of Post Office Workers and others* [1977] 3 All ER 70 per Lord Wilberforce at p. 79 and Lord Diplock at p. 97.
3. Article 12 (1) of the Constitution of Sri Lanka.
4. Article 14(1) of the Constitution of Sri Lanka.
5. See later discussion in this chapter, *infra*.
6. *Thassim v. Edmund Rodrigo* (Controller of Textiles)[48 N. L. R. 121.] (SC) and Nakkuda Ali v. Jayaratne [51 N. L. R. 457.] (PC) may suffice to serve as illustrations (when Sri Lanka (then Ceylon) was under the Soulbury Constitution and State Graphite Corporation v. Fernando [1981] 2 Sri LR 401 (at a time when the first Republican Constitution of Sri Lanka of 1972 was in operation) and Sirisena Cooray v. Tissa Bandaranayake and two others (1999) 1 Sri L.R. 1 (under the current Constitution of Sri Lanka).
7. Which so far successive governments in Sri Lanka have been reluctant to enact.
8. Pinto-Jayawardena (2008), p. 15.
9. Initially under the Chairmanship of Justice A.R.B. Amarasinghe (1994–2004) and more recently under the Chairmanship of Professor Lakshman Marasinghe, see Law Commission of Sri Lanka, *Report of the Law Commission on the Draft Freedom of Information Bill*, available at http://www.lawcomdept.gov.lk/info_English/index.asp-xp=723&xi=808.htm (last accessed on 15 January 2011).
10. Pinto-Jayawardena (2006).
11. (1991) 1 AC 696.
12. In that case the Secretary of State.
13. *Ibid.*, as per Lord Bridge.
14. Administrative Law (9th ed.), (Oxford, Ind. Ed.), p. 393.
15. That is, the purpose of challenging the justice of their convictions.
16. *R v. Home Secretary*, exp; Simms at p. 390.
17. Article 14(1)(a).
18. Most notably in *Fernando v. SLBC*, (1996) 1 Sri LR 157.
19. Which has been held to have the force of law, though such expansion does not extend to provisions of the Prevention of Terrorism Act No 48 of 1979. Vide *Thavaneethan v. Dayananda Dissanayake*, [2003] 1 Sri L.R. 74.

20. Review of legislation being out of the question in the context of the Sri Lankan situation (Vide: Article 80(3) of the Constitution).
21. Article 125 (1) of the Constitution.
22. Article 3 of the Constitution.
23. Vide: Article 83(a) of the Constitution.
24. (1978-80) 1 Sri LR 299.
25. *Ibid.* as per Samarakoon, CJ, p. 303.
26. *Ibid.* at p. 309.
27. 1983(2) Sri LR 311
28. ER Miscellaneous Provisions and Powers Regulations Nos.: 1, 2 and 3 of 1983.
29. An aspect that it is proposed to comment on later in this chapter.
30. An issue dealt with in 'Habeas Corpus in Sri Lanka; Theory and Practice of the Great Writ in Extraordinary Times', Kishali Pinto-Jayawardena and Jayantha de Almeida Guneratne (LST, 2011).
31. (1996) 1 Sri LR 157.
32. The SLBC under whose aegis the staff of the NEFS was conducting the said programme.
33. (1996) 1 Sri LR 157 per Fernando J, p.167.
34. *Ibid.*, per Fernando, J.
35. per Fernando, J. at p.172 read with Fernando, J.'s findings at p. 171.
36. At page 160, per Head Note, per Fernando, J.
37. 2000 (1) Sri LR 265.
38. As per Justice Amarasinghe.
39. 2000 (1) Sri LR 265 at p. 283, per Justice Amarasinghe.
40. *Ibid.*
41. 2000 (1) Sri LR 265, the decision under analysis.
42. No. 37 of 1966.
43. SLBC.
44. No. 6 of 1982.
45. SLRC
46. Later laws abrogate earlier contrary laws.
47. A general provision does not derogate from a special one.
48. See: at folio 1141 of the Parliament Hansard of 6 May 1997.
49. *Ibid.*
50. *Ibid.*
51. 'Independent' of the government.
52. At folio 1142, of the Parliament Hansard of 6 May 1997.
53. As stated in the Long Title of the Bill.
54. At folio 1143, of the Parliament Hansard of 6 May 1997.
55. At folio 1148 of the Parliament Hansard of 6 May 1997.
56. *Joseph Perera's case* (1992) 1 Sri LR 199.
57. *Ibid.*
58. *Thornhill v. State of Alabama* (31 US 88).
59. *Lamont v. Post Master General of US* (381 US 301).
60. *Stanley v. Georgia* (394 US 557). The case of Red Lion Broadcasting Co. v. F.C.C was also cited at folio 1150 of the Parliament Hansard of 6 May 1997.
61. In the United States, the 1966 Freedom of Information Act and the 1996 Electronic Freedom of Information Act have been pivotal to the campaigns of free information

advocates where federal agencies are concerned. Similar statutory provisions exist in regard to state agencies.

62. Folio 1150 of the Parliament Hansard of 6 May 1997.
63. Prescribed by law in the interest of racial and religious harmony or in relation to parliamentary privileges, contempt of court or incitement to an offence.
64. Prescribed by law in the interest of national security, public order, public health or morality which would include regulations made under the Public Security Ordinance by the Parliament.
65. What the court explained in terms of the 'Matrix Theory' (the indispensible condition) at folio 1151 of the Parliament Hansard of 6 May 1997.
66. (1978-80) 1 Sri LR 299.
67. 1983 (2) Sri LR 311.
68. (1996) 1 Sri LR 157.
69. *Ibid.*, at p. 160, per Head Note, per Fernando, J.
70. nn. 64–70.
71. SC(FR)47/2004-SC Minutes 28.11.05. This case is discussed in more detail in http://www.mediareformlanka.com/sites/default/files/core-research-articles/Dr%20Gunaratne.pdf.
72. (1992) 1 Sri LR 199.
73. nn. 88–107.
74. Right to Information Act No. 22 of 2005. Several other countries in the South Asian region also have similar laws.
75. (1966) US Code 552 (as amended) and the Open Government Act, 2007.

Part IV

Media Education and Reform

Part IV

Media Regulation and Reform

10

Media Education:
A Curricular Review

Kishali Pinto-Jayawardena and
Gehan Gunatilleke

Reviewing the Current System

The political crisis in Sri Lanka has had tremendous contextual impact on the discourse on media education. There are limits to what Sri Lankan reformers can achieve in the legal and institutional spheres in that regard. Many of the issues highlighted in Chapter 8 have dimensions that may be addressed only through long-term educational reform. For example, the profession's apparent insensitivity to gender issues or partisanship in terms of ethnicity cannot be transformed overnight. As identified by contemporary reform initiatives, such fundamental challenges may only be addressed in the classroom, where the future generation of journalists and media personnel is being moulded.[1] An interesting development in this regard is the introduction of communications and media studies into the school curriculum at GCE A/L and GCE O/L level from 2006. However, the impact of such revisions of school curricula is yet to be examined and evaluated.

In general, strengthening the training of journalists has commonly been seen as an answer to some of the systemic problems that plagued Sri Lankan society. Several attempts have been made to establish a training institute for journalists and other media personnel. One of the first initiatives in this respect was the appointment of a committee headed by Dr Gamini Corea in 1993 to set up a media-training institute. This initiative was followed by another government-appointed committee with the same objective in 1996 as well as by a government proposal for setting up a journalist training institute.[2]

Up until 2003, media training in Sri Lanka had been conducted at various universities, the Sri Lankan Television Training Institute, the Sri Lanka Foundation and within the internal training departments at SLBC and Rupavahini.[3] A uniform perception appears to be that media education in Sri Lanka is weak due to a wide gap between what is being taught and the reality of the functioning of the media.[4] It is rightly observed that media training must focus on ethics, principles and following a professional code.[5] There is, however, broad agreement that little of the training available at these institutions caters effectively for journalists in prioritising ethical standards.

One astute observation was that university courses tended to be too theoretical and focused more on abstract issues such as the relationship between media and society.[6] Hence, a real need for quality training—both theoretical and practical—had arisen during the early 2000s. Since 2003, two practical training institutions have been established, namely, the Sri Lanka College of Journalism (SLCJ) and the Media Training and Resource Centre in Jaffna. The functioning of these two training bodies will be discussed later. The current trends in media education will first be examined by surveying the teaching methodologies and curricula in universities and training colleges in Sri Lanka.

Universal Standards of Media Education

Prior to reviewing the current spectrum of curricula available amongst Sri Lankan universities and training colleges, the ideal standard in respect of media curricula ought to be briefly discussed. According to a recent study by the United Nations Educational, Scientific and Cultural Organisation (UNESCO), journalism education in universities is normally organised around three curricular axes or lines of development[7]:

(1) An axis comprising the norms, values, tools, standards and practices of journalism.
(2) An axis emphasising the social, cultural, political, economic, legal and ethical aspects of journalism practice both within and outside the national borders.
(3) An axis comprising knowledge of the world and journalism's intellectual challenges.

The first axis represents the core of any programme designed to prepare students for careers in journalism. The UNESCO study rightly points out that, on the one hand, a major weakness of journalism education 'arises out of a failure to grasp the degree to which education in university disciplines constitutes (with reporting and writing) the foundations of the practice of journalism'.[8] On the other hand, it was observed that journalism students require training in the techniques of journalism by having competent and respected practising journalists as members of the teaching staff,[9] and by including internships at local media organisations.[10] Moreover, it was recommended that media organisations be encouraged to provide journalists with the time to engage in further studies, and journalism instructors with the opportunity to upgrade their professional skills.[11]

The second axis 'elucidates the institutional and societal contexts within which journalists function and connects the practice of journalism to related human activities'.[12] The UNESCO study reveals that including such aspects in curricula strengthens professional identity, values and goals, and helps journalists understand their democratic functions and the legal and moral constraints relating to the profession. Hence, this axis emphasises professional and ethical attitudes and knowledge and the importance of independent journalism to democracy.[13]

Courses falling within this axis should introduce students to the range of national and international laws that affect journalists and the media. Moreover, such courses should include the following components[14]:

- Democratic and constitutional principles of openness and freedom of speech and expression.
- Access to information laws and procedures.
- Legal limitations to the state-imposed restrictions on media freedom such as restrictions based on national security and public order.
- Legal limitations to the protection of the judicial process, including contempt of court and publication bans.
- Legal limitations to the protection of social values and social groups, including blasphemy, expressions of racism and obscenity.
- Legal limitations arising from private rights, including defamation and privacy.

In respect of professional and ethical standards of journalism, the UNESCO study recommends that the curricula include:

> A critical examination of key ethical issues and values related principally to truth-telling, such as journalistic autonomy (including conflicts of

interest); evidence, fact checking, and corroboration; sources, named and anonymous; clarity, fairness and bias; photo and digital manipulation and misrepresentation; invention; speculation, rumours and gossip; cheque-book journalism; the Internet; quotations; plagiarism; 'objectivity' and stenographic journalism; sustained coverage of stories; corrections; etc.[15]

According to the study, the courses offered should also examine recurring ethical issues and challenges relating to civic duty, such as:

[N]ews judgment; diversity (including racial and cultural identities); gender and sexual orientation; stereotyping; children; coverage of state security issues; standards of taste, including suicides, funerals, and pictures of dead bodies; privacy issues, including public figures/private lives, celebrities, naming names, rape victims, consent, emergencies, high-jacking, kidnapping, terrorism, wars, massacres, [and] violence.[16]

The third axis exposes students to more contemporary knowledge. In this respect, the UNESCO study recommends a multi-disciplinary approach through which journalism studies are combined with education in the disciplines of arts and sciences. Moreover, such an approach requires journalism educators to collaborate with their colleagues in related fields.[17]

University Curricula[18]

Media education first emerged as a job-oriented course in the University of Kelaniya in 1973. Prior to this, media institutions were largely responsible for training journalists. One of the early pioneers of media education, Professor Wimal Dissanayake, has written that 'the Department of Mass Communication was established at Kelaniya University because there was a felt need at the time to introduce new courses that had an immediate applicability to daily life'.[19] But these early courses were taught in the language departments of the universities and were more concerned with writing and the print medium than with media and communication. Furthermore, there was hardly an applied and practical aspect to these courses.[20] According to Dr Tudor Weerasinghe, even the terms *jana sannivedanaya* and *jana maadya*, to denote mass communication and mass media, respectively, are conceptually wrong, as the word *jana* means 'folk' not 'masses', as in *jana kala* (folk art), *jana sangeethaya* (folk music), *jana natum* (folk dance). These terms were used in Europe, from where the early media teachers borrowed them, to generate different connotations and meaning. This clearly shows, he says, that they did not have a clear perception of the theories and concepts of media education.[21]

Today, at least three universities are known to offer degree programmes in mass communications and media studies, while several other institutions conduct courses with media and mass communication components. In November 2010, a National Media Summit (The Kelaniya Summit) was organised by the Department of Mass Communication, University of Kelaniya and the Ministry of Mass Media and Information to evaluate 'the nature, quality and relevance and the future of media education in Sri Lanka'.[22] The Kelaniya Summit saw the coming together of mass communication lecturers from around the country for the first time, as a result of which the Kelaniya Declaration was issued in late 2010. The Summit was preceded by a series of reviews of university curricula pertaining to media education. The reviews themselves appear to be reasonably comprehensive—though at times slightly generic[23]—and cover all academic courses offered by recognised universities in the country. The Kelaniya Summit itself was an extremely positive development in media education, which could lead to more structured and streamlined curricula across Sri Lankan universities. The next section of this paper summarises some of the key findings presented at the Summit by the reviewers.

The Department of Mass Communication, University of Kelaniya, offers special and general degrees in Mass Communication. The curriculum was revised in 2000, following which further programmes such as a Diploma in Mass Communication were introduced. One particularly interesting course offered at Kelaniya is 'Media Law and Ethics', which provides an overview of the relations between mass media, law and ethics.[24]

A recent review of the curricula in Kelaniya concluded that the offered courses in mass communication were 'sufficient academically and professionally' and that the structure and content of the degree programme ensured 'quality of education and opportunity to enhance the skills of the students'.[25] An important feature of the special degree courses offered at Kelaniya—an aspect that appears to attract a number of high quality students—is the opportunity given to students to train in private and public media organisations.[26] Moreover, close proximity to metropolitan areas has enhanced the employability of Kelaniya students, enabling them to find employment while in the last stages of their courses.[27]

As discussed below, the availability of practical training has become a key issue in media education and has often been the dividing line between high quality education that enhances career opportunities and mediocre education that leaves students detached from the industry. It has also been recommended that students be given additional opportunities to acquire proficiency in English and other foreign languages to enable them to find employment in local and international job markets with higher scales of remuneration.[28]

The Journalism Unit of the Faculty of Arts, University of Colombo, offers a variety of courses and course units with media and mass communication dimensions. The curriculum also specifically includes media policy studies, and media law and ethics. The Unit offers both a Diploma in Journalism and a general undergraduate degree with media components.

A 2008 review of the curriculum at Colombo noted that it 'carries a broad spectrum of subject areas [and] topics which are useful in producing quality graduates in the given discipline'.[29] Moreover, similar to the Kelaniya programme, it was observed that theoretical as well as practical components are incorporated into the curriculum in a balanced manner.[30] However, some of the weaknesses in the programmes offered at Colombo include the tendency for overlap, the lack of a research component and the lack of adequate course descriptions for the benefit of students.[31] Furthermore, it was noted that qualified and competent academic staff remain at the disposal of the university, and students with high 'Z-Scores' are attracted to the programme. Hence, the intellectual assets of the university remain in a healthy state. However, this advantage has not been adequately complemented by the provision of material assets. The reviewers observed that the amount of equipment currently available at the Journalism Unit was 'woefully inadequate'.[32]

Similar to the advantage seen in Kelaniya, the metropolitan location of the Colombo Campus enables easy interaction with print and electronic media organisations situated within close proximity. This advantage provides ample opportunity for the effective conduct of the practical components of course units[33] and certainly helps students build networks that benefit their career prospects.

The Department of Sinhala and Mass Communications, Sri Jayewardenepura University, offers both a diploma and a general BA degree with a specialisation in Mass Communication. The degree programme appears to be comprehensive, as it covers a variety of key topics and includes units on ethics and media law as part of the course on print media studies.[34] The programme also insists on the submission of a dissertation, which, unlike the Colombo and Kelaniya programmes, compels students to engage in more detailed research. The university also offers an MA programme with five units including one specifically on 'Media Law and Ethics'.

One criticism of the Sri Jayewardenepura curriculum for Mass Communication is that it fails to consider some of the new developments in the field and remains slightly outdated.[35] Moreover, the curriculum lacks a practical component, which denies students the opportunity to 'gain knowledge in the practical aspects of the subjects they learn in classrooms'.[36] Those involved in the professional training of journalists in Sri Lanka share this view on the basis that the university curricula are weighted towards the theoretical teaching of media rather than the practical aspects.[37] Reviewers of the curricula have also expressed concern over the standard of teaching at Sri Jayewardenepura, as teachers appeared to be averse to using any of the modern methods or technology in respect of teaching the subject of media.[38]

The Open University of Sri Lanka (OUSL) is virtually the only recognised university in Sri Lanka where students are permitted to pursue further education by distance education techniques in keeping with the philosophy of 'open and distance learning'.[39] Accordingly, the Department of Social Studies offers a unique programme through which students can engage in media studies at a self-governed pace.[40] A distinctive feature of the courses offered by the department is that they have 'a robust multi-disciplinary perspective'.[41] Yet the OUSL is observed to have outdated course material; hence major curriculum revision may soon be required.[42] Moreover, an unhealthy student–staff ratio at the department has caused the overburdening of academic staff members, possibly preventing them from designing and conducting new courses according to the contemporary demands of the media industry.[43]

The Department of Languages, Sabaragamuwa University, also offers a general degree programme with a Journalism Major and with a range of courses including 'Print Media Studies', 'Mass Communication and Society' and 'Print Media'.[44] As a programme conducted in the provinces, the Sabaragamuwa programme could potentially provide the vital leverage needed for the improvement of journalism skills outside the capital. A recent review of the curriculum suggests that the programme 'offer[s] good quality education and [...] provide[s] opportunities for students to enhance their skills'.[45] Furthermore, the department introduced a new syllabus in respect of Mass Communication in 2011, which aims to facilitate more specific media studies.[46] There has been animated discussion about the precise directions that these reforms will take and much openness on collaborating with experts, both domestic and regional in this effort.

However, compared to Colombo-based universities, the programme still seems to lack sophistication in terms of staff and facilities and may be a fair distance away from producing truly competitive media professionals. The Department of Linguistics, Faculty of Arts, University of Jaffna, offers a BA degree with a course in 'Communication and Media Studies'.[47] The programme contains a fairly detailed syllabus giving attention to both the theoretical and practical aspects of the field of journalism. This course also has a strong component of media law and ethics, including topics such as 'the right to information'. Despite obvious resource and infrastructural constraints, the academic staff appear to be highly committed to their students, while the students themselves have been observed as highly motivated in pursuing their studies.[48] This motivation is certainly encouraging in the post-conflict context, as journalism standards in the north would be expected to improve exponentially as the programme gathers momentum.

A number of other universities offer degrees with either mass communication specialisations or with media components. The Department of Mass Media, Sri Palee Campus, which is now affiliated to the University of Colombo, offers a four-year Special Degree in Mass Media.[49] The programme appears to be functioning well, notwithstanding limitations in terms of space facilities.[50] Similarly, the Department of Languages and Communication Studies, Trincomalee Campus, Eastern University offers a BA in Communication[51] and the Department of Social Sciences, South Eastern University of Sri Lanka offers a BA (special) degree with a specialisation in Sociology, which includes a course in 'Mass Communication'.[52] The Department of Humanities at the Rajarata University of Sri Lanka also offers a BA (general) degree in Mass Communication.[53] The programme, however, is not without its share of problems. A recent review of the curricula at Rajarata revealed that the programme suffered from over-dependence on visiting lecturers to conduct regular programmes[54] and also had inadequacies in terms of modern teaching technologies, and IT and library resources.

Training Institutes and Colleges

Interestingly, it was not a university but the state radio that started broadcast media training. Established with the cooperation of the BBC in the late 1960s, the Sri Lanka Broadcasting Corporation Training Institute provided skills development for its technical and programme staff. The

Institute also offered some sort of improvised practical training sessions of very short duration to students following communication studies at Kelaniya and Colombo universities. This had little impact on broadcast media education in the country as a whole, though those who later left the state radio to take up appointments in the newly expanded private broadcasting sector took with them certain aspects of this 'training'.

The Sri Lanka Television Training Institute (SLTTI), 'one of the educational wings of the Sri Lanka Foundation which came into being in 1984', is a national media training centre equipped to conduct professional training in the fields of television and radio. Its mission is 'to train media and film personnel in Sri Lanka and Asia in programming and technological aspects of TV, radio and principles of film art to improve the quality of electronic media and to make a more meaningful social impact'. SLTTI currently offers a 'vast range of training programs at different levels through Workshops, Certificate courses, advanced Certificate courses and Diploma and Higher Diploma courses'. The institute claims that 'the distinct feature of training is its inclination to equipment-based practical training', where the students get ample hands-on experience in each discipline, enabling them to confidently embark on a vocation. Considering its scope and focus, however, the impact of the SLTTI has been limited.

Amongst the other leading training institutes and colleges providing media education, the Media Research and Training Centre (MRTC), affiliated to the University of Jaffna, and the SLCJ require mention.

MRTC conducts two courses in journalism: (1) a part-time diploma course in journalism for working journalists and (2) a full-time course for university students. Both courses cover a range of key topics and include theoretical as well as practical aspects of journalism.[55] The courses also introduce students to the basics of media law and ethics. Crucially, the underlying thinking behind MRTC seem to be based on the idea that an '[i]ndependent, free and pluralistic media [has] a crucial role to play in the good governance of democratic societies, by ensuring transparency and accountability, promoting participation and the rule of law, and contributing to the fight against poverty'.[56] This ideology is important to the students at MRTC, since they are most likely to form the future backbone of journalism in the Northern Province. Given the post-conflict context, the proper training of these journalists would be crucial to the future reconciliation process.

SLCJ was established with the broad objective of furthering democracy and independent thinking through the development of journalism and the integration of the media industry.[57] SLCJ has three core programmes: a one-year diploma course at the entry level, short professional courses for working journalists, referred to as 'mid-career courses' and an extensive training program for provincial journalists. The unique feature of SLCJ is its novel approach of combining practical learning 'on the job' with the standard mass communication courses at universities which encourages more abstract reflection. This approach is the result of careful planning, as the institution has adopted a participatory process that involves designing and setting up the curricula through the contribution of prominent Sri Lankan journalists and lecturers, and a curriculum advisor provided by the donor agency, Fojo.[58]

Elmqvist and Bastian (2006) note that the methodology adopted at SLCJ is interactive and is based on continuous assessment rather than the standard 'lecture' model adopted in most universities.[59] Moreover, SLCJ has an internship component, where the student spends a significant period of time at a media organisation. This component has provided an additional dimension through which students could meet mentors and develop good relations within the industry, thereby enhancing their future career opportunities.[60] The authors intimate that the internships have been particularly helpful for women, since the industry can often be discriminatory in terms of providing equal job opportunities.[61]

One of the outstanding challenges faced by SLCJ remains the transforming of its Colombo-centric student base.[62] There is an undeniable need to provide sound training to journalists and media professionals in the provinces, as 'more and more newspapers have supplements from the provinces, and there is a commercial interest in improving the quality of provincial journalists'.[63] Moreover, coverage of provincial news has occasionally been limited due to the inability of Colombo-based journalists to cover issues in the provinces comprehensively. The main reasons for this inability include the lack of resources to travel outside Colombo and poor networks with provincial journalists, who themselves are grossly under-financed. Hence, the institution may need to focus more on facilitating the training of journalists from the provinces through specially designed scholarship programmes and by calling on newspapers to sponsor students from outside Colombo.[64]

The Sri Lanka Press Institute has already carried out a 'training needs assessment' for provincial correspondents in more than 20 districts and has identified critical areas that need to be addressed. As a result of this survey, SLCJ has begun to conduct at least one course for provincial correspondents every month. The subjects range from 'One-man Operation for Video Journalists' to 'Basic News Writing and Radio

Production'. SLCJ trainers acting as designers and co-trainers also carry out regional training programmes for the BBC World Service Trust.[65] By 2012, the SLCJ had trained close to 1200 provincial correspondents from all parts of the country including the north and east.[66]

Comparative Experiences from India[67]

Compared to Sri Lanka, there is little doubt that the teaching of media law and policy in India has advanced much farther in its reach and complexity. The rapid expansion of the Indian media during the last two decades has increased the demand for competent media persons well versed in the latest communication technologies. It has transformed media education in the country.

Two broad strands of teaching are in evidence across Indian educational institutions in this regard:

(1) University and academic programmes offered at the postgraduate level combining communication theory, social science research and practical skills.

(2) Professional courses that focus almost exclusively on skills with varying amounts of social theory included. New-age Journalism Schools, popularly known as 'J Schools', promise to teach the craft of journalism within a span of 10 months to 2 years. A good example of such cutting edge institutions is the Asian College of Journalism, Chennai (ACJ).[68]

Based on such categorisation, the content of the curricula in these institutions has also varied, resulting in different emphasis being placed on areas such as law and policy. The structural framework of the media curriculum in most of India's educational institutions begins with an overview of the Indian Constitution, followed by Press Laws, freedom of expression and reasonable restrictions in the second unit, Regulations and Acts in the third unit, TV, cable regulations, regulations governing advertisements and films in the fourth unit and ethical aspects in the last unit. This used to be the conventional course structure for a long time until the explosion of web-based media as a medium of communication. Thereafter, cyber laws came to occupy the fifth unit of the syllabus, resulting in the ethics component being delegated to the fourth unit, along with the regulation of TV and other media.

Media teachers have pointed, however, to obstacles in their efforts to reform curricula. Analysing the teaching of media law and policy in Southern India, for example, one perceptive commentator has observed that there are 'black holes' in the course. The content and constitutional aspects of the course have gradually become less important while vital legislation is not dealt with in sufficient detail.[69] As a result, the focus and interlinking of human rights with the teaching of media law and policy have been given a lower priority.

Second, the sequencing of content in university courses is far from ideal. In principle, media law should not be placed towards the end of the course, as its content is then overlooked. On the other hand, placing it too early in a course results in students not understanding the nuances and complexities of what is taught.[70] Many of the university courses, in particular, err on this point. Third, the media law courses today are fast being made more skill based and less theoretical. Students are more interested in vocational training for the future and are willing to compromise their theoretical understanding of the field in this light. Fourth, there are several challenges to finding an ideal method of instruction. The main difficulty is finding a balance between theory and practice to provide equal exposure to both. Teachers are often given too little time to cover important aspects of the subject comprehensively.[71]

This also gravely impacts on the teaching methods adopted. Case studies that are taken in the classroom are shorn of their context and historical background. Teachers do not have the freedom to undertake studies of cases that are closer to home and have to discuss issues such as the Watergate Scandal that does not have a local dimension. The incidents chosen are not contemporary and are not relevant to the contemporary media scenario. Fifth, teaching resources in universities are hard to locate and many institutions are unwilling to make the necessary financial investment to acquire materials for their students.[72]

Although there is a growing trend of using the Internet as a source of data and material, it cannot be said that the Internet has been used to the optimal extent. In short, there is considerable deficiency in innovation in the development of course material for media law courses. The absence of an interdisciplinary approach to media law in these courses has also attracted some concern. Most importantly, however, discussants point to the lack of critical study regarding the role and impact of the Indian media.

The manner in which the media law and policy is taught in India is not rigorously critiqued in the public space, either by journalists or by media analysts or by academics. There are some critiques of media practice and policy. But this is more from a feminist cum gender perspective and these critiques rarely have significant impact upon the media. The industry tends to react quite negatively to such critiques. For an example after the Mumbai blast, the media blamed the government for public criticism of their reportage and said this was because of the lack of guidelines issued to the media.[73]

Meanwhile an interesting aspect of these discussions is that many students who opt to take academic courses in the media do not intend to undertake a career in journalism after graduation; the reason is not simply lack of financial incentive but also a general perception that the India media had become corrupted.

We think that we would lose our idealism and belief in the ability of media to change society if we actually become professional journalists.[74]

Generally, there appears to be growing concern that the changes in the nature of the media have resulted in many students of journalism not opting for media studies after completing the course. This may also perhaps be because journalism is now offered as an undergraduate course. The students who opt for it do so without a firm conviction that they will pursue it later as a career. They are only interested in taking away the basic skills that such a study can offer.[75] Others think that the dwindling interest in the profession is caused by teachers being unable to make the important link between good journalism and society, and perhaps even weak remuneration structures.[76] Some also believe that students are averse to joining the media in India because they either want 'glamorous jobs' such as TV presenters that are hard to obtain or because they are disillusioned by the growth of paid news and are afraid of their future in the industry if these trends continue.[77] A refreshing counter point of view was expressed in the following terms:

Actually I feel that the good thing about the ACJ is the sizeable percentage from the college that does not go into practical journalism once they have finished studies. Instead, they adopt more critical avenues of work including even anthropology. Many students say that they do not want to enter mainstream media. Some others do enter the mainstream but leave after a while saying that they cannot do the job anymore. There is of course a number who do stay on and they rise to decision making levels in the Indian media institutions. In India, the struggle is different to the fighting against an authoritarian state. We are fighting against the corporate giants. This is as difficult a struggle as that which is carried on against a government.[78]

Certainly, dialogue amongst Indian media educators on devising appropriate pedagogical tools to train journalists and other media persons is being given increased importance. One suggestion being made is the need to bridge the glaring gap between the teaching of media law and ground realities. On these lines, some media teachers voice their belief that it is important that the broader legal curriculum be located in its social context and advocate a pedagogical structure which encourages students of media law to have a sense of their social role. As examples of this trend, the role of investigative journalism in filing public interest litigation and the interface between free media and constitutional liberties may be pertinent.[79] The result of an ideal education in media law and policy should involve equal exposure to the state, the private sector and the social sector which would make pedagogy not merely textual, but participative.[80]

Institutional and Attitudinal Challenges: A Comparative Analysis

The media industry in Sri Lanka appears to be attracting a strong and vibrant younger generation, as journalism still remains a reasonably viable career option. However, there are certain challenges faced by the industry that may significantly dissuade future job seekers from entering the profession.

One significant challenge that has already been discussed at length is the risk factor. Journalists and media personnel continue to be harassed, intimidated, assaulted and even assassinated for doing their job. The notion that working in the media is 'dangerous' has ultimately stigmatised the profession, and has possibly prevented a number of aspiring graduates from pursuing a media career. Apart from this quite obvious challenge, there remains the nagging issue of resources. Media personnel, in general, form a grossly underpaid class of professionals, which no doubt discourages new entrants.[81]

Apart from these entry-level challenges, media education in Sri Lanka faces certain distinct institutional and attitudinal challenges. One of the most significant challenges in this respect is the widening chasm between theory and practice. On the one hand, there is a dire need for sound practical training, as most journalists in Sri Lanka have received no formal training, either at the entry level or as working journalists.[82] Correspondingly, there appears to be a persistent problem in respect of university courses being too abstract or theoretical and lacking a practical dimension.[83] A common challenge faced by most universities—particularly those located outside Colombo—seems to be the lack of appropriate practical components.[84] According to the reviewers of the Mass Communication courses in the Kelaniya University, 'practical experience and multi-skills should be facilitated to the students so that they may be strong enough to compete with specialist[s] coming out from other institutions [*sic*]'.[85] In similar vein, the reviewers of the Journalism Unit of the University of Colombo have observed that opportunity for further development of students' talents is hindered by the dearth of exposure to practical aspects of the profession.[86]

This lack of practical training may have been addressed to an extent by the arrival of contemporary professional training institutions such as SLCJ, which has the potential to fulfil the role of a cutting-edge practical training institution. However, this institution is yet to penetrate the industry to the extent of creating systemic change.[87] Hence a fairly serious problem remains: university graduates lack practical training, while industry-trained journalists lack a sound theoretical grounding.[88] Practical and theoretical exposure in the international sphere would also enable the journalists to maintain international standards and ensure the professionalism expected of them in the media industry. Therefore, it would be necessary for the media education providers to understand their responsibility in this regard.[89]

Some key studies have revealed certain limitations in 'individual' media training. The focus on individual training may improve the skills of individual journalists, yet have very little impact on the institutions in which they function.[90] At the institutional level, it has been observed that 'the structures of hierarchy make it very difficult for trained staff to share their new competence with colleagues, unless in an informal way'.[91] As Elmqvist and Bastian (2006) rightly point out, 'institutional barriers make it difficult for individuals to practise what they learn'.[92] The authors further observe that 'many editors and gate keepers constitute the principal blockage to better journalistic practice'.[93] This hierarchical barrier certainly requires immediate attention.

The changing socio-economic context would require journalists to be prepared to face the changing nature of the post-war environment. Particularly, the end of the ethnic conflict in Sri Lanka means that journalists would be compelled to develop their expertise and professional skills to address a wider range of issues. Therefore, it is imperative that the review and enhancement of curricula in universities and institutions should be carried out to address these emerging circumstances.[94]

Media education in Sri Lanka also suffers from a sense of denial, as it appears to ignore the absence of media freedom in the country. There are two possible explanations for this inadequacy: first, the self-preservation agenda of certain educational institutions, and second, the influence of certain politically motivated elements within the university system. A good example of the first explanation comes from the Jaffna-based training institute, MRTC. During interviews conducted in Jaffna in December 2010, the MRTC educators admitted that they studiously avoided any reference to contentious issues such as the independence of the media from government, and attacks on journalists, to avoid the ire of the government. We also observed a similar pattern in November 2010 at the Department of Languages and Communication Studies, Trincomalee Campus, Eastern University. Educators at this institution cited inadequate facilities and university bureaucracy as major obstacles to upgrading the campus.[95] Ironically, nearly 80 per cent of the student population at this campus is of Sinhalese ethnicity, despite the fact that Trincomalee itself is celebrated for being multi-ethnic.

While this dysfunction is aggravated in the north and the east, it is also prevalent in Colombo and other places in the south. Self-preservation may partly explain this phenomenon in the south. Yet there also seems to be an element of politicisation within the system. A number of leading lecturers in Sri Lanka's departments of mass communications have been known to have political affiliations.[96] Such affiliations have an unhealthy impact on the development of curricula, as those charged with formulating curricula have vested interests in avoiding contentious issues. Since media education is vital to long-term reform, the absence of course content on media freedom and other contemporary issues facing the Sri Lankan media is of considerable concern.

The absence of an enlightened educational framework in Sri Lanka certainly weakens the potential of future journalists and media personnel to engage the state on key issues that affect their profession. This absence will ultimately impact on the quality of reform work in future. It is thus strongly recommended that educational institutions actively seek to include in their curricula a critical examination of current legal and institutional structures. Such frank discussion on these contentious issues will no doubt equip media workers to pursue reform far more effectively.

Furthermore, the situation in terms of education in media law and policy appears to be deplorable. Interviews that the research team conducted in Sabaragamuwa, Jaffna and Trincomalee Universities as well as conversations with media and mass communications lecturers in the Colombo Universities revealed that media law is taught by lecturers who are not lawyers and have no knowledge of how the law works in practice, and is generally dealt with in a superficial manner.

It appeared that one solution was to hire guest lecturers who were supposed to have knowledge in the area of media law; however, in actual fact, it was revealed that even those guest lecturers possessed very little knowledge about the subject matter of media law and policy. The dearth of qualified lecturers was indeed a problem. In addition, where the universities were concerned, bureaucratic red tape made it difficult for them to obtain the services of guest lecturers; as the Rector of the Trincomalee campus succinctly observed: 'we cannot pay guest lecturers very much due to the prevailing rules and regulations. Who will come all the way from Colombo to Trincomalee to teach media law and policy in this sort of situation?'[97]

At a different level, there appeared to be tensions between the academic and the practical spheres of education in mass communications and the media.[98] In private conversations with senior editors in Colombo, the courses offered by universities tended to be dismissed on the basis that they are academic and impractical in the actual world of journalism. On the other hand, there also appeared to be an undercurrent of resentment on the part of media educators in universities that the key media industry offices in Colombo give preference in awarding internships to students of the training colleges run by the industry rather than university students. Overcoming these tensions will be key to bringing educators and mass communication teachers together in the common objective of improving the system in which media and mass communications are taught in Sri Lanka.[99]

Educators have been enjoined to find a balance between the theory and the practice of media law. Further, it is of obvious importance that media training must have the widest possible contact with foreign media in order for journalists to have exposure to best practices.[100]

In conclusion, it may be reiterated that media reform in Sri Lanka requires an integrated approach, which addresses legal, industry and educational dimensions of the media through a comprehensive and all-encompassing strategy. It is mainly through such an approach that the Sri Lankan media could regain its independence and integrity and reclaim its rightful position as the fourth estate of democracy.

Notes

1. Continuous discussion among university lecturers, syllabus makers and media personalities is mandatory to identify what should be the final production of universities regarding Media Education [vide interview with. K. Janaranjana, 1 June 2012].
2. Elmqvist and Bastian (2006), p. 8.

3. See Grunnet et al. (2005); Nohrstedt et al. (2002).
4. Interview with Hiniduma Sunil Senevi, 1 June 2012, Sabaragamuwa University.
5. Interview with Kumar Nadesan, 20 February 2012.
6. Nohrstedt et al. (2002), p. 14.
7. UNESCO, Model Curricula for Journalism Education (2007), p. 7.
8. *Ibid.*
9. *Ibid.*
10. *Ibid.*, p. 8.
11. *Ibid.*
12. *Ibid.*
13. *Ibid.*
14. *Ibid.*, p. 22.
15. *Ibid.*, pp. 22–23.
16. *Ibid.*
17. *Ibid.*
18. Some portions of this discussion are based on the findings of Wijayananda Rupasinghe in his unpublished article: *Overview of Curricula Relating to the Teaching of Media Policy, the Law and Related Topics in Educational and Training Institutions in Sri Lanka* (October 2010).
19. See interview with Wimal Dissanayake, 10 March 2011.
20. See interview with Tudor Weerasinghe, 16 March 2011; interview with Bandula Dayaratne, 20 March 2011.
21. Interview with Tudor Weerasinghe. This section incorporates information from a research paper by Tilak Jayaratne and Sarath Kellapotha, available at: http://mediareformlanka.com/research-papers (accessed on 12 January 2011).
22. See Rupasinghe and Jinadasa (2010).
23. The authors note that a thorough comparison between different reviews conducted by the same individuals reveals a slightly generic trend, which may diminish the reliability of some of the reviews.
24. Course content includes: definitions and characteristics of mass communication law and ethics; ethics as a philosophical problem; aspects of social ethics; religious ethics; origin and development of ethics related to broadcasting, cinema, print media and other selected media; right to receiver (audience) communication rights; respect for privacy; impartiality; challenges and constraints on ethics; challenges and limitations of mass media usage with special reference to developing countries; acts and ordinances related to ethics; censorship; the Universal Declaration on Human Rights; the UNESCO Declaration on Mass Media Ethics; and Intellectual property rights. See New Curriculum (Special) Mass Communication, Faculty of Social Sciences, Kelaniya University; also see http://www.kln.ac.lk/social/maco/courses.htm (accessed on 12 January 2011).
25. Ismail et al. (2007), p. 8.
26. *Ibid.*, p. 10.
27. *Ibid.*
28. *Ibid.*, p. 11.
29. Rajapaksha et al. (2008), p. 6.
30. *Ibid.*
31. *Ibid.*
32. *Ibid.*, p. 7.
33. *Ibid.*

34. See Course Requirements to Consider Mass Communication as a Main Field for the BA (General) Degree, Department of Sinhala and Mass Communication, Faculty of Arts, University of Sri Jayewardenepura; also see http://www.sjp.ac.lk/fa/sinh/comass.html (accessed on 12 January 2011). The list of courses includes: Principles of Communication; Introduction to Mass Media; Evolution of Mass Media; News Gathering and Reporting; Public Relations; Advertising and Publicity Features, Columns and Interviews; Mass Media Law and Ethics; Fundamentals of Electronic Media; Effective Communication; Mass Media Effects; Inter-Cultural Communication; Television Production Techniques; Cinematography; Development Communication; Mass Media Research; Print Media Techniques; Radio Production Techniques; New Media Usage and Political Communication.

35. Meddegama et al. (2010), p. 5.

36. *Ibid.*

37. Interview with Imran Furkan, 9 February 2012, and Sukumar Rockwood, 14 February 2012.

38. Meddegama et al. (2010), p. 6.

39. Bandara et al. (2009), p. 12.

40. See the Open University of Sri Lanka, Department of Social Studies, Faculty of Humanities and Social Sciences, *Bachelor of Arts Degree Programme in Social Sciences— Prospectus for Students 2010-2011*, available at: http://www.ou.ac.lk (accessed on 13 January 2011).

41. Bandara et al. (2009), at p.4. The authors conclude: 'the academic staff members of the department strongly believe that the students should be well equipped with multi-disciplinary tools of analysis and applications to enable them to work effectively and efficiently in public, private or international institutions'.

42. *Ibid.*, p. 17.

43. *Ibid.*, p. 10.

44. See http://www.sab.ac.lk/Miscel/OurDegrees.htm (accessed on 13 January 2011).

45. Amunugama et al. (2006), at p.6. This observation is buttressed by a field visit made to the Sabaragamuwa University by the research team in 2010.

46. See New Syllabus for Mass Communication, Sabaragamuwa University.

47. See Syllabus for Communication and Media Studies, Faculty of Arts, University of Jaffna.

48. Amunugama et al. (2008), at p.11.

49. See Syllabus—Department of Mass Media, Sri Palee Campus, University of Colombo; also see http://www.cmb.ac.lk/academic/sripalee/index/media_syllabus.htm (accessed on 12 January 2011).

50. Rajapaksha et al. (2008), p. 12.

51. See http://www.esn.ac.lk/trincocampus/Departments/LCS.html (accessed on 12 January 2011).

52. See Course Syllabus of the B.A. (Special) Programme, available at http://www.seu.ac.lk/FAC/facpos. html#Sociology (accessed on 13 January 2011).

53. See Rajarata University of Sri Lanka (2008).

54. Gunatunge et al. (2007), p. 10.

55. See University of Jaffna, Sri Lanka, Faculty of Arts, Media Resources and Training Centre, Structure of the Diploma in Journalism Full Time and Part Time Courses (2010).

56. *Ibid.*, see Preamble.

57. SLCJ was founded in 2004 to provide training for potential and working journalists, to enhance their knowledge through skills and technology development. A senior

journalist stated that most journalists in Sri Lanka tend not to have any formal journalism education. In contrast, a large proportion of journalists in other countries in the subcontinent undergo professional or at least academic training before they commence practical work in the print or electronic media.

58. Elmqvist and Bastian (2006), p. 23.
59. *Ibid.*, p. 24.
60. *Ibid.*
61. *Ibid.*
62. Approximately, 60–70 students have been taken into the Sri Lanka College of Journalism each year since the start of the college in 2004. The college notches up a pass rate of 80–90 per cent entering the industry within the year of completing the diploma. Approximately, 5–10 students of the year enter university in pursuit of a BA degree (data obtained through an interview with senior administrator, Sri Lanka College of Journalism, 9 February 2012).
63. Elmqvist and Bastian (2006), p. 24.
64. *Ibid.*
65. Interview with a senior administrator, Sri Lanka College of Journalism Sri Lanka Collage of Journalism, 9 February 2012). In 2011, The SLCJ provided for six professional courses that were specifically asked for by the media organisations. Two courses were in relation of writing post-conflict articles and the other courses related to camera operations and training.
66. Sri Lanka College of Journalism, *Courses Offered: Provincial Correspondents*, available at http://www.slcj.lk/course_ditails.php?course_id=9 (accessed on 17 January 2012).
67. This is a synopsis of discussions with Indian media educators and academics conducted under the auspices of a grant by the Ford Foundation (Institute of International Education) during February–July 2012, including visits to the Asian College of Journalism, Chennai; Department of Media and Communications, University of Puducherry, Puducherry and the Centre for Culture, Media and Governance, Jamia Millia Islamia, New Delhi. In addition, perspectives from conference sessions on *Teaching Media Policy & Law—A Faculty Workshop (South Zone)* organised by the Alternative Law Forum, Bangalore and Centre for Culture, Media and Governance, Jamia Millia Islamia, New Delhi held on 24–25 April 2012, National Law School of India University, Bangalore (hereafter, NLSIU conference April 2012) have been particularly useful.
68. ACJ is considered to be a top ranking journalism school that offers post-graduate courses in journalism. ACJ offers a 1-year postgraduate diploma with specialisations in Television, Print, New Media and Radio. In the first trimester, all students, irrespective of their chosen medium, are taught the basics of broadcast, web and print. From the second trimester onwards, students of each stream are guided by a trained faculty to learn the nuances of reporting in their respective choice of medium. As observed in discussions with Sashi Kumar, a co-founder and Chairman, ACJ at Chennai (February 2012), emphasis is placed on looking at the 'how to' of journalism skills as well as the 'why' or the philosophical and idealistic components of journalism. Furthermore, the ACJ seems to be maintaining a cosmopolitan campus environment by granting scholarships to students from Afghanistan, Bangladesh, Bhutan, India, Maldives, Nepal, Pakistan and Sri Lanka.
69. Haneef (2012).
70. *Ibid.*

71. *Ibid.*
72. *Ibid.*
73. Discussions with Anuradha Sharma and Jamia Millia, New Delhi, July 2012.
74. Viewpoint of a student during guest lecturer and discussions at Department of Media and Mass Communications, University of Puducherry, February 2012.
75. Viewpoints of students during guest lecturer and discussions at University of Puducherry, February 2012.
76. *Ibid.*
77. *Ibid.*
78. Discussions with Sadan and Menon, Chennai, February 2012. His further point is equally interesting: 'I teach media and dance at the ACJ and my teachings are motivated by the critique of the media. I left journalism myself and became a radical activist due to the fact that the idealism which drove the Indian media in the past to rebel against the establishment no longer exists. In the 1970s, journalism was exciting and challenging. Now it has become market driven. The Indian corporate class maintains a stranglehold on the Indian media. There is a corporate takeover of the media. Even hardcore news is instantly converted into entertainment. India's most energizing thinkers in the media and on the media just moved away. Journalists have now become corporate salesman'.
79. Viewpoints put forward at conference sessions on *Teaching Media Policy and Law—A Faculty Workshop (South Zone)* organised under the aegis of the project '*Mapping Media Policy and Law*' supported by the Ford Foundation, by Alternative Law Forum, Bangalore and Centre for Culture, Media and Governance, Jamia Millia Islamia, New Delhi held on 24–25 April 2012, National Law School of India University, Bangalore.
80. *Ibid.*
81. As a senior administrator at the SLCJ observed, the conditions of work at media institutions need to be improved to promote professional and satisfactory standards in the media industry in Sri Lanka (Anonymous—interviewed on 9 February 2012).
82. *Ibid.*, p. 23.
83. The industry requirement for full-time journalists with academic qualifications and practical skills must be the main concentration point for the media education policy makers [vide interview with I. Furkan, 9 February 2012].
84. See, for example, the observations of Rajapaksha et al. (2008), at p. 12 and Gunatunge et al. (2007), p. 12.
85. Ismail et al. (2007), p. 12.
86. Rajapaksha et al. (2008), p. 8.
87. To create such a systematic change, it has been suggested that a National Diploma should be introduced for journalists. This course would take 18 months to complete and would be recognised as the pre-qualification to enter the profession [vide interview with S. Rockwood, 14 February 2012].
88. There exists a wide gap between the university education of students in mass media and mass communications and the practical trainings offered by media institutions such as the Sri Lanka College of Journalism [vide interview with D. Nesiah, 21 February 2012].
89. *Ibid.* The importance of maintaining good relationships with foreign media (not just in the western hemisphere) in countries like India, the Middle East, China and Russia was emphasised on the basis that there is a strong need to maintain a regional and international contextualised focus even in the reporting of national issues.
90. Elmqvist and Bastian (2006), p. 12.

91. *Ibid.*, at p.25. The authors observed that unless journalists occupied a higher position at the working place, they had few opportunities to '[apply] their new skills within a wider circle, or to provide in-house training to colleagues'.
92. *Ibid.*, p. 12.
93. *Ibid.*, p. 25.
94. The ability of journalists to change according to changing circumstances was identified as an important skill in the profession of journalism. For example, in the current context, journalists are required to specialise in greater business or financially related issues after decades of conflict and this has necessitated training in new skills (a senior administrator, Sri Lanka College of Journalism, interviewed on 9 February 2012).
95. Interviews of the research team with the Rector and the staff of the Mass Communications Department, Trincomalee Campus, 2010.
96. For example, Professors Ariyaratne Atugala and Sunanda Mahendra, both long-serving lecturers in mass media, continue to have political affiliations. Prof. Atugala is the former Head of the Department of Mass Media at Kelaniya University, who later became chairman of the SLRC and Director General of the Government Information Department. See http://www.news.lk/index.php?option=com_content&task =view&id=15111&Itemid=44 (accessed on 22 January 2011). Prof. Mahendra currently serves on the highly politicised Press Council. See Colombo Page, *Sri Lanka Press Council Born Again*, available at: http://www.colombopage.com/archive_091/ Jun1244821410RA.html (accessed on 23 January 2011).
97. Interviews of the research team with the Rector and the staff of the Mass Communications Department, Trincomalee Campus, 2010.
98. Mass communications degree holders with good knowledge of theory need to be empowered by including more practical aspects in the mass communications degree. Overall, the journalist needs to have the essential theoretical knowledge as well as the practical skills to become a successful professional [a senior administrator, Sri Lanka College of Journalism Sri Lanka Collage of Journalism, interviewed on 9 February 2012] and Prof. Ajantha Hapuarachchi—Head of the Journalism Unit—University of Colombo Interviewed on 30 April 2012).
99. 'The development of a critical mass of strategic and capability embedded professionals requires a much more focused and professional approach, delivered with excellence and commitment by all stakeholders. Effective Human Resource Development and Human Resource Management, with capable mentors, guides and gurus leading the way, are essential features that are lacking in Sri Lanka. The two areas where no emphasis is placed in capability and development are in connection with the development of correct attitudes and values/norms' [vide interview with C. Jayaratne, 4 March 2012]. Furthermore, it has been suggested that it would be more appropriate to combine all institutions providing media education to become one central education centre which would ensure common standards [vide interview with D. Lankapeli, 5 April 2012].
100. Interview with Devanesan Nesiah, 21 February 2012.

11

Media Education and the Tamil Community: A View from the North and the East

S. Raguram

As communication, in addition to food, clothing and shelter, has increasingly come to be seen as a basic need for the individual and society, the influence of the media and communications has grown in importance as a theme for research. Media education is vital in promoting an understanding of the media, reinforcing the utilisation of media as a means of meeting human needs, and encouraging a critical perspective on media usage. The practical issue is to consider what types of media education—formal or informal—should be pursued. Formal media education can be carried out within an institution, within a formal structure and with defined objectives. By contrast, media education for a wider public can be informal and use more flexible educational methods. In Sri Lanka, there are many informal educational approaches towards media at different levels. But formal institutional approaches to media education are comparatively weak.

At the initial stage, media education in the universities was introduced almost as a token subject and largely involved media appreciation. This proved a constraint in understanding the significance and potential of media education. A number of universities in Sri Lanka have a good record in considering the fundamentals of media education as part of their curricula. However, in the universities of the north and east, it is only recently that media education has become a major field of study.

There are many reasons for this. Colombo was considered as the hub of the mass media. Jaffna in northern Sri Lanka and Batticaloa in the eastern province have a long record of journalism both in Tamil and in English at the regional level. But compared with universities in Colombo, the northern and eastern universities were not pioneers in media education. In the north and the east, the media were rich in literary, cultural and religious content, but they were not the subject of structured media education. The long-standing war and its consequences played a major role in this. Media education was affected by a variety of factors, including continuous attacks on media outlets in Jaffna from the period of the Indian Peace Keeping Force, aerial bombardment and shelling during the 1980s and 1890s, and mass displacement and control over the local media by rebels. The economic embargo enforced by successive Sri Lankan governments on movements of goods and services to the north created additional obstacles to the development of the media during the war days. For all these reasons, media education could not (as in other parts of the island) reach the desired level. This was partly because education as a whole was disrupted, partly because for many Tamil inhabitants of these areas media education was not seen as a priority. During the war days, the Tamil media operated under considerable pressures. They were not generating large profits and journalism was a dangerous and poorly paid profession. In general, Tamil families encouraged their children to go into better paid professions and trades rather than taking the risks involved in entering the media field. The traditional mindset of Tamil families towards seeking government jobs also made them steer clear of a media education.

Universities, Affiliated Institutions and Working Journalists

The University of Jaffna (in the Northern Province) and the Eastern University of Sri Lanka and South Eastern University (in the Eastern Province) all come under the purview of the University Grants Commission, which in turn comes under the Ministry of Higher Education. Of these Universities, the University of Jaffna was established first and the other two came later. These regional higher educational institutions are highly valued by society in the Tamil community and Tamil speaking areas of Sri Lanka.

Any scholar doing research at the micro level about the history of the Tamils can easily identify the impact of these Universities on the Tamil community, notably through their contribution to the struggle for the political rights of the Tamil people. This social value is an essential feature of media education as a sector of social science.

University of Jaffna

In Jaffna University, media education was introduced first in the Faculty of Arts, as a part of literature studies, and the purpose was to improve the creative writing of the students. However, it is noteworthy that leading figures in the University of Jaffna and some well-wishers from Jaffna society also contributed to media education from a critical sociological perspective. As a result, the university organised societies for film appreciation, with external support from those concerned to promote social development. Furthermore, the Extra Mural Studies Unit of the University conducted a Certificate Course in Journalism, one of the pioneering courses for media education in the Northern Province.

The Certificate Course in Journalism, when it was introduced, did not purely depend on the university teachers but got help from professional journalists and media personnel. All those connected to journalism— chief editors, news editors, reporters, photo journalists, printers and distributors—were invited to share their experiences as guest lecturers, paving the way for the acceptance and utilisation by academics of the resources of the professional media. The course helped to educate not only the students of the University of Jaffna, but also different categories of media personnel. The course focused on the process and making of the media. But there was a lack of a critical approach to the media's role in society. Moreover, there was flexibility in recruiting the participants. This created concern among the academics and it led to the courses losing university recognition.

The same trend existed several years later when the Media Resources and Training Centre (MRTC) was set up in Jaffna with the assistance of the Danish Government and UNESCO. The selection of students was not carried out under university procedures and the teaching format was not in accordance with the norms of the university. So the centre's courses failed to get recognition as a 'university course of study'. It is also a matter of concern that so many students have been trained in the field of journalism in a region like Jaffna where the demand for journalists is limited and there is no assurance of employment. According to the information available, 33 full-time students and 32 part-time students have passed out since 2003. A further 31 full-time students and 12 part-time students completed their courses in 2012–2013 academic year.[1] The courses are conducted in the Tamil medium.[2]

The MRTC comes under the administration of the University of Jaffna but no effective action has been taken to recognise it as a unit or department within the university system. The centre is located away from the main campus and is physically and functionally isolated from the university environment. The visiting lecturers of the MRTC are paid below the amount approved for the normal visiting lecturers of universities. This was justified by the university administration on the grounds that the visiting lecturers of MRTC typically have a diploma qualification rather than a degree. The distinction has proved an obstacle to recruiting appropriate visiting lecturers to the MRTC and a barrier to the courses reaching the university standard. At the same time, the university administration, using only two Temporary Assistant Lecturers and without any permanent academic staff, has managed to offer a degree programme in Media Studies in the Faculty of Arts.[3,4] This experience of the MRTC illustrates the difficulty of providing media courses that are not under the auspices of the university.

Eastern University

The Department of Languages and Communication Studies on the Trincomalee Campus of the Eastern University has offered a degree programme in Communication Studies for the last 10 years. While the Department of Fine Arts on the main campus of the Eastern University handles subjects related to drama and theatre, and the Swami Vipulananda Institute of Aesthetic Studies (SVIAS) conducts programmes on Performing Arts, the Trincomalee Campus covers the larger area of Communication Studies. This includes an introduction to communication and interpersonal communication, communication and conflict management, advertising, film and television, print media, development communication, folk media, documentaries and short films, script writing and instructional media.[5]

Up to now, 200 students have passed out from the campus having followed this course of studies and it should be noted that among them a notable number of students are special degree holders. Another important point is that the Trincomalee Campus of the Eastern University of Sri Lanka is the only campus in Sri Lanka that admits students to study media education through the English medium. The students come from varied ethnic, religious and geographical backgrounds. The available facilities, which include a sound studio, editing suite, theatre and libraries with thousands of books on media education, are some of the special features of the Trincomalee campus, which distinguish it from its counterparts.

South Eastern University

Compared with the universities in the north and east, the South Eastern University in Amparai district has a very short history in media education. It provides diploma programmes for external students and subjects related to media for internal students.[6]

During 2007 and 2008, two batches of students passed out from the one-year diploma in journalism programme. The programme was subsequently discontinued because of a lack of academics with a background in media education. But the cooperation of local working journalists made a valuable and innovative contribution to the programme.

Despite a lack of lecturers in media studies, the Department of Languages and the Faculty of Arabic Language provide 'Tamil Journalism' either as a core or an optional subject for a number of students. A further programme with the title 'Diploma in Professional Journalism' has also been started by the university career guidance unit for students from all streams, with the aim of encouraging students to enter the media profession.

Challenges in Media Education

Media education in Sri Lanka is needed to prepare people to approach the media critically, to produce professional journalists, to protect democracy and good governance and to promote the practice of journalism in accordance with media ethics. In a country scarred by years of civil war and the polarisation of ethnic communities, the role of journalism is paramount. The media should point out the duties of the state—and its failures—and provide guidance to students, journalists and in particular to civil society. In achieving this aim, media education has an important role to play. As the media expands and is shaped and constructed by new influences, media education can help to create an understanding of what they mean. In the meantime, there is a practical requirement to train a younger generation of journalists for the job market. With so many alternative media, education is also needed to help ensure new media skills and technologies are available to a wider public. In the context of Sri Lanka this is an uphill task.

Media Education in Schools

In 2006, the new subject of 'Communication and Media Studies' was introduced in the school curriculum for the General Certificate in Education (GCE), ordinary level and advanced level, which is the entry point of university education in Sri Lanka.[7] But though 'Communication and Media Studies' has been introduced as a subject nationally, according to the available statistics[8] only a few schools in the north and east have the facilities to teach this subject. In Tamil districts such as Mullaithivu and Killinochi in the north, and Trincomalee, Batticaloa and Amparai in the east, no schools came forward to teach this subject. In the north, out of 144 schools, only five schools at the ordinary level (3.4 per cent) and two schools out of 84 schools at advanced level (2.3 per cent) provide the opportunity to learn this subject.[9] Many reasons for this disparity are put forward by the administrations of the schools in the north and east. The most important reasons include the lack of sufficient teachers with the background in media education to teach this subject, the non-availability of teachers' guides and a lack of reading materials.[10,11,12]

Even though there are some teachers willing to teach the subject, there are no in-service courses (educating the educators) for them. In the light of this, the Trincomalee Campus and the MRTC of the University of Jaffna began to conduct workshops for the teachers of media education.[13] However, many of the education officers from the school education system in the north and east think this subject will be an additional burden and have shown little interest in teaching it.

Media Education at University: Curriculum and Syllabus

In this section, we examine the different curricula and syllabi of the three major universities in the north and east of Sri Lanka: the University of Jaffna (including the MRTC), the Eastern University (Trincomalee Campus) and the South Eastern University in Oluvil, Amparai.[14,15,16]

The diploma in journalism, which is being conducted by the MRTC, under the patronage of the University of Jaffna and specially designed for a target group working in the media field, or working journalists,[17,18] can be seen as a role model. But to be sustainable, the course should reach university students and the general public as well as working journalists and should incorporate other areas of media education, along with the existing major area of 'print journalism'.

The MRTC was established with foreign funds and it has depended on assistance from outside for a long time. If the dependency on foreign funds changes and the MRTC becomes a part of the University of Jaffna, the courses conducted by the MRTC will get university recognition, which at present is restricted. Moreover, if through the MRTC it is possible to establish a department of media and a venue for research, this will pave the way for an innovative and creative course of studies in media education.

The Trincomalee Campus offers a degree in communication studies with a broad syllabus, via the Department of Languages and Communication Studies.[19] Its main feature is the opportunity given to the students to familiarise themselves with the components of a wider range of media education. In the first two years, students have the chance to study the basic theoretical subjects essential to an understanding of communication, such as Communication and Persuasion, Interpersonal Communication, Organisational Communication, Mass Communication and Society, Communication Theories and Media Literacy, Instructional Media, Development Communication and Communication, Gender and Society. In the third and fourth years, students are given an opportunity to apply what they have learnt. Subjects such as Writing for Media, Communication and Conflict Management, Film and Television, Folk Media, Print Media, Video Production and Advertising are offered to the students.

Further, in the field of research methodology, subjects such as Critical Media Theory, Media Ethics and Semiotics are also in the curricula and they lead the students to become involved more effectively in media research.

Of the universities in the north and east, Trincomalee is the only one to offer a three- or four-year degree programme in communication studies, with specialisation through the English medium. The Faculty of Arts of Jaffna University provides a degree programme in media studies through the Tamil medium. Its first batch completed the course in 2013.[20] The longer degree course gives time to the student to comprehend the subject and learn the appropriate skills.

Most of the available textbooks for the Trincomalee course are in English, which makes it possible for the students to update their knowledge according to global trends. Because of their skills in communication in English, degree holders of the Trincomalee campus are more easily employable than other students. But the Trincomalee Campus also needs to prepare its graduates for further education by offering more specialisation at undergraduate level, as well as postgraduate MA programmes, and the chance to do research in a relevant field.

The next challenge in designing curricula and syllabi is to get professionals in different fields, related to the print media, the electronic media, traditional media and new media to engage with the teaching in the universities. Another gap in the present curricula is a lack of attention to issues relating to media policy and media freedoms and the legal and constitutional protection for media activities. There is apparently only limited space at the present time to accommodate these subjects, or media ethics, in the university curricula.

Teachers: Educational Background and Professional Experience

In Trincomalee Campus, three PhD holders are working in media studies: one as a senior lecturer and the other two as visiting lecturers. The campus has also recruited four lecturers from among its own graduates. These academics cover the range of subjects on offer and are in a position to provide the media education satisfactorily. However, the University of Jaffna lacks these resources. It has no senior lecturers to expand its media education syllabus. The Department of Tamil in the South Eastern University has a senior lecturer with a doctorate in print media studies but it lacks lecturers to teach media education as a full-fledged subject.[21]

With regard to media education, however, theoretical knowledge is not sufficient. Academics should also have had working experience in the field of journalism to be able to develop a capacity for constructive criticism in their pupils and to impart media education more usefully and realistically. Currently, the academics of the north and eastern universities do not consider professional experience as a necessary requirement. A kind of 'university mentality' has grown up in which practical experience is not regarded as educational.

Though the MRTC in Jaffna was established to cater to working journalists, the irony is that most directors of the MRTC have had no professional experience.[22] This has been a major constraint on understanding the needs of the students, who are mostly working journalists, and utilising the centre to meet its goals. A theoretical knowledge of media education alone will not contribute to the betterment of society or the media. Like medical practitioners, teachers of media studies should also have internships with practice and experience throughout their teaching life to be able to achieve the desired results.

With regard to the universities in the north and east, especially the University of Jaffna and the Eastern University at Trincomalee, there are veterans of media without degrees who are willing to serve from the local regions but there are administrative obstacles to obtaining their services. Among the barriers to the recruitment of personnel from the professional media field, as has been noted, is an inadequate pay structure.[23] The universities cannot justify this disparity between those with degrees and those with practical experience.

Medium of Learning

The medium of media education in the north and east is Tamil and English. In the University of Jaffna, courses are taught in Tamil, the medium of the Faculty of Arts. Outside the campus, the MRTC also teaches courses in Tamil. The same situation prevails in the South Eastern University. Students of both universities are from Tamil speaking communities.

Trincomalee Campus caters to both Sinhala and Tamil speaking students and it uses English as a lingua franca to teach media education. The Trincomalee Campus considers the ability of students to learn and create in their mother tongue and gives them the opportunity to submit their assignments for the subjects of 'script writing' and 'short film making' using their mother tongue and English. Education is language-oriented, and if the language of instruction hinders media education, we must adjust the environment of the learning group in a practical way. The majority of Sri Lankan students, having completed their degrees in media education, prefer to work in their mother tongue. The medium of learning should not be a hindrance to media education and teaching.

A constraint from a language point of view in teaching media education at ordinary and advanced levels is the lack of textbooks on the subject in Sinhala and Tamil.[24] It is the same problem in the universities. Textbooks on media education are more widely available in Sinhala than in Tamil. The state of Tamil Nadu in India is close to Sri Lanka and its official language is Tamil, but even in Tamil Nadu there are fewer textbooks in Tamil than in English. Although Tamil textbooks have been translated, they are often not comprehensible. This type of translation forces students to go back to the original versions because the translated materials are often difficult to understand.

We should not ignore the fact that the new and growing trends in media education are available to Sri Lankans only in English. But if we want to create a curriculum to represent the traditions and experience of Sri Lanka, there must be space for our own ideas, which should be channelled through the texts. Without ignoring English, we should use our mother tongue as much as possible to teach media education by creating new texts and research.[25] It is the need of the time.

Internships and the Job Market

Without opportunities to apply it, media education would be of little use to students. But in the universities in Sri Lanka, it is difficult to get opportunities to acquire the professional practical knowledge or to arrange internships. The students and institutions have difficulty in getting training from media outlets based in Colombo.

Media outlets are very sensitive. Their policy is to keep to themselves and when students are sent by the universities to these outlets they are treated as strangers.[26] The same attitude prevails both in the private and public sectors.

Although some institutions do take trainees, the length of internship is generally not adequate to familiarise them with the trade. It is unfortunate that some students who cannot get access to recognised media outlets become apprentices at institutions not related to their field. The universities should aim to bridge the gap between themselves and the media entrepreneurs, and make greater efforts to get the cooperation of professionals in the field.

Another solution to this would be for the universities to provide training for students on their campuses by establishing their own infrastructure instead of sending students for internships outside. Trincomalee Campus has established laboratories for media education such as a Sound Studio, Editing Suite and Theatre, and has a plan to set up a Television Studio and Community Radio Centre. The MRTC at the University of Jaffna has also set up some facilities related to the electronic media with funding from the Danish Government.

The students of Trincomalee Campus can benefit from training in two ways. One is through practical sessions on the campus related to their respective subject areas with the guidance of the lecturers and the support of technical persons such as audio-visual and sound studio technicians. This is mandatory for the completion of their degree programme. The second way is for internships to be provided. Trincomalee Campus has an arrangement with the State Television 'Rupavahini', and every year it sends students for internship for three consecutive months.

Research

There are difficulties in maintaining a culture of research in the universities for the following reasons: inadequate remuneration, the practice of going on strike to meet the teachers' basic needs, the lack of freedom of expression and above all the influence of politics on the higher education system. There are few if any research reports from Sri Lanka which are up to international standards. Although some academics have made serious efforts in the research field, they have not received much international exposure.

Apart from using media education as a qualification for jobs, there should be a mechanism to encourage a research culture in universities and to provide staff and students with the opportunity to analyse the functions of the media critically. At present, very limited research is being done on issues related to media freedom, media ethics, and the role and responsibility of the state, parliament and the judiciary in the development of media laws and regulation.

Threats, Influences and Restrictions

The influence of party politics in the universities—and the consequent interruption of studies—has had a notable and unnecessary impact. It has paved the way for politicians to involve themselves in education and try to sabotage the system without knowing what it is trying to achieve. There are many hidden pressures and restrictions from external forces on the public discussion of problematic areas in media education, such as media freedoms, human rights, the reporting of elections, conflict-sensitive journalism, communication and conflict management and media ethics.

To ensure a healthy and constructive atmosphere for media education, attempts should be permitted to examine the present condition of media freedom. It is vital to accept these activities as motivated not by opposition to the authorities but for the well-being of the public. If we do not advocate a genuinely free and fair media environment in the country, we cannot make students reflect on these issues of media education on our campuses. At the same time, we can only protect media freedoms if we produce a generation of energetic young professionals and academics through an effective media education programme.

Proposals and Suggestions to Improve Media Education at University Level

The following proposals and suggestions, based on the shared opinions and ideas analysed in this article, could provide solutions to the challenge of media education in the universities.

(1) As part of the effort to advance and promote media education in universities, the talents and knowledge of media professionals should be incorporated in the teaching programme.

(2) Media education should be provided at different levels, according to the needs, expectations and goals of the target audience.

(3) The curriculum and syllabus should be reviewed from time to time according to the requirements of the job market.

(4) There must be increased opportunities to study the different aspects of media education.

(5) An appropriate mechanism should be arranged by university academics to cater to the educational needs of schools. Teachers and students should be encouraged to engage in the 'Communication and Media Studies' subject at GCE ordinary and advanced levels.

(6) Research efforts should be increased to find a system of media education suitable for Sri Lanka. Texts for media education in local languages should be provided where required.

(7) Master's degrees and research programmes should be started in universities and lecturers appointed at a senior level.

(8) Arrangements should be made with professional media outlets to provide work experience for academics if they do not have such background.

(9) The selection of the language of learning should be flexible and students should be allowed to deal with creative sections of media education through their mother tongue as they choose.

(10) Journalists, who are working in the professional field, but without the academic qualifications expected by the university system, should be allowed to share their experiences and to take part in discussions and other informal teaching sessions, and their services should be properly recognised.

(11) There should be a good rapport with professional media outlets, to ensure that internships and training for students become mandatory.

(12) To avoid complete dependency on professional media outlets for internship opportunities for the students, universities should have basic facilities and infrastructure to provide media training at least to a certain level.

(13) Interest in media research should be encouraged in the academic and the professional field.

(14) Media freedoms and activities designed to protect freedom of expression should be supported.

Notes

1. Mr K. Pathytharan, Media Analyst, Former Trainer, MRTC, Jaffna (interviewed on 28 December 2012) and Mr K. Rushangan, Director/Media Trainer, Sikaram Media House, Jaffna (interviewed on 17 October 2012).
2. Report 'About MRTC' (2012).
3. Ms Kiruthiga Tharumarajah, Assistant Lecturer, Unit of Media Studies, Faculty of Arts, University of Jaffna (interviewed on 20 January 2013).
4. The Handbook of Faculty of Arts, Eastern University, Sri Lanka, 2012.
5. The Handbook of Faculty of Communication and Business Studies, Trincomalee Campus, Eastern University, Sri Lanka, 2012.
6. Dr M.A. Mohamed Rameez, Senior Lecturer, Department of Tamil, South Eastern University (interviewed on 10 January 2013 and 18 January 2013).
7. Harischandra, S. and Rupasinghe, W. (2012).
8. Abeygunasekara, G. (2012).
9. *Ibid.*
10. Mr V. Senthan, Teacher in 'Communication and Media Studies', Union College, Jaffna (interviewed on 18 December 2012).
11. Ms Sutha Rushangan, Teacher in 'Communication and Media Studies', Uduvil Ladies College, Jaffna (interviewed on 20 December 2012 and 20 January 2013).
12. Mr K. Pathytharan, Media Analyst, Former Trainer, MRTC, Jaffna (interviewed on 28 December 2012).

13. Mr T. Thevananth, Director, Media Resources and Training Centre (MRTC), University of Jaffna (interviewed on 11 January 2013).
14. The Handbook of Faculty of Communication and Business Studies, Trincomalee Campus, Eastern University, Sri Lanka, 2012.
15. Dr M.A. Mohamed Rameez, Senior Lecturer, Department of Tamil, South Eastern University (interviewed on 10 January 2013 and 18 January 2013).
16. The syllabus of Diploma in Journalism (Part time Programme), Media Resources and Training Centre (MRTC), University of Jaffna, 2012.
17. The syllabus of Diploma in Journalism (Full time Programme—two years), Media Resources and Training Centre (MRTC), University of Jaffna, 2012.
18. Report on 'MRTC Action Plan' (2012).
19. The Handbook of Faculty of Communication and Business Studies, Trincomalee Campus, Eastern University, Sri Lanka, 2012.
20. Ms Kiruthiga Tharumarajah, Assistant Lecturer, Unit of Media Studies, Faculty of Arts, University of Jaffna (interviewed on 20 January 2013).
21. Dr M.A. Mohamed Rameez, Senior Lecturer, Department of Tamil, South Eastern University (interviewed on 10 January 2013 and 18 January 2013).
22. Report on 'MRTC Action Plan' (2012).
23. The Report of the National Media Summit (2010).
24. Raguram (2012).
25. Kelaniya Declaration on Mass Media, Communication Study, and Media Industry in Sri Lanka, National Media Summit (2010), 9–10 November 2010.
26. Mr Wijayananda Rupasinghe, Senior Lecturer in Media Studies, Department of Mass Communication, University of Kelaniya (interviewed on 12 November 2012).

12

Putting the Citizen First: New Approaches to Media Literacy

Tilak Jayaratne and Sarath Kellapotha

Of all the issues relating to media education, it is the issue of media literacy that should receive the utmost attention, as it is a very important factor for active citizenship in today's information society. Unfortunately, in Sri Lanka, this is not the case, though the topic is quite familiar in international circles. We present our case for media literacy for all with supporting evidence from institutions and authorities working in this field.

Media Literacy for All

The proliferation of mass media has brought about decisive changes in human communication processes and behaviour. Media education aims to empower citizens by providing them with the competencies, attitudes and skills necessary to comprehend media functions. Media education can be contextualised within two UNESCO advocacies—the Human Rights-based approach to programming and the creation of Knowledge Societies. Access to quality media content and participation in programming are principles that are among the cornerstones of the universal right to free expression.

UNESCO has long-standing experience in enhancing media literacy, from the passing of the Grünwald Declaration of 1982, which recognised the need for political and educational systems to promote citizens' critical understanding of 'the phenomenon of communication'. The organisation has since supported a number of initiatives to introduce media and information literacy as an integral part of people's lifelong learning. In June 2008, it brought together experts from various regions of the world to catalyse processes to introduce media and information literacy components into teacher training curricula worldwide.

Renée Hobbs, Professor at the School of Communications and the College of Education at Temple University, points out that The Knight Commission's report, *Information Communities: Sustaining Democracy in the Digital Age* 'recognised that people need news and information to take advantage of life's opportunities for themselves and their families. To be effective participants in contemporary society, people need to be engaged in the public life of the community, the nation and the world. They need access to relevant and credible information that helps them make decisions. This necessarily involves strengthening the capacity of individuals to participate as both producers and consumers in public conversations about events and issues that matter. Media and digital literacy education is now fundamentally implicated in the practice of citizenship'.[1] Hobbs describes digital and media literacy as a set of skills necessary for full participation in society today and she defines media literacy as the ability to do the following:

- Make responsible choices and access information by locating and sharing materials and comprehending information and ideas.
- Analyse messages in a variety of forms by identifying the author, purpose and point of view, and evaluating the quality and credibility of the content.
- Create content in a variety of forms, making use of language, images, sound and new digital tools and technologies.
- Take social action by working individually and collaboratively to share knowledge and solve problems in the family, workplace and community, and by participating as a member of a community.[2]

She further explains that

[F]or all aspects of daily life, people today need a constellation of well-developed communication and problem-solving skills that include these competencies:

These five competencies work together in a spiral of empowerment, supporting people's active participation in lifelong learning through the processes of both consuming and creating messages.[3]

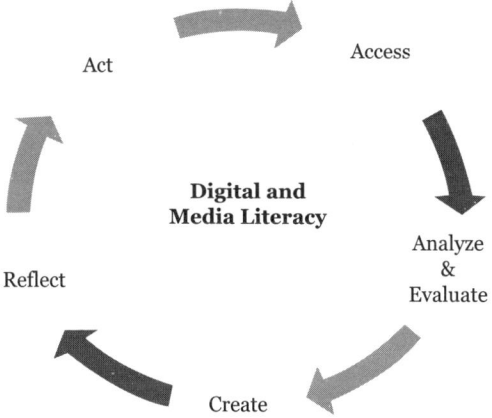

The Commission of the European Communities' Recommendation of 20 August 2009 on media literacy[4] in the digital environment includes the following:

- Media literacy relates to the ability to access the media, to understand and critically evaluate different aspects of the media and media content and to create communications in a variety of contexts.
- The diffusion of digital creative content and the multiplication of online and mobile distribution platforms create new challenges for media literacy. In today's world, citizens need to develop analytical skills that allow for better intellectual and emotional understanding of digital media.
- Media literacy includes all media. The aim of media literacy is to increase people's awareness of the many forms of media messages encountered in their everyday lives. Media messages are the programmes, films, images, texts, sounds and websites that are carried by different forms of communication.[5]
- Media literacy is a matter of inclusion and citizenship in today's information society. It is a fundamental skill not only for young people, but also for adults and elderly people, parents, teachers and media professionals. Thanks to the Internet and digital technology, an increasing number of Europeans can now create and disseminate images, information and content. Media literacy is today regarded

as one of the key prerequisites for an active and full citizenship to prevent and diminish risks of exclusion from community life.

• A media literate society would be at the same time a stimulus and a precondition for pluralism and independence in the media. The expression of diverse opinions and ideas, in different languages, representing different groups, in and across societies has a positive impact on the values of diversity, tolerance, transparency, equity and dialogue. The development of media literacy in all sections of society should therefore be promoted and its progress followed closely.

• Democracy depends on the active participation of citizens in the life of their community and media literacy would provide the skills they need to make sense of the daily flow of information disseminated through new communication technologies.

• Media literacy should be addressed in different ways at different levels. The modalities of inclusion of media literacy in school curricula at all levels are the Member States' primary responsibility. The role played by local authorities is also very important since they are close to the citizens and support initiatives in the non-formal education sector. Civil society should also make an active contribution to promoting media literacy in a bottom-up manner.[6]

Media Literacy for School Children

In the school class room, a variety of practices can help to build digital and media literacy. Socratic questioning, for example, promotes critical thinking about the choices people make when consuming, creating and sharing messages.

Although comparatively late in introducing universal education concepts like 'Education for All' or 'Lifelong Education', Sri Lankan schools are now teaching media literacy. But the attention it receives from the relevant authorities (Education Ministry, Education Department) is to say the least insufficient.

Media Education and Training

Many talk about the rapidly deteriorating media situation in Sri Lanka. But few venture to seek out the root causes. Lack of effective media education and training can be considered a major contributory factor to the decline in the media culture. Most of the early broadcast practitioners were chosen from the print media and they brought with them 'the good, the bad and the ugly'. And when television 'arrived', again it was an exodus from the radio. So the traditions remained and continue up to the present day. These are reflected not only in the skill and the craft, but also in the approaches and attitudes towards media education. In these circles, change is abhorred and many hold on to their views without budging an inch. Early media educational attempts focused on writership. It is true that this was a worldwide phenomenon and not limited to Sri Lanka. But then, in the west, the print media traditions fostered freedom, independence, tolerance and other democratic values. Nurtured during the colonial rule, the journalist traditions of Sri Lanka were focused on different ideals.

The main factor affecting the situation was lack of proper media education for broadcast journalists. Media education and training was not a priority for the state sector broadcast institutes and even less for the private media. Even in the early attempts by a few universities in the country, considerations were different, with the focus on 'improving employability skills'. There are many issues related to media education and media studies. The issues that we have identified and prioritised are presented briefly below:

- There seems to be no interest on the part of the major actors, namely the state, media owners and media practitioners, in media education. The government controlled media need no education for their broadcasters for what they are doing. Indeed, training may even prove counterproductive. The private media owners have trust in new technologies to maximise profits rather than investing in 'human capital'. For media personnel, media education is not an entry requirement to obtain employment or even for promotions. The educationalists, including university teachers, the intelligentsia and the civil society, are not far behind them. Media education is also low down on their agenda. This lack of interest does not encourage them to study and understand the requirement for media education and the role of the media as an enabling tool for democracy. Hence, few individuals and organisations undertake research to explore this aspect. Lack of commitment and sponsorship on the part of stakeholders automatically follows. Needless to say, this affects media education badly and in turn causes further deterioration of media education and practice.
- It is obvious to any casual observer that there is no clear vision or direction in whatever media education occurs. Thus, the curricula

of the existing media education institutes and organisations do not reflect the needs of the industry and the country, nor do they cater to these needs. Attempts are not made to bridge the gap between media education and media practice.

- Lack of funds and resources—both physical and human—is a major stumbling block. Almost all the institutions that provide media education lack facilities for practical training. On the other hand, most of the media organisations that provide on the job training do not have facilities for teaching. Thus, it is difficult to achieve expected results.

- As is the case in other areas, there exists a huge imbalance in both media coverage and media education as regards minorities and the marginalised. This does not come as a surprise, as it is known that media in Sri Lanka, both print and broadcast, cater mainly to the elite, irrespective of racial differences. Media education is provided mainly in the Sinhala language and occasionally English and Sinhala. Echoing these sentiments, Sri Lankan human rights defender, Sunila Abeysekara[7] posited that independent and autonomous institutions that could provide strong professional frameworks as well as play a creative training and capacity building role 'should have a special focus on outreach to provincial journalists; there should also be a special focus on strengthening access to media training for marginalised groups such as women and members of minority communities'.[8]

- Another point to note is that most of the media studies are conducted in and around the capital city of Colombo. Excepting university courses, it is mostly short duration workshops/seminars for the outstations. In the Tamil medium, that too is limited. The war situation was blamed for this 'injustice' to Tamil medium journalists and would be journalists. But since the war ended there is hardly any improvement in the status quo. This imbalance should be considered a huge impediment to establishing a free, fair, independent and pluralistic media in the country.

Media Studies and Curricula

Curriculum evaluation is a specialist's job which needs expertise in the field of curriculum theory and practice. We do not propose to venture into an exercise of that sort. Instead, we record below our concerns and observations. At the time of this research, most of the Sri Lankan universities were in the process of revising their curricula and our comments should be validated in that context. However, we do not expect radical changes, as we found hardly any drastic shift in academic thinking in the course of the research and interviews we conducted.

- A mechanism must be in place to provide vision and direction as well as to establish a wide framework within which media institutions could set their goals and organise their teaching/pedagogy. This could perhaps take the form of a free, independent advisory/regulatory body to guide, advise and assist in curriculum development and revision. It should unquestionably be free from government and corporate control.

- A critical examination of present media practice in Sri Lanka (and our personal experience) suggests that a huge gap exists in 'what is taught' and 'what is practised'. Available curricula do not offer effective means to bridge the gap. What happens is those who manage to make it across the 'bridge' invariably forget what they learn and become willing (and rarely unwilling) collaborators. Those who fail to go across the bridge leave the profession. It is a matter of choice for survival. We do not suggest that media education courses should teach ways and means to 'cross the bridge'; rather the curricula should be designed so that the learner would be able to take with her to the 'employment environment' the change that occurred in herself as a result of her training and make her presence and the change felt there. It is this aspect more than the high quality alone (as aspired to by academics) that would help to change the face of media practice in the country.

- Journalism training curricula must consciously attempt to draw together two traditions too often in conflict. There is the dominant newspaper culture in Sri Lanka, which stresses the learning of skills 'on the job'. Then, there is a universalist tradition, embedded in many mass communications courses in colleges and universities around the world, which encourages a more reflective, critical approach to the media. The research findings available worldwide are too distant to media practitioners in Sri Lanka and, as a result of this, journalists and media theorists seem to inhabit different worlds, speaking different languages. To effectively confront these issues, media training institutions must draw on some of the theoretical writings to inject helpful new insights into journalists' routines, skills and news values. Since all practice is based, consciously or unconsciously, on theory, journalists' standards would improve if they reflected more on the values that underpin their work and the press in general.

- We need media training courses designed with a difference to provide broadcast and print media journalists with further opportunities to enhance their capacity to perform as ethical and responsible professionals who do their best to avoid being manipulated in offering accurate, balanced and impartial information in keeping with accepted journalistic norms.

- There is a sense of mismatch that exists between media practitioners' and media educators' perceptions of the competencies that journalism education must instil in its alumni in keeping with market realities and curriculum fundamentals. The 'cold war' continues to haunt journalism education and the oft-cited theory/ practice dichotomy is far from being resolved within academia. Instead, the 'theory-practice gap' comes into sharp relief for media educators considering how to advance journalism education on the professional 'skills' side of the curriculum. With the industry having to bear economic pressure and the impact of technological advancement, how might journalism programmes re-orient pedagogical practices and adapt curricula so that those who come out of media educational faculties and institutions will no longer be socialised into replicas of earlier-generation journalists? How can they be 'transformed' into a new generation of self-actualising innovators, capable of maintaining professional relevance in rapidly changing societal, industrial and democratic contexts? These are questions not only for curriculum developers, but also for other stake holders, especially media institutes.

- In the early days, the emphasis of university courses was on communication studies, which involves 'preparing students for the academic study of the way people and organisations communicate through the mass media' rather than the practice of journalism. Although several more universities have entered the field of media education, the earlier trend seems to persist. While it cannot be denied that communication studies is a vital element in any comprehensive media study curriculum, from the points of view of both the industry and the academics, it is best to strike a fine balance between the two.

- Needs analysis is important for two necessary and complementary elements of curriculum development, namely 'technique and curriculum conscience'. Information about actual needs is required for the development of the programme and can also help the curriculum designer in making the required value judgments that are part and parcel of critical consciousness. Needs analysis is important for both these elements of curriculum development. By incorporating needs assessments in their curricular decisions, curriculum developers can select options that benefit both the learners and society. In Sri Lanka, experience tells us that no such importance is attached to needs assessment.

- As F. Morgan of the University of Newcastle in Australia observes: 'the evident need and widespread demand for better media and communication practice has led variously to the introduction of academic programmes in universities and colleges and industry training programs in a range of other settings and institutions. Frequently, however, academic courses have been too abstract to be useful and industry training has been largely bereft of ideas. Both have failed to meet the need fully and have been expensive to provide'.[9] So we join Morgan in articulating the need 'for a new approach to curriculum that would strengthen the professional education of media and communication practitioners by taking due account of what is to be learned, who is to learn it and the context in which they have to do so'.

- The relationship between communication and culture is a very complex and intimate one. Cultures are created through communication; that is, communication is the means of human interaction through which cultural characteristics—whether customs, roles, rules, rituals, laws or other patterns—are created and shared. Without communication and communication media, it would be impossible to preserve and pass along cultural characteristics from one place and time to another. It can be said that culture is created, shaped, transmitted and learned through communication. The reverse is also the case; that is, communication practices are largely created, shaped and transmitted by culture.

- Wimal Dissanayake sees the role of culture in communication as an extremely important topic. Quoting the eminent anthropologist Clifford Geertz, he told us that 'culture refers to the webs of meaning that human beings weave around themselves. Meanings are made, un-made and re-made in the terrain of culture. Culture can best be understood as a struggle for meaning. Therefore a sound theoretical understanding of culture and how it impacts media pedagogy should be explored'.[10] We too endorse this suggestion.

- Dr Kalinga Seneviratne, the Head of Research at AMIC, has observed that 'the challenge for Asian communication scholars is to come up with new theoretical perspectives to describe the function of Asian media systems with reference to Asian philosophy and modes of traditional communications. We need to analyse and theorise such communication models using our own cultural perspectives'. This presents an angle which is definitely worth considering.[11] He says that 'it is a matter of being focused on developing collaborations within Asia and realising that we need to develop Asia-centric material for communication or media studies. But this does not mean that we ignore western material. What we need to do is use both hand in hand. It will enrich our standards not weaken them'.[12]

Media Education and Research: Some Conclusions

We believe that media education in the country is in a sort of disarray, as it lacks a national policy. It is too much confined to certain requirements of the industry and not the needs of the country as a whole. Though wide publicity is given to what ails the media, this aspect receives scant attention even in the media itself. At first glance, it may appear that there are more critical and burning issues in the country that need greater and more urgent attention. If one looks deeper, however, it should be apparent that media literacy has links to both the causes and results of many issues. Thus, in this sense, media literacy should not be the concern of media people and educationalists only, but of a whole range of stake holders, including media freedom fighters, human rights activists, legal affairs professionals, the civil society, religious leaders, intelligentsia and academia and most of all the citizens.

Wijeyananda Jayaweera, a former Director of Communication at UNESCO, describing the attributes of a media literate person, says that such a *person* should be able to:

- Describe the Article 19 of Universal Declaration of Human Rights and its relevance to individuals and to the society.

- Describe normative functions attributed to media in a democracy in the light of the above right.
- Describe how news matters to society.
- Identify what is newsworthy.
- Identify representation of viewpoints in news.
- Identify how news media use certain words.
- Describe how images can influence news.
- Assess advertisements in the media in the light of international codes of practice.
- Describe what is media pluralism and why it is important.
- Explain journalism as a discipline of verification and self-accountability of the media.
- Explain functions of journalistic ethics and values, and why they are important.
- Explain why safety of journalists should be a collective concern of the society.
- Explain the concept of editorial independence and how to assess media content.
- Describe the functions of a broadcast media regulator.
- Describe the difference and complementarity between Public Service Broadcasting, Community Broadcasting and Commercial Broadcasting.
- Critique media content in the light of representation and under-representation.
- Evaluate the media as a system which comprises different competing and complementary elements.
- Engage with media based on basic journalistic principles.[13]

This is the picture painted by many media scholars worldwide. If we are to go by this definition, media literates are the ideal persons to bring about the changes to society we so much desire. Wimal Dissanayake sees it this way: 'The study of mass media should be directly related to the promotion of a vigorous democratic polity. This is certainly the case in most advanced countries. It is very important that media education in Sri Lanka should be directed towards this end. For this to happen, media studies should develop as a social science paying very close attention to empirical research'.[14]

To put in place appropriate and effective media education, we propose the establishment of a completely independent institute comprising representatives of all relevant stakeholders to formulate, guide, monitor and update media education programmes in the country. As Wijeyananda

Jayaweera has argued 'it is important [that] media literacy becomes an engaged civic education movement in Sri Lanka. It is true that media itself can be a partner of media literacy campaign but media literacy is a fundamental obligation of the education system'.[15]

Compared to media education, media research in Sri Lanka has received only scant attention. Considering the fast growth of the media industry in the country, it is perplexing why media research fails to attract the consideration it deserves. Perhaps it may be due to lack of orientation towards research as a discipline. Some even tend to equate market research with media research. Research is conducted ad hoc and most of the time for a very specific and limited purpose. Whatever research is done in the country is largely done by foreign researchers and local civic organisations and sometimes by both parties in collaboration. In the universities, media research is mostly restricted to students' dissertations, which are deemed to be a mandatory requirement. University teachers are guided in most cases by personal interests and enthusiasm and such academic exercises have limited applicability to media practice and the media industry. How much of this work is channelled back to media education and curriculum development is anybody's guess. Moreover, there is a lack of an institutional base to coordinate even the work of this small number of researchers. Critically missing is a systematic and comprehensive research agenda.

In spite of all this one cannot say the need for media research has lessened; on the contrary, efforts in this direction must be doubled or trebled. Hence, we propose that a media research and study centre be set up as an autonomous and independent body modelled, perhaps, on the Sri Lanka Press Institute. This could consist of representatives of academia, the media industry, media practitioners' organisations, policy planners and civil society organisations. It should act as a resource centre which can provide not only facilities, but also guidance and direction, assistance and encouragement. Media students could be employed on a voluntary basis so that they could obtain knowledge and experience. A venture of this nature would receive blessings from all quarters as none could perceive it as a threat or danger. But the benefits it would bring would be immense.

Notes

1. Hobbs (2010).
2. *Ibid.*, pp. vii–viii.
3. *Ibid.*, p. 16.

4. Official Journal of the European Union (L 227/9) of 29 August 2009 [English version].
5. *Ibid.*
6. *Ibid.*
7. Interview with Sunila Abeysekara, 22 March 2011.
8. *Ibid.*
9. Morgan (2000), pp. 4–21.
10. Interview with Wimal Dissanayake, 10 March 2011.
11. Kalinga Seneviratne, Speech made to the Royal Asiatic Society, Colombo, 16 May 2011.
12. *Ibid.*
13. *Ibid.*
14. See interview with Wimal Dissanayake, 10 March 2011.
15. See interview with Wijeyananda Jayaweera, 4 April 2011.

Part V

Future Prospects

13

Challenges Ahead and a Call for Action

Kishali Pinto-Jayawardena and Gehan Gunatilleke

Introduction

Bolin (2006) observes that viewed from a normative perspective, the role of media is to deepen and strengthen democracy.[1] This role may involve four distinct functions: first, to serve people with sufficient information; second, to comment on contemporary economic, social and political issues in society; third, to act as a watchdog, controlling and scrutinising people with power; and finally, to encourage communication between groups within political, technical and non-profit organisations.[2] This role could only be effectively fulfilled by an independent, pro-active and professional media that is sensitive to the needs of a pluralist society. This section reflects on some of the major challenges faced by the Sri Lankan media today. Such reflection may better explain why the media in Sri Lanka has struggled to effectively fulfil its role.

We discuss contemporary challenges facing the Sri Lankan media and try to identify the direction in which the media in Sri Lanka is heading as well as define the proper scope for future intervention at the legal, institutional and educational levels. The analysis also attempts to interrogate sensitive questions of editorial independence from government and management, the nature of free media activism, interactions between the academic teaching of media studies and professional courses, the explosion of web-based media, as well as the way forward in law and industry reforms.

The objective is to move the debate from an exclusive focus on the excesses of authoritarian governments (tempting as this may be in the current context), to a broader look at the very nature of the media industry itself, its successes and challenges. The objective is not to limit the discussion to matters of theory and analytical interest but to fuse the theoretical analysis with practical observations not only by media practitioners themselves but also by the public at large.

In looking for a way forward for Sri Lanka's media, the link between these reform efforts and the overall democratic structure of governance is crucial. There is an imperative need to restore rights of speech and expression, along with other concomitant rights, through the joint efforts of civil society and committed media groups. However, as part of this process it remains an overriding responsibility of the media itself to put its own house in order. In the alternative, there is little doubt that the Sri Lankan media, once hailed as among the best in South Asia, will be driven to the ground, a victim of its own loss of public credibility.

Independence of the Media

The extent to which the Sri Lankan media has enjoyed independence from political influence has been largely contingent on the regime in power. For example, it has been observed that the ideological changes in the media policy of the government under President D.B. Wijetunge stood in stark contrast to the governmental policy of media control under President R. Premadasa.[3] While the Premadasa government's position on media control relaxed during the latter stages of his presidency, few real advances in media freedom could be observed during this period.[4] Following President Premadasa's assassination in 1993, President D.B. Wijetunga took significant steps to reduce media controls, one of which was to withdraw the previous president's order for the compulsory telecast of Rupavahini news bulletins on all television channels simultaneously.[5]

In 1994, the election mandate of the People's Alliance included a pledge to establish a free media. However, some commentators observe that following the elections, the newly established regime 'was quick to harness and abuse the power of the media' in the lead-up to the presidential elections, scheduled to take place later that year.[6] Since then, the issue of independence has haunted the Sri Lankan media.[7] In July 1995, the

UN Human Rights Commission, in its Concluding Observations on Sri Lanka, recommended that the government 'should take the necessary steps to prevent control and manipulation of electronic media by the Government'.[8] This was essentially a corollary to the Commission's finding that state ownership and control over much of the electronic media could 'undermine the right of everyone to seek, receive and impart information and ideas of all kinds', which is a clear violation of Article 19 of the International Covenant on Civil and Political Rights.[9] Jayaratne et al. (2005) comment that despite these clear recommendations, 'no changes have been introduced to bring the legal and regulatory regimes for broadcasting in Sri Lanka into line with international law'.[10] Domestic committees and pressure groups have raised similar concerns. In 1996, the R.K.W. Goonesekere Committee observed:

> [R]adio and television broadcasting by the state should be undertaken by separate corporations as now but with necessary changes in the law to guarantee both the independence of their governing bodies and their editorial independence. They should be governed by boards which are independent of government; members should see themselves as independent trustees of the public interest in broadcasting and not as representatives of any special interests. They should be appointed for a fixed term according to specified criteria. The selection process should be such as to ensure it is fair and not subject to political or other pressure...[11]

This view stems from a much more fundamental observation regarding the role of the state in ensuring media independence. The Committee pointed out that merely permitting private stations to proliferate could not satisfy the duty of the state to ensure that the state-funded media enjoys editorial independence. It was accordingly observed:

> It is important that private broadcasting exists; this is one way of promoting pluralism in sources of information and preventing media monopolies. It would be a mistake however to think that pluralism can be ensured simply by permitting private broadcasting. Commercial stations are often unwilling to criticise government policy for various reasons; they are influenced by business considerations and the need to earn advertisement revenue. ... While media diversity is important ... granting licences to private broadcasters should not be viewed as a substitute for ensuring the pluralism and independence of public-funded broadcasting. The State will continue to be the main and significant component of broadcasting. Amendments should seek to achieve the public's right to receive information and opinion on matters of public interest.[12]

Moreover, due to diminished profit expectations, private media organisations have become heavily dependent on the government for loans as well as revenues from advertisements. Such economic circumstances tend to weigh heavily on the overall independence of the industry.[13] Thus, future reform efforts[14] must take stock of two very important considerations regarding the independence of the media in Sri Lanka: first, that state regulation of licences needs to be liberalised and undertaken by an independent licensing authority; and second, that private media institutions may not necessarily be as inherently independent as usually presumed, thus requiring the institutional restructuring of state-run media institutions to ensure greater independence from the government.[15]

Governmental Regulation vis-a-vis Self-regulation

It is accepted that the effective regulation of the media is a key factor impacting on the credibility of the media institutions in any country. In Sri Lanka, excessive governmental regulation has always been a serious problem facing the media, print and electronic. Where the electronic media is concerned, as discussed above, many stakeholders actively sought the amendment of the Sri Lanka Broadcasting Authority Act, which empowers the minister to issue licences for the establishment and maintenance of private broadcasting stations. Other major concerns relate to the specification of qualifications and criteria for the appointment and removal of board members to the Sri Lanka Broadcasting Corporation (SLBC), as the current framework grants excessive powers of appointment and removal to the minister. Additionally, the Sri Lanka Telecommunications Act[16] (as amended)[17] established a Telecommunications Regulatory Commission (TRC) empowered to control the use of the radio frequency spectrum; to issue and revoke licenses to use radio frequencies in Sri Lanka and to maintain all telecommunication apparatuses. The present law also provides for an appeal to the Court of Appeal against the refusal to issue a licence or against a revocation of a licence.[18]

Like the SLBC, the TRC is also subject to extensive governmental control. By virtue of Section 3 of the Amendment Act, the membership of the TRC comprises the Secretary to the Minister of Telecommunication, the Director General of the Commission, and three other members appointed by the minister.[19] Moreover, the Director General of Telecommunications is appointed by the minister without any criteria being specified for such appointment, and the officer remains in office virtually at the minister's pleasure.[20] Hence, commentators including Jayaratne et al. (2005) insist on the expeditious introduction of reforms in respect of the TRC.[21] The authors call for the amendment of the existing law to ensure that the TRC consults with an independent broadcasting authority, as well as other interested stakeholders, when determining the use of the radio frequency spectrum.[22] Furthermore, it was recommended that the power to issue and revoke licences in respect of radio frequencies or operation of radio transmission apparatus should be vested in an independent broadcasting authority.[23]

In late 2008, during the height of military operations in the north and east, the then Minister of Mass Media and Information issued certain regulations under Section 31 of the Sri Lanka Rupavahini Corporation (SLRC) Act.[24] The regulations were intended to establish a new licensing regime pertaining to private television broadcasting stations and to monitor and regulate such broadcasting stations. Regulation 13(e) provided that a television broadcasting licence could be cancelled on the grounds that programmes aired by a licensee were detrimental to the interests of national security; incited breakdown of public order; incited ethnic, religious or cultural hatred; violated any laws of the country; were morally offensive or indecent; were detrimental to the rights and privileges of children or violated the code of ethics, standards and practices of television broadcasting. Regulation 19 empowered the minister to suspend the permission granted to a licensee to operate any channel for a specified period, in the interest of the public or in the interest of national security. Furthermore, Regulation 28 empowered the minister to appoint a Consultative Committee with certain broad powers including the power to hold inquiries to determine whether programmes broadcast by licensees were detrimental to the interests of national security.

These regulations appeared to establish a mechanism through which the government could regulate *programme content*—a largely unprecedented regime of control. The regulations were met with widespread criticism, mostly on the grounds that they were ultra vires and that they would lead to excessive governmental control over private broadcasting stations. Critics argued that the regulations went beyond the 'technical, financial and professional' grounds for regulation stipulated in Section 28 of the SLRC Act.[25]

An interesting point of contention in the case was whether the government was within its rights to regulate television programming on the grounds of national security. Article 15(7) of the Constitution permits the restriction of the freedom of speech and expression if such restrictions are prescribed by law inter alia in the interests of national security. The said Article also declares: 'For the purposes of this paragraph 'law' includes regulations made under the law for the time being relating to public security'. A question thus arose as to whether regulations under the SLRC Act could form a legitimate basis for restricting fundamental rights under Article 14(1)(a) in the interests of national security. In its petition to the Supreme Court challenging the regulations, the Centre for Policy Alternatives (CPA) argued that the impugned regulations were in fact not 'law'.[26] CPA cited the Supreme Court judgment in *Thavaneethan v. Dayananda Dissanayake, Commissioner of Elections and Others*,[27] which conclusively held:

> The word 'includes' in Article 15(7) does not bring in regulations under other laws. 'Law' is restrictively defined in Article 170 to mean Acts of Parliament and laws enacted by any previous legislature, and to include Orders-in-Council. That definition would have excluded all regulations and subordinate legislation. The effect of the word 'includes' was therefore only to expand the definition in Article 170 by bringing in regulations under the law relating to public security.[28]

The Supreme Court responded positively to the series of petitions filed on behalf of private telecommunication companies, political parties and the civil society. Upon the direction of the court, discussions were initiated to establish a vastly watered-down regulatory regime, which adopted a consultative process involving numerous stakeholders. Despite the fact that the court never made an official pronouncement on the matter, as it was settled out of court, the case remains one of the few recent examples of successful campaigns against excessive governmental control over the media.

The success of the campaign may be attributed to several key factors. First, the Supreme Court during the later years of the Sarath Silva period grew fairly antagonistic towards the government and was prepared to strike down regulations it deemed unconstitutional. Second, the court opted not to grant leave to proceed in the matter, which enabled it to provide a pragmatic remedy without becoming mired in long-drawn proceedings. This approach may present its own set of problems, as the lack of a proper precedent is not always welcomed. However, the approach, at least as far as this case was concerned, seems to have provided the petitioners with an expeditious remedy. Third, the multi-stakeholder litigation campaign that ensued drew extraordinary attention towards the case and raised its profile significantly. This no doubt expedited the negotiations that were to follow. It remains one of the only occasions on which the government was forced into a consultative process with such rapidity.

Government regulation of the print media has been a long-standing feature of Sri Lanka's media history. The Press Council of Sri Lanka, set up under Law No 5 of 1973, established a seven-member council to regulate the press—six appointed by the president with the director of information as the ex officio seventh member. Out of the six appointees, there was nominal representation afforded to the media industry. The member representing the working journalists must be selected from a panel of seven persons nominated by the journalists' associations in Sri Lanka. Similarly, there must be an appointee representing the interests of the employees of newspaper businesses, such person being selected from a panel of not more than three persons nominated by each registered trade union of such employees. The Press Council was given quasi-judicial powers to inquire into complaints against the press and possessed a wide range of draconian powers, including imposing a strict prohibition on publishing matters vaguely defined as official secrets, material relating to cabinet meetings and fiscal policy. Though the council was not vigorous in its enforcing of these powers, their enabling by law had a sufficiently 'chilling' effect on the media in particular.

In 1999, a Parliamentary Motion 218/99 on legal anomalies affecting the press introduced by the combined opposition included a recommendation to replace the Press Council with a Media Council. From this point on, even though a Media Council was not established, the movement within the media industry bodies to put into place effective self-regulatory measures grew stronger.[29] The concept of self-regulation of journalism standards has been described as a 'novel concept' for Sri Lanka.[30] After the establishment of the Press Council in 1973[31]—an institution essentially controlled by the state—the established practice was for the Press Council to regulate the conduct of the media. This arrangement provided the government with ample opportunity to interfere with press freedom. The idea of self-regulation is therefore quite germane to the reduction in the high levels of governmental interference observed during the functioning of the Press Council.[32]

First, journalists have to accept the idea of self-regulation and support a code of practice. Second, the public has to be made aware of it. Third, the mechanism should deliver satisfactory results that warrant the confidence of both journalists and the public.[33] In an evaluation conducted on behalf of the Swedish International Development Cooperation Agency, Elmqvist and Bastian (2006) observed that there is 'almost universal acceptance of the notion of self-regulation within the journalist community'.[34] Almost all the journalists that the authors interviewed during the evaluation appeared to accept that self-regulation was better than being subjected to the Press Council. Moreover, a slow process of disseminating the idea of effective self-regulation among the public has begun to take shape.[35]

In this context, the Press Complaints Commission of Sri Lanka (PCCSL) was established to introduce a mechanism for self-regulation within the print media.[36] The objective of establishing the PCCSL was to provide a body independent of the state to which citizens, aggrieved by actions of the press, could appeal without 'the arduous procedures and prohibitive costs that accompany court actions'.[37] Foremost in this initiative was, once again, the joint efforts of the three main media institutions in the country, the Editors Guild, the Newspaper Society and the Free Media Movement (FMM).[38] The PCCSL is an 11-member entity established under the Companies Act No. 17 of 1982, entrusted with the task of interpreting and implementing the Code of Professional Practice that was formulated by the Editors Guild.[39] The primary task of the institution is to entertain complaints on editorial content from members of the public and resolve the disputes through conciliation, mediation or arbitration.[40] Enforcement of PCCSL decisions takes place through the courts under the provisions of the Arbitration Act[41] in the event of non-compliance by erring newspapers.[42] The lack of willingness demonstrated by certain newspaper editors and journalists to abide by the decisions of the PCCSL has been one of the major drawbacks regarding the effectiveness of the mechanism. The lack of commitment from the very constituents on whose behalf the mechanism has been introduced may even be used to question the legitimacy and legality of the concept of self-regulation.[43] At the outset, the PCCSL functioned at a reasonably satisfactory level,[44] as it received numerous complaints to which the newspapers concerned responded.[45] The PCCSL received 181 complaints between October 2003 and December 2004.[46] However, the number of complaints reduced to 111 the next year and has steadily declined since, indicating a 'certain degree of ineffectiveness of the PCCSL'.[47] Figure 14.1 depicts the extent of this decline.

One possible explanation for this worrying trend is 'the weakening of the PCCSL activities due to staff resignations'.[48] The PCCSL may require a comprehensive strategic plan to respond to some of these institutional challenges.[49] Other challenges remain such as the refusal on the part

Figure 14.1

Complaints chart of the PCCSL 2003–2011

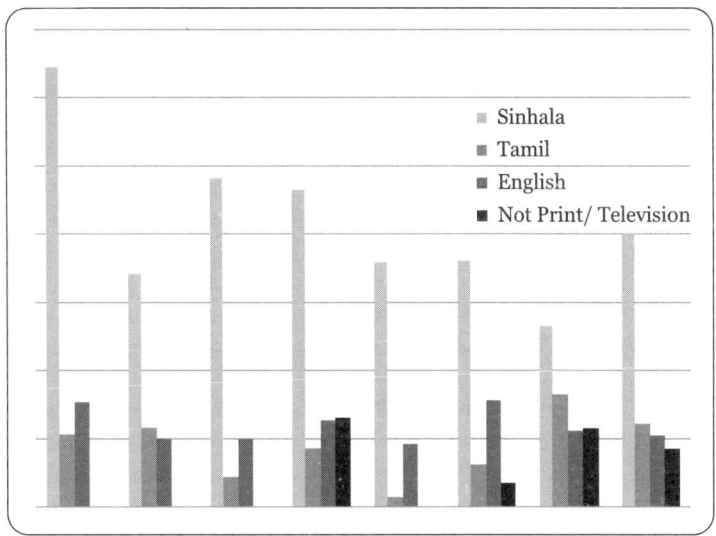

of some newspapers to submit themselves to the voluntary reach of the PCCSL.[50] However, it has been observed that the independent self-regulatory mechanism of the PCCSL is widely accepted by the vast majority of the registered newspapers printed in Sri Lanka. Similarly, editors have now largely accepted the 'Right of Reply' culture, which is a positive result and helps to reach the objectives of the PCCSL.[51]

It is important to note in this regard that the overall success of any self-regulatory scheme is possible only though the participation of the whole industry and not just a part of it. But this position must not in any manner be construed as undermining the progress made by the PCCSL during the last 7 years when compared to the history of the government imposed regulatory mechanism within which the media industry operated for more than 150 years.[52] There is little doubt that the PCCSL carries out an indispensable function within the media sector today; hence the maximum allocation of effort and resources to maintain its institutional integrity and overall efficiency is highly justified.[53] It is certainly the better alternative to government regulation.[54]

The Press Complaints Commission of the UK was the model followed by Sri Lanka at the time of establishing the PCCSL. More recently, however, the scandal of hacking by journalists working in Rupert Murdoch's media empire led to strong criticism of the inability of the UK's self-regulatory body to play an effective role. These events have dented public trust in the Press Complaints Commission of the UK, where the effectiveness and applicability of self-regulatory measures have been questioned.[55] Procrastination, contrived delay and a lack of pro-activity warranted the reference to that body as a 'toothless poodle of the press',[56] and following the report of the Leveson enquiry, commitments were made to replace it with a new regulatory body. However, positive recognition of the continued importance of the Press Complaints Commission and the service rendered during the last 20 years for the betterment of the UK media industry cannot be discounted.[57]

A media self-regulatory scheme in Norway had faced similar disputes in the 1990s. The Norwegian response to serious breaches of ethical codes by journalists in 1990s had been to establish a 'one-stop committee' known as the 'Press Industry Committee'[58] which deals with ethical complaints against media of all formats. The Dispute Resolution Council of PCCSL can be identified as the Sri Lankan counterpart of the 'Press Industry Committee' where the membership consists of 11 members representing academia, civil society and journalists.[59]

The success of the Ombudsman model in the Sri Lankan context in relation to financial services, insurance and tourism has given rise to speculation as to the possibility of establishing an Ombudsman for the media industry.[60] The similarities between an Ombudsman scheme and the PCCSL in relation to the voluntary nature of the scheme, its independence based on reliance on a Consolidated Fund, its cost effectiveness and a less time-consuming alternative dispute resolution process, have been identified as facilitating such a process of conversion. This has been seen as a means of addressing the issues encountered by the PCCSL currently in relation to non-compliance with its directives by some of the editors, the non-availability of monetary relief and the doubtful position as to the status of an arbitration award by the High Court.

The difficulties encountered by journalists who also work as government servants (mostly provincial journalists who engage in part-time journalism while working as a full-time employee somewhere else) would also have to be taken into account, as it is necessary to ensure job security for those who are willing to criticise and be involved in investigative journalism. The opportunities and leeway granted to other professions, including government doctors and lawyers, may also have to be considered for the journalists as well. Media organisations would have to take the lead to initiate discussions and negotiations in this regard with government entities. For such purpose, it would be important to ensure that journalists also be given the right to form trade unions to protect their professional interests.[61]

The apparent lack of motivation for self-regulation is another challenge that the PCCSL would have to be prepared to address in future as the present system does not provide for 'a carrot and stick' approach to motivate compliance. 'Sticks' are very limited in a self-regulatory scheme (may be to the extent of expulsion or reprimand which is not strictly relevant to the media industry), and there appear to be no 'carrots' to induce the journalists to comply with codes of ethics.[62]

Furthermore, it would be necessary to extend the reach of PCCSL by the inclusion of regional publications, periodicals and magazines, which are still not within its purview. The initiation of a discussion between such publications to bring them within the scope of the PCCSL would be important, as these publications also exercise a powerful influence over the public.[63]

Worryingly, in recent years, the government has begun to discredit the 'self-regulatory approach' under the PCCSL. The reactivation of the Press Council was announced in 2009.[64] During the public debate that took place as a result of this announcement, the then Media Minister, Lakshman Yapa Abeywardena, alleged that the self-regulatory mechanism was not an ideal tool to address public grievances.[65]

There appear to be concerted efforts to restore the Press Council as the primary, and perhaps even the sole, arbiter of complaints against the media. The main issue with the Press Council, as currently constituted under the Press Council Law, is the nature of its composition. Section 3 of the Press Council Law empowers the President to appoint the members of the Council[66]—a provision prone to open abuse. In comparison, the Indian model contains certain safeguards that ensure some level of independence from the government.[67] The Chairman of the Council is by convention a retired judge of the Supreme Court of India.[68] The Council has 28 members, of whom 20 are appointed from among the newspaper industry, five are Members of Parliament and the remaining three are nominated by the Sahitya Academy, the Bar Council of India and the University Grants Commission.[69] Moreover, the Council is reconstituted every three years and has its own source of revenue, such as levies collected from the registered newspapers and news agencies. The Press Council of India is an established autonomous quasi-judicial body, largely independent from the government. Hence, any argument for the reactivation of the Sri Lankan Press Council, which places reliance on the Indian model, is wholly capricious.[70]

There is a further issue in regard to the current composition of the Press Council. As observed previously, Section 3(1)(b) (I) of the Press Council Law states that, out of six members (other than the ex officio member) the member representing the working journalists must be selected from a panel of seven persons nominated by the journalists associations in Sri Lanka. Section 3(1)(b) (II) stipulates that, out of the six members, one shall be a person to represent the interests of the employees of newspaper businesses, such person being selected from a panel of not more than three persons nominated by each registered trade union of such employees.

However, in the reactivation of the Press Council by the incumbent President, two representatives of journalists associations and newspaper businesses were not appointed as statutorily mandated.[71] The question then arises as to whether the composition of the Council is in accordance with the enabling law.[72]

The existing National Media Policy discussed above also refers to the establishment of a 'Media Development Council' to identify and address some of the pertinent issues that face the media today. On what seems to be the same line of thinking, the government recently announced plans to set up a Media Development Authority (MDA).[73] The stated objectives of the proposed authority are to formulate guidelines in accordance with media ethics, to promote professionalism and to ensure clear, consistent and predictable regulatory policies and guidelines to protect core values and safeguard public interests. Ominous among such core values is the aim to uphold 'the unity and integrity of the country',[74] which may easily be interpreted to justify curtailing political dissent.

Probably modeled after the Singapore MDA,[75] the proposed authority has been described as an attempt to suppress the private media through yet another regulatory mechanism.[76] One commentator observes that the MDA was announced by Minister Keheliya Rambukwella, who headed the MCNS during the last phase of war against the Liberation Tigers of Tamil Eelam (LTTE).[77] It was further observed that since the MCNS is now defunct,[78] the MDA is likely to replace the MCNS and thereafter spearhead media control for moral policing and economic development.[79]

Though the media community may be able to counter or halt new government proposals for media regulation, the ability of stakeholders to influence the *content* of governmental proposals seems to be grossly inadequate. One reason for the success of the campaign against the 2008 SLRC regulations was the unanimity of the stakeholder group, which included powerful entities within the private sector. Thus, future campaigns to influence the content of proposals and establish true independence within the media should focus heavily on garnering the support of a wider range of stakeholders, including the more influential opinion makers.[80]

Institutional Structures and Policies within the Non-state Sector

Sri Lankan media organisations face many of the same challenges as media organisations the world over. However, in an environment of excessive governmental control, the additional pressure placed on editors by owners seems to accentuate the already severe constraints on editorial freedom.[81] Where good journalism is not backed by owners, the system is forced to rest on the shoulders of individual dedicated journalists. Yet with scarce resources and constant influence from the hierarchy above, even these few dedicated journalists are likely to wilt under the pressure.[82]

Despite official talk from owners about being completely independent from outside political or economic influences, journalists are often required to withdraw or substantially change articles that are critical towards advertisers or towards political allies of the owners.[83] Moreover, journalists allege that owners often engage in the unsavoury practice of micro-managing the daily operations of the newsroom. In some private media organisations, daily news bulletins are broadcast only after the direct consent of the owners.[84] Such vested interests are often reflected in the news carried by various news agencies.[85]

It is of interest that trade unions do not flourish within private media organisations. However, a number of institutions that focus on safeguarding the interests of media stakeholders (i.e., journalists, editors, owners, employees, etc.), improving media freedom, and maintaining professional standards do exist as part of an institutional support base. Among these institutions, the Sri Lanka Press Institute (SLPI), the PCCSL, the Editors Guild, the Newspapers Society, FMM, the Federation of Media Employees' Trade Union, the Sri Lanka Working Journalists' Association, the Sri Lanka Muslim Media Federation and the Sri Lanka Tamil Journalists' Association take precedence.

SLPI's role in this regard is crucial, as it is one of the only organisations that could potentially bring various stakeholders within the media industry under one umbrella. However, SLPI still faces a challenge in terms of unifying the print media with the electronic media. It is hence unlikely that the objective of finding greater consensus within the media community would be achieved unless this representational issue is appropriately addressed. The role of the SLPI to nurture an informed public and to create a more professional, independent media[86] remains of pivotal importance in increasing media professionalism in Sri Lanka.

As observed previously, no systematic studies have been conducted in regard to private interests that control the non-state media sector. Such a study is important in examining the issues that persistently challenge the Sri Lankan media today. Threats to media independence may emanate not only from state actors, but also from private interest groups. In addition, the support base provided to the media by civil society actors has not been adequately utilised for the benefit of journalists and editors. In this context, expecting profit-oriented organisations to drastically improve in the area of social responsibility and provide editorial independence may ultimately prove futile. Hence, there is an undeniable need to introduce and enforce best practices and standards within the industry to ensure greater institutional support for media professionals.

The proposed recommendation for a Charter of Editorial Independence to be adopted in media organisations would be a welcome initiative as this Charter would constitute a written agreement between the owners and the editorial staff. This would separate the proprietor from the day-to-day preparation and presentation of news and opinion.[87] Furthermore, the creation of a board of trustees which would be a buffer between the editor and the owners would also be important to safeguard the interests of both proprietor and the editorial staff. Though this may not be a perfect solution, as any one of the signatories to the Charter may decide not to abide by the terms and conditions, it would at least result in building confidence among the public in relation to the news or information they receive.

Media Standards, Best Practices and Professionalism

The level of professionalism in reporting is considered by many to be quite low in Sri Lanka.[88] A recent study conducted by the International Federation of Journalists[89] reveals that journalists are well aware of universal journalism norms—such as impartiality, accuracy and diversity of sources—but admit that they fall well short of these standards. Elmqvist and Bastian (2006) rightly observe:

> The most evident problem in the media is the lack of the adherence to internationally recognised basic standards of accuracy, impartiality and responsibility. Overall, there remains a very high level of partisanship, little attempt to distinguish facts from opinions, [and] little analytical journalism or investigative reporting.[90]

Some efforts, however, have been undertaken to improve media standards and produce a professional and well-trained class of journalists. For instance, the establishment of SLPI[91] is highly germane to such efforts to promote media professionalism. According to its initial donor proposal, the objective[92] of SLPI was to develop 'a group of trained journalists demonstrating the highest quality, commitment and standards of professionalism'.[93]

Moreover, as discussed above, reformers have attempted to establish a culture of self-regulation through the PCCSL and the Code of Practice of the Editors Guild.[94] In its preamble, the Code of Practice states:

> This code of practice, which is binding on all Press institutions and journalists, aims to ensure that the print medium in Sri Lanka is free and responsible and sensitive to the needs and expectations of its readers, while maintaining the highest standards of journalism.[95]

It is noted that this Code is a significant improvement on the previous Press Council Code.[96] The notion of ethics and related codes have been recognised as the best methods to regulate the professions, as there should be a certain degree of freedom for professionals to act within their respective spheres of work.[97] The Editors Guild Code consists of eight sections covering accurate reporting, corrections and apologies, opportunity to reply, confidential sources, general reporting and writing, privacy, harassment and subterfuge and dignity. Additionally, the Rules and Complaints Procedure of the PCCSL covers the process of entertaining complaints, evidence, the award, correction or change of award and the enforcement and interpretation of the code, and also specifies who could speak on behalf of the PCCSL.[98] The ethical code of journalists differs from most of the other professional codes as it is a non-binding document, which does not impose mandatory disciplinary proceedings against a journalist. This freedom and privilege can be seen as a recognition of the unique and special nature of the journalism profession which is considered as a means of enforcing the rights of the public.[99]

Recently, a committee was appointed with the objective of revising the Code of Practice. This is in fact consistent with the Code itself, which states: '[t]he Editors Guild shall review the provisions of this Code from time to time, but not less than once each year'.[100] The Code of Practice, together with the self-regulation scheme facilitated by the PCCSL states that aggrieved parties will be given an opportunity to voice their concerns and to obtain a remedy in that regard. The education level of the new entrants to the media industry has shown a significant increase due to the growth of higher education and this has resulted in the creation of a generation of journalists who are well aware of the applicable ethical considerations. The success of this Code would essentially depend on the awareness and acceptance of the code among journalists, the general public and all the other industry stakeholders.[101]

More recent attempts by the government to impose a Code of Ethics on the Sri Lankan media were met with substantial criticisms of its proposed contents and its general incoherent nature. Such a Code appeared incongruous in the context of the state media continuing to be blatantly used for government propaganda purposes, and an open disregard by state journalists of basic norms of decency and fairness in reportage. This proposal was subsequently to all intents and purposes shelved, though the possibility of its resurrection is still present.

From a different perspective, it is clear that a Code of Practice (however excellently drafted) would not be able to eradicate the possibility of human error. Therefore, it is necessary to address the grievances of those who are affected by such conduct. The personal pride of journalists and editors may sometimes prevent them from retraction or correction. But it would be important to understand that such measures not only create credibility, but also a certain level of respect and trust in regard to such newspapers.[102] Certain personal qualities are also expected from professional journalists. As professionals whose task is to show the wrong doings and mistakes of others, journalists also have to be humble enough to accept their own mistakes.[103]

Any consideration of the professional state of the media in Sri Lanka needs to take account of the marked disparity between journalists from Colombo and those from the provinces. Interviews conducted by a Colombo-based NGO with provincial journalists revealed that they often lacked proper journalism training and seldom received training on media ethics.[104] Furthermore, provincial journalists are isolated from mainstream media outlets and often from their peers and editors who are mostly based in Colombo.[105] It was found that most provincial journalists did not even receive copies of the Code of Practice from their respective media organisations.[106] Thus, journalism standards across the country may vary considerably. In response to these concerns, reformers must ensure greater circulation of the Code of Practice among provincial journalists and also provide them with better access to training. Some media organisations have recognised their responsibility in this regard by the implementation of initiatives towards a better compliance with ethics and professional norms.[107] Such initiatives have already been undertaken by SLPI in particular, and have proved to be reasonably successful.

The need to have more frank exchanges on key issues between the journalists and the industry is another important element in ensuing greater professionalism. Grossly inadequate payments, delay in making payments, the inability of journalists to form and organise trade union activities and the insecure nature of their personal and professional interests have resulted in the failure of the media industry to achieve any real solidarity.[108] The relative size of the industry when compared to the Indian print media industry and the special circumstances of the Tamil print media are crucial matters of concern. The issue of safety of the source in the absence of shield laws to protect sources and whistle-blowers has also been a significant problem.[109]

Access to Means of Transmission and Distribution

It seems clear that the general public has reasonable access to the print media in Sri Lanka, particularly to Colombo-based mainstream newspapers. It has been observed that compared to other developing countries, where regional and community media often play an important role, Sri Lanka possesses very little regional and local media.[110] In this context, Sri Lanka does not have an extensive community radio industry. Since 1992, four successive governments have refused to grant broadcasting licences to non-profit, non-governmental or cooperative groups, including the country's largest local development organisation—Sarvodaya.[111] The explanation for this refusal seems to be political, since the government has often feared the political agendas of some of these organisations, particularly those that may take 'an anti-government stand on social and political issues, such as human rights abuses, corruption, welfare policy and ethnic issues'.[112]

The projects that ultimately did get governmental approval, such as the Mahaweli Community Radio, lacked independence, as they depended heavily on the goodwill and partnership of SLBC.[113] A report published by the CPA in 2008 notes that the Mahaweli Community Radio, among other similar ventures, was never truly independent, as its contents were kept 'artificially non-political' through a policy which prevents any criticism of the government.[114] Likewise, an earlier World Bank Study conducted by Jayaratne et al. (2005) revealed that almost every aspect of broadcasting in Sri Lanka is tightly controlled by the Central Government.[115] The occasional collaboration between the Central Government and certain Provincial Councils was not seen as evidence of de-centralising control. A good example of this phenomenon is the Uva Community Radio (UCR), established jointly by SLBC and the Uva Provincial Council.[116] Jayaratne et al. (2005) rightly conclude that Sri Lanka's political culture is antagonistic towards community radio initiatives. This antagonism was evident in the case of UCR, which eventually witnessed a 'marked decrease in community-driven programming, ostensibly as part of an effort to stay on the air'.[117]

In stark contrast to Sri Lanka, the experience in India has been far more positive. For decades, the broadcast media was under the complete monopoly of the Government of India.[118] However, in 1995, in *Secretary, Ministry of Information and Broadcasting v. Cricket Association of Bengal*,[119] the Supreme Court emphasised that the airwaves are public property, that every citizen has a fundamental right to impart and receive information and to have access to telecasting for that purpose, and that the government had no monopoly over such media.[120] As a result of such jurisprudential developments and persistent campaigning by civil society organisations, the broadcasting sector in India has gradually become more open and accessible to the citizens, though restrictions remain on local news broadcasts. In November 2006, the government released a Community Radio Policy, which allowed agricultural centres, educational institutions and civil society organisations to apply for community-based FM broadcasting licences.[121] These non-transferable licences were to be valid for a period of five years and were to be used for community development purposes only. The government envisaged 4000 stations across the country but progress in granting licences has been slow, with only 167 stations on air by 2013.[122]

Jayaratne et al. (2005) recommend that to overcome political impediments, future community radio initiatives in Sri Lanka should be redesigned.[123] The authors claim that such initiatives should be 'relatively smaller and established in cohesive communities that have articulated common goals and are thus able to successfully surmount destabilising influences'.[124] However, significant reform may not be possible without the overhaul of the present licensing regime. Thus, the proliferation of community radio in Sri Lanka may ultimately be contingent on broader reforms that culminate in the establishment of an independent broadcasting authority.

Ethnicity and Language

Issues of ethnicity and language are obviously relevant to the media in Sri Lanka, particularly in the context of a savage ethnic conflict and long-standing language-related tensions. In the private sector, the co-relation between ethnicity and media ownership is clearly revealed when one examines *who* really invests in Tamil media. Apart from a solitary non-Tamil investor, that is, Asian Broadcasting, which runs a Tamil radio station, all other Tamil language media are results of investments by Tamil entrepreneurs. It is observed that none of the leading private sector media houses such as the Wijaya Group or Upali Group in terms of print, or well-known stations such as Swarnavahini in terms of electronic media, cater to the Tamil-speaking people.[125] In fact, some of the newspaper groups were established explicitly for the purpose of representing the views of a particular ethnic group. For example, the Upali Group represents the interest of the Sinhala population, and the Express Group represents Tamil interests. With the exception of the Maharajah Group, there seems to be little incentive for a capitalist class to invest in the media with the objective of cutting across ethnic segregations.

However, in this polarised environment, there have been a few attempts to break ethnic barriers. One example is the advent of multi-lingual newsrooms where journalists of different language groups work together. The Maharaja Group pioneered this approach and established an environment where journalists of each ethnic group are compelled to confront the opinions of colleagues from the other groups. Moreover, it is somewhat encouraging to note that certain regional services of the state-owned SLBC radio, such as the UCR, have introduced multi-lingual programmes.

Diversity of ethnic representation in media houses is a key issue which needs to be addressed to ensure good public service journalism. Effective public service journalism should be reflective of the views expressed by all communities in society. Thus, it is '*vital that a newsroom should include all types of Sri Lankans to ensure diverse mix of gender, ethnicity, religion, language and background*.[126] In Sri Lanka, English language newspapers appear to maintain the most diverse newsrooms which include Sinhala journalists together with Tamil, Muslim and Burgher journalists. Though there has been official recognition as to the trilingual language policy in the country, the absence of a conducive environment for the implementation of such policies is a major obstacle.[127] A content analysis of the print media in 2005[128] revealed that Tamil, Sinhala and English newspapers focus on the same topics quite differently.[129] A good example of this phenomenon was the reporting of killings, abductions and armed attacks during the ceasefire period, where a great dearth in credible information on such acts existed. The English-speaking press habitually attributed all killings to the LTTE, whereas the Tamil media tended to blame the government. Another study[130] revealed a similar result concerning thematic content and sources. The Sinhala press focused on the CFA[131] violations by the LTTE and much less on government attacks, whereas the Tamil press focused on the peace process. Furthermore, the Sinhala and English press relied heavily on military and police sources, whereas the Tamil press relied on more unconventional sources, including the LTTE.

> In a common paradox, the mass media in Sri Lanka has been one of the prime violators of freedom of expression in practising ethnic exclusivism in its reportage and commentary. This is borne out, for example, by the language medium playing a selective role in the manner in which ethnic issues are represented.[132]

This inherent ethnic gap is also confirmed by S. Nadarajah in his study on the reporting of the vernacular press.[133] The author observes that the Tamil press generally tended to cover more Tamil concerns such as the ethnic conflict, while the Sinhala press covered Sinhala concerns such as intra-Sinhala party politics. However, the author concedes that in specific respects, the Sinhala and Tamil papers have deviated from the norm, where Sinhala papers have criticised the government and Tamil papers have criticised the LTTE.[134] Yet, it seems that the radicalisation of positions over the past few years has ultimately contributed to ethnicity becoming the most essential issue, particularly in Tamil media, even leading to the neglect of other factors.

Today, ethnicity and language continue to act as highly divisive levers within the media machinery.[135] Though the representational nature of journalism will continue to influence the 'angle' from which journalists report on issues, the ability to engage readers across ethnic lines remains an important part of the broader democratic role of the media. Direct measures for reforming the system have proved to be largely ineffective. However,—as discussed later in this chapter—there may be some scope for achieving long-term reform by fostering a future generation of media personnel more sensitive to complex ethnic and language issues.

Gender

Sri Lanka's record of gender empowerment in the public sphere has often been grossly over-valued, perhaps as a result of certain 'visible' achievements in the past, such as producing the world's first woman prime minister in 1960.[136] Despite some advances since then, 'the actual impact that women [have] in the political and public sphere has continued to be minimal'.[137] Jayaratne et al. (2005) comment:

> Despite one or two women assuming the uppermost levels of political leadership, the overall participation of women in the formal political process has sunk to the lowest levels yet experienced in the South Asian region, as compared to India, Pakistan and Bangladesh.[138]

This lack of substantive progress is certainly evident in the media profession as well. For instance, the workforce is still highly male-dominated, as female journalists have limited opportunities in the newsroom.[139] The following graph provides an indication as to the male–female participation in the print media.[140]

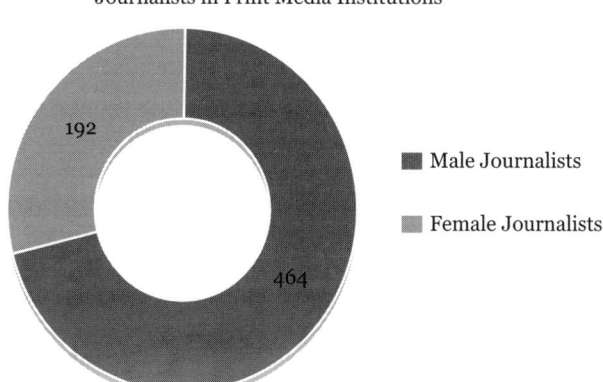

Male–Female Breakdown of Journalists at Newspapers
Journalists in Print Media Institutions

192
464
■ Male Journalists
■ Female Journalists

The paucity of representation in the profession is also reflected in the choice of content. A good example of this phenomenon may be observed in Sri Lanka's limited foray into community radio. Some commentators suggest that the community radio experience in Sri Lanka has failed to provide a space for the vigorous articulation of women's voices on their specific concerns.[141] Research has instead indicated that '[p]rogramming that was systematically targeted at empowering the women of the communities was conspicuously lacking'.[142]

A recent survey conducted on behalf of SLPI reveals that the number of female journalists entering the media industry and the media education institutions in Sri Lanka has significantly increased over the years.[143] Unfortunately, the study also reveals that despite these encouraging developments, female participation in media in Sri Lanka is still less than that of their male counterparts[144]; a trend clearly visible in the Sinhala and Tamil print media and to a lesser extent in English print media. Furthermore, the increased number of female entrants to the industry has not been reflected at the managerial and decision-making level where the progress of female journalists to such positions has been very slow.[145]

However, the concluding remarks in the SLPI Report indicate positive changes in future. Most participants to that survey have expressed the view that:

> There was a time when female journalists could only go up to heading a magazine or programme section of media organisations. Now there are several who have managed to break through and rise to the top and in time more females will follow suit.[146]

The existence of intimidation and harassment, tight work schedules, multiple roles expected to be performed by women and their consequential discouragement are some of the issues which need to be addressed to ensure the positive participation of the female journalists in the media industry.

In terms of academia and professional training, some institutions such as the Sri Lanka College of Journalism hold sessions on topics such as 'Women in Media and their Role' and 'Development Journalism and Women's Issues'. The objectives of these sessions are to provide an insight to students on gender issues and expose them to sensitive areas of reporting which concern women. The importance of gender sensitising in journalism cannot be overstated. Accordingly, it has been observed that gender-related training can equip journalists and editors to quickly detect glaring gaps in stories in terms of perspectives that may have been overlooked.[147]

Hence, it is crucial that journalists are made more aware of the different needs of men and women, which in turn should be adequately reflected in media coverage.[148] The reform agenda, once again, ought to be mainly focused on education, as changing the mindsets of the existing generation of media professionals is improbable. However, some attitudinal, and consequently structural, changes may be introduced through strategic curricula reform and gender training.

A new generation of female media professionals has slowly emerged over the last decade or so. Thus, the combination of greater gender sensitivity within the profession and an exponential growth in the number of female journalists entering the profession should result in tangible improvements over time.

Market Context

The lack of extensive and multi-faceted research on the Sri Lankan media has led to a dearth in information on media economics in the country. Credible and systematically generated figures on revenues from advertising or on overall profitability are scarcely available today.

The excessive duties imposed on newsprint have no doubt adversely affected the cost of newspapers. The signatories to the Colombo Declaration on Media Freedom and Social Responsibility raised this concern while pointing out that the import duty ultimately acts as a barrier to the distribution and dissemination of knowledge.[149] It was hence concluded: 'As a direct result of escalating newsprint prices, publishers of developing economies like Sri Lanka, are compelled to increase the cover price of newspapers thus impacting on the dissemination of news and views'.[150]

A common view held among media professionals is that the industry is heavily dependent on advertising.[151] Concerns are often expressed with regard to the volatility of the market and the effects an economic crisis may have on advertising budgets, and consequently on the already limited profitability of newspapers. Though some media houses belong to larger conglomerates, which can sustain their businesses through cross-financing strategies, most other organisations effectively survive on a knife edge.

The social responsibility of media stakeholders in relation to advertising content is another aspect which needs to be taken into account. The responsibility of all stakeholders, including newspapers, advertising agencies, business and consumers, is imperative in this respect. In practice, the dependency of the newspapers on advertising income has prevented editors and/or journalists from commenting on the advertising content. Recently, advertising campaigns run by a certain financial company offering extravagant interest rates, which ultimately turned out to be a financial scam, had raised many concerns among the general public as to the duty of respective parties to prevent incidents of this nature. The perspective of the business community in regard to maximisation of profits would seem to act as a barrier to responsible advertising. Though there is a Code of Ethics by which the advertising agencies are self-regulated, such measures have been found to be inadequate. In this context, the responsibility of the consumer has been emphasised as the ultimate decision maker regarding any product or service.[152]

American researcher J.H. McManus points out that most of the news around the world today is produced by profit-seeking enterprises.[153] It is observed that in this model of 'market-driven journalism', audiences cease to be citizens, but rather become consumers. Moreover, news becomes a commodity and has to prioritise the needs of the market rather than reflect reality. Thus, the entire process becomes a 'transaction' in which consumers exchange their attention for money to get news, where upon the media company sells their attention to the advertisers.[154]

This model appears to be prevalent in Sri Lanka as well, particularly in respect of the broadcasting media. Bolin (2006) rightly surmises:

> For the time being most of the television programmes are for the upper economic groups, while there are no programmes for minorities, homeless, single parents or underprivileged groups. The quality is compromised to save costs, and the programmes promote consumerism with the aim to maximise a wealthy audience and get more advertisers.[155]

The extent of the commoditising of the media was amply demonstrated during the civil war. As J.B. Disanayaka observes, the Sri Lankan media often treated the war as a commodity, 'helping to increase sales figures rather than increase understanding of the situation'.[156] The author notes that throughout the 1980s and 1990s, the media focused on presenting the conflict as a series of sensational incidents rather than on covering its long-term implications.[157]

The proper response to this phenomenon must come from within the journalism profession itself. As noted above, journalists often come under severe pressure from owners with purely economic interests. Only a sound profession that uncompromisingly adheres to high professional and ethical standards could prevent market forces from dictating terms.

If high standards are maintained, the consumer's expectations would also be shaped in a positive fashion, thereby creating a demand for balanced news and credible analyses. In this context, public discourse would govern the market, rather than vice versa, consequently compelling media organisations to strive for a better quality of reporting to sell their 'commodity'.

Erosion of Media Freedom in Sri Lanka

Censorship

The issue of media censorship in Sri Lanka has evolved significantly during the past decade. While in the early 2000s, the government often overtly resorted to censorship, its strategy for imposing restrictions on the media has grown more sophisticated during recent times. Today, censorship laws are scarcely imposed. Yet, even with the decline of such overt measures, the government has succeeded in creating an environment in which self-censorship is routinely practised.[158]

An early example of overt censorship is the case of *Leader Publications (Pvt.) Ltd. v. Ariya Rubasinghe, Director of Information and Competent Authority and Others.*[159] The background to this case involves the appointment of the first respondent to be the 'Competent Authority' under Regulation 2 read with Regulation 14(2)[160] of the Emergency (Miscellaneous Provisions and Powers) Regulations No. 1 of 2000. On 22 May 2000, the first respondent, purporting to act in terms of Regulation 14(2)(b)(i), sent a letter to the petitioner prohibiting the petitioner from printing, publishing and distributing its newspaper *Sunday Leader* or any newspaper for a period of 6 months from the date of the order. Further by an order purporting to be under regulation 14(2)(b)(ii), he directed the Inspector General of Police to take possession of the petitioner's printing press and its premises. The petitioner filed a Fundamental Rights Application in the Supreme Court complaining that the said orders violated its rights under Articles 12(1), 14(1)(a) and 14(1)(g) of the Constitution. At the hearing, the validity of the first respondent's appointment as 'Competent Authority' was taken up as a preliminary matter.

The Supreme Court was of the view that the 'first respondent was not entitled to make the orders he did, for he was not empowered by the regulations to do so within the meaning of Section 6 of the Public Security Ordinance'.[161] It was further held that the means chosen for the appointment of the Competent Authority, namely by a notification published in the Official Gazette, was 'not an effective exercise of the delegated power conferred by parliament by Section 6 of the Public Security Ordinance'.[162] Thus, it was held that the first respondent had no power or authority to act under regulation 14 and the document dated 22 May 2000 addressed to the petitioner was a nullity and was of no force or avail in law.[163]

Though many welcomed this somewhat unusual ruling in favour of the petitioner, the narrow technical scope of the judgment was instantly revealed. By relying on a legal technicality rather than on a substantive legal principle, 'the Supreme Court left the door open for the government to re-impose media censorship'.[164] The government immediately promulgated a set of emergency regulations under which it became mandatory for all media—both domestic and foreign—to submit their reports to the 'Competent Authority' prior to publication or broadcast.[165] Amidst protest by both domestic and international journalists, the government lifted the requirement of pre-publication vetting. However, the Competent Authority still possessed broad sweeping powers to ban material on a wide range of grounds, including the interests of national security and the preservation of public order.[166]

The strategy of the government for imposing media censorship slowly changed over the next few years, particularly after the resumption of hostilities in the north and east of the country. As observed by an 'insider' familiar with media practice in the north and east:

> It is true that there is no official censorship or banning of newspapers now, but the effects of these two stringent measures are achieved in a subtle way through various devices by the authorities. Even steps are taken to cripple certain newspapers to force them to close down due to lack of resources. Therefore, it is evident that real press freedom does not exist here in practice.[167]

Examples of government-backed elements strong-arming the media in the north and east into ceasing operations are many. A good example of this de facto censorship was a July 2006 incident where such unruly forces stopped the distribution of all the Tamil newspapers in the eastern districts of Batticaloa and Amparai.[168]

Another critical issue in this regard is the emergence of self-censorship within the private media.[169] Despite the fact that the government has not imposed censorship laws during the past few years, the Sri Lankan media is afflicted by self-censorship.[170] The issue of editorial freedom in Sri Lanka is complex and the responsibility of editors and owners in this regard needs to be better scrutinised.[171] The issue of self-censorship is very real, as continued interference in the newsroom by owners has severely hampered the space for free, accurate and balanced reporting. Thus, ascribing responsibility for the erosion of media freedom through censorship is a complex task. Though the government is largely responsible for creating an ambience of fear and paranoia,[172] the media industry itself is also responsible for becoming easily malleable and resorting to self-censorship.

Killings and Disappearances; Prevention of Terrorism and Emergency Law

The UN Human Rights Committee has observed that states must appreciate the importance of a pluralistic media in the nation-building process. Restricting media freedom to advance apparently noble goals such as 'national unity' ultimately violates the freedom of speech and expression. The Committee further observes:

> The legitimate objective of safeguarding and indeed strengthening national unity under difficult political circumstances cannot be achieved by attempting to muzzle advocacy of multi-party democratic tenets and human rights.[173]

Such observations remain largely unheeded in the Sri Lankan context. At the end of 2006—perhaps during a period when preparations for a full-blown military confrontation between the government and the LTTE were set in motion—Reporters without Borders referred to Sri Lanka as one of the world's most dangerous countries for journalists.[174] This predicament continued to prevail throughout the rest of the decade, with only small improvements observable following the end of military operations in May 2009. Although Sri Lanka's Constitution provides for freedom of expression, the comprehensive legal framework 'leaves wide discretion for the government to impose restrictions'.[175]

Apart from the government's over-arching power to issue licences for radio and television stations, it possesses a variety of mechanisms to hinder the work of an independent media. The Prevention of Terrorism Act (PTA)[176] and the Emergency Regulations under the Public Security Ordinance[177] remain the most outstanding of these mechanisms. These laws and regulations have been indiscriminately used to impose censorship of the media, seize printing presses and jail journalists. The PTA, in addition, specifically prohibits the printing, publishing and distribution of a particular publication without the prior approval in writing of a competent authority, and prohibits publication of any matter, which may perceivably lead to the incitement to violence.[178] Similarly, the Emergency Regulations permitted inter alia the detention of suspects without charge or trial, and entry search and seizure of property.[179] Though the regulations were temporarily suspended during the Ceasefire Agreement of 2002, they were promptly re-introduced by the then President Chandrika Kumaratunga in August 2005 following the assassination of the then Foreign Affairs Minister Lakshman Kadirgamar.

During the ceasefire period, media freedom began to slowly improve. Not surprisingly, some quarters in the media and civil society called for the repeal of the PTA altogether. Following the breakdown of the peace process in late 2006 and the resumption of the war between the government troops and the LTTE, media freedoms came to be increasingly under threat by both protagonists with several incidents involving violations of human rights and attacks on journalists.[180]

This new era of media restrictions witnessed incredible pressure being applied on southern journalists by the government and also on Tamil journalists by the LTTE, which contributed heavily to the systematic silencing of moderate voices.[181] The culture of fear engendered in the south also led to a number of Sinhala journalists being identified as unpatriotic, traitors or LTTE sympathisers and as a threat to national security. As mentioned above, this environment caused many journalists to resort to self-censorship, which no doubt adversely affected journalistic standards during the period.

Countless incidents of repression of the freedom of speech and expression, including extortion, abduction, assault and even the murder of journalists have taken place over the past decade.[182]

Some notably egregious incidents of violence against media personnel require mention:

a. Jaffna-based freelance journalist, Mylvaganam Nimalarajan, was killed in October 2000 inside a high security zone controlled by the Sri Lankan Army. Some have argued that his assassination was due to his public opposition to the activities of the Eelam People's Democratic Party (EPDP), a government-backed political party opposed to the LTTE. He was also noted for criticising the government for its repressive policies in Jaffna. Though some arrests of suspects belonging to the EPDP were made, 'the investigations petered out' by the end of 2002.[183]

b. Dharmeratnam Sivaram, a Tamil journalist most noted for being the Editor of controversial news website Tamilnet.com, was kidnapped in April 2005 in Colombo and extra-judicially executed soon after. Many analysts have speculated that the Tamil Makkal Viduthalai Pulikal (TMVP)—a breakaway faction of the LTTE that enjoyed considerable governmental support—was responsible for the assassination, thereby insinuating government complicity. Once again, no suspects were apprehended or tried in respect of the crime.[184]

c. Manusamy Parameshwari,[185] a translator of Tamil ethnicity at the *Standard* newspaper was arrested and the newspaper labelled as LTTE funded with frequent government raids and the arrest of its publisher.[186]

d. Namal Perera, Deputy Director Advocacy at the SLPI at that time, and a friend with whom he was travelling were severely assaulted sustaining serious injuries.[187] Attacks on media personnel including Keith Noyahr, *Rivira* Editor, Upali Tennakoon, *Uthayan* Editor, N. Vidyadharan, and media activist Poddala Jayantha confirmed this dangerous trend. Many journalists fled the country.

e. The brutal assassination of Lasantha Wickrematunge, the Editor of the strongly anti-government newspaper, the *Sunday Leader*, in January 2009, was perhaps the most shocking of all recent attacks on media personnel. Wickrematunge was a prominent figure in the media and often described as a 'virulent critic of the Mahinda Rajapaksa government'.[188] The journalist also clashed with Defence Secretary, Gotabaya Rajapaksa, over a defamation suit, in which Wickrematunge's business was being sued for ₹2 billion. Following the assassination, a number of suspects, mostly linked to the armed forces, were taken into custody for their alleged involvement. However, no formal charges have been instituted against any individual.

f. On 29 July 2011, the news editor of *Uthayan* newspaper, Mr G. Kuganathan, was assaulted with iron rods in Jaffna.

g. On 15 February 2012, Prasad Purnimal Jayamanne, a freelance journalist working for the BBC's Sinhala service and a member of the South Asian Free Media Association, was attacked and badly beaten while filming a demonstration by fisherman in Chilaw, in protest against the death of a fisherman at the hands of the police.

The above examples only serve to amplify the dismal state of journalistic freedom in Sri Lanka during the prosecution of the war as well as in the post-war period. The post-war situation has unfortunately failed to witness much improvement. Even five years after the end of hostilities in the north and east of the country, the PTA continues to be in force, even though the state of emergency has been allowed to lapse.

The Tissainayagam Case

Perhaps no other case better reflects the tension between the freedom of speech and expression and the government's obsession with controlling the dissemination of information in the media than the case of journalist J.S. Tissainayagam. The Terrorism Investigation Division (TID) of the Sri Lanka Police arrested Tissainayagam in March 2008. The journalist was charged inter alia with inciting the commission of acts of violence or racial or communal disharmony by publishing certain articles in the *North-Eastern Monthly* Magazine in 2006 and 2007.[189] During his trial, Tissainayagam claimed that he was harassed and threatened by the TID while under detention, which had led to an involuntary confession.[190]

In August 2009, the High Court sentenced Tissainayagam to a total of 20 years rigorous imprisonment—the maximum sentence—for arousing 'communal feelings' by writing and publishing articles that criticised the government's treatment of Sri Lankan Tamil civilians affected by the war, and for raising funds for a magazine in which the articles were published in furtherance of terrorism.[191] Soon after, Tissainayagam appealed the ruling, and was granted bail on 11 January 2010 pending the outcome of his appeal.[192] Eventually, in May 2010, the government announced that he would be pardoned by President Mahinda Rajapaksa to mark the 2010 World Press Freedom Day. The case of Tissainayagam was conveniently swept under the rug and discussion on the matter soon ended.

The High Court judgment has been severely criticised at several levels. One major issue related to the judge's acceptance of the confession, despite a host of evidentiary discrepancies put forward by the defence, and also her own official's contention that the prosecution had presented tampered evidence. Moreover, the judge appeared to disregard the fact that no prosecution witnesses were summoned to prove the articles could incite ethnic disharmony, but instead relied on her own judgment and on a defence witness's evidence that the articles were factually incorrect.

Surprisingly, the judge dismissed the evidence of four other witnesses on the basis that they were of the same political beliefs as the accused. It may reasonably be said that the judge failed to adhere to the fundamental principles of a fair trial including the requirement of placing the burden of proof on the prosecution.

Tissainayagam's case does not merely highlight the lack of media freedom in Sri Lanka; it also reveals a much deeper systemic problem. The three charges against Tissainayagam under the PTA were: (1) that he intended to cause the commission of acts of violence or racial or communal disharmony through the printing or distribution of the magazine '*North-Eastern Monthly*'; (2) that he intended to cause the commission of acts of violence or racial or communal disharmony through the publishing of particular content in the said magazine and (3) that he collected funds from *non-governmental organisations* for the publishing of the said magazine (emphasis added). One is immediately struck by the absence of any reference to the LTTE or any terrorist group in the indictment.

One of the editorials relied on in the indictment was headlined: 'Providing Security to Tamils now will define northeastern politics of the future'. The excerpt specifically cited in the indictment reads: 'It is fairly obvious that the government is not going to offer them [Tamil Civilians] any protection. In fact it is the state security forces that are the main perpetrator of the killings'. By analysing the three charges and the excerpt in the indictment, it becomes fairly obvious that the conviction of Tissainayagam on the first and third charges was contingent on his conviction on the second charge, which was the only charge that was 'content based'. The entire case therefore rested on proving in terms of Section 2(1)(h) of the PTA No. 30 of 1981 that the article, and more specifically the excerpt, was published with the intention of 'causing the commission of acts of violence or racial or communal disharmony'.

The sole contention of the state in the case—and this is often omitted in propaganda statements—was that an article written by a *Tamil* journalist accusing a predominantly *Sinhalese* Army is likely to incite the commission of acts of violence by Sinhalese readers against Tamils, or lead to racial or communal disharmony. This proposition is absurd and, at the very least, imposes an enormous evidentiary burden on the prosecution. Yet this aspect of the trial seldom found its way into the media, as the government successfully distorted the controversy into one revolving around Tissainayagam's links to the LTTE. Even those in the civil society who campaigned for Tissainayagam's release focused on the issue of journalistic freedom, while being divided on whether he actually had links to the LTTE.

It was rarely emphasised that Tissainayagam's purported links to the LTTE had nothing to do with his indictment. The government achieved this feat through the relentless use of propaganda on official governmental websites during the pendency of the case—an act which would constitute contempt of court in most jurisdictions.[193] In the courtroom, however, there was simply no link that could be drawn between the accused liaisons with the LTTE—albeit during the ceasefire period where even government officials habitually liaised with the LTTE—and the actual indictment.

Today, very few commentators identify the media ruse orchestrated by the government during the trial. Through its control of the media and effective hold over public discourse, the government successfully avoided having to defend the unconvincing position that Tissainayagam's articles were intended to incite reasonable readers into committing acts of violence or to cause racial or communal disharmony. Hence, the case revealed the extent of the government's influence over public opinion and the government's ability to define the parameters of discourse on controversial issues. The end result was the conviction of an innocent individual and the confusion of the general public.

The Post-conflict Context

Post-2009, the media environment has continued to witness serious challenges. Following a long line of similar indictments,[194] Reporters without Borders downgraded Sri Lanka in its World Press Freedom Index, 2011–2012, citing impunity and official censorship of websites[195] as leading to pervasive self-censorship.[196] Reports abounded that Sri Lanka's government was seeking the assistance of the Chinese government to block and filter websites.[197] In early 2012, protest demonstrations by media organisations in Colombo were blocked and impeded by hostile pro-government groups holding clubs,[198] despite a recommendation by the government-appointed Lessons Learnt and Reconciliation Commission made public in December 2011 that media freedom should be enhanced in keeping with democratic principles and relevant fundamental rights obligations. It affirmed that harassment and attacks on media personnel should be prevented, cases should be properly investigated and prosecuted as well as deterrent punishments imposed.

For its own part, media activism has faced serious challenges to its integrity and continuing dissension between media advocacy bodies has damaged the public credibility of these organisations. Today, one of the most urgent contemporary issues facing the media is the need to maintain its status as a vehicle for systemic change and as a facilitator of public debate. To retain this status, reporting standards need to dramatically improve, that is, journalists need to be more analytical, more considerate of ethnic dimensions and to represent more divergent perspectives on various issues. In effect, the media needs to adhere to universal journalistic standards and adopt best practices to ensure a fair and balance culture of reporting.

The end of the nearly 30-year military conflict brought with it certain legitimate expectations of a rapid improvement in media freedom. Yet more than five years after the end of hostilities, the state of media freedom in the country remains ambiguous. In this context, two scenarios require analysis, as priorities for interventions may greatly differ depending on whether media freedom is re-established or not.[199]

In the context of continued media restrictions and curtailment of the freedom of speech and expression, the highest priority should be the protection of journalists by measures such as increasing the already existing safety funds for journalists and training journalists to produce content while minimising risks.

In the context of an improved situation where more public debate is possible, more activities for enlarging background reporting and political analysis with comprehensive views may be possible. Media reformers should look to support activities in influential spheres by maintaining existing training programmes and enlarging them by adding components such as political analysis, studies on ethnicity, conflict analysis and gender studies. Reformers should also look to strengthen in-house training efforts for media organisations. Moreover, the space created by the relaxation of restrictions should be exploited to lobby for reforms in respect of media laws and regulations.

There is little doubt that the media is likely to reflect heavily on its proper role during the next few years. The government would no longer have the luxury of citing emergency conditions or terrorism as an excuse for restricting media freedom, though it does have other means of exercising influence on media organisations. The media, much weakened by years of state control, is still to come out of its shell. For instance, newspapers and radio and TV stations have for the most part remained apathetic towards the government's continued restrictions on media freedoms, despite the end of military operations. Likewise, strong collective action, either to discredit corrupt politicians or to advance the enactment of a Right to Information Law, is simply not visible within the media today. Hence, one could only hope that as peace in the country solidifies and journalistic space widens, the media would seize the opportunity for much-needed reform.

Notes

1. Bolin (2006), p. 16.
2. *Ibid.*
3. Senadhira (1996). The author observes that President Premadasa kept an iron grip on the media, a policy demonstrated in the president's use of media during an opposition bid to impeach him in August 1991.
4. See Brady (2005).
5. *Ibid.*
6. *Ibid.* See also the following point of view: 'the early years of the Chandrika Kumaratunga government were identified as a period during which the media was allowed to function with a certain amount of freedom. However, the latter part of her tenure was marked by assaults on journalists, torture, murder and disappearances engaged in by those with certain agendas, compounded by many cases of self-exile under the threat of death. Since then the media in Sri Lanka has been crushed into a state of 'self-censorship and docility' [vide interview with A.C. Visvalingam, President, Citizens Movement for Good Governance (CIMOGG), interviewed on 13 April 2012, views expressed in personal capacity].
7. 'In the present context, intimidation, assaults, murder, the denial of the right to information, withdrawal of government advertisements and providing unsecured finance to sympathizers to take over control of the less friendly media companies have been identified as the most powerful weapons deployed to make the media submissive' [*Ibid.*].
8. UN Doc. CCPR/C/79/Add. 56, 27 July 1995.
9. Article 19(2) reads: 'Everyone shall have the right to freedom of expression; this right shall include freedom to seek, receive and impart information and ideas of all kinds, regardless of frontiers, either orally, in writing or in print, in the form of art, or through any other media of his choice'.
10. Jayaratne et al. (2007), p. 14.
11. Report of the Committee to Advise on the Reform of Laws Affecting Media Freedom and Freedom of Expression (R.K.W. Goonesekere Committee Report) (1996), hereafter the R.K.W. Goonesekere Committee Report, at p. 39.
12. *Ibid.*, p. 38.
13. Though physical attacks against journalists have declined post 2008–2009, the climate of fear in the industry has been a major concern, as the financial stability of a media house would be at risk if the government in power is offended [vide interview with I. Furkan (former) CEO, Sri Lanka Press Institute (SLPI), 9 February 2012].
14. 'The success of any reform effort would be dependent on the restoration of basic democratic rights and accountability to the public at large by those vested with power. Furthermore, it is important to establish independent institutions in the form of judicial, regulatory and professional associations comprised of and led by men and women of integrity, independence, commitment and capability. Independent civil society groups need to be established to ensure intellectual, open and transparent debate in regard to

issues of predominant concern to society' [vide interview with Chandra Jayaratne, civil society member, 4 March 2012].

15. The Government of Sri Lanka was one of the signatories to the Colombo Declaration on Media, Development and Poverty Eradication (2006). The government's commitments under this Declaration included the promotion of a free, pluralistic and independent media committed to social justice and development.

16. Act No.25 of 1991.

17. Act No.27 of 1996.

18. See Section 22(4) of the Sri Lanka Telecommunications Act (as amended).

19. See Schedule to the Act; Section 3 of the Act.

20. See Section 22B of the Act.

21. See Jayaratne et al. (2005), pp. 56–57.

22. *Ibid.*

23. *Ibid.*

24. Act No.6 of 1982. The said regulations were published in the Gazette of the Democratic Socialist Republic of Sri Lanka (Extraordinary) No. 1570/35 on 10 October 2008,

25. *Centre for Policy Alternatives v. Minister of Mass Media & Others*, SC (F.R.) Application No. 478/2008, Petition.

26. *Ibid.* CPA cited the case of *Sunila Abeysekera v. Ariya Rubasinghe, Competent Authority and Others*, [2000] 1 Sri L.R 314, which held that 'exceptions to Article 14(1)(a) must be narrowly and strictly construed for the reason that the freedom of speech constitutes one of the essential foundations of a democratic society'.

27. [2003] 1 Sri L.R. 74.

28. *Ibid.*, p. 98.

29. 'Formulation of regulations by bureaucrats (mostly as a response to a crisis) has been viewed as short-sighted action which would result in a framework that is oppressive to those who are regulated and would inevitably be presented as constituting an unnecessary interference. Furthermore, such measures have been criticised for being disguised censorship which is burdensome and unnecessarily expensive in terms of compliance cost'. National Conference on Self-Regulation (2011) Session on Policing the Media: Statutory or Self-Regulatory? at p.17 (presentation by Arittha Wickramanayake, Attorney at Law and former Director General, Securities and Exchange Commission).

30. Elmqvist and Bastian (2006), p. 20.

31. See Sri Lanka Press Council Law, No. 5 of 1973.

32. It was a given therefore that the argument for complete abolition of the Press Council depended significantly on the success of the self-regulation initiatives.

33. Elmqvist and Bastian (2006), p. 20.

34. *Ibid.*

35. *Ibid.*

36. The Sri Lankan media industry introduced and implemented a Press Complaints Commission with the intention of allowing the public to voice grievances and petition for redress. The PCCSL was created as an outcome of the Colombo Declaration, 1998.

37. Pinto-Jayawardena (2003), p. 16.

38. *Ibid.*

39. *Ibid.*

40. See http://www.pccsl.lk (accessed on 3 January 2011).

41. Act No.11 of 1995. The arbitration Council of the PCCSL is a vital element of the self-regulation exercise. When complaints cannot be resolved through reconciliation or mediation, arbitration is carried out by three members of this special council.

42. Pinto-Jayawardena (2003), p. 16. 'Certain doubts have arisen as to the possibility of successful enforcement of an arbitration award due to the informal nature of the arbitration process'. National Conference on Self-Regulation (2011) Opening Session, pp. 8–9 (presentation by Dr Wickrema Weerasooriya, Insurance Ombudsman).

43. 'It has been said that the self-regulation has been utilised as an alternative paradigm whenever the government initiates a regulation process. But the great flurry of enthusiasm, usually motivated with the intention of diverting the government imposed regulations, fades away as the time passes and stakeholders generally drift away to follow their own interests'. *National Conference on Self-Regulation: Speeches and Interactive Sessions* (September 2011), Press Complaints Commission of Sri Lanka (PCCSL) (hereafter National Conference on Self-Regulation (2011)), pp. 18–19 (presentation by A. Wickramanayake).

44. 'There has been a steady and slow growth of complaints received by the PCCSL' [vide interview with S. Rockwood, CEO of the Press Complaints Commission of Sri Lanka, 14 February 2012].

45. *Ibid.*

46. PCCSL Complaints Chart received from the PCCSL on 14 February 2012.

47. Elmqvist and Bastian (2006), at p.22. This was further noted as a disappointing trend. As was succinctly observed, complaints made to the PCCSL are decreasing not because of the media has improved but because people are not sufficiently interested to follow up (vide interview with D. Nesiah, retired senior civil servant and member Press Complaints Commission of Sri Lanka (PCCSL) interviewed on 21 February 2012).

48. *Ibid.*

49. One such instance would be to inquire into the complaint process and investigative mechanism. The existing requirement in the Complaint Form to the PCCSL requires a complainant to identify the clause in the Media Code of Professional Practice that has been breached. Furthermore, the complainant is expected to provide the details and evidence and the burden is placed on him to provide copies of the alleged newspaper publication. Requirements of this nature mandate a standard which is neither practical nor fair to be expected from ordinary people. National Conference on Self-Regulation (2011), Wickrema Weerasooriya. Yet another cause of the Press Council not receiving sufficient complaints over past years may be because the guidelines of the body have not been explicit (vide interview with D. Nesiah, 21 February 2012).

50. The PCCSL faces challenges in dealing with editors who do not want to comply with the PCCSL mandate as it does not have mandatory legal standing (vide interview with S. Rockwood, 14 February 2012).

51. Press Complaints Commission of Sri Lanka Annual Report 2010, p. 63. But the conduct of certain editors has been subject to criticism based on their unsupportive behavior coupled with the unwillingness to adopt corrective measures [vide interview with S. Rockwood, 14 February 2012].

52. National Conference on Self-Regulation (2011) Session on Policing the Media: Statutory or Self-Regulatory?, at p.24 (response made by Kamal Liyanarachchi, Acting CEO, PCCSL).

53. For this purpose, it would be necessary to ensure the independence of the entity by the appointment of independent, credible, professional and well-respected members of the industry to the PCCSL. Furthermore, issues relating to funding, staffing and infrastructure and support service will also have to be addressed.

54. This is an opinion almost universally supported by those interviewed for this study with the exception of state media officials. To ensure the due functioning of the Press

Complaints Commission it is necessary for media personnel to have faith in the institution and ensure that the functions are performed as per the mandate given to it (vide interview with D. Nesiah, 21 February 2012).

55. National Conference on Self-Regulation (2011) Session on The World Outside, p. 58 (presentation by William Gore, Director, Public Affairs, PCC UK).

56. These observations were made by the speaker in relation to his personal experience regarding two articles published in the *London Sunday Times* by a well-known journalist, the late Marie Colvin. National Conference on Self-Regulation (2011) Session on The World Outside, at pp.61–66 (presentation by Neville de Silva, Senior Journalist).

57. National Conference on Self-Regulation (2011) (William Gore).

58. National Conference on Self-Regulation (2011) Session on The World Outside, at pp.67–68 (presentation by Hana Ibrahim, Editor, Ceylon Today). The Press Industry Committee consists of four industry members, that is, two journalists and two editors together with three members to represent the public. This format has been recognised as in line with the concept of 'Readers' Clubs' in the UK, where public participation has been emphasised as vital for the balance of different interests.

59. National Conference on Self-Regulation (2011) Session on The World Outside, p. 68 (Sukumar Rockwood).

60. National Conference on Self-Regulation (2011) (Wickrema Weerasooriya).

61. National Conference on Self-Regulation (2011) Session on The Role of Media Organisations in Self-Regulation, at p.76 (presentation by Gnanasiri Koththigoda, Acting President, Sri Lanka Working Journalists Association).

62. National Conference on Self-Regulation (2011) Session on Policing the Media: Statutory or Self-Regulatory?, at p.18 (A. Wickramanayake).

63. National Conference on Self-Regulation (2011) Session on The Role of Media Organisations in Self-Regulation, at pp.86 and 87 (Imran Furkhan and Gnanasiri Koththigoda).

64. See Colombo Page, *Sri Lanka Press Council Born Again*, available at: http://www.colombopage.com/archive_091/Jun1244821410RA.html (accessed on 23 January 2011).

65. LankaTimes.com, *Dayasiri and Yapa at Loggerheads over Press Council*, available at http://www.lankatimes.com/fullstory.php?id=18616 (accessed on 23 January 2011).

66. See Sri Lanka Press Council Law (No. 5 of 1973), Section 3, which reads: '(1) The Council shall consist of—(a) the person for the time being holding office as the Director of Information (in this Law referred to as 'the Director') and (b) *six other members appointed by the president*, of whom—(i) one shall be a person to represent the working journalists, such person being selected from a panel of not more than seven persons nominated by the journalists associations in Sri Lanka and (ii) one shall be a person to represent the interests of the employees of newspaper businesses, such person being selected from panels of not more than three persons nominated by each registered trade union of such employees' (emphasis added).

67. See Press Council Act 1978 (India).

68. See Citizen's Charter of Press Council of India, available at: http://presscouncil.nic.in/Citizen%20Charter-Modified.pdf (accessed on 23 January 2011).

69. *Ibid.*

70. Sukumar Rockwood (PCCSL) and Imran Furkan (formerly SLPI) both observed that there is little need for the restoration of the Press Council as the PCCSL has been successful in dealing with complaints brought against newspapers. It was opined that

there is a lack of public faith in the Press Council as it is perceived to be working under the umbrella of government (vide interviews with Imran Furkan, 9 February 2012, and Sukumar Rockwood, 12 February 2012).

71. The *Sunday Times* challenged the legality of the Press Council on this basis following a complaint lodged against the newspaper by the government's Director General of the Media Centre for National Security (MCNS) (May 2011). The press industry has taken a collective decision to refrain from appointing the required number of members to the Press Council as it may be interpreted as an acceptance of the validity and legality of the decision to revive the Press Council (Dharmadasa Lankapeli, media dissident [interviewed on 5 April 2012]). On 24 November 2014, the President appointed the Chief Editor of the *Thinakaran* newspaper, S. Thillainathan, to the Press Council presumably in a bid to forestall further objections.

72. The legality of the Press Council was vehemently defended by its Chairman W. Dayarathne, PC (vide interview with W. Dayarathne on 12 June 2012).

73. See Official Government News Portal of Sri Lanka, Media Development Authority, available at: http://www.news.lk/index.php?option=com_content&task=view&id=15 940&Itemid=44 (accessed on 23 January 2011).

74. *Ibid.*

75. Patranobis (2010).

76. See Kannangara (2010).

77. Deshapriya (2010).

78. Despite this assertion, this body continues to be routinely used for repressive measures imposed by the government. One illustration was the fact that as notified by the MCNS, prior approval needs to be obtained for SMS news alerts related to the security establishment.

79. *Ibid.*

80. This was a common expectation voiced by interviewees.

81. 'In practical terms, editorial independence is generally observed. Where conflicts arise, such situations are responded to on a consensual basis and with a view to achieving a compromise [vide K. Nadesan, Publisher, Express Newspapers interviewed on 20 February 2012]. The fact however that the ultimate control of news content and editorial freedom in a publishing house rests with the publisher or the owner of such media house is an inevitable reality (vide interview with Ranjit Wijewardene, Publisher, Wijeya Newspapers interviewed on 21 February 2012 and Harendra Jayalal, former news head, Swarnavahini television channel, interviewed on 12 February 2012).

82. Malik Chaminda Dharmawardena—Dinamina Newspaper (interviewed on 24 March 2011).

83. This position was affirmed by a senior administrator at the Sri Lanka College of Journalism, who observed that both state and private media have political affiliations. Some of the media houses are more overt in their views (interviewed on 9 February 2012).

84. The general consensus among the public and different stakeholders in the industry acknowledges that the control of media freedom in the private media lies in the hands of the owners/investors (e.g. in views expressed by C. Jayaratne and A.C. Visvalingam views expressed in personal capacity). It is interesting to note however that the institutional structure and the unique nature of the ownership scheme of the *Ravaya* newspaper have been identified as placing the *Ravaya* newspaper in a different context to other newspapers insofar as investor control of newspapers is concerned (vide interview with K. Janaranjana, senior journalist, Ravaya newspaper, interviewed on 4 January 2011).

85. The existence of such interests has been identified as a practical reality. 'Given such political affiliations, there is a need to ensure the availability of a variety of newspapers which would ensure the balance of views between different interests (vide interview with D. Nesiah, 21 February 2012.).

86. Vide interview with Imran Furkhan, 9 February 2012.

87. Dobbie (2007), p. 16.

88. Self-regulators in Sri Lanka share this view. The generally low standards of professionalism in Sri Lanka is commonly attributed to the lack of higher educational training. However, it cannot be denied that vulnerability to persistent attacks and intimidation have driven out professional journalists and rendered others nervous to join the profession.

89. International Federation of Journalists (2004).

90. Elmqvist and Bastian (2006), p. 23.

91. The SLPI was founded in 2004 and is the umbrella organisation that brings together the PCCSL and the Sri Lanka College of Journalism. A major aim of the SLPI's mandate was to establish links with fraternal international organisations around the world (Colombo Declaration on Media Freedom and Social Responsibility, International Symposium, 1998).

92. The overall aim of SLPI is to create and nurture an informed public committed to democratic ideas and the creation of a professional, independent and unbiased media [vide interview with I. Furkhan, 9 February 2012].

93. *Ibid.*, p. 10.

94. Vide interview conducted with K. Nadesan, 9 February 2012

95. Code of Professional Practice (Code of Ethics) of the Editors' Guild of Sri Lanka adopted by the Press Complaints Commission of Sri Lanka, available at http://www.pccsl.lk/includes/downloads/files/file_09081732403.pdf (accessed on 3 January 2011).

96. See The Press Council (Code of Ethics for Journalists) Rules, 1981. The said Rules were formulated by the Sri Lanka Press Council setting out the Code of Ethics for Journalists under Section 30(i)(a) of the Sri Lanka Press Council Law, No. 5 of 1973, and approved by Parliament under Section 30(3) of the said Law.

97. National Conference on Self-Regulation (2011) Session on Media Ethics: Fact or Fiction, at p.37 (presentation by Wijedasa Rajapaksha, PC, MP and former Chairman, Press Council of Sri Lanka).

98. Elmqvist and Bastian (2006), p. 21.

99. National Conference on Self-Regulation (2011) (Rajapaksha).

100. See Code of Professional Practice, section entitled 'Review'.

101. National Conference on Self-Regulation (2011) Session on Media Ethics: Fact or Fiction, p. 31 (presentation by N.M. Ameen, President, Muslim Media Forum and Editor, Navamani newspaper).

102. National Conference on Self-Regulation (2011) Session on Media Ethics: Fact or Fiction, p. 34 (presentation by Seetha Ranjanee, senior journalist and former convener, Free Media Movement).

103. In one incident, a newspaper based in London published an inaccurate report about a Sri Lankan living there and after getting to know about the inaccuracy that newspaper company had been quick in taking corrective measures even before the person involved had seen the newspaper report. Consequently, a representative of the company had come to his place, apologised and had paid compensation to the aggrieved person. Sri Lankan journalists must strive to attain professionalism of such high standards,

National Conference on Self-Regulation (2011) (Rajapaksha). See Code of Professional Practice (Code of Ethics) of the Editors' Guild of Sri Lanka, section entitled 'Review'.

104. CPA and IMS, at p.19f. Also see Bolin (2006), p. 10.

105. IMPACS, CPA and IFJ., p. 10.

106. *Ibid.* See also Transparency International Sri Lanka and Friedrich Ebert Stiftung (2011), p. 15.

107. Transparency International Sri Lanka and Friedrich Ebert Stiftung (2011), at p.15 'Some media organisations have voluntarily moved to the next level. The Sinhala alternative publication, Ravaya, introduced its own house rules and introduced an ombudsman to the newspaper. Some media organisations have evolved their own organisational policies on gifts'.

108. 10th Anniversary of the Colombo Declaration (2008) Session on Press Freedom in Sri Lanka: What's Happening?, p. 34 (panel discussion).

109. Transparency International Sri Lanka and Friedrich Ebert Stiftung (2011), p. 92. '...a story published in The *Sunday Leader* in 2007 about a group of police officers who were falsely accused and indicted of crimes in retaliation for raiding a well—known Colombo drug ring that had been operating with the approval of police superiors. The story quoted several of the falsely accused officers including IP Douglas Nimal. The day after the story ran, Nimal called the reporter and thanked her profusely for her work. He also said he was on his way to the Supreme Court to file a fundamental rights petition challenging his wrongful suspension. He promised to come over to the newspaper office with additional information exposing even more wrongdoings of his superiors. He never made it. Nimal and his wife were killed in Athurigiriya on their way to the Supreme Court in Hulfstdorp'.

110. Bolin (2006), p. 8.

111. *Ibid.*, p. 10.

112. *Ibid.*

113. *Ibid.* The author notes: 'Two groundbreaking projects have met with considerable success—the Mahaweli Community Radio (MCR) established in 1981, and its offshoot Kothmale Community Radio Internet Project, established in 1991. Both of these stations were developed with foreign aid and the support of UNESCO, and were designed to engage local rural communities. In MCR's case Mahaweli Radio was to broadcast in communities involved in the government's ambitious irrigation scheme to divert the Mahaweli River. Meanwhile the Kothmale Community Radio Project set in Sri Lanka's hill country was designed to use radio broadcasts as a conduit between the local community and the new technology of the Internet. But while these stations were considered 'community radio' in terms of their content and philosophy, they relied on the goodwill and partnership of the SLBC to survive'. Also see Gunawardene (2007).

114. See Centre for Policy Alternatives (2008), p. 37.

115. Jayaratne et al. (2005), p. 10.

116. *Ibid.*

117. *Ibid.*, p. 43.

118. See Basu (2003).

119. (1995) 2 SCC 161.

120. *Ibid.*, p. 122.

121. See UNESCO.org, *India to Establish 4000 Community Radio Stations under New Community Radio Policy*, available at: http://portal.unesco.org/ci/en/ev.php-URL_ID=24250&URL_DO=DO_TOPIC&URL_SECTION=201.html (accessed on 23 January 2011).

122. See http://qsl.net/vu2jos/fm/cr.htm (accessed 14 June 2013).
123. Jayaratne et al. (2005), p. 43.
124. *Ibid.*
125. Currently, the mainstream media (Sinhala and English language) versions are mostly controlled and administered by ethnic Sinhalese, both Buddhist and Christian. In the post-conflict era, it would be necessary for all media to consciously avoid the continued propagation of ideas that militate against an inclusive Sri Lankan mentality [vide interview with A.C. Visvalingam, 13 April 2012].
126. IMPACS, CPA and IFJ., p. 12.
127. *Ibid.*
128. Hettiarachchi (unpublished).
129. The negative impact of the significant influence and control exercised by extremists in Sinhalese and Tamil language media has been worsened by the limited impact of the English media (which is generally considered as moderate in its approach) on the majority Sinhala speaking public in the country.
130. IFJ (2004)
131. This refers to the ceasefire agreement (CFA) signed between the United National Front (UNF) government of Ranil Wickremasinghe and the Liberation Tigers of Tamil Eelam (LTTE) in 2002, which brought in the Nordic-dominated Sri Lanka Monitoring Mission (SLMM) to monitor the implementation of the ceasefire. In the wake of multiple violations of the ceasefire agreement by both parties, in April 2003, the LTTE announced that it was withdrawing from the ceasefire. Some years thereafter, active hostilities resumed between the successor government of Mahinda Rajapaksa and the LTTE.
132. Pinto-Jayawardena (2003), p. 17.
133. S. Nadarajah (2005).
134. *Ibid.*
135. Vide interview with A.C. Visvalingam, 13 April 2012.
136. Jayaratne et al. (2005), p. 44.
137. *Ibid.*
138. *Ibid.*
139. Bolin (2006), p. 10.
140. Sri Lanka Press Institute (2011), p. 21.
141. Jayaratne et al. (2005), p. 45.
142. *Ibid.*
143. SLPI Report, p. 34.
144. *Ibid.*
145. *Ibid.,* p. 35.
146. *Ibid.,* p. 36.
147. Elmqvist and Bastian (2006), p. 30.
148. *Ibid.*
149. See Colombo Declaration on Media Freedom and Social Responsibility (October 2008).
150. *Ibid.* 'The cost of paper and print is one of the most significant obstacles to the increased professionalism of the media industry' [vide interview with D. Nesiah, 21 February 2012].
151. 'The dependency of media institutions on the revenue generated through advertisements and the inability of media institutions to oppose such investors is a practical reality which needs to be accepted by the media industry' [vide interview with B. Padmakumara, Chairman, Lake House, interviewed on 8 January 2011].

152. 10th Anniversary of the Colombo Declaration (2008) Session on Press Freedom in Sri Lanka: Business Ethics—Is There Such a Thing? (Panel discussion).

153. McManus (1994), p. 21.

154. *Ibid.*, pp. 1, 37 and 61. Also see Bolin (2006), p. 22.

155. Bolin (2006), p. 23.

156. Disanayaka (1999), p. 268.

157. *Ibid.* Also see Bolin (2006), p. 23.

158. The present context has been identified as an era where the 'media has caved in' (vide interview with D. Nesiah, 21 February 2012). The following observation was made by Chandra Jayaratne in relation to the present context. 'The 'fear' and 'reward' structures in force primarily along with legal regulatory and extra regulatory measures hand in hand with the lack of effective, independent and committed public institutions, lack of effective codes of conduct and ethics and disinterest and fear amongst key civil society actors and willingness to ignore amber lights around—the present calcification and labeling of all independent persons to be either 'patriots' or 'traitors' merely by their spoken, written or other actions—the net result of all this is to cripple free and fair media in operation (both state and non-state media) leading even to the non-state media imposing on themselves self-censorship governance practices' (vide interview with C. Jayaratne, 4 March 2012).

159. [2000] 1 Sri. L. R. 265.

160. Regulation 14(2) provides inter alia that 'Competent Authority' in relation to any emergency regulation means, unless otherwise provided for in such regulation, any person appointed, by name or by office, by the President to be a Competent Authority for the purpose of such regulation'.

161. [2000] 1 Sri. L. R. 265, p. 278.

162. *Ibid.* Section 6 of the Public Security Ordinance No. 25 of 1947 declares: 'Emergency regulations may provide for empowering such authorities or persons as may be specified in the regulations to make orders and rules for any of the purposes for which such regulations are authorised by this ordinance to be made, and may contain such incidental and supplementary provisions as appear to the president to be necessary or expedient for the purposes of the regulations'. Accordingly, the court held that such authorities and persons must be appointed through a substantive enactment.

163. *Ibid.*, p. 282.

164. Sturgess (2000).

165. *Ibid.*

166. *Ibid.* The author cites the new regulations as banning 'any material which would in the opinion of the Competent Authority be prejudicial to the interests of national security or the preservation of public order or the maintenance of supplies and services essential to the life of the community or inciting or encouraging persons to mutiny, riot or civil commotion or to commit the breach of any law for the time being in force'.

167. 10th Anniversary of the Colombo Declaration (2008) Session on Press Freedom in Sri Lanka: What's Happening?, p. 28 (presentation by E. Saravanapavan, Chairman, Mass Media Syndicate [Pvt] Ltd).

168. *Ibid.*, p. 29.

169. A predominant problem currently affecting the Sri Lankan media is self-censorship which has prevented effective reporting and commentary on a range of issues, not only in regard to defence-related matters, but also in reference to general non-observance of the Rule of Law and the prevalence of widespread corruption.

170. 10th Anniversary of the Colombo Declaration (2008) Session on Press Freedom in Sri Lanka: What's Happening?, p. 32 (presentation by Sunanda Deshapriya [former] Head, Media Unit, Centre for Policy Alternatives).
171. *Ibid.*
172. Government interference in the media as well as threats and intimidation of the media has increased during the last few years [vide interview with D. Nesiah, 21 February 2012].
173. See *Mukong v. Cameroon*, Communication No. 458/1991, at para 9.7. Also see Jayaratne et al. (2005), p. 14.
174. Centre for Policy Alternatives (2007), p. 7.
175. Amnesty International (2008), p. 8.
176. Act No. 30 of 1981.
177. Ordinance No. 25 of 1947.
178. Pinto-Jayawardena (2003), p. 4.
179. The requirements that other jurisdictions insist on prior to the exercise of power to issue emergency regulations, including but not limited to the principle of exceptional threat, principles of legality, principles of proportionality, the principle of necessity in a democratic society and the principle of non-discrimination, have not been made prerequisites under the Sri Lankan Constitution. 10th Anniversary of the Colombo Declaration (2008) Session on Freedom of Expression in Period under Emergency Regulations, at pp.72 and 73 (presentation by Asanga Welikala, Senior Researcher, Legal Unit, Centre for Policy Alternatives).
180. See Amnesty International (2008), pp. 12–27. Also see Free Media Movement (2007).
181. 10th Anniversary of the Colombo Declaration (2008) Session on Press Freedom in Sri Lanka: What's Happening?, pp. 32 and 38 (presentations made by Deshapriya and Saravanapavan).
182. Vide interviews with S. Rockwood, 14 February 2012, and K. Nadesan, 21 February 2012
183. Pinto-Jayawardena (2003), p. 19. Also see Committee to Protect Journalists (2001).
184. Reporters Without Borders (2006 and 2010). Also see International Press Freedom and Freedom of Expression Mission to Sri Lanka (2007), p. 8.
185. Lanka Business Online (2007b).
186. http://www.thesundayleader.lk/20090301/exposive.HTM (accessed on 11 January 2011).
187. Free Media Movement (2008).
188. Reddy (2009).
189. See CNN (2009).
190. See Law and Society Trust (2009).
191. The *Sunday Leader, Convicted*, available at: http://www.thesundayleader.lk/archive/20090906/convicted.htm (accessed on 15 January 2011).
192. See BBC (2010).
193. See Ministry of Defence, Sri Lanka (2010a and 2010b)
194. International Federation of Journalists (2010); http://en.rsf.org/press-freedom-index2010,1034.html (accessed on 11 January 2011); Freedom House (2011b). Both Chandra Jayaratne and Sukumar Rockwood agree that the threats have increased significantly, with a certain marginal downturn since the end of the war (vide interviews with C. Jayaratne, 4 March 2012, and S. Rockwood, 14 February 2012).
195. PCCSL has commenced discussions with different web managers to formulate guidelines for the websites to regulate themselves (vide interview with S. Rockwood, 14 February 2012).

196. Reporters Without Borders, http://en.rsf.org/IMG/CLASSEMENT_2012/C_GENERAL_ANG.pdf (accessed on 11 January 2011).

197. http://ict4peace.wordpress.com/2010/02/11/sri-lankan-government-to-block-internet-and-censor-independent-web-media/ (accessed on 11 January 2011); among the websites blocked were lanka-e-news, lanka dissent, srilanka guardian. Websites were requested to register with the government and many declined to do so.

198. *The Sunday Times*, 29 January 2012.

199. This assertion is made in reference to an analysis carried out during a recent evaluation of the media industry in Sri Lanka which however cannot be quoted due to its confidential nature.

14

Conclusion: Media Reform in a National and Global Context

This book emerged from an initiative which had a number of specific objectives: to look at the present status of the media and of media freedoms in Sri Lanka; to assess the role of the fourth estate in the functioning of Sri Lankan democracy; to look at the role of universities and training institutes in developing a critical appreciation of the role of the media and in training a class of professional journalists to play that role; to generate a body of material about the Sri Lankan media to inform discussion and debate and for teaching and training purposes.

The project and the book have highlighted a number of key areas of concern for the future. One is about the place of freedom of expression within the wider framework of Sri Lankan constitutional experience. It does not exist in a vacuum; it is intimately related to constitutional development, the exercise of power by political parties in government; and ultimately on the preservation of a proper balance between the main branches of government: presidency, parliament and judiciary. In Sri Lanka, over the past 30 years, there have been special circumstances, which have distorted some of these relations and created semi-permanent constraints on some of these freedoms. And many of those distortions continue, though the war is now over.

Constitutions are not just legal documents. They are about power and culture, nationalism, ethnicity and identity and how they are mediated in terms of legal processes and rights through the institutions of the state. Over the past 30 years, the making and remaking of constitutions in the image of particular political leaders has undermined confidence in constitutions per se and a new generation of Sri Lankans has grown up knowing only a permanent State of Emergency and restrictions on their rights. During this time, the role of the judiciary as the key arbiter of constitutional rights has been critically weakened by a process of politicisation.

The exercise of political power to reshape constitutions, to reduce the scope of judicial review, to politicise appointments to offices of state, much of it justified in terms of the prolonged civil war and the real threat to the state it posed, has strengthened the political dominance of particular parties or ethnicities at the expense of inclusive notions of citizenship and has further alienated sections of the population who needed to be won over to bring peace to the country.

The media in Sri Lanka—particularly the private print media and the private television media—have unfortunately got caught up in the political in-fighting and internecine war of the last few decades. The state used a whole battery of legal instruments to restrict media coverage of the war and tended to see any criticism of its conduct as a sign of treachery. At the height of the war, the assassination of journalists reached epidemic proportions and many more fled the country for fear of their lives. A great number of those affected were Tamil journalists, seeking to report on the impact of the war on their own community. But journalists working for the English and Sinhala media and for international news agencies were not exempt from such pressures, as the testimonies of journalists in this book make clear.

The fact that the media profession has got caught in the crossfire of the war means that it has come under massive scrutiny from the public as well as the politicians. Like the other institutions of Sri Lankan democracy, confidence in the role of the media has also come to be questioned. All this underlines the critical need for agreement across the political spectrum on the role of the fourth estate in Sri Lankan democracy and the importance of a free flow of information if the public is to be well informed and in a position to hold the government to account. Without that, there is little chance that the checklist of desirable changes to existing laws required by media pressure groups will be accepted and implemented by the political class.

The Direction of Reform

Most commentators go back to the R.K.W. Goonesekere report for their text on Sri Lankan media reform. At a particular moment of political change in the mid-1990s, there was a window of opportunity for open and thoughtful consideration of the fundamentals. But the window was only open for a short period before short-term political advantage closed off those promising prospects. There was a similar moment in the period of political co-habitation from 2002 to 2004, when the Prime Minister, Ranil Wickremasinghe, was able to bring in some limited reforms. But for most of the last 40 years, power has not been on the side of the reformers. The R.K.W. Goonesekere report identified almost all the key issues which have continued to be at the forefront of efforts for reform since that time. It made recommendations to strengthen constitutional guarantees of freedom of expression; to remove parliamentary privilege as grounds for restricting media freedom; to pass a Contempt of Court Act, which offers more protection to reporting in the public interest and to bring in a Freedom of Information Act to make government more transparent. The report also identified the need for an Independent Broadcasting Regulator and a Media Council to hear complaints. Only its recommendations to remove the Criminal Defamation provisions of the Penal Code from the statute books and to amend the Parliamentary Privileges Act to return the power to determine grave breaches of privilege exclusively to the Supreme Court have so far been fully implemented.

A great deal of thinking and drafting work has been done on these various issues since that time—by governments, parliamentary select committees, the Law Commission, the Bar Council and by media pressure groups. Different draft laws on Freedom of Information and on Contempt of Court have been prepared and refined over the past 10 years. But so far they remain firmly in the domain of aspiration. Governments have not seen fit to bow to pressures for change.

As far as the role of the courts is concerned, there have been some progressive judgements, such as the judgement of the late Dr Justice Mark Fernando in the case of Wimal Fernando v. the Sri Lanka Broadcasting Corporation, which broadened the interpretation of the rights to freedom of thought and information in the context of broadcasting. But for the most part, the courts have tended to be cautious in their pronouncements. They have generally upheld rights to freedom of expression but on a case-by-case basis. They have not acknowledged any specific 'freedom of the press' nor extended any special rights to the journalistic community. Rather, they have explicitly denied these rights. Jayantha Almeida de Gunaratne shows in his analysis of case law that in their interpretation of Article 14(1)(a) of the Sri Lankan constitution, the courts have not upheld any unqualified right to freedom of information, which persuades him that a Freedom of Information Act needs to be put on the statute book. An equally clear, if sobering, conclusion is reached by Kishali Pinto-Jayawardena and Gehan Gunatilleke in Chapter 8 after their review of judicial responses to the media reform agenda. They write that 'reformers cannot—and indeed should not—expect the judiciary to be the vehicle of change'. Reform efforts have to focus on 'alternative strategies to litigation, including collective advocacy, institutional improvement and educational reform'.

Perhaps the most encouraging aspect of Sri Lanka's record in this area has been the constant and dynamic civil society involvement in debates on issues of free speech and freedom of expression. Strong media industry and civil society initiatives such as the 1998 Colombo Declaration and its review and revision in 2008 (as described by Sinha Ratnatunga in Chapter 2) have exercised a powerful and lasting influence on the debate in the face of contrary pressures. Other prominent declarations, such as those made at Tholangamuwa in 2005 and Weligama in 2006, also testify to a remarkable solidarity in the media profession—journalists, editors and owners' organisations—in the defence of a beleaguered industry and to restore freedom of expression and democratic rights.

These have been extremely hazardous times to be a journalist in Sri Lanka, as a stream of critical reports from international bodies like Reporters without Borders have testified. But there have been many examples of extraordinary commitment and courage, despite the dangers to life and livelihood involved in doing what in normal times would be regarded as a professional job.

At the same time, the newspaper industry particularly has recognised that it needs to do more to unite the profession and to improve standards. In the aftermath of the Colombo Declaration, a number of key bodies—the Editors Guild, the Newspaper Society and the Free Media Movement—came together, with support from Scandinavian countries, to create the Sri Lanka Press Institute (SLPI) with a commitment to improved self-regulation, training and advocacy for media reform. Out of this collaboration came a new code of conduct developed by the Editors Guild, a Press Complaints Commission, which has made the industry more accountable to its readers, and the Sri Lanka College of Journalism, which is providing courses for new entrants and mid-career professionals. Sinha Ratnatunga, who has been very much involved in this process, gives a graphic account in the book of the creation of these institutions and their contribution to a more effective and responsive profession. But more still needs to be done to bring the same benefits to the television sector and to the neglected provincial press.

On the other side of the balance sheet, there has been a significant deterioration of editorial freedom and a widespread practice of self-censorship in the face of emergency laws and dangerous and unpredictable extra-legal sanctions and threats against editors and individual journalists who do not toe a government-defined line. As Namini Wijedasa points out in Chapter 5, even prominent women editors have been sent death threats; and while there is optimism that the present low number of women in senior positions will increase, they face the same obstacles as their male counterparts.

The offices of media institutions seen as critical of the government have been attacked, and little or no attempt has been made to discover or bring to book those responsible. The situation has improved to some extent since 2009. But new government controlled bodies such as the revived Press Council and the proposed Media Development Authority do not encourage advocates of free expression and a more liberal media environment. Neither does a recent proposal to bring in a government-imposed Code of Ethics for journalists which contains vague and ill-defined language with potential to hamper freedom of expression still further.

There has also been a worrying concentration of media power in the government's own hands. This has restricted both the quantum of credible journalism and the scope for discussion and debate. With the state-owned print media and the state-controlled TV and radio broadcasters being prime sources of information for the public and the means through which such restrictions are operated, there is a dilemma which remains unresolved. On one side is the politician's wish to harness the media in a drive for effective government. On the other is the imperative for a media institution to retain its credibility with its audience and with the public. Arguments for operational autonomy for the state broadcasters have been weakened by the growth of competition from private broadcasters, as governments argue that they need their own voice. In reality, however, Sri Lanka's state media have degenerated considerably, often carrying out crude and vituperative attacks on prominent dissenters. Moreover, state control extends into the private sector as well, both by formal and informal means. Financial pressure is exercised on media owners through their wider business interests. Media institutions can be bought outright by new owners who make editorial appointment in accordance with their own and the government's preferences. Beyond that, the practice of self-censorship limits the terms of policy debate.

Efforts to persuade the government to give up the power to licence TV and radio channels and to set up a regulator with a broader public interest brief have so far fallen on deaf ears. Sri Lankan experience is not unusual in this respect. Even where regulators have been set up—supposedly at arms' length from government—they have sometimes proved less independent than was expected. Even in the best circumstances, issues of regulation of the media, both new and old, raise difficult conflicts of purpose and interest. Rights of free expression are agreed to have limits: child pornography is one area in which the protection of children overrides other considerations. Similarly, national security may be perceived to take precedence over the personal privacy of an individual, though official use of surveillance methodologies worldwide is coming under increasing scrutiny following the recent revelations of some very prominent whistle-blowers in western countries. The agency and purposes of media regulation are a key point of policy making; and beyond the decision making is a further contested area of who needs to know what the decisions are. All this pushes advocates of media reform to agree on the importance of freedom of information legislation, and the right to know.

The rapid spread of the Internet and of mobile phones in Sri Lanka has opened up new, potentially freer spaces for public discussion and for citizen journalism. However, the government has blocked access to some websites for security reasons and, whatever the technological challenges, suffers from minimal legal restrictions in maintaining detailed surveillance of web communications. In Chapter 7, Nalaka Gunawardene has pointed to the slow and hesitant appreciation of the revolutionary character of new media, particularly among those with 'old mindsets', including those working in 'old media'. He has also reflected on the significance of what he sees as present-day public apathy in Sri Lanka with regard to media rights. He surmises that three decades of restrictions have created 'an entire generation that does not know what normalcy is'. Whatever the reason, his conclusion is of massive relevance for advocates of media reform. It is that 'they have not paid sufficient attention to this demand side of the freedom equation'.

Media Literacy: A Way Forward

Several authors stress the importance of civil society to the media reform agenda. Universities, schools and the public at large have to take part in this debate if it is not to become one of narrow media self-interest. Journalists and the media generally do not necessarily enjoy pubic trust to the extent that their arguments would prevail in a battle with a powerful government which enjoys electoral support.

One key objective of the Media Reform Lanka initiative has been to engage with the universities, training institutes and with civil society about the role of media education in producing well-informed citizens and a professional class of journalists, producers and media managers. Unfortunately, the difficult situation on the ground in Sri Lanka made this kind of engagement more problematic than we had originally anticipated. The challenges faced by the universities due to extensive politicisation of educational structures, not to mention the antagonisms between government and the media profession, and indeed between government and civil society, made it necessary to explore many issues on a personal basis rather than in open discussion with a range of stakeholders. Those constraints in themselves indicate how much work needs to be done to restore a more normal political environment in the country.

In the universities themselves, we had some valuable conversations with professors and lecturers on different campuses in Colombo and in Kandy. Other authors in this volume have commented on the existing media curricula of universities across the island or specifically in the north and east. What seems clear is that media and communication studies do not have a very coherent profile at the moment. As a subject, communication studies began tentatively at Kelaniya in the early 1970s, as an extension of the language department, with a practical emphasis on writing for the print media. Since then, media studies, broadly defined, have found a place in many different faculties from modern literature to sociology, from agricultural extension to law, and sometimes more comprehensively in degree courses with a range of different modules. In most of the degree courses, there continues to be a tension between equipping students for the job market and a more analytical approach to issues of society, economics, democracy, law, regulation and media reform. Some institutes, such as the Jaffna Media Resources and Training Centre or the College of Journalism in Colombo, now provide professional training with a heavy emphasis on what the industry needs. But some universities still fall between two stools, offering training without adequate facilities or professional manpower to deliver the skills and falling short on the broader curriculum as well. If teaching and research in media, policy and law, which is a key focus of this book, is a touchstone for university investment in greater understanding of the role of media and society, then the view of Kishali Pinto-Jayawardena and Gehan Gunatilleke is that no university in Sri Lanka or in southern India passes the test with flying colours. The research output of Sri Lankan universities on these kinds of critical issues remains very limited, even in Sinhala and Tamil, while the number of academics publishing internationally in these fields is more limited still.

Professor Sasanka Perera, who headed the Sociology Department at Colombo University until 2010 and is now Dean of the Faculty of Social Sciences at the recently established south Asian University in New Delhi, believes that the university system in Sri Lanka, particularly in the social sciences and humanities, has been in decline since the 1960s and that media studies have suffered from a difficult birth at a bad time in the cycle. In his view 'one of the most serious issues in Sri Lankan society today is not really the nature of journalism itself, but the non-existence of a critical intellectual tradition and the institutional structure to sustain it, that could generate serious debate, research and knowledge about journalism and its local practice'. Sasanka Perera would argue that media studies have tended to follow 'a highly utilitarian, technical paradigm' which has proved 'manifestly detrimental to democratic politics'.[1]

In terms of the universities' present-day contribution to research and knowledge in these fields, it is difficult to contest this view. In fact, this book itself testifies to the difficulty of commissioning research papers in English from academics in Sri Lanka on these subjects. It is not without interest that lawyers, journalists and broadcasters have taken up the pen with greater facility than their academic counterparts. There are, however, some positive signs. The 'Kelaniya summits' which began in 2010, have been a valuable initiative to bring lecturers in media studies together, to exchange ideas and to extend the boundaries of the subject as currently taught. There is a dissatisfaction among many lecturers with the existing curricula and a thirst for more relevant, Sri-Lanka focused material to replace some of the foreign text books which do little to bring the subject to life. There are a number of motivated and capable young academics who are keen to move the subject forward and would benefit from stronger international linkages. It is to be hoped that they will find this book and some of the other material generated by the Media Reform Lanka initiative of relevance to their teaching and their future research.

The contribution of Tilak Jayaratne and Sarath Kellapotha, both professional broadcasters of long standing, is to move the spotlight away from higher education to the population as a whole. Important though the universities are, after 30 years of emergency rule, there is an urgent need to re-educate the wider Sri Lankan community about the role of the media and to ensure that the average citizen is media literate, aware of his or her rights and in a position to be an effective citizen and voter. They emphasise the importance of teaching the subject in schools, something which is not well done at the moment, particularly in the north and east of the country, where Dr Raguram shows that the take-up of the subject, from ordinary level onwards, is handicapped both by a lack of trained teachers and of text books in Tamil. Others have stressed the need for more outreach to professional groups, like policemen and civil servants, who require re-education about the rights of the public and the duties of public servants in normal times as well as the role of the media itself. One of the problems here is that there has been little recognition of this need by the authorities themselves.

The Global and Regional Context

The focus of this book has been to examine the possibilities and approaches to reform of the media in Sri Lanka. What it has shown very clearly is that the content of government policy and the response of the media industry and civil society have been determined by the very specific political and cultural context of the past 30 years. It has been a time of extraordinary political division and upheaval, of threats to the state from insurrections and insurgencies, both in the north and the south; a time when Sri Lanka's national experience has led it to look inwards. It is a small country. Its major language Sinhala is not an international language. The minority language Tamil has a more international profile, spoken in a state and by a population within India which is many times larger than the population of Sri Lanka, and by an extensive and politically influential diaspora in South East Asia, North America and in Europe. At times, the majority community has almost developed a minority complex and the government has seen itself not only fighting for survival against powerful enemies at home, but also criticised for its human rights record by those it felt should be its friends and allies. It has not been a propitious time for media reform.

But many of the long-standing issues that Sri Lanka faces are shared with its regional neighbours and reflect worldwide changes brought about by technological advances and the globalisation of communication. As the country returns to more normal times, it should be better placed to draw on others' experience in addressing its own challenges. The global spread of satellite television was the challenge of the 1990s. In the 21st century, the viral spread of the Internet as a means of communication has overtaken most of the previously established media and journalistic norms. Many existing systems of media regulation have been rendered virtually obsolete on a global scale. Every state is affected by these changes which impact drastically both on national security, commerce and cultural communication. The debate on these issues reflects the widest international concerns. At the same time, there has been a practical value in sharing experiences across south Asia.

In terms of the broadcasting landscape, the case for autonomy for state broadcasters has lost some of its force. But the case for regulation of the media sector in some form, whether state regulation or self-regulation, has grown stronger. In all countries of south Asia, the media scene has become more complex. In countries where political patronage plays a large part in the allocation of licences, there is a growing realisation that more transparency would provide greater insurance against political change. In Bangladesh, the example of Ekushey TV, which was granted a licence under one government and lost it under the next, was a matter of serious concern among media owners. In that instance, it was the courts that ruled the proper licensing procedure had not been followed. But the courts are not a guarantee of freedom from political pressure.

From the point of view of professional broadcasters and journalists across South Asia, there are clear advantages in having a better regulated media sector. Proprietors may and do intervene in ways which are damaging to the integrity of the output and to the morale of staff. The importance of media education can be taken to apply to encouraging media owners themselves to take more account of their responsibilities to the public.

In all these countries, there is an aspiration for effective regulation of broadcasting in the public interest. But experience so far has also induced wariness of government intervention or of government-inspired national media policies, as both have tended to mean more not less control. In most democracies, there is no formal media policy. A report by the Human Rights organisation Article XIX in 2007[2] suggested that such a policy is not essential to guide the media and that such a policy may derive from a wish to use legislation to limit the independence of the media, and to change the balance power in the government's favour.

As in Sri Lanka, fear of creeping state control has forced the media industry in other south Asian countries to think more strategically about effective self-regulation. In India, the government's heavy-handed attempt at regulation in July 2007 acted as an immediate spur to the broadcasting industry to put its own house in order. The News Broadcasters Association was formed a few days later, with leading news broadcasters in the forefront. Agreement was reached on a code of ethics and a new News

Broadcasting Standards Authority was set up to implement it, with a former Chief Justice of India as Chairman. These developments mirror very closely the emergence of the SLPI a few years earlier and underline the value of comparative approaches and shared experience.

In India, the issue of self-regulation was highlighted by the TV coverage of the Mumbai terror attacks in November 2008. The TV channels were accused of compromising military operations by showing them 'live' and of putting the lives of the hostages at risk by showing the terrorists where they were. Other governments were quick to draw lessons from this experience which would aim to restrict reporting in similar circumstances in future. The idea of freedom of speech and expression has been changing substantially in the contemporary context, especially in face of the threat of terrorism. The global media provide an increasingly diverse information environment. In the regulation of broadcasting and the Internet, governments have aimed to counter media influences by developing and applying new technologies which increase the power of the state. These are issues which are common to all the south Asian countries.

Fundamental to a common approach is a long-term commitment to media diversity, to allow for both global, national, minority and personal perspectives. While the media can never be defined as a purely legal forum, the legal and constitutional protection of freedom of expression remains a central part of media freedoms. The social media and the Internet have opened up a whole new area of communication which tends to create its own rules. Even where it may be seen as citizen journalism, the reporting is essentially unmediated or weakly mediated and may be characterised as editorially anarchic. Where freedom of expression appears to clash with other fundamental freedoms, they can best be reconciled within an open and democratic framework. The question is being asked whether Sri Lanka will retain its liberal democratic traditions, accepting (in the words of the Nobel prize-winning Indian economist, Amartya Sen), that 'using democratic means to remedy endemic problems ... demands sustained deliberation, political engagement, media coverage, popular pressure. In short, more democratic process, not less'.[3] There is certainly a strong historical basis for this, though much is going to depend on wider and more critical support across Sri Lankan society for the restoration of democratic values and the institutions which uphold them.

From a south Asian perspective, national legal frameworks for rights to expression and information reflect a common colonial inheritance, adapted in different ways in each country. There are many shared problems and the research undertaken for this book has shown the value of a comparative perspective. If the book has a central conclusion as far as Sri Lanka is concerned, it is that an integrated approach to media reform—which looks at the legal, the institutional and the educational—is the only one which stands any chance of success. But in adopting such an approach, Sri Lankans have much to learn from other countries in South Asia and elsewhere which face similar challenges and are also wrestling to find workable solutions.

Notes

1. Perera, S. (2012).
2. Article XIX and the Centre for Policy Alternatives (CPA) Sri Lanka 2007. Note on Sri Lanka's Proposed National Media Policy, September 2007, http://www.tamilnet.com/img/publish/2007/09/National_Media_Policy.pdf (accessed in May 2014).
3. Amartya Sen writing in the *New York Times*, 20 June 2013, http://www.nytimes.com/2013/06/20/opinion/why-india-trails-china.html?partner=rss&emc=rss&smid=tw-nytimesworld&_r=3& (accessed in May 2014).

Glossary

Aggregator	In digital technology, meaning an Internet-based application that collects related, frequently updated content from different sources and consolidates it in one place.
Ahimsa	Buddhist principle of non-violence.
Article 19 (or Article XIX)	International media watchdog, named after Article 19 of the International Covenant on Civil and Political Rights (ICCPR).
Balagiridosha	Sinhala phrase 'Always tomorrow not today'.
BBC *Sandeshaya*	Current affairs programme of the BBC Sinhala Service.
BBC *Tamilosai*	Current affairs programme of the BBC Tamil Service.
Bloggers	Columnists and writers of opinion pieces on the Internet.
Broadcasting Regulator	An official or official body charged with allocating frequencies and determining the scope of media freedoms and responsibilities.
Cause celèbre	An issue of public importance and controversy.
Civil society	Non-government civil institutions, activists and organs of public opinion.
Co-habitation	Collaboration in government between political opponents, for example, when President and Prime minister come from different parties, as in Sri Lanka 2002 2004.
Colebrooke Commission	Commission set up in 1829 by the British government to report on the administration of Ceylon (Sri Lanka).
Colombo Declaration on Media Freedom and Social Responsibility, 1998	Statement of principles for safeguarding media freedoms drawn up by independent Sri Lankan media and civil society organisations.

Communications Convergence Bill (India 2000)	Draft bill to regulate communications in India; never implemented.
Community Radio and Television	Broadcasting run by or on behalf of a community rather than by private commercial bodies or the state.
Contempt of Court	Acts or speech which may prejudice a fair trial or bring the legal system into disrepute.
Digital Divide	The division between those with access to digital communications and those without.
Digital Immigrants	New entrants and learners in the use of digital communications.
Digital Natives	The generation brought up with digital communications and the Internet.
Donoughmore Reforms	Commission set up in 1927 to recommend constitutional reforms for Ceylon (Sri Lanka) under British rule. Reforms incorporated in 1931 Constitution; lasted to 1946.
Dr Jekyll and Mr Hyde	A split personality, one good one evil.
Eastern Province	Mixed ethnic Tamil, Muslim and Sinhala region of Sri Lanka.
ECHR	European Convention on Human Rights (formally the *Convention for the Protection of Human Rights and Fundamental Freedoms*). An international treaty to protect human rights in Europe, drafted in 1950 by the then newly formed Council of Europe; all member states are party to the Convention.
Editors' Guild of Sri Lanka	Professional body set up by newspaper editors to set out principles for self-regulation of the media.
Embedded journalism	Journalism in a high security or war context that relies predominantly on military or official sources of information.
Emergency	The supersession of normal laws and of rights in times of national crisis, as in India under Mrs Gandhi from 1975 to 1976 or in Sri Lanka for most of the period from 1971 until 2011.

Establishments Code of Sri Lanka	Principles of public administration administered by the Sri Lanka Administrative Service.
Ethno-nationalism	a sense of national identity based on ethnic origin.
Free Media Movement	Independent journalists' organisation and media watchdog to protect media freedoms; set up in 1991.
Fourth estate	Term to describe the media as an influence on government.
Freedom House	US-based International democracy monitoring organisation.
Generalia specialibus non-derogant	Legal term; general principles do not nullify or detract from specific principles or exceptions.
Government Gazette	First newspaper in Sri Lanka started under British rule in 1802; now publishes official version of new laws, government regulations, notifications, appointments, etc.
Harare Declaration	Statement of principles of democratic governance by member states of the Commonwealth agreed at Harare in 1991.
Hartal	Politically motivated strike that closes shops and public services.
Impunity Index	CPJ international register of unsolved or unpunished violence or crimes against media personnel.
Jana maddya	Sinhala term for 'mass media', literally 'folk media'.
Jana sannivedanaya	Sinhala term for 'mass communication', literally 'folk communication'.
Kavi kola	Poems praising the dead at a funeral.
Lake House	Headquarters of the Associated Newspapers of Ceylon Ltd, leading Sri Lankan media organisation, originally a public company; nationalised in 1973.
Latimer House principles	Commonwealth principles proposed at Abuja conference 2003, setting out the relationship between parliament, the judiciary and the executive in member countries; launched 2004.

Leges posteriores priores contrarias abrogant	Legal maxim, meaning later laws supersede earlier laws.
Leveson enquiry	A government appointed independent investigation into the practice of phone hacking by sections of the British media; set up in July 2011, which reported in November 2012.
Mahaweli Project	Major hydro-electric and agricultural development project in north central Sri Lanka which expanded rapidly with international support in the 1980s.
Mahinda Chinthana	Mahinda Rajapaksa's presidential election manifesto of 2005.
MCNS	Media Centre for National Security— government-appointed media regulator which played an important role during the war but was allowed to lapse in 2013.
Media Accountability	The principle that media freedoms should be exercised in the public interest and subject to an ethical responsible editorial policy.
Media Development Authority	Plans to replace the MCNS with a Media Development Authority on a Singapore model were announced in 2010, but not implemented.
Media literacy	A critical understanding and awareness of the nature and impact of the media and media content on culture and society.
National Media Policy	A draft government media policy proposed in 2007, which attracted strong criticism from the Sri Lankan media.
New media	Term used to describe the Internet and other digital telecommunications media.
nisi rule	Legal term; a Latin phrase where the ruling of a court becomes final unless one or both parties show cause for it not to be.
Obiter dicta	In legal usage, arguments or statements of reasoning included in but not forming part of a substantive legal judgement.
Official Secrets Acts	Laws to restrict access to or prevent publication of sensitive information. In Sri Lanka, first passed in 1955.

Ohama Yan	'Let's just go like this', an old Sinhala axiom meaning to maintain a course in the face of adversity.
Ombudsman	A public advocate usually appointed by a government or parliament but with a significant degree of independence, who is charged with representing the interests of the public by investigating complaints of maladministration or violation of rights. In Sri Lanka, an ombudsman was first appointed in 1978. Separate ombudsmen for different sectors (e.g., finance, insurance) have been appointed since.
Op-eds	Short for 'opposite the editorial page' in newspapers—opinion articles by named columnists which do not necessarily reflect the opinion of the editor.
Parliamentary privilege	A right given to parliamentarians to disclose information in parliament which could be subject to legal action if published outside parliament.
People's Alliance	An alliance of Sri Lankan political parties, led by the SLFP, which won the national elections of 1994 and 2000 and the Presidential elections of 1994 and 1999 under Chandrika Kumaratunga.
People's Sovereignty	Concept defined as the predominant characteristic of the Sri Lankan Constitution.
Pluralist society	One in which different languages, ethnic identities, religions and cultures are given recognition and opportunity to develop alongside that of a majority or dominant group.
Proportionality	Legal criterion of fairness and justice used to ensure that a penalty is appropriate to the crime committed.
Public Interest Broadcasting	Broadcasting which aims to promote open and impartial information and high standards of cultural and entertainment programming.
Puligalinkural	Voice of the Tigers, the LTTE radio station.
Realpolitik	A style of governance based on power rather than principle.

R.K.W. Goonesekere Committee Report	Recommendations for the reform of media law and regulation put forward in 1996, which have formed the basis for much subsequent lobbying and debate on media freedoms.
Simpliciter	Legal term; without qualification.
Sirasa	The name of the Sinhala-language TV and radio stations of the Maharajah group. Sirasa TV was founded in 1998 and Sirasa FM in 1994.
Spectrum management	Distribution of available broadcast frequencies.
Sri Lanka Penal Code Section 479	Section relating to criminal defamation.
Stakeholders	People and organisations with an interest in the operation or regulation of an institution.
Sub-judice rule	Legal requirement not to comment on a case currently under trial or awaiting trial.
Sword of Damocles	A constant threat to life or existence hanging over an individual or institution.
Tamil diaspora	Ethnic Tamils settled outside Sri Lanka or India, mainly in North America, Britain and South East Asia.
Tamil separatism	Political advocacy and up to 2009 insurgency in support of a separate Tamil state in Sri Lanka known as Tamil Eelam.
Tamilnet	Web-based Tamil information service.
Taraki	*Nom de plume* of Dharmaratnam Sivaram writing in The Island and Tamilnet.
Tholangamuwa Declaration	A Charter for a Democratic and Pluralist Media Culture and Social and Professional Rights for Media and Journalism in Sri Lanka passed by journalists' associations in September 2005.
Universal suffrage	Electoral franchise for all adults; in force in Sri Lanka since 1931.
Veerakesari	Sri Lanka's oldest Tamil paper.
Veritas Radio	Roman Catholic radio station operating in Sri Lanka since 1969.
Watchdog groups	National and international organisations set up to monitor the extent to which institutions conform to best practices and international standards, especially in the field of democracy and human rights.

Weligama Declaration	A declaration in 2006 by members of Sri Lanka's media industry and practitioners on the Role of the Media for National Unity.
Whistle-blower	Someone who without authorisation reveals confidential inside information relating to his or her employment or position within an organisation.
White van syndrome	Term used to describe the threat to journalists and political activists picked up (often in unmarked white vans) by unofficial (but believed to be officially supported) vigilante groups, for interrogation and in many cases torture and death. Practice prevalent during the LTTE insurgency, much reduced since 2009.

Bibliography

Books, Papers and Articles

Abeygunasekara, G. (2012) *Performance of Candidates at GCE Ordinary Level Examinations 2007–2011 in Communication and Media Studies*, Presented at 'Media Summit 2012', University of Kelaniya 24.05.

Abeysekara, S. (2011) *Writing Against the RSF/JDS Appeal to Boycott the Galle Literary Festival, Groundviews, 24 January*. Available at: http://groundviews.org/2011/01/24/writing-against-thersfjds-appeal-to-boycott-the-galle-literary-festival/ (accessed on 13 September 2011).

Alternative Law Forum, Bangalore, and Centre for Culture, Media and Governance (2012) *Jamia Millia Islamia, New Delhi, Teaching Media Policy & Law—A Faculty Workshop (South Zone) held on 24–25 April 2012*, National Law School of India, Bangalore.

Amnesty International (2008) *Silencing Dissent*. London: Amnesty International.

Amunugama, Sarath, Premaratne, Asoka and Ismail, S.M.M. (2006) *Subject Review Report—Department of Languages and English Language Teaching, Faculty of Social Sciences and Languages, Sabaragamuwa University of Sri Lanka*, (p. 6).

Amunugama, Sarath, Ven, Ayangama, Vijitha and Hapuarachchi, Ajantha (2008) *Subject Review Report—Department of Linguistics and English, Faculty of Arts, University of Jaffna* (p. 11).

Aronoff, C.E. (Ed.) (1989) *Business and the Media*. Santa Monica, CA: Goodyear Publishing.

Article XIX 'Access to the Airwaves' Section 5 (2002). Available at: http://www.article19.org/resources.php/resource/2633/en/broadcasting:-access-to-the-airwaves (accessed in May 2014).

Article XIX and the Centre for Policy Alternatives (CPA) Sri Lanka (2007a) *Note on Sri) Lanka's) Proposed) National) Media) Policy September) 2007*. Available at: http://www.tamilnet.com/img/publish/2007/09/National_Media_Policy.pdf (accessed in May 2014).

Article XIX and the Centre for Policy Alternatives (CPA) Sri Lanka (2007b) *Reporting Human Rights in Sri Lanka: A Handbook for Media Professionals*. Available at: http://reliefweb.int/sites/reliefweb.int/files/resources/A113B5C306EAEE16C12574CF00309913-Full_Report.pdf (accessed in May 2014).

Article XIX Report (1997) *Reforms at Risk? Continuing Censorship in Sri Lanka*. Available at: http://www.unhcr.org/refworld/docid/475418af0.html (accessed on 13 September 2011).

Arulvarathan, Subha (29 November 2006) *Press Freedom Struggles in Sri Lanka*. Available at: http://www.iataj.org/pressfreedom.pdf (accessed in 2013).

Asia-Pacific Telecommunity (1998, 1999) *The APT Yearbook*. Bangkok, Thailand: APT.

Asian Media Information and Communication Centre (1998) *Mass Media Laws and Regulations in Sri Lanka* (compiled by N. Selvakumaran and Rohan Edrisinga with a commentary by Sinha Ratnatunga and Kishali Pinto-Jayawardena, 1998).

Asian Tribune (2005) *Presidential Race Begins with Mahinda Rajapakse as the People's Alliance Candidate.* Available at: http://www.asiantribune.com/news/2005/07/28/presidentialrace-begins-mahinda-Rajapaksa-people%E2%80% 99s-alliance-candidate (accessed on 13 September 2011).

Asoka, J. (2010) *To Question or Not to Question, Sri Lanka Guardian* (9 March 2010).

Barker, C. (2004) *The SAGE Dictionary of Cultural Studies.* London: SAGE Publications.

Basu, A. (2003) *Media Laws—An Overview.* Available at: http://www.legalserviceindia.com/articles/media.htm (accessed on 22 January 2011).

BBC (2010) *Sri Lankan Editor JS Tissainayagam Gets Bail.* Available at: http://news.bbc.co.uk/2/hi/south_asia/8451413.stm (accessed on 15 January 2011).

Begoyan, A. (2009) *State versus Private Ownership: A Look at the Implications for Local Media Freedom.* Article XIX. Available at: http://www.article19.org/data/files/pdfs/publications/poland-article-19-report-onmedia-ownership.pdf (accessed on 13 September 2011).

Berger, G. (2011) *Beyond Broadcasting: The Future of State-owned Broadcasters in Southern Africa.* Available at: http://www.highwayafrica.com/media/guyberger/fesreport.pdf (accessed on 13 September 2011).

Bolin, A. (2006) *In Whose Interest? A Study of Journalists' Views of Their Responsibilities and Possibilities within the Mainstream Press in Sri Lanka.* Sweden: Institute for Journalism and Mass Communication, University of Gothenburg.

Brady, L. (2005) 'Colonials, bourgeoisies and media dynasties: a case study of Sri Lankan media', *E Journalist,* Vol. 5, No. 2. Available at: http://ejournalist.com.au/ejournalist_v5n2.php (accessed on 1 January 2011).

Center for Democracy and Governance, Bureau for Global Programs, Field Support, and Research, USAID (1999) *The Role of Media in Democracy: A Strategic Approach.* Washington DC: USAID.

Central Bank of Sri Lanka (1998) *Economic Progress of Independent Sri Lanka.* Colombo: Central Bank of Sri Lanka.

Centre for Policy Alternatives (2003) *Media Law in Sri Lanka.* Colombo: Centre for Policy Alternatives.

Centre for Policy Alternatives and International Media Support (IMA) (2005) *A Study of Media in Sri Lanka.* Copenhagen K, Denmark.

Centre for Policy Alternatives (2007) *Background Note Prepared for International Press Freedom and Freedom of Expression Mission to Sri Lanka.* Colombo: Centre for Policy Alternatives.

Centre for Policy Alternatives (2008) *Best Practices and Potential for Improved Information Flows in Media and Civil Society.* Colombo: Centre for Policy Alternatives and Hivos.

Ceylon Daily News, 4 September, 2010.

Chandraprema, C.A. (1991) *Sri Lanka: The Years of Terror—the JVP Insurrection 1987–1989.* Colombo: Lake House Bookshop.

Chandrika Kumaratunga (2000) Speech on State Radio and TV, 3 January 2000. Available at: http://www.sangam.org/NEWSEXTRA/CBKonTVJan00.htm (accessed on 13 September 2011).

Clarke, A.C. (1999) '2001: A Cyber Odyssey', in: *Himal Southasian,* Available at: http://himalmag.com/component/content/article/2347-2001-A-Cyber-Odyssey.html (accessed in October 2013).

CNN (2009) *Jail Sentence for Dissident Sri Lankan Reporter Condemned.* Available at: http://edition.cnn.com/2009/WORLD/asiapcf/09/01/sri.lanka.journalist (accessed on 14 January 2011).

Colombo Page (2011) *Sri Lanka Press Council Born Again.* Available at: http://www.colombopage.com/archive_091/Jun1244821410RA.html (accessed on 23 January 2011).

Colombo Telegraph (February 2012). Available at: http://colombotelegraph.com/2012/02/03/wikileaks-looked-like-epdp-and-sl-navy-burnt-the-uthayan-basil-to-us/ (accessed in 2013).

Committee to Protect Journalists (2001) *Attacks on the Press 2000: Sri Lanka.* Available at: http://cpj.org/2001/03/attacks-on-the-press-2000-sri-lanka.php (accessed on 5 January 2011).

Committee to Protect Journalists (2012) 'Getting Away with Murder', Special Report. Available at: http://cpj.org/reports/2012/04/impunity-index-2012.php#more (accessed in June 2013).

Coomaraswamy, R. (1981) 'Regulatory framework for the press in Sri Lanka', *Marga Quarterly Journal,* Vol. 6, No. 2, pp.66 96.

Coperahewa, S. (1997) *Bhashanuragaye Deshapalanaya.* Colombo: S. Godage & Brothers.

Curran, J. and Seaton, J. (1997) *Power without Responsibility: The Press and Broadcasting History in Britain* (5th edition). London: Routledge.

Daily Mirror Editorial (2011). Available at: http://print.dailymirror.lk/editorial/106-editorial/49088.html (accessed on 13 September 2011).

Das, B. and Parthasarathi, V. (2011) 'Media research and public policy: Tiding over the rupture', in: R. Mansell and M. Raboy (Eds.) *Handbook on Global Media and Communication Policy,* Wiley-Blackwell.

David, M.J.R. (1993) *Mahaweli Community Radio: A Field Producer's Notebook.* Los Banos, California: University of the Philippines.

De Alwis, Dinidu (2012) 'Media should exercise self-censorship—Lakshman Yapa', *Ceylon Today.* Available at: http://www.ceylontoday.lk/16-3780-news-detail-media-should-exercise-self-censorship-lakshman-yapa.html (accessed on August 20, 2014).

De Mel, V.S.M. (1980) *Through the Vistas of Life.* Colombo.

Democracy Asia (2011) *State of Democracy in South Asia Study—Thinking About Democracy in a Democratic Way.* Available at: http://www.democracy-asia.org/readthereport.htm (accessed on 13 September 2011).

De Samarasinghe, S.W.R.A. (1997) Reading, Listening and Watching: A National Sample Survey of the Sri Lankan News Media, in G. H. Peiris (Ed.), *Studies on the Press in Sri Lanka and South Asia.*

Deshapriya, S. (2010) *Media Development Authority: Another Name for Media Control in Sri Lanka? Groundviews.* Available at: http://groundviews.org/2010/07/28/media-development-authority-anothername-for-media-control-in-sri-lanka/ (accessed on 23 January 2011).

De Silva, H.L. (1992–1993) 'Free Press and Fair Trial', *OPA Journal,* Vol. 15.

De Silva, N. (2011) 'Sri Lanka is neither Egypt nor Libya'. *The Island,* 22 March 2011.

De Silva, M.A. and Siriwardena, R. (1977) *Communication Policies in Sri Lanka.* Paris: UNESCO.

Disanayaka, J.B. (1999) 'Ethnic perceptions and media behaviour in Sri Lanka', in: A. Goonasekara and Y. Ito (Eds.), *Mass Media and Cultural Identity.* London, UK: Pluto Press.

Eapen, K.E., Thakur, B.S. and Sanjay, B.P. (1990) *Journalism/Communication Education in SAARC Countries.* Department of Journalism and Mass Communication, University of Tampere, Finland.

Editor and Publisher International Year Book (1999). Irvine, CA: Editor and Publisher.

Elmqvist, M. and Bastian, S. (2006) *Promoting Media Professionalism, Independence and Accountability in Sri Lanka, Sida Evaluation 06/50*. Available at: http://www.sida.se/ publications (accessed on 30 December 2010).

Fernando, A. (2008) *My Belly is White*. Colombo: Vijitha Yapa Publications.

Fernando, B. (1997) 'Harmonizing Asia's cultural values and human rights: The validity of the approach—Sri Lankan experience', *FOCUS*, Vol. 9. Available at: http://www. hurights.or.jp/archives/focus/section2/1997/09/harmonizing-asias-cultural-valuesand-human-rights-the-validity-of-the-approach—sri-lankan-experience.html (accessed on 13 September 2011).

Fernando, B. (2010) *Sri Lanka: Impunity, Criminal Justice & Human Rights, in the State of Human Rights Report*. Hong Kong: Asian Human Rights Commission.

Ferdinando, S. (2010) *SLFP Gen. Secretary Discusses Past Plots in the Party. The Island* (online) 28 May. Available at: http://www.island.lk/2010/05/28/news24.html (accessed on 13 September 2011).

Fernando, W.L. (1973) *The Press in Ceylon*. Colombo: Trade Exchange.

Francis, W.E. (1986) *First Amendment; Theory and Practice, Mass Media Law and Regulation* (4th edition).

Freedom House (2010) *Countries at the Crossroads 2010, Country Report Sri Lanka*. Available at: http://www.freedomhouse.org/modules/publications/ccr/modPrintVersion.cfm?e dition=9&ccrpage=43&ccrcountry=198 (accessed on 13 September 2011).

Freedom House (2011a) *Methodology, Freedom of the Press*. Available at: http://www. freedomhouse.org/uploads/fop 11/FOTP2011Booklet.pdf (accessed on 13 September 2011).

Freedom House (2011b) *Death Threat Deals New Blow to Free Expression in Sri Lanka*. Available at: http://www.freedomhouse.org/template.cfm?page=70&release=1066 (accessed on 15 January 2011).

Freedom of the Press (2011) Freedom House, http://www.freedomhouse.org/uploads/fop 11/FOTP2011Booklet.pdf.

Free Media Movement (2007) *The Death of Media Freedom in Sri Lanka*.

Free Media Movement (2008) *On the Criticism of Daily Mirror by Hon. Ranil Wikramasinghe, Leader of the Opposition*. Available at: http://freemediasrilanka.wordpress.com/page/3/ (accessed on 13 September 2011).

Free Media Movement (2008) *Assault on Journalist Mr. Namal Perera*. Available at: http:// freemediasrilanka.wordpress.com/?s=Wickramasinghe (accessed on 10 January 2011).

Free Media Movement (1997) Statement in the *Sunday Observer*, 14 April 1997.

Frohardt, M. and Temin. J. (2007) 'The use and abuse of media in vulnerable societies, in the media and the rwanda genocide', A. Thompson (Ed.) Pluto Press—London, Fountain Publishers Ltd—Kampala and International Development Research Centre—Ottawa.

Goodman, A. and Goodman, D. (2004) 'The exception to the rulers: exposing oily politicians, war profiteers, and the media that love them', *Hyperion*.

Goodman, A. and Goodman, D. (2005) *Why Media Ownership Matters. The Seattle Times* (3 April 2005). New York: Hyperion.

Grunnet, H., Yakoob, U. and Weiss, L. (2005) *Assessment of the Need for a Radio and TV Journalist Training Unit in Sri Lanka*. Sri Lanka Press Institute.

Gunaratne, S.A. (1970) 'Government-press conflict in Ceylon: freedom versus responsibility', *Journalism Quarterly*, Vol. 47, pp.530–543.

Gunaratne, S.A. (1975) 'The Taming of the Press in Sri Lanka', *Journalism Monographs*, Vol. 39.

Gunaratne, S.A. (1978) 'Sri Lanka (Ceylon)', in: J.A. Lent (Ed.), *Broadcasting in Asia and the Pacific: A Continental Survey of Radio and Television*. Lexington, Kentucky: Association for Education in Journalism.

Gunaratne, S.A. (1997) 'Sri Lanka and the third communication revolution', *Media Asia*, Vol. 24, pp.83 89.

Gunaratne, S.A., Hasim, M.S. and Kasenally, R. (1997) 'Small is beautiful: informatisation potential of three Indian Ocean rim countries', *Media Asia*, Vol. 24, pp.188–205.

Gunasekera, A. (1994) 'Sri Lanka forges a new framework', *Asian Communications*, Vol. 8, No. 8, pp.38–43.

Gunasekara, H.M. (1997) *Media as Bridge Maker*. Colombo: Friedrich Ebert Stiftung.

Gunasekera, L. (1998) *Freedom of Expression and Media Freedom, in Law & Society Trust, Sri Lanka: State of Human Rights 1998*. Colombo: Law and Society Trust.

Gunawardene, N. (1997) *Communication Ethics: A South Asian Perspective*. Singapore: AMIC.

Gunawardene, N. (2007) *The Sri Lankan Government's Broadcast Stranglehold*. Available at: http://www.asiamedia.ucla.edu/article.asp? parentid=57939 (accessed on 3 January 2011).

Haneef, M.S.M. (2012) 'Teaching media law and ethics in Communication Departments in Tamil Nadu and Puducherry', *LST Review*, Vol. 22, No. 295, pp. 1–16.

Harischandra, S. and Rupasinghe, W. (2012) *Writing Textbooks on Communication and Media Studies for the G.C.E. Ordinary Level: A Content Analysis*, Presented at 'Media Summit 2012', University of Kelaniya.

Harrison, F (2012). *My Double Life as Mother and Foreign Correspondent*. Available at: http://www.journalism.co.uk/news-features/frances-harrison-my-double-life-as-mother-and-foreign-correspondent/s5/a548236/.

Harrison, F. (2012) *Still Counting the Dead Survivors of Sri Lanka's Hidden War*. London: Portobello Books.

Hettiarachchi, R. (unpublished) Content Analysis of Print Media on Peace Process (without title).

Hobbs, R. (2010) *Digital and Media Literacy: A Plan of Action*. Washington, D.C: The Aspen Institute.

Hulugalle, H.A.J. (1960) *The Life and Times of D. R. Wijewardene*. Colombo: Associated Newspapers of Ceylon.

ICT for Peacebuilding (2011) *Sri Lankan Government to Block Internet and Censor Independent Web Media?* Available at: http://ict4peace.wordpress.com/2010/02/11/sri-lankan-government-to-block-internet-andcensor-independent-web-media/ (accessed on 15 January 2011).

Dobbie, M. (2007) 'Reporting for all: Developing a public service journalism culture in Sri Lanka', *A Handbook for Journalists*. IMPACS, CPA and IFJ.

Induruwa, A. (1996) *High Performance Computing: The Next Wave of IT Development in Sri Lanka*. Available at: http://www.cs.ukc.ac.uk/people/staff/asi1/cssl/papers/paper. htm (accessed in June 2013).

International Federation of Journalists (2010) *End of a Deadly Decade: Journalists and Media Staff Killed in 2009*. Available at: http://www.ifj.org/assets/docs/059/046/c93b13b-7a4a82e.pdf (accessed on 15 January 2011).

International Press Freedom and Freedom of Expression Mission to Sri Lanka (2007) *Press Freedom and Freedom of Expression in Sri Lanka: Struggle for Survival*.

International Telecommunication Union (1997) *Challenges to the Network: Telecoms and the Internet*.

International Telecommunication Union (1999) Yearbook of Statistics: Telecommunication Services 1988–1997.

Ivan, V. (2011) *President Rajapaksa is an Authoritarian Leader but not a Dictatorial Ruler.* Available at: TransCurrents: http://transcurrents.com/tc/2011/04/president_rajapaksa_is_an_auth.html (accessed on 13 September 2011).

It's a Tough Job Being the Champ (2011) Available at: www.lakbima.lk (accessed on 19 June 2011).

James, W. (1907) *Pragmatism: A New Name for Some Old Ways of Thinking.* New York: Longman Green and Co.

Jayaratne, T. (2005) *Post-Tsunami Media coverage: Sri Lankan Experience.* Colombo: Transparency International Sri Lanka.

Jayaratne, T., Pinto-Jayawardena, K., de Almeida Guneratne, J. and de Silva, S. (2005) *Sri Lanka Enabling Environment Study: A Paper based on a Study for the World Bank.* Colombo.

Jayaratne, T., Pinto-Jayawardena, K., de Almeida, G.J. and de Silva, S. (2007) 'Legal challenges and practical constraints: A comprehensive study of community radio in Sri Lanka (undertaken for the World Bank)', *LST Review*, Vol. 18, No. 241, p.14.

Jayathunga, N. P. (2010) *Mahinda Rajapaksa—The Statesman, The Island, 28 January 2010.* Available at: http://infolanka.asia/opinion/sri-lanka/mahindarajapaksa-the-statesman (accessed on 13 September 2011).

Jayawardena, S. (1999) *Radio in Sri Lanka, Media Development Loan Fund.* Available at: www.mdlf.org.105

Joint Civil Society Submission to the UN Universal Periodic Review (Sri Lanka) Second Cycle (2012) 14th Session 2012.

Jeffrey, R. (2000) *India's Newspaper Revolution: Capitalism, Politics and the Indian-language Press, 1977–99.* London: Hurst.

Jeffrey, R. and Doron, A. (2013) *The Great Indian Phone Book.* London: Hurst.

Jeyaraj, D.B.S. (May 2008) *Did Karuna Personally Kill 'Taraki' Sivaram?* Available at: http://www.tamilweek.com/Karuna_Sivaram_0010.html (accessed in 2013).

Joshi, I. (Ed.) (1998) Asian Women in the Information Age: *New Communication Technology, Democracy and Women.* Singapore: Nanyang Technological University.

Kadirgamar, L. (1992–1993) 'Freedom of expression and sub judice', *OPA Journal*, Vol. 15.

Kadirgamar, L. (2012) *Democracy Sovereignty and Terror: Lakshman Kadirgamar on the Foundation of International Order, IB Tauris, London* (Sir A. Roberts; Ed.).

Kannangara, N. (2010) 'An Act of Suppression,' *The Sunday Leader.* Available at: http://www.thesundayleader.lk/2010/07/25/%E2%80%9Can-act-of-suppression%E2%80%9D/ (accessed on 23 January 2011).

Karunanayake, N. (1996a) *Broadcasting in Sri Lanka; Potential and Performance.* Colombo.

Karunanayake, N. (1996b) *The Press in Sri Lanka: Towards a Sound Policy Framework.* Colombo.

Keune, R. (2010) *Models of Public Service Broadcasting. Kuala Lumpur: Asian Institute for Broadcasting Development.* Available at: http://www.aibd.org.my/node/290 (accessed on 13 September 2011).

Kovach, B. and Rosenstiel, T. (2001) *The Elements of Journalism: What News People Should Know and the Public Should Expect.* New York, USA: Three Rivers Press.

Lanka Business Online (2007a) *Asia Defies Global Newspaper Meltdown.* Available at: http://www.lankabusinessonline.com/fullstory.php?nid=1625284934 (accessed on 10 January 2011).

Lanka Business Online (2007b) *False Arrest*. Available at: http://www.lankabusinessonline. com/fullstory.php?nid=899765082 (accessed on 10 January 2011).

LankaTimes.com (2011) *Dayasiri and Yapa at Loggerheads over Press Council*. Available at: http://www.lankatimes.com/fullstory.php?id=18616 (accessed on 23 January 2011).

Law and Society Trust (2009) *Briefing Note on Tissainayagam Case: 17 September 2009 Case of J.S. Tissainayagam*. Available at: www.lawandsocietytrust.org/web/images/PDF/ briefing%20note.doc (accessed on 15 January 2011).

Law Commission of Sri Lanka (2011) *Contempt of Court Law: Explanation*. Available at: http://www.lawcomdept.gov.lk/info_English/index.asp-xp=723&xi=1129.htm (accessed on 16 January 2011).

Liyanage, G. (1993) *Lankaawe Puwathpath Mellakireema (The Taming of Newspapers in Sri Lanka)*. Colombo.

Mahendra, S. (1996) 'A Note on Television in Sri Lanka', in: D. French and M. Richards (Eds.), *Contemporary Television: Eastern Perspectives*. SAGE Publications.

McChesney, R.W. (2008) *The Political Economy of Media: Enduring Issues, Emerging Dilemmas*. New York: Monthly Review Press.

McManus, J.H. (1994) *Market-driven Journalism: Let the Citizen Beware?* SAGE Publications.

Media and Democracy in Asia (Conference Papers) (2000).

Meinardus, R. (2004) *Democracy, Democratization and the Challenges of Sustaining and Promoting Democratic Governance*, Paper presented at the Democratic Pacific Assembly (DPA) Taipei, Taiwan, 12–25 August 2004. Available at: http://www.fnf.org. ph/liberallibrary/democracy-democratization.htm (accessed on 13 September 2011).

Melody, W.H. (1978) 'Mass media: The economics of access to the marketplace of ideas', in: C. Aronoff (Ed.) *Business and the Media*. Santa Monica, CA (Goodyear).

Mendel, T. (2001) *A Model Freedom of Information Law*. Article XIX.

Merrill, J.C. and Fisher, H.A. (1980) *The World's Great Dailies: Profiles of 50 Newspapers*. New York: Hastings House.

Metzl, J.F. (1997) 'Information intervention: when switching channels isn't enough', *Foreign Affairs*, Vol. 76, No. 6.

Michaels, Henry (5 March 2003) *CNN Imposes New 'Script Control'*. Available at: http:// www.wsws.org/articles/2003/mar2003/cnn-m05.shtml (accessed in 2013).

Ministry of Defence, Sri Lanka, (2010a) *Background: Tissanayagam Case and Others*. Available at: http://www.defence.lk/new.asp?fname=20081222_01 (accessed on 15 January 2011).

Ministry of Defence, Sri Lanka, (2010b) *Tissanayagam Found Guilty of Terrorism: Sentenced 20 Years' Imprisonment*. Available at: http://www.defence.lk/new.asp ?fname=20090831_07 (accessed on 15 January 2011).

Ministry of Mass Media and Information (2007) *National Media Policy* (Draft). Colombo: Ministry of Mass Media and Information, Government of Sri Lanka.

Ministry of Mass Media and Information (2011) *Ongoing Projects*. Available at: http://www. media.gov.lk/ongoing-projects.php (accessed on 18 January 2011).

Moonesinghe, G. (2011) *Small Country Diplomacy, Groundviews*. Available at: http:// groundviews.org/2011/03/23/small-country-diplomacy/ (accessed on 13 September 2011).

Morgan, F. (2000) 'Recipes for success: curriculum for professional media education', *Asia Pacific Media Educator*, Vol. 8. Available at: http://ro.uow.edu.au/apme/vol1/iss8/2 (accessed on 13 September 2011).

Muthulingam, P. (1997) 'Evolution of the Tamil press of Sri Lanka', in: G. H. Peiris (Ed.), *Studies on the Press in Sri Lanka and South Asia*. Kandy: International Center for Ethnic Studies.

Muttulingam, T. (2012) *Fighting the Good Fight for Feminism*, The Personal Story of a Woman—Tamil Journalist Dushyanthi Kanagasabapathipillai. Available at: http://www.ceylontoday.lk/35-3226-news-detail-fighting-the-good-fight-for-feminism.html (accessed in June 2013).

Nadarajah, S. (2005) *Sri Lanka's Vernacular Press and the Peace Process 2000–2005*. Washington, D.C.: The Asia Foundation.

National Conference on Self-Regulation (2011) *Speeches and Interactive Sessions* (Press Complaints Commission of Sri Lanka PCCSL, September 2011).

Neumann, A.L. (1998) 'Sri Lanka: Reform's key moment—journalists face off with the military', *Columbia Journalism Review*, Vol. 37, pp.59–60.

NGO Files (2012) *Free Media Movement Hides 40 Million Fraud, Colombo Telegraph*, 2 June 2012.

Nissan, E. (1994) *An Agenda for Change—The Right to Freedom of Expression in Sri Lanka*. Article XIX.

Nissan, E. (1995) Sri Lanka, State of Human Rights 1995, Law and Society Trust, Colombo.

Nohrstedt, S.A., Bastian, S. and Hök, J. (2002) *Journalism Training and Research in Sri Lanka*. SIDA, Department for Democracy and Social Development.

Official Journal of the European Union (2009) (L 227/9) of 29 August 2009 (English version).

Official Website of Mahinda Rajapaksa (2004) *Mahinda's Appointment, A Wish Come true Mahanayake Theras*. Available at: http://www.mahindarajapaksa.com/sworn_in.php (accessed on 13 September 2011).

Oorukku Nallathu Solven (2010) Published by Puravalar Hassim Omar.

Page, D. and Crawley, W. (2001) *Satellites over South Asia: Broadcasting, Culture and the Public Interest*. New Delhi: SAGE Publications.

Patranobis, S. (2010) 'A media development authority for Lanka', *The Hindustan Times*. Available at: http://www.hindustantimes.com/A-media-development-authority-for-Lanka/Article1-575360.aspx (accessed on 23 January 2011).

Peiris, G.H. (1997) 'Media in Sri Lanka: Recent trends of change', in: G.H. Peiris (Ed.), *Studies on the Press in Sri Lanka and South Asia*. Kandy: International Center for Ethnic Studies.

Perera, J. (1994) *An Intolerant Climate, in Press Systems in SAARC*. Singapore: AMIC.

Perera, K. (2005) *A Double Error Choosing an Opposition Leader*. My Thoughts blog [blog]. 22 July. Available at: http://kusalperera.blogspot.com/search?updated-min=2005-01-01T00:00:00-08:00&updated-max=2006-01-01T00:00:00-08:00&max-results=20 (accessed on 13 September 2011).

Perera, S. (1997) 'Articulating human rights in the context of Buddhist ethics in Sri Lanka', *FOCUS*, Vol. 9. Available at: http://www.hurights.or.jp/archives/focus/section2/1997/09/articulating-human-rights-in-the-context-of-buddhist-ethics-in-sri-lanka.html (accessed on 13 September 2011).

Perera, S. (2005) 'Media practice as a problem of representation', in: *Post Tsunami Media Coverage: The Sri Lankan Experience —A Study of the Media Behaviour*. Colombo: Transparency International.

Perera, S. (2009) *Keynote Address, Viluthu*. Colombo: Centre for Human Resource Development, Restaurant Hall, BMICH.

Perera, S. (2010) *Contemporary Social Sciences and Humanities in Sri Lanka: Towards a Reflexive Reading of the Disciplines of Sociology/Anthropology*, delivered at the

Sabaragamuwa University of Sri Lanka on 26 August 2010. Available at: http://sasankaperera.com/?page_id=44 (accessed in May 2014).

Perera, S. (2012). *Media Practice, Media Education and Politics in Sri Lanka.* Available at: http://www.mediareformlanka.com/sites/default/files/core-research-articles/Sasanka%20Perera.pdf (accessed in May 2014).

Pieris, G.H. (1997) Studies on the Press in Sri Lanka and South Asia. International Centre for Ethnic Studies, Kandy.

Pinto-Jayawardena, K. (1988), in: Ila Joshi [Ed.], *Asian Women in the Information Age— New Communication Technology, Democracy and Women.* Singapore: Asian Media Information and Communication Centre, Nanyang Technological University, (p. 28).

Pinto-Jayawardena, K. (2000) 'Freedom of expression and media freedom', in: E. Nissan (Ed.), *Sri Lanka, State of Human Rights 2000.* Colombo: Law and Society Trust.

Pinto-Jayawardena, K. (2003) 'Freedom of expression and media freedom', in: E. Nissan, (Ed.), *Sri Lanka, State of Human Rights 2003.* Colombo: Law and Society Trust.

Pinto Jayawardena, K. (2004) 'Law reform for media freedom in Sri Lanka', in: *The Right to Information and Freedom of the Mass Media, South Asian Free Media Association.*

Pinto-Jayawardena, K. (2006) 'Right to information; illusionary court victories and its continuing denial', LST Review, Vol. 17, No. 229, November 2006, pp.1–9.

Pinto-Jayawardena, K. (2008) *Colombo Declaration on Media Freedom and Social Responsibility—1998: Background Paper.*

Pinto-Jayawardena, K. (2010) *Post-War Justice in Sri Lanka; Rule of Law, The Criminal Justice System and Commissions of Inquiry, International Commission of Jurists.*

Pinto-Jayawardena, K. (2009) 'Collapsing bridges and collapsing public trust', *The Sunday Times.* Available at: http://sundaytimes.lk/090802/Columns/focus.html (accessed on 24 January 2011), p.107.

Pinto-Jayawardena, K. and Guneratne, J. de A. (2004) 'Contempt of Court in Sri Lanka', National Human Rights Commission.

Press Complaints Commission of Sri Lanka (2011) Available at: http://www.pccsl.lk (accessed on 3 January 2011).

Raguram, S. (2012) *School Curriculum of Communication and Media Studies and its Challenges,* Presented at 'Media Summit 2012', University of Kelaniya.

Rajakarunanayake, L. (2005) *Recommendation on Policy for Media Freedom and Media Practice.* Colombo.

Rajapakse, W. (2000) *Media Freedom and Responsibility.*

Ramaphosa, C. (1999) *South Africa's Financial Mail, of 14 May 1999.* Johannesburg.

Ranasinghe, N.E. (1996) 'Radio spectrum management in Sri Lanka', *APT Journal,* Vol. 8, No.2, pp.20–22.

Reddy, B.M. (2009) *Editor of Sri Lankan Daily Assassinated.* Available at: http://www.thehindu.com/2009/01/09/stories/2009010956091400.htm (accessed on 17 January 2011).

Reporters Without Borders (2006) *Tamilnet Editor's Murder Still Unpunished After One Year.* Available at: http://en.rsf.org/sri-lanka-tamilnet-editor-s-murder-still-28-04-2006,17503.html (accessed on 17 January 2011).

Reporters Without Borders (2010) *Press Freedom Index 2010.* Available at: http://en.rsf.org/press-freedomindex2010,1034. Html (accessed 15 January 2011).

Reporters Without Borders (Reporters Sans Frontieres [RSF]). (2012a). Available at: http://en.rsf.org/sri-lanka-sri-lanka-12-03-2012,42068.html (accessed on 8 September 2012).

Reporters Without Borders (Reporters Sans Frontieres [RSF]). *With Media Gagged or Threatened, No Progress for Freedom of Information.* (2012b). Available at: http://

en.rsf.org/sri-lanka-with-media-gagged-or-threatened-no-28-02-2012,41946.html (accessed in June 2013).

Robertson, G., and Nicol, A. (1992) *Media Law* (3rd edition). London: Penguin Books.

Rupasinghe, W. and Jinadasa, M.P. (Eds.) (2010) *National Media Summit 2010*, University of Kelaniya.

Rupasinghe, W. (unpublished) *Overview of Curricula Relating to the Teaching of Media Policy, the Law and Related Topics in Educational and Training Institutions in Sri Lanka* (October 2010).

Samarajiva, R. (1997) 'Institutional reform of Sri Lankan telecommunications: The introduction of competition and regulation, in: E.M. Noam (Ed.), *Telecommunications in Western Asia and the Middle East* Oxford University Press (p.244).

Samarajiva, I. (2011) 'Freedom of expression in Sri Lanka, Circa 2011', *The Sunday Leader*. Available at: www.google.lk/url?sa=t&rct=j&q=&esrc=s&source=web&cd=12&ve d=0CFEQFjABOAo&url=http://www.thesundayleader.lk/2011/01/30/freedom-of-expression-in-sri-lanka-circa-2011/&ei=xfLeT_SPMpGzrAeG2aDKDQ&usg=AFQj CNE9w2Kkct78tR6HuMtmNaRNJ-x1Kg.

Selvakumaran, N. and Edrisinha, R. (1998) (Comps.) Mass Media Laws and Regulations in Sri Lanka (with a commentary by Sinha Ratnatunga and Kishali Pinto Jayawardena). AMIC.

Senadhira, S.P. (1996) *Under Siege: Mass Media in Sri Lanka.*

Seneviratne, K. (2011) Speech Made to the Royal Asiatic Society, Colombo, 16 May 2011.

Shah, N. and Jansen, F. (Eds.) (2011) *Digital Alternatives—With a Cause, Centre for Internet and Society, Bangalore and Hivos Knowledge Programme*, The Hague Netherlands, July 2011.

Sivaram, D. (1999) *Media Bias and Censorship in Conflict Reporting in Sri Lanka*. Available at: http://tamilnation.co/conferences/cnfCA99/taraki.html (accessed in 2013).

Sri Lanka Media Development Authority (2011) *Official Government News Portal*. Available at:http://www.news.lk/index.php?option=com_content&task=view&id=15940&Item id=44 (accessed on 23 January 2011).

Sri Lanka Press Institute (SLPI) (2008) *10th Anniversary of the Colombo Declaration on Media Freedom and Social Responsibility—International Symposium: Speeches and Interactive Sessions, October 2008.*

Sri Lanka Press Institute (2011) *An Assessment of Female Participation in Mainstream Media in Sri Lanka [pdf]* Colombo: Sri Lanka Press Institute. Available at: http://www.slpi.lk/ downloads.php (accessed on 6 May 2012).

Sturgess, D. (2000) *Court Decision Expresses Rifts in Ruling Circles: Media Censorship in Sri Lanka Ruled Invalid then Re-imposed*. Available at: http://www.wsws.org/articles/2000/ jul2000/sri-j18.shtml (accessed on 24 January 2011).

Sumathy, S. and Thiruvarangan, M. (2011) *Boycott Calls and International Engagement –'Dissenting Dialogue'*. No. 2. Available at: www.srilankademocracy.org/files/ dissenting_dialogues_Feb_2011.pdf (accessed on 13 September 2011), p.30.

The Nation, Reactivating Press Council (2009) *Criminal Defamation Best Approach for Press Regulation S.L.* Available at: http://www.nation.lk/2009/07/19/newsfe1.htm (accessed on 23 January 2011).

Thillainathan, S. (1997) 'Contemporary Tamil media scene in Sri Lanka', in: G.H. Peiris (Ed.), *Studies on the Press in Sri Lanka and South Asia*. Kandy: International Centre for Ethnic Studies.

Transparency International Sri Lanka and Friedrich Ebert Stiftung (2011) *Resource Book on Investigative Journalism.*

Udagama, N.D. (1986) *Freedom of the Press in Sri Lanka, Master of Laws Dissertation*. Berkeley: University of California. (Unpublished).

Udagama, N.D. (1996) 'Freedom of expression and media freedom', in: E. Nissan, (Ed.), Sri Lanka, State of Human Rights 1995, Law and Society Trust, Colombo.

UN Democracy (2000) *UN General Assembly (Session 57 Meeting 15)*. Available at: http://www.undemocracy.com/generalassembly_57/meeting_15 (accessed on 13 September 2011).

UNESCO (2007) *Model Curricula for Journalism Education, UNESCO Series on Journalism Education*. Paris: UNESCO.

UNESCO.Org (2011) *India to Establish 4000 Community Radio Stations under New Community Radio Policy*. Available at: http://portal.unesco.org/ci/en/ev.phpURL_ID=24250&URL_DO=DO_TOPIC&URL_ECTION=201.html (accessed on 23 January 2011).

UNESCO Statistical Yearbook (1998).

UNHCR Eligibility Guidelines for Assessing the International Protection Needs of Asylum Seekers from Sri Lanka (2010) *United Nations High Commissioner for Refugees (UNHCR)*. 5 July 2010.

United Nations Human Rights Commission, Concluding Observations on Sri Lanka, UN Doc. CCPR/C/79/Add. 56, 27 July 1995.

Wattegama, C. and Sreekanth, K.M. (1998) *Proliferation of Internet in Sri Lanka and India: A Comparative Study*, Paper presented at the 17th Annual Session of the Computer Society of Sri Lanka.

Weerakoon, B. (2004) *Rendering unto Caesar*. Co-published in Sri Lanka, Colombo: Vijitha (Yapa Publications).

Weiss, Jessica (2009) 'How Can Women Journalists Achieve a Healthy Work-life Balance?' *International Journalists' Network*. Available at: http://ijnet.org/community/groups/10189/how-can-women-journalists-achieve-healthy-work-life-balance (accessed on 20 August 2014).

Wesumperuma, D. and Ranasinghe, C.S. (Eds.) (1993) *Mass Communication in Sri Lanka: Some Salient Aspects*. Colombo: Sri Lanka Foundation Institute.

Wickramatunge, L. (2009) 'And then they came for me', *The Sunday Leader*, 11 January 2009.

Wijedasa, N. (2011) *Law to Protect Right to Information is Unnecessary—President*. Sri Lanka Brief, 4 July. Available at: http://www.srilankabrief.org/2011/07/law-to-protect-right-toinformation-is.html#more (accessed on 16 July 2011).

Wijedasa, N. (2012) *Keynote Address Delivered Prior to the AGM of the CIMOGG Held in the Auditorium of the Organisation of Professional Associations, Colombo*. Available at: http://cimogg-srilanka.org/2012/05/pre-agm-keynote-address/ (accessed May 2014).

Wijetunga, W.M.K. (1996) 'Mass media, elective politics and multi-party democracy in Sri Lanka', *Asian Journal of Communication*, Vol. 6, No. 2, pp. 92–118.

Wijetunga, W.M.K. (1998) 'Sri Lanka', in: A. Goonasekera and D. Holaday (Eds.), *Asian Communication Handbook*. Singapore: AMIC, Nanyang Technological University.

World Association of Newspapers (2006) *World Press Trends*.

Reports

Asian Human Rights Commission, Hong Kong (2010) The State of Human Rights Report.

Bureau of Democracy, Human Rights, and Labor (2008) United States Department of State.

Bureau of Democracy, Human Rights, and Labor (2008) United States Department of State. Sri Lanka Country Reports on Human Rights Practices—2007.

Central Bank of Sri Lanka, Infrastructure and Services (1998) Communication and Mass Media, in Economic Progress of Independent Sri Lanka 1948–1998.

Devanesan, R. (2006) Sri Lanka Broadcast Media Report: June–August 2006: An Investigation into the closure of CBN Sat and Implications for Sri Lankan Broadcast Media.

Global Report on the Status Women in the News Media (2011) International Women's Media Foundation. Available at: http://iwmf.org/pdfs/IWMF-Global-Report.pdf (accessed in June 2013).

International Federation of Journalists (2004) On the Road to Peace Reporting Conflict and Ethnic Diversity: A Research Report on Good Journalism Practice in Sri Lanka.

International Federation of Journalists (2011) Free Speech in Peril. Press Freedom in South Asia 2010–11, Ninth Annual IFJ Press Freedom Report for South Asia 2010–11, Delhi.

International Telecommunication Union (1998) World Telecommunication Development Report 1998.

Law Commission of Sri Lanka (2011) Report of The Law Commission on The Draft Freedom of Information Bill. Available at: http://www.lawcomdept.gov.lk/info_English/index.asp-xp=723&xi=808.htm (accessed on 15 January 2011).

Media South Asia: Media, Policy and Law in South Asia—Scoping Report 2008. Available at: http://www.mediasouthasia.org/research_report.asp (accessed in June 2013).

National Conference on Self-Regulation (2011) Print Media in Sri Lanka.

Press Complaints Commission of Sri Lanka (2010) Annual Report.

Report of the Committee to Advise on the Reform of Laws Affecting Media Freedom and Freedom of Expression (1996) R.K.W. Goonesekere Committee Report.

Report of the National Media Summit—2010 (2010) University of Kelaniya.

Report on the Findings of the Investigation with Respect to the Effective Implementation of Certain Human Rights Conventions in Sri Lanka (2009) Commission of the European Communities. Brussels, 19 October 2009.

The Access Initiative (TAI) (2007) Sri Lanka Report: Access to Environmental Information, Public Participation and Access to Justice.

Declarations, Covenants and Codes of Ethics

Citizens' Charter of Press Council of India. Available at: http://presscouncil.nic.in/Citizen%20CharterModified.pdf (accessed on 23 January 2011).

Code of Professional Practice (Code of Ethics) of the Editors' Guild of Sri Lanka, adopted by the Press Complaints Commission of Sri Lanka. Available at: http://www.pccsl.lk/includes/downloads/files/file_09081732403.pdf (accessed on 3 January 2011).

Colombo Declaration on Media, Development and Poverty Eradication (2006).

Colombo Declaration on Media Freedom and Social Responsibility (1998).

Colombo Declaration on Media Freedom and Social Responsibility (2008).

International Covenant on Civil and Political Rights, GA res. 2200A (XXI), 21 UN GAOR Supp. (No. 16) at 52, UN Doc. A/6316 (1966); 999 UNTS 171; 6 ILM 368 (1967).

Kelaniya Declaration on Mass Media, Communication Study, and Media Industry in Sri Lanka, National Media Summit—09 and 10 November 2010.

Media Charter for a Democratic and Pluralist Media Culture and Social and Professional
    Rights for Media and Journalism in Sri Lanka (Tholangamuwa Declaration) (2005).
    Available at: http://www.unesco.org/new/fileadmin/MULTIMEDIA/HQ/CI/2.%20
    Tholangamuwa%20Declaration.pdf (accessed June 2013).
The Press Council (Code of Ethics for Journalists) Rules (1981).
Universal Declaration on Human Rights, GA res. 217A (III), UN Doc A/810 at 71 (1948).
Weligama Declaration on the Role of Media for National Unity (2006).

Constitutions and Legislation

Arbitration Act No.11 of 1995.
Associated Newspapers of Ceylon (Special Provisions) Law No. 28 of 1973.
Code of Criminal Procedure (Amendment) Act No.52 of 1980.
Code of Criminal Procedure Act No.15 of 1979.
Establishment Code of Sri Lanka, Official Secrets Act No.32 of 1955.
Parliament (Powers and Privileges) (Amendment) Act No.17 of 1980.
Parliament (Powers and Privileges) Act No.21 of 1953.
Penal Code (Amendment) Act No.12 of 2002.
Penal Code Ordinance No.2 of 1883.
Press Council (Amendment) Act No.13 of 2002.
Press Council Act of 1978 (India).
Press Council Law No.5 of 1973.
Prevention of Terrorism Act No. 30 of 1981.
Public Performance Ordinance No. 7 of 1912.
Public Security Ordinance No. 25 of 1947.
Sri Lanka Broadcasting Authority Act No. 5 of 1974.
Sri Lanka Rupavahini Corporation Act No. 6 of 1982.
Sri Lanka Telecommunications (Amendment) Act No.27 of 1996.
Sri Lanka Telecommunications Act No.25 of 1991.
The Constitution of the Democratic Socialist Republic of Sri Lanka.

Gazettes, Regulations, Policies and Draft Laws

Draft Contempt of Court Law. Available at: http://www.lawcomdept.gov.lk/info_English/
    index.aspxp=723&xi=1129.htm (accessed on 16 January 2011).
Draft Freedom of Information Bill. Available at: http://www.lawcomdept.gov.lk/info_
    English/index.aspxp=723&xi=808.htm (accessed on 15 January 2011).
Emergency (Miscellaneous Provisions and Powers) Regulations No. 1 of 2000.
Gazette of the Democratic Socialist Republic of Sri Lanka (Extraordinary) No. 1570/35 of
    10th October 2008.
Ministry of Mass Media and Information, National Media Policy (2007).
The Constitution Bill of 2000.

Cases: Sri Lankan

Amaratunga v. Sirimal and Others [1993] 1 Sri L.R. 264. Application 47/2004, S.C. Minutes 28.11.2005.

Athukorale and Others v. The Attorney General (Sri Lanka Broadcasting Authority Case) [1997] 2 BHRC 610.

Centre for Policy Alternatives v. Minister of Mass Media and Others, SC (F.R.) Application No. 478/2008.

De Silva and Others v. Jeyaraj Fernandopulle and Others [1996] 1 Sri L.R. 22.

Deshapriya and Another v. Municipal Council, Nuwara Eliya and Others [1995] 1 Sri L.R. 362.

Ekanayake v. Herath Banda, SC Application 25/91, S.C. Minutes, 30 October 1996.

Environmental Foundation Ltd v. Urban Development Authority of Sri Lanka and Others, SC (F.R.).

Hewamanne v. Manik De Silva [1983] 1 Sri L.R. 1.

In Re Garuminige Tillekeratne [1991] 1 Sri L.R 134.

In Re Hulugalle, 39 NLR 294.

In Re the Broadcasting Authority Bill, S.D. No 1/97 15/97, delivered on 5 May 1997.

In the Matter of a Rule on De Souza 18 NLR, 41

Joseph Perera v. The Attorney General [1992] 1 Sri L.R. 199.

Karunatilleka and Another v. Dayananda, Commissioner of Elections and Others [1999] 1 Sri L.R. 157.

Leader Publications (Pvt.) Ltd. v. Ariya Rubasinghe, Director of Information and Competent Authority and Others [2000] 1 Sri L. R. 265.

Neville Fernando and Others v. Liyanage and Others [1983] 2 Sri L.R. 214.

Palihenage Don Saranapala v. S.A.D.B.R. Solanga Arachchi, Senior Superintendent of Police, Police Headquarters, Colombo 1 and Others, SC Application No: 470/96, SC Minutes of 17/07/1997.

R.P. Wijesiri v. The Attorney General [1980] 2 Sri L.R. 317.

Ratnasara Thero v. Udugampola [1983] 1 Sri L.R. 461.

Sri Lanka Broadcasting Authority Bill—Supreme Court Determination 1/97 15/97.

Sumith Jayantha Dias v. Reggie Ranatunge, Deputy Minister of Transport [1999] 2 Sri L.R. 8.

Sunila Abeysekera v. The Competent Authority and Others, SC Application No 994/99, decided on 15 May 2000.

Thavaneethan v. Dayananda Dissanayake, Commissioner of Elections and Others [2003] 1 Sri L.R. 74.

The Democratic Socialist Republic of Sri Lanka v. Sinha Tissa Migara Ratnatunge, High Court Case No. 7397/95.

Victor Ivan v. Sarath Silva, Attorney General [1998] 1 Sri L.R. 340.

Visuvalingam and others v. Liyanage and Others [1983] 2 Sri.L.R. 311.

Wimal Fernando v. Sri Lanka Broadcasting Corporation [1996] (1) Sri L.R. 157.113.

Cases: Foreign Jurisdictions

Autronic AG v. Switzerland (1990) 12 EHRR, 485.

Gaskin v. UK (1989) 12 EHHR, 36.

Glasenapp v. Germany (1986) EHHR, 25.
Leander v. Sweden (1987) 9 EHHR, 433.
Mukong v. Cameroon, Communication No. 458/1991, at para 9.7.
R V Metropolitan Police Commissioner ex parte Blackburn (No 2) 1968, QB 150.
Secretary, Ministry of Information and Broadcasting v. Cricket Association of Bengal (1995) 2 SCC 161.

University and Training College Curricula, Handbooks and Reports

Amunugama, S., Premaratne, A. and Ismail, S.M.M. (2006) Subject Review Report— Department of Languages and English Language Teaching, Faculty of Social Sciences & Languages, Sabaragamuwa University of Sri Lanka.

Bandara, H.M., Hapuarachchi, A. and Karunathilake, K. (2009) Subject Review Report— Department of Social Studies, Faculty of Humanities and Social Sciences, Open University of Sri Lanka.

Eastern University, Sri Lanka (2011) Available at: http://www.esn.ac.lk/trincocampus/ Departments/LCS.html (accessed on 12 January 2011).

Eastern University, Sri Lanka (2012) *Handbook of Faculty of Communication and Business Studies*, Trincomalee Campus.

Eastern University, Sri Lanka (2012) *Handbook of the Faculty of Arts*.

Gunatunge, R.S., Atapattu, D. and Endagama, M. (2007) Subject Review Report—Department of Humanities, Faculty of Social Sciences & Humanities, Rajarata University of Sri Lanka.

Ismail, S.M.M., Weerasinghe, T. and Hapuarachchi, A. (2007) Subject Review Report— Department of Mass Communication, Faculty of Social Sciences, University of Kelaniya.

Meddegama, U., Rajapaksa, C, Weerasinghe, T. and Ven. Agalakada Sirisumana (2010) Subject Review Report—Department of Sinhala and Mass Communication, Faculty of Arts, University of Sri Jayewardenepura.

NALSAR (2011) Subject and Curriculum Content—PG Diploma in Media, Available at: Laws http://www.nalsarpro.org/ml_cc.htm (accessed on 23 January 2011).

NUJS (2011) Entertainment and Media Law: Course Overview—NUJS. Available at: www. nujs.edu/courses/entertainment-and-media-law-course-overview.pdf (accessed on 23 January 2011).

Open University of Sri Lanka (2011) Department of Social Studies, Faculty of Humanities and Social Sciences, Bachelor of Arts Degree Programme in Social Sciences—Prospectus for Students 2010 2011. Available at: http://www:ou.ac.lk (accessed on 13 January 2011).

Rajapaksha, C., Hapuarachchci, A. and Ismail S.M.M. (2008) Subject Review Report— Department of Mass Media, Sri Pali Campus.

Rajapaksha, C., Weerasinghe, T. and Dissanayake, C. (2008) Subject Review Report— Journalism Unit, Faculty of Arts, University of Colombo.

Rajarata University of Sri Lanka (2008) Faculty of Social Sciences and Humanities, Prospectus. Available at: http://www.rjt.ac.lk/ssh/index.php?option=com_content&view=article& id=12&Itemid=18 (accessed on 13 January 2011).

Report 'About MRTC' (2012) By T. Thevananth, Director, Media Resources and Training Centre (MRTC), University of Jaffna.

Report on 'MRTC Action Plan' (2012) Prepared by K. Rushangan and Others, Jaffna.

Sabaragamuwa University. New Syllabus for Mass Communication, Sabaragamuwa University.

Sabaragamuwa University (2011) Available at: http://www.sab.ac.lk/Miscel/OurDegrees. htm (accessed on 13 January 2011).

South Eastern University (2011) Course Syllabus of the B.A. (Special) Programme. Available at: http://www.seu.ac.lk/FAC/facpos.html#Sociology (accessed on 13 January 2011).

Sri Lanka College of Journalism (2011) Courses Offered: Provincial Correspondents. Available at: http://www.slcj.lk/course_ditails.php?course_id=9 (accessed on 17 January 2011).

Sri Palee Campus (2011) Syllabus—Department of Mass Media, Sri Palee Campus, University of Colombo. Available at: http://www.cmb.ac.lk/academic/sripalee/index/ media_syllabus.htm (accessed on 12 January 2011).

SRM University (2011) Available at: http://www.srmuniv.ac.in/downloads/pgdj-curriculum-2009-10.pdf (accessed on 23 January 2011).

St. Xavier's College (2011) Available at: http://www.xaviercomm.org/diploma-courses/ courses-jr.htm (accessed on 23 January 2011).

University of Calcutta (2011) Available at: http://www.caluniv.ac.in/academic/academic_ frame.htm (accessed on 23 January 2011).

University of Colombo (2011) Course Units for Under Graduate Programs. Available at: http:// www.cmb.ac.lk/academic/arts/journalism/cunits.htm# (accessed on 12 January 2011).

University of Colombo (2011) General Degree Course Syllabus, Journalism Unit, Faculty of Arts, University of Colombo; Also see Course Units for Under Graduate Programs. Available at: http://www.cmb.ac.lk/academic/arts/journalism/cunits.htm# (accessed on 12 January 2011).

University of Colombo. Diploma in Journalism—Course Syllabus, Journalism Unit, Faculty of Arts.

University of Jaffna (2012) Syllabus of Diploma in Journalism (Full time Programme—2 years), Media Resources and Training Centre (MRTC).

University of Jaffna (2012) Syllabus of Diploma in Journalism (Part time Programme), Media Resources and Training Centre (MRTC).

University of Jaffna, Sri Lanka (2010) Faculty of Arts, Media Resources and Training Centre, Structure of the Diploma in Journalism Full Time and Part time Courses.

University of Jaffna. Syllabus for Communication & Media Studies, Faculty of Arts, University of Jaffna.

University of Kelaniya (2011) New Curriculum (Special) Mass Communication, Faculty of Social Sciences, Kelaniya University. Available at: http://www.kln.ac.lk/social/maco/ courses.htm (accessed on 12 January 2011).

University of Sri Jayewardenepura (2011) Available at: http://www.sjp.ac.lk/fa/sinh/comass. html (accessed on 12 January 2011).

University of Sri Jayewardenepura. Course Requirements to Consider Mass Communication as a Main Field for the B.A. (General) Degree, Department of Sinhala and Mass Communication, Faculty of Arts.

Interviews and Discussions

Ms Anne Abayasekara, 20 February 2012.
Ms Sunila Abeysekara, 22 March 2011.
Anonymous Senior Administrator, Sri Lanka College of Journalism, 9 February 2012.

Mr W. Dayarathne, 5 April 2012.
Mr Bandula Dayaratne, 20 March 2011.
Mr Malik Chaminda Dharmawardena, 24 March 2011.
Prof Ganganath Dissanaike, 19 March 2011.
Prof Wimal Dissanayake, 10 March 2011.
Mr Imran Furkan, 9 February 2012.
Prof Ajantha Hapuarachchi, 30 April 2012.
Mr Senani Harischandra, 16 March 2011.
Ms Mandana Ismail, June 2012.
Mr K. Janaranjana, 4 January 2011.
Mr Harendra Jayalal, 12 February 2012.
Mr Chandra Jayaratne, 4 March 2012.
Mr Wijeyananda Jayaweera, 4 April 2011.
Mr Dharmadasa Lankapeli, 5 April 2012.
Lecturers of the MRTC, Jaffna (names not disclosed on request), 15 December 2010.
Mr Kumar Nadesan, 20 February 2012.
Dr Devanesan Nesiah, Ret. Senior Civil Servant and member of PCCSL, 21 February 2012.
Mr Bandula Padmakumara, 8 January 2011.
Mr K. Pathytharan, 28 December 2012.
Ms Indrani Peiris, March 2012.
Prof Sasanka Perera, 23 March 2011.
Ms Seetha Ranjani, 23 March 2011.
Mr Kingsley Ratnayake, 20 March 2011.
Mr Sukumar Rockwood, 14 February 2012.
Mr Wijeyananda Rupasinghe, 17 March 2011.
Mr K. Rushangan, 17 October 2012.
Dr M.A. Mohamed Rameez, 10 and 18 January 2013.
Mr Wijayantha Rupasinghe, 12 November 2012.
Ms Sutha Rushangan, 20 December 2012 and 20 January 2013.
Mr Hiniduma Sunil Senevi, 1 June 2012.
Mr V. Senthan, 18 December 2012.
Ms Kiruthiga Tharumarajah, 20 January 2013.
Mr T. Thevananth, 11 January 2013.
Mr A.C. Visvalingam, 13 April 2012.
Dr Tudor Weerasinghe, 16 March 2011.
Discussions with Indian media educators and academics conducted under the auspices of a
grant by the Ford Foundation (Institute of International Education) during February–
July 2012, including visits to the Asian College of Journalism, Chennai; Department of
Media and Communications, University of Puducherry, and the Centre for Culture,
Media and Governance, Jamia Millia Islamia, New Delhi [Anuradha Sharma (Jamia
Millia, New Delhi, July 2012) and Sadanand Menon (Chennai, February 2012)].

Websites

Journalists for Democracy in Sri Lanka. Available at: http://www.jdslanka.org (accessed
in 2013).

Media Reform Lanka Initiative Website: http://www.mediareformlanka.com (accessed in June 2013).

Media South Asia Website: http://www.mediasouthasia.org (accessed in June 2013).

Ministry of Mass Media and Information. Available at: http://www.media.gov.lk/ (accessed on 29 June 2011); Technical and Vocational Education and Training. Available at: http://www.tvec.gov.lk/sa/index.htm (accessed in June 2013).

Source Watch Website: http://www.sourcewatch.org/index.php?title=Embedded (accessed in 2013).

Sri Lanka Campaign: http://www.srilankacampaign.org/media-freedom.htm (accessed in June 2013).

Committee to Protect Journalists: http://cpj.org/killed/asia/sri-lanka/ (accessed in June 2013).

The Hoot: Watching Media in the Subcontinent: http://www.thehoot.org (accessed in June 2013).

About the Editors and Contributors

Editors

William Crawley is Senior Fellow at the Institute of Commonwealth Studies, University of London, and Co-director of the Media South Asia Project (www.mediasouthasia.org). After completing his doctorate at Oxford University, he was a journalist, editor and manager in the BBC World Service for 23 years until 1994. Since leaving the BBC, he has written articles and edited publications on the BBC and India, and on the media in South Asia. He and David Page collaborated with partners in India, Pakistan, Sri Lanka, Bangladesh and Nepal in researching and writing *Satellites over South Asia: Broadcasting, Culture and the Public Interest* (SAGE, New Delhi, 2001). The Media South Asia Project also commissioned a documentary film *Michael Jackson Comes to Manikganj*, directed by the Indian Journalist and Film-maker Nupur Basu. He was Secretary of the Charles Wallace Pakistan, Bangladesh and Burma Trusts from 2002 to 2007. He is on the Editorial Board of *Asian Affairs*, the journal of the Royal Society of Asian Affairs.

David Page is Senior Fellow at the Institute of Commonwealth Studies, University of London and Co-director (with William Crawley) of the Media South Asia Project. After taking his doctorate in South Asian History at Oxford University, he joined the BBC in 1972 and worked for more than 20 years as a journalist, editor and manager in the BBC Eastern Service. Since leaving the BBC, he has worked as a consultant and researcher on communication issues in South Asia. He and William Crawley collaborated with partners in five South Asian countries in researching and writing *Satellites over South Asia: Broadcasting, Culture and the Public Interest* (SAGE, New Delhi, 2001) and in organising conferences and seminars on broadcasting policy in the region. In 2012, he co-authored a BBC Media Action publication *The Media of Afghanistan:*

The Challenges of Transition. He is a trustee of Afghanaid, a British charity working with rural communities in Northern Afghanistan.

Kishali Pinto-Jayawardena is a Sri Lankan legal analyst whose work encompasses advocacy, research and litigation in the protection of civil liberties. After graduating with honours from the Faculty of Law, University of Colombo in 1993 and upon being admitted to the Bar, she appeared in several media law cases in the appellate courts and challenged the Sri Lankan State before the United Nations Human Rights Committee on violations of international standards. She has drafted Right to Information and Contempt of Court laws and authored local and internationally referenced books on Sri Lanka's Rule of Law challenges. The editorial (legal) consultant for the *Sunday Times* since 2000, she contributes a law-based column 'Focus on Rights' for the newspaper. A 2001 Salzburg Fellow, a 2003 WISCOMP (New Delhi) Scholar of Peace Fellow and the 2007 Sri Lankan recipient of the International Woman of Courage award by the United States Department of State, she was conferred a Distinguished Visitor Fellowship by the Research School of Asia and the Pacific, Australian National University (ANU), Canberra in 2013.

Contributors

Jayantha de Almeida Guneratne, PhD, is a President's Counsel with expertise in administrative, constitutional and land law, a former Law Commissioner and Visiting Lecturer and Examiner, University of Colombo/Sri Lanka Law College. Currently serving in a visiting judicial capacity overseas, he was a member of the 1995–1997 Presidential Commission on Involuntary Removals and Disappearances of Persons in the Southern, Western and Sabaragamuwa Provinces. He has written extensively on the concept of peoples' sovereignty in constitutional law which constituted his doctoral thesis. The author of *The Swiss Constitution: Lessons for Sri Lanka,* (Centre for Policy Research and Analysis, University of Colombo: 1995), he is co-author (with Kishali Pinto-Jayawardena) of *Habeas Corpus in Sri Lanka; Theory and Practice of the Great Writ in Extraordinary Times* (LST: 2011) as well as (with Kishali Pinto-Jayawardena and Gehan Gunatilleke) of *The Judicial Mind in Sri Lanka,* (LST: 2014). He is a Salzburg Fellow (2002).

Gehan Gunatilleke is an attorney-at-law and researcher based in Colombo, Sri Lanka. He has done LLB (Hons) from the University of Colombo and is an LLM from Harvard Law School. He is presently the regional coordinator of the Master of Human Rights and Democratisation (Asia Pacific) Programme jointly offered by the University of Sydney and the University of Colombo. He is also the Head of Legal Research at Verité Research. His recent publications include: *The Right to Information: A Guide for Advocates* (Sri Lanka Press Institute; UNESCO: 2014), *The Judicial Mind in Sri Lanka* (co-authored with Jayantha de Almeida Guneratne and Kishali Pinto-Jayawardena; LST: 2014), and *Reporting on Human Trafficking and Forced Labour: A Practical Guide for Journalists in Sri Lanka* (ILO: 2012).

Nalaka Gunawardene has been associated with media, communication and development for 25 years in a multitude of roles including reporter, feature writer, TV host, journalist trainer and communication consultant. He has written widely on the social and cultural impact of information and communications technologies (ICTs). From 2003 to 2009, he was a Sri Lanka contributing editor for *Digital Review of Asia Pacific*, www.digital-review.org. He was also a researcher and co-writer of *Sri Lanka Human Development Report on ICTs*, published by UNDP in 2004. He now writes weekly columns on science, development and information society issues for two Sunday newspapers in Sri Lanka (*Ravaya* and *Ceylon Today*), and contributes op-ed essays to other print and online media outlets at regional and global levels. He hosts a TV show on innovation on national TV, and blogs at http://nalakagunawardene.com.

Ameen Izzadeen is Editor, International Desk, Wijeya Newspapers Ltd, Sri Lanka, and Deputy Editor, the *Sunday Times*, Sri Lanka, as well as Columnist, *Daily Mirror*. He began his career as a print media journalist in 1986 as a sub-editor in the now defunct Sun/Weekend newspaper group, Colombo. His specialities are international affairs, effective editing and editorial administration. From 2005 to August 2008, he was the Sri Lanka correspondent for the Dubai-based *Khaleej Times*, filing news stories and writing a weekly opinion column. He is a Harry Brittain fellow of the London-based Commonwealth Press Union and won the Japan Foreign Press Centre fellowship in 1993. He is also a visiting lecturer in journalism at the Colombo University and the Sri Lanka College of Journalism; a visiting lecturer in international relations at the Bandaranaike International Diplomatic Training Institute, Colombo, and a visiting lecturer in Middle Eastern politics at the Defence Services Staff College, Batalanda, Sri Lanka.

Tilak Jayaratne was a veteran broadcaster and Sri Lanka's community radio pioneer, spearheading the Uva Community Radio initiative which was supported by UNESCO. He founded the Educational Service of the Sri Lanka Broadcasting Corporation and was instrumental in taking radio to the people through innovative programmes and content which marked a turning point in Sri Lanka's broadcast media. He was the first director of the College of Journalism, Sri Lanka. His tenure with the country's state broadcaster, Sri Lanka Broadcasting Corporation (SLBC) and consequent dismissal from the Non-Formal Education Programme (NFEP) of the SLBC resulted in the seminal Supreme Court judgment, *Wimal Fernando v. Sri Lanka Broadcasting Corporation* ([1996] 1 Sri LR 157), which even today remains a standard setter for independent governance of the airwaves. Ably representing a generation of honourable broadcasters serving Sri Lanka with integrity and commitment, he passed away on 7 September 2012. The Media Lanka Reform Initiative recalls his valuable contribution to the work despite his illness with much gratitude.

Amal Jayasinghe is the Bureau Chief, Agence France-Presse (AFP), Sri Lanka/Maldives. He joined the agency in August 1987 after working for over five years as a reporter for Sri Lanka's main English-language newspaper, the *Daily News*. He has been on special reporting assignments for AFP in war-torn areas of the world, including Afghanistan and Iraq. His reporting on Sri Lanka's drawn-out Tamil separatist conflict earned him accusations of bias by both sides of the ethnic divide and a medal and title, Chevalier, Order National du Merite (Knight of the National Order of Higher Merit), from the Government of France in 2005.

Sarath Kellapotha is a senior broadcaster, researcher and writer, with more than 30 years of experience in Sri Lanka's broadcasting regime. He worked for more than 20 years at the SLBC and alongside Tilak Jayaratne as a senior trainer at numerous community radio stations. After leaving the SLBC, he and Tilak Jayaratne engaged in a review of the regulatory aspects of Sri Lanka's community radio at the request of the World Bank in 2004.

S. Raguram is currently Dean of the Faculty of Communication and Business Studies, Trincomalee Campus, Eastern University, Sri Lanka. He was educated at Madras, Madurai Kamaraj and Gandhigram universities in India, specialising in journalism and visual communication. He wrote his doctoral thesis on the use of Tamil folk media in development communication. He has worked as a master trainer and as a manager of the Media Resources and Training Centre of Jaffna University. He was an editor of the Jaffna Tamil daily *Yarl Thinakural* in 2004/2005 and served as an associate producer for Vijay TV in India and as an executive producer at MTV in Sri Lanka. He was appointed as a senior lecturer in Trincomalee in 2006. He has worked on a number of projects to improve communication, democratic governance and budget transparency in the Eastern province and has presented many articles and papers on the media's socio-economic and cultural role. He was a Panos South Asia fellow in Media and Conflict in 2004/2005 and a Commonwealth scholar from 2007 to 2010.

Sinha Ratnatunga is Editor-in-Chief of the *Sunday Times* and Executive Director at Wijeya Newspapers Ltd. A former President of the Editors' Guild of Sri Lanka (TEGOSL), he is a Director of the Sri Lanka Press Institute (SLPI) and Director of the Press Complaints Commission of Sri Lanka (PCCSL). He played a leading role in founding of the TEGOSL and the SLPI. His conviction on criminal defamation charges in the late 1990s became the catalyst for a media campaign to abolish provisions regarding criminal defamation in the penal laws which culminated in their repeal in 2002. His conviction was later set aside by the Supreme Court. These events provided the impetus for the creation of a wider platform for media law reform conceived around the Colombo Declaration on Media Freedom and Social Responsibility which was signed by TEGOSL in April 1998 together with the Newspaper Society of Sri Lanka and the Free Media Movement, and revised thereafter in October 2008. This document remains the road map for media freedom in Sri Lanka. He serves on the Board of the World Association of Newspapers and News Publishers (WAN-IFRA). His book, *Politics of Terrorism: The Sri Lanka Experience*, published by the International Fellowship for Social and Economic Development, Canberra, in 1988, remains essential reading for those wishing to understand the complex roots of Sri Lanka's ethnic conflict.

Namini Wijedasa is Assistant Editor at the *Sunday Times*. She also writes for the *Economist* and works for NHK Japan TV. She began her career in 1994 as a junior reporter on the *Island* newspaper, the English-language daily run by Upali Newspapers. She also freelanced as a news reporter and presenter with Capital Radio, a private broadcaster. In 1998 she joined the *Midweek Mirror*, a publication of Wijeya Newspapers Ltd, and was part of the team that helped the *Midweek Mirror* transition from a weekly to a daily newspaper, the *Daily Mirror*. She was a correspondent for the Associated Press from 2000 to 2001. She joined the *Sunday Island* in 2001 and was promoted to an assistant editor. In 2007, she joined *Lakbima News* where she was an assistant editor till 2012, when she joined the *Sunday Times*. She has received national and international awards for journalism, including the 2005 Lorenzo Natali Journalism Prize. She served as a board member of the Sri Lanka Press Complaints Commission from 2007 to 2009.

Index